The User's Manual for the Brain
Volume II
Mastering Systemic NLP

L. Michael Hall, Ph.D.
Bob G. Bodenhamer, D.Min.

Crown House Publishing
www.crownhouse.co.uk

First published by

Crown House Publishing Ltd
Crown Buildings, Bancyfelin, Carmarthen, Wales, SA33 5ND, UK
www.crownhouse.co.uk

and

Crown House Publishing Ltd
P.O. Box 223, Williston, VT 05495-2223, USA
www.CHPUS.com

www.crownhouse.co.uk

Primary website for the Society of Neuro-Semantics:
www.neurosemantics.com

British Library of Cataloguing-in-Publication Data
A catalogue entry for this book is available
from the British Library.

ISBN 1899836888

LCCN 2003101230

Printed and bound in the UK by
The Cromwell Press
Trowbridge
Wiltshire

From L. Michael Hall

In honor of two Neuro-Semantics/NLP trainers who have been excellent partners:

Stephen Campbell

Alan Woodhouse

From Bob G. Bodenhamer

In loving memory of my "Mentor in Ministry"

Reverend Doctor Hoyle Allred

And to my "Second Mother"

Mrs. Hoyle "Dot" Allred

Contents

Introduction..v

Part One: Introduction to Mastery 1

Chapter One   Thinking Systemically About NLP...................................3

Chapter Two   The Cinema of the Mind....................................11

Chapter Three   The Pathway to Mastery 37

Part Two: Mastering the Four Meta-Domains of NLP..65

Chapter Four   Mastering the States Our Movies Create 67

Chapter Five   Mastering Meta-States....................................81

Chapter Six   Meta-Stating Mastery....................................111

Chapter Seven   "Sub-Modalities" as Editorial Meta-Levels.................133

Chapter Eight   Meta-Modalities 147

Chapter Nine   Mastering Programs of Perception 159

Chapter Ten   An Advance Listing of Meta-Programs 177

Chapter Eleven   The Meta-Representation System 205

Chapter Twelve   Meta-Magic and Extended Meta-Model......................219

Part Three: Systemic NLP 231

Chapter Thirteen   Systemic NLP....................................233

Chapter Fourteen   Meta-States as a Unifying Field Theory.......................253

Chapter Fifteen   NLP Unified Field Theories....................................267

Part Four: Modeling with Systemic NLP **289**

Chapter Sixteen   The NLP-Enriched Strategy Model 291

Chapter Seventeen   Modeling Using Meta-Levels 309

Part Five: Personal Mastery **331**

Chapter Eighteen   Mastering Trance...333

Chapter Nineteen   Mind-Lines: Conversationally Reframing....................357

Chapter Twenty   Using Mind-Lines in Everyday Life 377

Chapter Twenty-One   Presuppositional Languaging: Part I.............................395

Chapter Twenty-Two   Presuppositional Languaging: Part II 413

Chapter Twenty-Three   Practical NLP 433

Chapter Twenty-Four   NLP Mastery 451

Bibliography...**455**

The authors **460**

List of Figures

2.2	Basic NLP communication model	18
2.3	Meta-levels of internal production	21
4.1	Three-fold division of personality	68
4.2	The components of neuro-linguistic magic	69
4.3	State journaling	72
4.4	Emotion scale	77
5.4	Second-order abstractions or states-upon-states	90
5.6	From "thought" to "belief"	95
5.7	The levels of the mind	99
6.1	Dragon slaying	122
6.2	Continuum of welcoming	125
7.1	Validating a thought	143
7.3	"Sub-modalities": The cinematic symbols of sensory	146
8.1	Awareness of awareness	149
10.1	Levels of thought and language	179
11.5	The Meta-Model	215
12.2	The extended Meta-Model	228
13.1	Old hag/beautiful woman	245
14.1	The multiple feedback loops	263
15.1	The Jungle Gym	269
15.3	Overview of the 5 models forming the Dilts' unified field theory	270
15.4	System of models	271
16.2	Diagram of TOTE model	294
16.3	Spelling TOTE	296
16.4	The TOTE model	297
17.1	Modeling I and II	310
17.2	Meta-levels in the spelling strategy	312
17.5	The neuro-logical levels or levels of beliefs	318
17.6	Neuro-logical levels	319
17.9	Imprints and developmental stages of intelligence	321
17.10	Re-modeling the neuro-logical levels	322
17.11	Modeling using meta-levels: frames all the way up	329
18.1	The hypnotic state	335
18.2	The feeling of trance	337
18.5	The logical levels of "time"	347
19.1	The magic box or cube	365
19.2	Pascal Mind Lines	369
21.2	The "directions" of the mind	407
22.1	Inclusive/exclusive or	417

Introduction

Becoming a master

Becoming a practitioner of NLP (Neuro-Linguistic Programming) begins an adventure—an adventure of learning to fully "run your own brain". On this adventure, you will discover the structure of experience and become more resourceful in using your mind-body states. In the adventure you first learn the basic NLP model. After that comes abundant practice and application in order to become knowledgeable and skilled.

We described all of this in the first volume of *The User's Manual for the Brain*. There we introduced the adventure as we presented the model and content of NLP. There we set forth the components that comprise NLP, how it models the structure of subjectivity, the foundational linguistic model of NLP (the Meta-Model of language), the foundational neurological model (states and strategies), and the basic Representational Model (the sensory modalities and sub-modalities), which is also known as the communication model. Along with all of that, we included scores and scores of transforming patterns. *The User's Manual*, as a practitioner course, introduced you to the language of hypnosis (the Milton Model), the use and play of "sub-modalities", and the heart and soul of Meta-States, which explains how the meta-levels of NLP work so powerfully.

Having done that, we are now excited about adding more to the field of NLP and about the sharing of the newer advancements in his field, especially about Neuro-Semantics (NS). Accordingly, this book presents what we call the NLP Master Practitioner level. As such, it invites you into the adventure of *mastering* NLP both in skills and in attitude. With this second volume of *The User's Manual for the Brain* we invite you to move beyond the practitioner level and on to the master's level, where you will not only know NLP, but you will develop the very *spirit* of NLP. As we do this, we shift our focus to facilitating the processes that will transform you from a *practitioner* of this art to a *master* in running your own brain and modeling the structure of excellence.

The User's Manual for the Brain, Volume I contains the foundation of this work. Here we introduce additional facets of the NLP model that are vital for operating with a full understanding and level of skill. What are these additional pieces? What is new in this volume?

- Meta-Programs
- Meta-States
- "Sub-modalities" as meta-level framing
- Advanced Meta-Model distinctions
- Mind-Lines as conversational reframing patterns (previously known as the "sleight of mouth" patterns)

- Advanced language distinctions (presuppositions)
- Trance as a meta-level phenomenon
- Advanced Time-Lines patterns
- Systemic thinking about NLP
- The Meta-Domains systemic model
- Practical applications of NLP

Yet, above and beyond all of that, in *The User's Manual for the Brain, Volume II*, the master's level, our focus is on presenting and installing something even more important, and that is the very attitude that enables a person to use this model powerfully.

For anyone who has experienced NLP, there's no doubt about the magic and wonder of this approach to working with the human dimension. NLP does provide numerous models and patterns that work magic in human minds and hearts. Yet, if we want to use this transformative power in profoundly magical ways, we have to operate from a mind and state of power ourselves. There's a reason for this: NLP is not for the timid.

To master this model of the mind-body system, you will need a good dose of courage, boldness, and passion. These patterns will not work their full magic if you attempt to use them while you are hesitating, fearful, and/or unmotivated. The power of any wizard not only involves the tools that he or she uses, but also the attitude of love, courage, and passion that drives the use of the tools. This is where the artistry of the magician comes in to supplement the science of the technology.

The spirit of NLP involves a passionate commitment to self and others, a belief in possibilities and discovery, a responsibility to excellence and mastery, a "go for it!" attitude of curiosity, playfulness, and respect. And that's just the beginning. It involves an attitude of abundance that enables us to operate from a win win orientation. It is a spirit that's not afraid to make mistakes but, in fact, welcomes and celebrates mistakes as informational feedback. It's a spirit that experiments, explores, embraces ambiguity, and gets more excited as things become more difficult and challenging.

It is exciting for us to present this work. Other books (including some of our own) cover much of the content here. Yet few, if any, even touch on the *attitude* or *spirit* of NLP in the way we have presented it here. And this makes the difference between, on the one hand, those who use it with power and respect and who have fun doing so and, on the other hand, those who lack such power and presence. This makes the difference between those who give NLP a good name and those who misuse it. That NLP can be misused is obvious. Any tool, model, and technology as powerful as NLP invites misuse, and even abuse. Yet that, in itself, does not argue against the model. It rather challenges us to make sure we handle it with the right kind of spirit.

To that end, we have layered the discussions, case studies, seminar demonstrations, patterns, and trances so that they will assist you in developing:

- The kind of passion tempered by respect and honor of others;
- The kind of motivation tempered by awareness of the other contexts and values in your life;
- The kind of dedication needed by the quality of mind and emotion that serves to truly honor your life and the lives of others.

Conscious and unconscious training

As trainers, we seek to install the knowledge and skill not only at the conscious level, but also at the unconscious level. We seek to do both. It is our conviction that practitioners need to know and understand the model and the kind of thinking that both created and works best with the processes, and to then feel totally confident that they can *do* the corresponding skills. Then knowledge and expertise will go together to form a persuasive package.

Some NLP trainings aim only to *install* directly at the unconscious mind. We question whether that's even possible. Can you install a simple skill such as riding a bicycle directly without conscious practice and understanding? How about typing? Even learning a language, which is about as unconscious a skill as there is, involves hours and hours of practice. Watch a small child play for hours and have lots of fun pointing to things and naming them and trying out new sounds. That's called *practice*. And, even if you could stick some piece of high-level expertise into someone's behavior, if they don't have conscious control over it who would be driving the bus? Is the person running his or her own brain? NLP is truly about running your *own brain* and not delegating that to someone else, not even to an NLP trainer and being conscious of how you do this.

This underscores the importance of cognitive understanding of the model and for developing an articulate knowledge about *why* you choose this pattern over that one, and what you hope to achieve by doing so. To be able to perform the skills yet to lack guiding knowledge does not describe mastery. Such would actually leave a person unskilled when the environmental conditions and cues change. Automatic, unconscious learning is great for motor habits and skills in areas where the environment and contexts are fairly constant. But, when we have an ever-changing environment, we need the flexibility to *not* respond in only an unthinking and unconscious automatic way. We need the mindful flexibility that arises from conscious understanding that can choose and invite new choices.

The best *installation of skills of excellence* arises from and involves a healthy combination of conscious and unconscious skillfulness. We have designed our trainings and this book to provide both information and programming and to engage both your conscious and unconscious mind. We believe that you will make better use of the materials and have them more readily available if you not only experience the patterns, but also understand the meta "whys" and "wherefores".

To facilitate conscious and unconscious understanding, we will continually ask throughout this work the following types of questions:

- What is its purpose?
- What use can we put it to?
- How does it work?
- How does it relate to other patterns and models?

Expanding the practitioner training

As you examine the basic NLP Communication Model in Chapter Two (Figure 2.2), you will see the broad areas of NLP practitioner training. With this work, we broaden the brush to paint a larger picture. In this work, we do this primarily by fully introducing the Meta-States model and showing how it relates to the Meta-Model of language and the Meta-Programs model of perception. We will show how the meta-levels of the mind, in creating our conceptual frames about so many things, play a role in the overall matrices of our mind. These frames involve conceptual categories as time and space, as the framing of the cinematic features of our internal movies ("sub-modalities") and much more.

Of course, all of the models presented here are metaphors. We will exchange the metaphor for trance and go *up* into the higher reaches of mind and notice what happens. We will change the metaphor of "sleight of hand" (sleight of mouth) and talk about magical lines that cast spells in the mind (Mind-Lines). We will utilize the metaphorical concept of "the Place of Pure Potentiality" and "the Void" as metaphors for some of the higher conceptual frames so that you can take a magic-carpet ride to some truly new and exciting territories in your mind. And knowing, as you do, that "the map is not the territory", you can enjoy the realization that all language operates metaphorically. None of it is real. It doesn't have to be. It has only to be effective in achieving more life-enhancing outcomes. Our words do not even have to reference externally real things. They need only to offer us more useful and empowering maps for navigating, so that we can move out into new areas for exploration, performance, and enjoyment.

Becoming masterful

We want to be crystal-clear as we begin that a master in any field does *not* "know it all". Not at all. Masters are masters precisely because they recognize that they do *not* know it all and so become explorers of what they don't know. What they don't know excites them and triggers them to curiously explore. They become masters because they are forever learning, discovering, practicing, experimenting, finding out the edges of the maps and patterns, and looking at this from a learner's point of view. Becoming a true master means becoming a perpetual learner. That's why it takes humility to become truly masterful. The arrogant know-it-alls never get there: they spend their energies on creating, maintaining, and defending a know-it-all image.

To date, NLP has only touched the hem of the garment about what is possible in modeling excellence, finding and detailing more of the structure of subjectivity, and forging new patterns for reaching the full human potential. To date, NLP does not even have a fully articulated model of itself, a "unified field theory" about human psychology and functioning. Two attempts have been made and in this work we offer a third attempt at articulating a unified field theory using the four meta-domains of NLP. Yet this is only the beginning, and not the last word.

It is our privilege, having explored so many of the subjects of the Master Practitioner Course in other works, to put together this volume. You will find other facets of this course in the following books:
The Spirit of NLP (1996, 2000): the Master Practitioner Course as presented by Richard Bandler in the late 1980s.

Mind-Lines (1997, 2001): the sleight-of-mouth patterns reformulated to use logical or meta-levels.

Time-Lining (1997): advanced Time-Line patterns.

Secrets of Personal Mastery (2000): introduction to the three-day Meta-States training, Accessing Personal Genius.

Meta-States (1995, 2000): the Meta-States model.

Hypnotic Language (2001): hypnotic language using Gestalt and developmental psychology.

Figuring Out People (1997): extensive analysis and listing of 51 Meta-Programs.

A word about this manual and the writing style

We have attempted to avoid writing this text in "textbook" style. Instead, we have aimed primarily to present it as a training workbook. This means that rather than employ an academic tone, we will "speak" in the writing pretty much as we would speak the same ideas in a training.

Treat this book also as one that you will read repeatedly. We have written it to be read sequentially from beginning to end. Once you have overviewed the content, then feel free to skip around, filling in your knowledge and skills.

We have also included lots of exercises. These are *not* fillers. Our intention is that you use them, that you stop … right then and there and *use* the exercises as thought experiments and a human laboratory of experimentation. Some of the exercises require a partner and some even a "meta-person" to observe, record, and/or to keep you on track. If you have or can find some others to create a study group, that would enrich your experience of this manual. If not, you can still use most of the exercises, even though we have written them as if you were doing them with a partner. At least you can use them to some extent.

When you do so, remember that everything about representation systems, calibrating, pacing, state management, and so forth—all of that still counts. Always begin by orienting yourself to the task, get rapport with your partner or partners, and then go for it.

Did you notice the ellipses just a moment ago? You know those three dots (…) in the middle of a sentence? We use this to indicate not only missing material in a quotation, but to get you to slow down … and stop speed reading … and experience the words. This is especially true for inductions … for state inductions … for trance inductions.

In terms of spelling, we use hyphens to denote relationships, and en dashes (small dashes) a lot to reconnect what could easily be misunderstood as a dichotomized and elementalized world. Hence neuro-linguistic, neuro-semantic, mind-body, mind-emotion-body, time-space, and similar constructions. When we refer to a formal model, we use capital letters, Meta-Model, Meta-Program, Meta-States, but, when using these terms in another way, we use small letters. The @ symbol is used throughout this book to mean "about".

We have used other linguistic devices in the writing itself. You will find these explained in Chapters Eleven and Twelve on the Meta-Model.

L. Michael Hall
Bob G. Bodenhamer
2002

Part One

Introduction to Mastery
Mastering the Attitude and Skills of NLP

Chapter One
Thinking Systemically About NLP

NLP is Itself a Systemic Model About the System of Our Neuro-Linguistics

To master using and working effectively with NLP, we have to *think systemically* about the model. This is because NLP itself is a systemic model. It is not only *about* systems (for instance, the human mind-body system, the mind-language system, the sensory and meta-representational systems, the person within a culture system), and not only did it come from modeling several systems (e.g., Satir's family systems, Alfred Korzybski's non-Aristotelian system), but NLP itself operates systemically and is structured systemically.

This is one reason why many people have found the early NLP books so difficult. The early developers, caught up in systemic thinking, did not (perhaps could not at the time) present the materials in a nonlinear way. The materials did not follow a strictly linear process. A person has to think more systemically to fully appreciate some of those early works (e.g., *Frogs into Princes, Reframing, Trance-formations*). If that's true of NLP generally, it is especially true with regard to the master practitioner level, when we begin working with the four meta-domains of NLP and using the Meta-Model, the meta-modalities ("sub-modalities"), the Meta-Programs, and Meta-States to describe, model, and interact with subjective experiences.

Systemic thinking

To a great extent, *systemic thinking* defines the difference between the practitioner level of NLP—for instance, knowing the parts and pieces of the model, using the technology, following the patterns—and the master practitioner level. Beyond the parts and pieces is the mastery level of knowing how to put it altogether as a system. This means *thinking systemically*. Thinking systemically is essential for truly mastering this mind-body, non-Aristotelian model. It is one of the primary objectives we have in this book.

Getting there, however, is another matter. So how do we learn to think systemically? How do we integrate systemic thinking into our NLP skills and processes?

It begins with looking freshly at NLP as a system: the parts and pieces that go together into the model, how these elements fit together, and how they operate as a system. It also means zooming in and out of the materials. Zooming *in* to the details of this or that pattern or understanding, then zooming *out* to get a sense of the larger gestalt, the emerging pattern that arises from the sum of the parts and that is yet *more* than the sum of those parts. Yet it involves something different as well as more.

To think systemically, we have to move beyond "parts thinking". Parts thinking stands in opposition to systems thinking. You can know all of the parts, the elements, even the mechanisms and processes that tie the parts together, and still not be able to see or sense the *system*.

Systems are not see-hear-feel things. They involve the invisible relationships, patterns, and processes that occur between the parts. So, as we shift to systemic thinking, we will be moving above and beyond *detail thinking*. We will be accessing the meta-program of global thinking, and then on to *gestalt thinking*. The more your awareness stays glued to the details, to the content, the more difficult you will find the challenge of mastering NLP. Yet, if you are committed to mastery, then this learning will change this facet of your thinking; you will become much more global in your awareness.

Actually, you'll become more skilled at what we call *meta-detailing*. It's not that you will become more global rather than detailed. That description itself is linear thinking, either/or thinking, and thinking along a continuum. *Either* global *or* specific. Instead, you will become more flexible in shifting your awareness from details to global and from global to details. Merely being more global in processing information does not make you a better systems thinker, either. Global thinking alone (as a driving meta- program) is not the same as systems thinking. It typically makes it a bit easier, yet it is not the same. We've met many people who are highly global in their thinking but who do not think systemically, and so are not masters of NLP.

In systemic thinking we are able to step back, go meta, and get a sense of the whole. That's an essential part. Yet it is not the whole story. Systemic thinking involves the reflexivity that we speak about in Meta-States that allows us to effectively *go round in circles*.

The key word here is "effectively". We can all go in circles. That's simply a description of how consciousness works, yet a lot of people don't like it. In fact, they hate it. They try to stop themselves from doing it. Yet in failing to embrace ambiguity, not knowing, and complexity, they make a big mistake. To think systemically, we have to learn how to enter the looping, even the spiraling, and to enjoy the process. Only then can we learn how to effectively manage it. This is a torture to those who prefer and are driven by "procedure" as a meta-program.

Processing and sorting by procedures is a great last step of systemic thinking. After we have entered, explored, experienced, danced around in the loops of consciousness, and modeled the system, then we need to sort out the steps that put it all together. Then we can create a linear step-by-step process that allows others to replicate the experience. We need to bring all of the rich awareness of our modeling together in the final step to create new patterns and processes. That's certainly a crucial part of mastering NLP as it enables us to create new things and extend human knowledge.

But too much of that too early in the process will kill *systemic thinking*. First we have to live with ambiguity, we have to live with feeling overwhelmed by the wonder and magic of the experience we wish to understand and model. First we need to access and use the sorting style of options and free-floating. Bateson (1972), in *Steps to an Ecology of Mind*, called it "loose thinking".

When Bateson would begin researching a new area of concern, such as a new anthropological survey, or of the subject of culture itself, he would invent some words that would give him a sense of the "stuff" of culture and the "feel" of culture. He would intentionally use such vague terms as "stuff" and "feel" to cue himself that he was engaged at the loose level of thinking and that he would later revisit the terminology to make it more precise after he had more thoroughly surveyed the new territory. The looseness of the terms, metaphors, and ideas enabled him to survey an area of exploration without knowing all of the details and without demanding it be right. He used it to get started. He used it to begin the research process, and he used it so he did not become attached to his own ideas or terminology.

Loose thinking and terminology allows us to enter a realm without the demand or pressure of needing to know it all or needing to get it right first time. This promotes the kind of creativity where we can truly use feedback to refine, hone, and sharpen the ideas and model over time. It is systemic in that it traces a broad outline and then reflectively feeds back new data into the model.

We begin with loose thinking that allows us to enter into a new realm of study or another person's neuro-semantic reality and then we follow the loops. From a Meta-State point of view, this necessitates *tolerating ambivalence*. It means living with *not-knowingness*. We set supporting frames: "It's okay; we're just exploring, we'll tie it all together later." To do otherwise is to impose structure too soon and to delete the processes of the system before we become fully acquainted with it.

Thinking systemically about the NLP systems

In this book, we have introduced the four meta-domains of NLP:

- The Meta-Model
- The Meta-Programs
- The Meta-States
- The Meta-Modalities ("sub-modalities")

These four models, which govern the meta-domains of consciousness and subjective experience, give us four windows to human reality. The first three follow the historical discovery of these models; the fourth was there from the beginning but not recognized as a meta-domain. The first model involves the domain of *language* and how we language our internal worlds and encode our experiences, neurology, and skills in language. NLP began here. When Bandler and Grinder first wanted to model the therapeutic magic of Perls, Satir, and Erickson they began with how they talked. From that came the Meta-Model and its inverse, the Milton or Hypnotic model.

This led to the basic NLP communication model and model of human functioning as well as many of the techniques for altering, transforming, and renewing the models of the world that people live by. All of the early NLP patterns focused on challenging and updating people's impoverished models of the world to evoke a richer and more resourceful model.

Eventually, however, they began finding weaknesses in the model. As they put their Meta-Model to the test, their patterns for meta-modeling, hypnotizing, and so forth, they began to find that sometimes the classic NLP patterns just didn't work. As Leslie Cameron-Bandler [AA1] kept discovering these problematic points, she and Richard Bandler began identifying meta-programs that were getting in the way. This introduced the second meta-domain of NLP.

They discovered that sometimes a pattern won't work, owing to *the way a person thinks and sorts information*. They said it was as if the person had a program at some higher level that was getting in the way, that interfered with the pattern, that discounted the technique. From this they identified nine meta-programs; others extended it to 14, then 21, and later we extended it to 51 (*Figuring Out People*, 1997).

Meta-programs gave NLP a model of thinking patterns, perceptual filters, or neurological sorting devices. This opened the way for profiling people—the NLP Lab profile—and for taking into consideration the way that people's styles of perceiving can become an operational program, operating above awareness yet shaping and formulating how they think, what they see, and so on. This domain further enriched the NLP Communication model as well as the Strategy model.

Another area of inadequacy was discovered over the years that eventually gave birth to the Meta-States model. This time it came about from finding problems of inadequacy in the Strategies model. In modeling the complex state of resilience, I (MH) found that the mostly linear NLP-enriched TOTE (test-operate-test-exit) model failed to account for higher states of mind that are always there governing the experience.

People who were highly resilient experienced the same roller-coaster emotional ups and downs as the nonresilient. Yet, *at a higher state of mind* they knew they would come through and bounce back. They also had other thoughts about their discouraging thoughts and emotions while in a setback. They just knew, as a frame of mind, that emotions are emotions, that negative things happen, that there's no failure, just feedback, that they have the power to bounce back. As I kept modeling the resilient, more and more meta-levels of states and frames were discovered. Yet the Strategy Model didn't have anything within it to account for these higher states and frames of mind that endured over time. This led to the discovery and description of Meta-States (1995/2000). Meta-States, in turn, opened up more about modeling and then about profiling neuro-semantic networks of beliefs, frames, personality, and so on.

The fourth domain remained hidden until recently. It was hidden under the unfortunate label that it received. By the term "sub-modalities" we all thought that this domain was at a lower "logical level" to the representational systems and our mental movie, not higher. But that was just a trick of language, a wrong label, as you will discover in Chapters Seven and Eight.

With these four meta-domain models, NLP now has four avenues that give us redundant formatting and framing of subjective and personal reality:

- *Language:* the linguistic descriptions that map sensory-based realities
- *Perception:* the ways of thinking and perceiving that get into our eyes as our way of sorting and paying attention to things
- *States:* the layered states or frames of mind that enable us to stabilize thoughts and emotions into meta-phenomena that we can carry with us
- *Cinematic features:* the ways we encode and frame our internal cinema made up of our sensory representational systems

The Systemic III Model

When we put these models together in this way a number of years ago, we realized that we can put together a beginning description of a *unified field theory*, as it were, for NLP. We called it the "Systemic III Model" for two reasons.

First and foremost, it involves the *three* (now four) meta-domains that unite the field of NLP and give us the necessary redundancy that allows us to model subjective experiences using four avenues or channels. The first three models redundantly describe the same territory from three different points of view, thereby creating a very special richness to the model. Later we added "sub-modalities" as the fourth meta-domain, thereby adding yet another redundancy.

Second, it was historically the *third* attempt at a unified field theory among NLP trainers. The first was Robert Dilt's attempt with his "Jungle Gym" approach. Dilts took the three "time" positions as one axis, the three perceptual positions as another axis, and then the six Neuro-Logical levels as his vertical axis to create a cube that he called a jungle gym. The second was Richard Bandler's attempt using "sub-modalities" that he called Design Human Engineering (DHE). We will cover these models in a later chapter, where we will fully present the Systemic III Model (Chapter Fifteen).

Mastering systemic NLP

To think systemically about NLP so that we can truly become masterful in our use of this model, we have to *go meta* to content and truly learn to think in structural terms. A great deal of the material in this second volume deals precisely with this. We have included a chapter on the use of presuppositions. Above and beyond the details of that section is the kind of thinking that you will have to shift to in order to understand presuppositions, namely, meta-thinking about structure and process over content.

To think systemically also necessitates thinking *holistically*. This means learning to see and work with processes as interactive, hyphenated, and operating holographically over time and space. It means recognizing neuro-linguistic states of mind-and-body-and-emotion of a person as an-organism-as-a-whole in the context of relationships-in-a-culture, and so on. Such thinking allows our neuro-linguistic mastery to become truly non-Aristotelian.

When we go meta and think holistically, we are able to experience the systemic thinking that we describe as a *gestalt*. And this is no surprise since NLP arose from Perl's Gestalt therapy, which came from the earlier Gestalt psychology.

Structurally, we present the four meta-domains of NLP in separate chapters in Part Two of this book as "Mastering the Four Meta-Domains of NLP":

- Meta-States: Chapters Four, Five and Six
- "Sub-modalities": Chapters Seven and Eight
- Meta-Programs: Chapters Nine and Ten
- The Meta-Model: Chapters Eleven and Twelve

From there we present Part Three, "Systemic NLP":

- Systemic NLP: Chapter Thirteen
- Meta-Stating and a Unified Field Theory: Chapter Fourteen
- Unified Field Theories and the Systemic III Model: Chapter Fifteen

Because the heart and soul of NLP is *modeling*, Part Four, "Modeling with Systemic NLP", is on using strategies and meta-levels in modeling as our way to find and articulate the structure of experience. So, using the four meta-domains, we more fully introduce the NLP Strategy Model and then integrate the NLP Enriched-TOTE model with meta-levels to talk about using such for modeling (Chapters Sixteen and Seventeen).

Part Five is called "Personal Mastery". We devote this final section of the manual to NLP applications and especially to applying the entire NLP model to the theme of personal mastery.

We begin with the mastery of trance states by introducing meta-trance. By exchanging metaphors and thinking of the trance states as *up* rather than down, we describe and facilitate going in and then up, up, and away into the highest regions of the mind for engineering even more resourceful states. And we throw in some new time-lining processes for the fun of it (Chapter Eighteen).

We then shift to the personal mastery of reframing and so introduce our work with mind-lines. After all, how masterful would a master practitioner really be without the ability to conversationally perform his or her neuro-semantic magic? So we will conclude with a chapter on mind-lines. This refers to the way that we have taken the sleight-of-mouth patterns and rigorously applied logical or meta-levels to them to create the Mind-Lines model. This brings together the three meta-domains of NLP and the patterns so that we can talk about it conversation-ally and perform the magic of transforming meaning (Chapters Nineteen and Twenty).

Next comes the personal mastery of presuppositional elegance. To that end we introduce the use of presuppositions in everyday language. The chapter on the use of presuppositional language takes a practitioner into the mastery of recognizing the "frames by implication" that occur in using the terms and phrases that we do. We have applied its usage to trance work as well as to sales, managing, and being more resourceful (Chapters Twenty-One and Twenty-Two).

In the final chapter, we more directly apply NLP to therapy, business, coaching, communication, and other everyday uses (Chapter Twenty-Three).

Summary

The key to mastering NLP lies in shifting from linear thinking to nonlinear think-ing, to thinking systemically. When we can do that, then we can truly understand neuro-linguistic states and the mechanisms that drive them.

For most people, thinking systemically does not happen suddenly or overnight. It is an application of NLP to ourselves, and involves non-Aristotelian thinking.

Meta-detailing practice on this adventure into mastery

1. Meta-detail this manual
As an accelerated-learning technique, quickly scan through the chapters of this book until you have a sense of the overview of the manual.

What is the *meta* perspective that you sense about *The User's Manual for the Brain, Volume II?*

What is the essence or heart of this approach?

2. Mind-map the *details* of the overview

Create your own mind map in any way you desire to sketch out a sense of the direction that this manual is going. Remember, it doesn't have to be right. As you read and study, as you do the thought experiments and play with your brain, you can use every experience as feedback to refine your meta-detailing process.

3. Compare your meta-detailing discoveries with those of a partner

Chapter Two
The Cinema of the Mind
Rising Up to Edit, Direct, and Produce Quality Cinematography Productions

While we presented an extensive description of the NLP Communication model in *The User's Manual for the Brain, Volume I*, we here will summarize the elements of the NLP model, with a twist. While the component pieces of the model will remain the same, how we package and format them will be different. These are the elements that we use in exploring or modeling "the structure of subjective experience", to quote the title of Robert Dilts's 1980 classic. And these are still the key features that make NLP so magical, the features that we have to know and understand thoroughly in order to develop mastery in recognizing and using these features. Yet we will offer a new simplification of the model that will make it more user-friendly. In this chapter we present the NLP model in terms of *cinematography*.

Part I

First we will identify all of the pieces that make up the model and reformulate it in terms of the cinema of the mind. Then, we will play with using the cinematography to take charge of these neuro-linguistic dynamics.

The pieces that make up subjectivity

It begins with *neurology*, with the DNA genetic structure that encodes the most fundamental information about how our cells should grow and split and specialize to become the organisms that we are. We are neural creatures, detained in bodies with boundaries and nervous tissue that model the energies out there in the world. Via our nervous systems, end receptors, and basic senses we begin our map making as we "abstract" (or summarize) from the world.

This gives us a *neurological map of the world*. We sense things in terms of the structures of our body—in terms of sights, sounds, smells, sensations, tastes, equilibrium, and so forth. After many more levels of abstraction, we experience the "sense" of, for instance, internal sight, sound, sensation, and smell in such a way that it seems like we actually are *re-presenting* what we saw, heard, felt, or otherwise experienced. We do not *literally* have these sensory modalities on an actual screen in our mind, but it seems as if we had them. It seems as if we had images, sounds, and other sensations on the inside.

In NLP we call this internal "sense" of the sensory modalities our Visual, Auditory, Kinesthetic representations (the VAK). As our first conscious mapping of the world, this experience is our primary sense of "knowing" the world. We used this NLP jargon freely in *The User's Manual, Volume I*, but here we are exchanging this jargon for a more simple and more user-friendly language. So, instead of VAK, modalities, representations, and so on, we will here speak about our *internal movie*, the movie that plays on the screen of the mind.

To perform the task of mapping the external world inside our minds, we have to leave out (delete) a lot of information—most information in fact. We also generalize, summarize, abstract, which leaves us with summaries of things, things rounded off. We also alter, change, or distort things. We call these the modeling processes.

Here's an example. Consider sight itself. What impinges upon our eyes is electromagnetic radiation, light. We cannot see that energy for what it is, so we distort it via our rods and cones. This gives us the sense of "color". Our two eyes give us the sense of "depth". We have 100,000,000 light-sensitive cones, but only 1,000,000 nerve impulses to the brain. So we reduce what we receive to a hundredth. That leaves a lot out. It also changes the form from electromagnetic radiation to cell activation, to a nerve impulse, to the exchange of neurotransmitters, and so on. What goes in at one end (the eyes) does not show up at the other (the brain).

Our neurological mapping changes, deletes, generalizes, distorts things all the way through. Yet it is in this way that we end up with a map *of* the territory. We end up with our first-level *neurological map*. When we become aware of it, we have the internal sense (a map) of the territory. That is, we create a sensory-based internal movie and play it in our mind.

"I see a dog; I hear the dog barking; I feel the dog's soft hair and wet nose; I smell

Figure 2.1

NLP jargon	User-friendly conversational language
The VAK	Mental or internal movie
Sense modalities	Screen of the mind/of consciousness
Representational systems	The cinema
"Sub-modalities"	Cinematic features/movie magic
"Sub-modality" mapping across	Editing the movie
Chunking up and down	Zooming in to the details in the movie
	Zooming out to notice the frames of the movie
Strategy, strategy analysis	Order or sequence of the movie frames

the dog ...″

At this point the movie isn't very detailed or clear. It's more general. Yet we have a *sense* of the visual features, a *sense* of the soundtrack, and of the feel, smell, taste, balance tracks. Yes, that's weird. Theater owners are still working on adding other sensory tracks to the audiovisual tracks. But in the mind—in the theater of our consciousness—we have *multidimensional tracks in all sensory systems*. Of course, this is what makes the internal cinematic world of mind so magical. There we can represent these sensory features and step into the movie so that all of our neurology responds.

Next comes language. We not only attach sounds, music, tones, and pitches to our cinema, but also a language track, so that we hear the words of the people in the movie and our own internal movie narrator and critic. For "mind", this offers even more internal magic. We can (and do) encode our mental movie not only with one soundtrack, but multiple tracks. We not only have our own voice saying things, but we can also have other narrative voices occurring: Mom's, Dad's, a teacher's, a religious figure's, that of a vague historical narrator, whatever.

Our mental movies are first made out of sense modalities and sensory-based language. Yet this is just the beginning. We never stop with that. As we abstract from see-hear-feel words to more abstract terms to create higher-level ideas, concepts, and knowledge systems, the words on the soundtrack become richer and more complex. This can change the quality and even the very nature of the movie.

Consider the language soundtrack playing in the mind of an infant or small child. "See doggie. See Dick and Jane. Look! Doggie is running after the duckie!" The same scenario playing in the movie of the mind of an adult would undoubtedly have a different set of words in the soundtrack.

"When we brought home the first puppy that we got for the children, the pup was full of excited energy, especially when the neighbor's duck came into his line of sight ..."

The *visual scenario* that we represent and "see" in the theater of our mind is just part of the content; the *auditory soundtrack* can supply more of that content, or it can operate at a higher level that sets a frame about the movie. What we hear being said *in the soundtrack* of the movie differs from what a narrator may say about the movie. "The child spoke in short succinct statements. More as commands, similar to those that fill up the child's world."

The words we use in the soundtrack influences our mind's way of *framing* things. Childish words and tones can set a frame, as can academic words, journalistic terms, poetry, or rap. Our choice of language, style, or tone can set frames about the movie playing and cueing us about how to encode the movie. When I look at the puppy chasing the duck or jumping upon the child with its wet nose and licking its face ferociously, what language plays out *inside* the movie, what words do I hear playing out as if *narrating* the movie, and what words may an *editor's* voice be saying, or another spectator's to the movie? If you were watching another movie, what words would you use to describe that movie?

From inside the movie, the child is laughing and giggling.

From the back of the movie, my voice is sorting for the degree of the dog's roughness or playfulness and how the child is experiencing it. "Just as long as its play and fun; I don't want anyone to get hurt."

From the edge of the movie, an editor's voice says, "Zoom in on the shot of the child's laughing and delight."

Because our *linguistic mapping* of the world in our movies shifts us up to higher levels, this is our primary way of *framing* the cinema. Every movie screen, play, and picture occurs inside of a frame. In fact, we use the frames to contribute to the meaning of the cinema. How much the movie fills the screen or recedes into the background, how clear or fuzzy, how bright or dim—these facets of the movie create a certain frame. How we use the curtain (raising it or lowering it), whether we see the screen as a still picture or a movie, as a flat picture or a 3-D holographic image, whether we see inside or outside the image, the kinds of borders we see, whether it's a panoramic view—all these are editorial distinctions that we can make about the movie.

We can do the same with words: real, not real; vivid, dull; interesting, boring; significant, irrelevant; about me, not about me; escapism, science fiction, documentary; educational, entertainment. The terms we use about the movie, or any feature of the movie, enable us to frame it with different meanings. Some framing affects perception, other framing affects conception. Both influence feelings.

Because our sensed mental movie arises as a neurological process within our physiology, all of our internal moviemaking is inescapably *neuro-linguistic*. This means that what we represent, map, encode at the sensory-based or evaluative-based level, we experience and feel in our body. Though the words we use are not real externally, they are impactful and significant inside our mind-body system. That's why NLP can use either the tools of mind (words, language, linguistics, symbols) or those of body (movement, posture, breathing) to improve, correct, and transform our everyday experiences. These two facets of our functioning give us two royal roads to our everyday states of mind-body-emotion:

1. Mind in the form of internal representations, and;
2. Body in the form of all of our neurological and physiological responses.

Ultimately, we need an alignment of both to be fully congruent.

Information processes within our neuro-linguistic system

We are information processors. From the DNA coding in our genes, to the neuro-transmitters, peptides, glands, central nervous system, immune system, all the way up to brain anatomy and mind functioning, we code, encode, decode data. This is what gives us "life" and separates life from nonlife. We respond to the world and do so by abstracting information from the world, encoding it as a map, and responding according to our model of the world.

Most of all, this information processing of inputs and outputs occurs outside the level of awareness—in our *embodied* flesh. It is part of our "cognitive unconscious" (Lakoff and Johnson, 1999) and cannot be accessed. Some of it lies below awareness and can be brought into consciousness. Consciousness is a narrow band of awareness severely limited by how much data it can hold at any given time. George Miller (1956) described it as the "the magical number seven, plus or minus two" in his classic paper by that title, and this suggests the numbers that make up that limit.

What we can become aware of is that "sense" of our internal cinema full of sights, sounds, smells, and other sensations (the VAK that makes up our *sensory represen-tational systems*). Our choice here to use a different terminology is designed to make it more accessible in everyday language. The cinematic movie that plays on the screen of our mind is, of course, not literal. We do not literally see or hear this movie: we only "sense" that we do. It is not real, but phenomenological. Our representational screen of awareness—what we "sense" inside in the theater of our mind—is the map that we use to navigate the world. It is the only contact we have with the reality "out there" that Korzybski (1933) called "the Territory". This "sense" of the see-hear-feel world gives us a *seeming awareness* of things, philosophically what we call phenomenology.

In speaking about our maps in this way, NLP uses such language as "sensory modalities", "representational systems", "VAK", and "strategies". Here we will simply speak about the *internal cinema* that plays out on the screen of our consciousness as we think, and make sense of things. Inside, we sense by seeing, hearing, and feeling the movie. Bateson used the phrase of a "screen of conscious-ness" and so we use it here. We expand it to speak about the video track, the soundtrack, the feel track, the smell and taste tracks, the balance track (a sense of being upright or upside down, dizzy or clear, for instance) of our vestibular sensory system.

Our sense of things in terms of our internal movie allows us to apply all the of the *cinematic features of a movie* to the way we process sensory-based information. That is, the movie metaphor for thinking and information processing translates into modalities and their distinctive qualities. These "sub-modalities" (an unfortunate term, as you'll discover in Chapter Seven) describe the cinematic features of our movies. So when we step back from our movie we are then able to frame it as close or far, bright or dim, in color or not, fuzzy or clear, loud or quiet. This allows us to use the cinematic features to make multiple adjustments to our "thinking". That is, to the way we map our mental movie that makes up our model of the world.

We map the world using our internal movie as young children, and only later, as we mature, do we begin using more abstract symbols and notations. This brings us to the meta-representation system of more abstract symbols (language, mathematics, music). With language we enter into the symbolic world at a much more abstract level. Then we use images of words and sounds as words to *stand for* and *to represent* entire movies of things, people, events and even more abstract things of the mind such as classes, categories, and concepts.

Noam Chomsky's (1957) contribution in linguistics was his theory that we have an innate language-acquisition device that allows us to acquire language and to do so more rapidly than any stimulus-response conditioning process could provide. Our ability to encode things symbolically, and to create human linguistics, enables us to create levels of semantic meanings.

From movie to meaning

How does "meaning" enter into the picture of representing sensory data and then abstract data about our mental movies? What is the relationship between our sensory movies and the phenomenon of "meaning"?

First, *meaning* at the first level of representation is *associative meaning*. Things become associated or linked together as events occur, and then we think or feel things. Given these two different phenomena, we associate them in our mind by making a movie that sees and hears first one, then the other. As we map it this way, so it becomes real to us inside our neuro-linguistics. We map the event as leading to, or triggering, our internal mind-body state. This creates the first kind of "meaning"—associative meaning.

As an example, we commonly link fear to things. We can just as well link love to things: arousal, anger, joy, playfulness, and so on. At the primary level meaning, it's a stimulus-response world. It's a world where we see one thing on the screen of our mind and then another. One triggers or anchors the other. We then conclude that the first causes the second, the first equals the second. In linguistics this shows up as cause-effect and complex equivalence statements—Meta-Model distinctions.

A new and higher level of "meaning" emerges when we use an associated reference like that as the way we frame other things. What began as a mere referent that we mapped by making a movie of a thing (noun) and action (verb) now becomes a frame of reference, a way to think about the thing (the noun) and the way it works (the verb).

This indicates a change in how we *use* the internal movie. It is not just a recording of one event (an external one) that we connect to another (an internal one). No. We now elevate the reference so that it *stands for* a whole category or classification. We do this by abstracting or generalizing from the event and using it as a category of the mind. This creates *contextual meaning*.

For example, the movie may have started by the way Dad yelled at us, which triggered fearful feelings in us. But, over time, we come to use that movie not merely for recoding the sequence of events: we use it for a different purpose. We might conclude, for instance, that "Dad" is typical of all "people in authority" and so use that movie to think about the class of authority figures. Now we have a movie ready for how to make sense of, understand, and have a map for how to respond to any authority figure we meet today. Or we could take the movie of "yelling" and use "yelling" to be our way to think about the entire class of "humiliation", "put-down", "control", or whatever category we create.

It is in this way that we begin to refer to, and reference, our history of memories of previous references and use them for abstract reasoning. This creates all of our *frame-of-reference meanings* that make up the matrix of our mind.

The basic NLP Communication Model

These features of how we input and process information give us the core of NLP, the Communication Model, which lies at the heart of NLP, which we use to describe human functioning or psychology. Our "psycho-logics" result from how we process information. That's because the only thing that ever enters into "mind" or "consciousness", as Bateson noted, is *information* or *news of difference*. "Things" cannot enter. There are no "things" in the mind. What enters is information.

Movie frames

Movies comprise not only the objects (nouns) moving about on the screen and doing things (verbs), but also frames. From *referent experience* we create our internal represented reference (our sensory-based internal movie). Then we create our first *frames of reference*. Eventually, with the habituating of our frames, we develop our *frames of mind*, our habitual patterns for perceiving. We call these our meta-programs.

Every representation within every frame affects us. The framed movies invite us to experience the movie in some way and so evoke mind-body-emotion states. Even when the frame of the movie is that of "just watching", witnessing, and observing, we do not experience that without some emotion or physiological state. The emotion may be mild, calm, relaxing, and hardly noticeable. But we are breathing, moving, exper-iencing some posture. We are not disembodied. Even when we feel "numb", that's still a feeling.

Every sensory-rich movie that we construct on the screen of our mind affects us

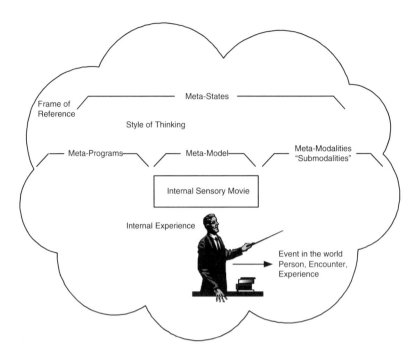

Figure 2.2: Basic NLP communication model

neurologically and so influences our state of mind, emotion, and body. While we so readily use these terms as if they were separate elements, they are not. It is our language that so easily tricks us here. Korzybski suggested that when we encounter such terms we use the hyphen to reconnect their systemic world.

Every thought and representation that we encode on the cinema of our mind and frame evokes mind-body *states*. That's why we cannot dismiss or discount our internal movies as innocent, harmless, or irrelevant. They are not. *States*, as in neuro-linguistic and neuro-semantic states, make up the very heart of all our experiences. When we process information from reading, listening, or communicating, we go into states. And, while our physiology and neurology certainly contribute to these states, it is our internal cinemas that primarily govern our states.

Now you know why it is so important that we learn how to "run our own brain". The movies that we run in our brains and the ways that we frame those movies centrally determine our experiences, self, skills, destiny, relationships, and health. So at the heart of the communication model is *state*.

Yet it doesn't end there.

Our neuro-linguistic states, governed by the movies (or programs) that we run, can reflect on themselves to create meta-states. We create layers of states by relating a state to itself or to another state. This means that, as we run one movie on the screen of our mind, we have enough "mind", or awareness, so that we can step back to notice the movie and run a movie about that one.

This is the way of "mind". Mind reflects upon itself and so builds up layers of embedded frames or what we call meta-states. Prior to the development of the NLP and NS models, we called these higher-level states of mind-body by many, many names. This, in itself, created confusion and falsely led theorists and psychologists to think that these different terms referred to different "things". They did not.

So what we call beliefs, values, identity, decisions, understandings, expectations, paradigms, knowledge, mission, purpose, or intention are just nominalizations of *mind* in action processing different perspectives of information. None of these are "things" or actual "entities" at all. At best we might say that they are "things" of the mind. Yet we are the ones who call them into existence and we do so by *thinking* them into existence. They are "real" to that extent.

They are all but symbols and they are made out of the same "stuff" we make our primary state movies out of: the sensory modalities of what we see, hear, feel, smell, taste, and the words that we use. As we move up "the levels" and layer thought upon thought, feeling upon feeling, physiology upon physiology and all of these in various combinations, we are simply *framing* the main movie. Doing this programs different qualities and features into the movie. In this sense, it is *symbols* all the way up, *frames* all the way up, *beliefs* all the way up.

These higher frames (meta-states) make up our attitude, our neuro-semantic reality, and the matrices of our mind. They have no immediate connection with anything "out there". They are our mental framing of information as we build up the higher levels of our mind.

This description begins to give an idea of how the Meta-States model provides a unifying format for NLP and will be further explored in later chapters. The idea of layering frames upon frames on our movies describes a unifying structure that suggests meaningful ways to explain, understand, and work with the higher layers of our minds. It unifies how to think about how to gain transformational leverage over the neuro-semantic system for greater personal resourcefulness.

NLP/NS cinematography

NLP excels as a model of cinematography. This was the genius of Bandler and Grinder in their original creation, although, by using the computer metaphor of "program" (and therefore "programming") and the engineering metaphor of "mapping," they missed out on fully utilizing the movie metaphor. Representation systems and the use of the visual, auditory, kinesthetic modalities were revolutionary as the "language" of the mind. Bateson noted that in his preface to the first NLP book (Bandler and Grinder). Eye accessing cues and linguistic markers of the sensory systems add to this revolutionary impact in psychology, education, and modeling. It gave us a "way in" to "the Black Box" of the mind that behaviorism said was undecipherable.

Using Your Brain—For a Change (1985) explicitly tapped into the movie metaphor and more fully described the process of "running your own brain" by working with the cinematic features of our movies. While there were previous works on "sub-modalities," this initiated a more formal exploration that brought new excitement to NLP.

Yet there was a flaw in the model of "sub-modalities". The name was wrong. The name was not only wrong, but it misdirected our understanding of what these cinematic features were, how to understand them, and how to use them effectively. Todd Epstein originally called them "pragmagraphics". And, since it's the *graphic* features of the movies that have *pragmatic* effects on our states, that was a much better label than "sub-modalities". In Chapters Seven and Eight, we will fully explore this domain and show how these cinematic features are in actuality, meta-frames for editing our mental movies.

Directing the cinema of your mind

Thinking about the way we use our sensory cinema to represent the things we see, hear, feel, smell, taste, and otherwise experience moves us to a meta-level about our mental movies. As we run with this metaphor, it moves us to an editor's role, a director's role, a producer's role, and on up.

We can move back to the movie we have in our mind of an embarrassing moment at work, school, or with friends and notice the default settings we use in framing and formatting the movie. This takes us to what we call the "sub-modalities" distinctions. We can notice if we portray the movie as still pictures or moving, as black and white or in color, as close or far, and so forth. This moves us to the *editor's perspective* of our mental movies. As an editor, what have we put in the foreground? In the background? What perspective have we used in viewing the movie? How dim or bright? From above or below? From the back or front?

Here we can use all of the techniques that any editor uses in producing a cinematic effect: multiple images, transparency, speeding up the film, slowing it down, whatever. We can even use various "movie magic" tricks.

When we move back from direct *editing* of the mental movie in our mind, we move back (or up) to the director's role. Here we are not so concerned with the particular cinematic features but with the attitude, intent, design, and focus that we want to convey through the movie. By way of comparison, consider what a director does in directing the making of a film. While the director may ask the camera people to zoom in or out, say, or to fade out with a fog coming in, the director mostly asks the actors to play their parts with more or less flare, boldness, anger, or fear. The direc-

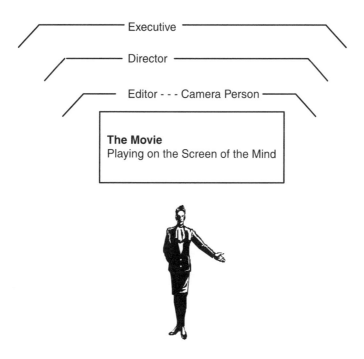

Figure 2.3: Meta-levels of internal production

tor may ask for more or less eye contact, a different speed of voice, or forcefulness of expression. In doing this he or she directs the *qualities* that texture the film in a certain way. This corresponds to the higher frames of mind that make up the meta-state *attitudes* that seep into our mental movies.

When we take yet another step back or up, we move to the position of the producer. With each step there's a paradox. The actors in the movies are a lot more involved than the camera people and editors, who are more involved than the director, who is more involved than the producer … yet the producer has more long-term and pervasive influence than the director, who has more influence than the editor and camera people, than the actors. "Control" moves down the levels to the actors who just play the parts.

This means that, ultimately, how we experience a film depends not on what happens, but how it is produced, directed, and edited. The movie *Mystery Theater 3000* provided a great illustration of that. Here in a futuristic theater aboard a spaceship zooming through the galaxy there are a human and two robots watching old B-movies, frequently old sci-fi films of Godzilla, Wolfman, and the like. But now the B-movies *feel* different: they are more like comedies than scientific dramas or horror pictures. Why? Because you see the back of the human's head and the outline of the robots and they won't shut up with all of their snide remarks about the old films.

Cinematic exercises

It's time to play. This is the end of the first part of this chapter. Take time now to explore and play with the following exercises as a way to become more fully acquainted with the cinemas of your mind. These exercises are designed to empower you to truly "run your own brain" as you become the editor, director, producer, and executive CEO of the movies that play in your brain. If you're serious about mastery, do not skip this.

EXERCISE: Exploring insult movies

Have you ever been insulted? Has anyone ever in your entire life ever said something to you that was sarcastic, degrading, or unpleasant? From your archives of video features, pull out an instance of such and let us explore the "insult movie" in terms of its cinematic features.

1. Access a resourceful state of curiosity, interest, and learning.
Think about something that evokes curiosity in you and anchor the feeling.

Think about a time when you were really fascinated and interested in something and anchor that as well.

2. Now pull out the insult movie and curiously explore it.
Examine the default settings in how you have it encoded.

Consider each sensory track (visual, auditory, and so forth) in terms of its qualities and properties. If you need to use a "sub-modality" list, do so. There's one in Chapter Seven.

What are the key editorial features ("sub-modalities") that you have used to encode this film?

How resourceful or unresourceful do you find your default settings?

If unresourceful, how would you like to change them?

3. Step back to examine the frames on this movie.
How have you framed this movie in terms of attitude? That is, what is your attitude *about* this insult movie? What do you think about it, believe about it, expect, understand?

What state do you find yourself in and how do you feel about this state?

Find a more empowering state and now step back and examine the frames of this movie.

How resourceful or unresourceful are these frames?

If unresourceful, what would be a more resourceful frame?

4. Step back one more level from the movie.
As you move to the producer level in your mind, what are your purposes, motivations, and intentions in producing this movie?

Do you need to update your intentions?

Do you need to update how to better fulfill the intentions?

5. Step back (or up) one more level.
From the executive level of your mind, do you need this insult movie?

If so, then how do you need to encode it so that it works to enhance your life?

6. Confirm, solidify, and future pace.
As you alter your movie, its default settings, and the frames at the higher levels of your mind, are you now satisfied with it? Would it now serve as a useful and enhancing reference?

EXERCISE: *Resourceful movie marathon*
1. Identify five favorite states.
What are five of your most favorite mental and/or emotional states? It could be confidence, playfulness, laughter, challenge, or something else. Pick five of your favorites.

2. Match movies to states.
Which movies elicit these states in you? Identify actual movies that elicit the states in you or your own mental movies of events, experiences, and situations that have or that could elicit these states in you.

3. Edit each movie for maximum elicitation.
Take one state and one movie at a time. First, step into it to see how well the movie, as you now have it encoded, elicits that resourceful state for you. Then step back from the movie and up into the editor's and director's role and update it so that it strongly elicits that favorite state in you. Continue until just the thought of that mental movie puts you into the state. Make sure you have it well anchored in as many sensory systems as you can.

EXERCISE: *Editing your screenplay*
1. Identify a serenity movie.
Have you ever been in a state of calm peacefulness? Have you ever experienced a getaway from life's everyday hassles and stresses where you just relaxed fully and completely?

Scan through your mind until you identify the place, situation, or experience that allowed you to experience such serenity and go there, turn on that video again and step into the movie to re-experience it fully.

2. Test the power and usefulness of your serenity movie.
While still inside your serenity movie, think about some of the current challenges, difficulties, stresses, and pressures that you face in your everyday life.

How well does the serenity feelings hold when you invite the stress thoughts into that movie? Gauge on a scale of 0 to 10.

3. Update the production of your serenity movie.
Rise up in your mind to the level of editor and director and check out the script that occurs when you think about life's everyday stresses. Notice the voice, the tone, the volume, the words, and other indicators.

Do you need to update the soundtrack and screenplay that occur when you think about the stressors?

If so, then do that. Eliminate every word or phrase that interrupts the calm serenity and replace it with a more neutral or positive term. Add a soothing voice that's strong, confident, and resilient.

What else do you need to re-edit so that, while you're facing life's everyday stresses, demands, and pressures, you can operate from a serene center?

4. Quality-control the end result and future pace.
Would you like to take this into all of your tomorrows?

Will you?

Are you fully aligned with this?

Part II

Lights, sound, action!

"Communication" as the evocation of our cinematography
Given the way we make sense of information by *representationally tracking* from words to the mental movie in our mind, what we call "communication" is evoking a similar movie on another's mental screen to the one playing on ours. When we communicate well, the other says, "I can *see* that!"; "I *see* what you mean"; "I can *hear* that and it does *feel* good." What we do in attempting to communicate is to get others to turn on a cinema in their mind that's similar to the one in ours. The closer our mental and emotional words and history of referent experiences, the easier it is

to do this. The more different our experiences and beliefs, the more challenging and difficult.

Why is that? Because we never receive the communications of others directly and simply. Rather, the "screen of consciousness" that we use to *track over* from the words of another person to our own internal movie has its own default settings. We have our own way of producing, directing, and editing. We have our own references, frames, beliefs, and values. We don't have to marshal these and consciously use them. We have learned them so well that they are now automatic. It's our reference system and style for understanding things.

From when we first began to see, hear, feel, and otherwise perceive, we developed our own preferences for which senses to use (visual, auditory, kinesthetic). We develop our preference for which cinematic features to use (close/far, bright/dim, large/ small). We developed our preferences for which frames to use: pains to avoid or pleasures to approach; things practical and useful or things right and correct, choices or procedures, things fun or things that bring pain, and so forth. We even develop preferences and beliefs about why and how to produce our mental movies: to be loved, for instance, or to get approval, to be powerful, to win, not to lose, to show someone up, to be right, to just survive, to discover truth.

In communicating our ideas, thoughts, and experiences to another and receiving theirs, the messages are always filtered and contaminated by our *models of the world*. That's why we really never do know how a person is editing, directing, or producing the words and gestures we use or what movie is playing in another's mind. We know how we mean the words to be used, what films we are trying to evoke and what cinematic features we would like the other to use. But we never know how it all gets filtered.

That's why we are much more likely to miscommunicate than to communicate accurately or effectively. Our models of the world get in the way. They get in the way as our cinema's default settings. It is in this way that our frames interfere. These are not just different thoughts: they actually make up our neuro-semantic reality that governs the movies we see and can see. We actually live inside our mind/emotion/body/culture structures that map our reality. It's not just that we *have* a "mental screen of consciousness": we mostly live inside it and operate from out of it. This more fully describes what we mean by "state"—by our neuro-semantic state.

So what?

The "so what?" here is very important. We experience the world out there and the world of others *through* our cinema as our story, our narrative, our life script, our programming, and our belief frames. All these terms and phrases describe the same phenomenon. We don't deal with the world directly, but indirectly through our maps. As we realize this we are truly able to understand and use the NLP Communication Guideline: *The meaning of your communication is the response you get, regardless of your intention.*

This no-fault, nonblaming model of communication helps us open our eyes and ears, move into uptime state of sensory awareness and more clearly recognize the responses we receive. It helps us to stop reading everything solely through our mental movie. It helps us to recognize that there are other films playing, other stories, narratives, life-scripts, programs, and beliefs. And, with that, we can use the "screen of our mind" in a new and powerful way, to just track from what others actually say and welcome their movies inside our heads so that we can actually understand what is playing in their world:

- Did the message this person receive match the message I sent?
- Are the sender and the listener watching the same movie inside?
- What did the receiver hear? Which movie did it evoke in that person's mind?
- What does the editor, director, and producer inside that person's processing style do with the screenplay that I offered?
- Which words and gestures can I use to convey the film or message I want to convey?
- Which filters or cinematic settings influenced this person to hear and translate things in that way?

Explorative questions about the communication process enable us to *avoid* taking *mis*communication personally. They allow us to focus more exclusively on clarifying the messages and on developing the flexibility to vary our messages until we can get through. Until message sent is message received. This model also highlights the importance of checking out what is happening on the inside. What is the message received? Does it match message sent? How is it off? How do I need to vary my signals? We never "fail" in the communication process: we just continually receive feedback about processing style and the effect it has in another.

Recognizing that everybody has their own way of filming, editing, and producing the things that occur on the screen of their mind frees us from the impoverishing idea that just because we *said* something in a certain way it has to be *received* in that way or make sense to the other in the way it does to us. Knowing that then frees us for greater flexibility.

Framing the communication process in this way eliminates blame, judgment, and negative feelings. Communication is *not* moral or immoral in itself. It's just an information-transfer process. There is no "right" or "wrong" way to input and process information. In communication we are simply sharing symbols that stand for referents that we map onto the movie theater of our mind. And, ultimately, each of us is responsible for what we do with the *symbols*. Ultimately, we are responsible for the meanings, frames, cinematic settings, and states that our movies induce in us. We try to blame others for *making* us create our internal movies and seeing them so that they make us feel bad. But it's our brain. It's our mental movie. It's our choice about how to represent things.

Framing communication in this way also turns the exchange of words and symbols into a *process of discovery*. It also empowers us to become more resourceful in our communicating, more professional, and, over time, much more effective and persuasive.

To increase your own confidence of running, editing, directing, and producing your own internal cinemas, use and practice this model for a period of time. If you know that you have been doing what does not work, and you keep doing it, you will just get more of the same. Is that what you want? If not, then try something new. Something different. Anything. Experiment. By flexibly shifting our use of symbols and openly receiving and playing with the symbols of others, we increase our chance of succeeding in accurately transferring our messages and at least understanding each other.

This highlights yet another facet of the NLP Communication Guideline: *There is no failure: there is only feedback.*

So we keep at it. Identifying and clarifying to ourselves our message and developing a clear outcome, acting by speech and behavior, noticing results, calibrating to others, flexibly adapting to generate other responses, checking feedback. And we keep at it until we succeed.

"Success" as mapping a movie that you can use

Suppose we run with the movie metaphor for "thinking," information processing, framing, making sense of things, developing knowledge, and so on. Then how does this fit into our understanding of "success"?

First of all, it says that *successful* understanding of others, of books, of trainings, of knowledge means *mapping an accurate film*. As I get out of myself, and hear you clearly, without all my frames and settings getting in the way, then I can video-record what you say in all the sensory systems and with all the necessary frames. This doesn't mean I agree with it, believe it, or condone it. It just means I can accurately represent it. Of course, to let it in I do have to let go of my prejudgments and empathically seek first to understand the other. In NLP we use the know-nothing state and the Meta-Model questions to do this. We simply *model* the symbols offered, make a movie of it, and then we evaluate it. We call this "getting the structure of the experience."

Second, all *successful* replication of a learning, skill, behavior, or expertise means starting with pacing or *matching* the movie that we have imported. As we accurately and vividly film a set of high-quality performances and reset our frames so that we can "try it on," we can then begin to replicate the strategy. In NLP, this is the utilization part of strategy work.

Third, to *successfully* learn, develop, and master anything using NLP, we employ our mental movies to encode and represent two locations: present state and desired outcome state. From there we can then create a mental movie of the resources that we need in order to move from one to the other. We call that the SCORE model in

NLP (Symptoms, Causes, Outcome, Resources, Effects). It helps us to think strategically. Where am I now? Where do I want to be? How can I get there? What resources do I need? Every NLP process as a technology for "running your own brain" has that basic structure.

These descriptions of the NLP system and the component elements involved in that system offer us a general description of how to *succeed* in anything. Since everything involves information, which involves representation, which involves state, this model gives us a way to think about and sequence becoming masterful with any set of behaviors or skills. It gives us a prototype for how to succeed in accomplishing any of our outcomes. The early NLP developers summarized how to think about and use NLP for success in the following way:

1. Create and clarify a well-formed outcome of your intention. Make a vivid and accurate film of the desired outcome.
What do you want?

Make an internal movie of it so that you have a clear, vivid, and specific description of what you want.
What resources do you need to make this become a reality?

2. Use your behavior and speech to obtain that outcome. Play the movie in your mind, step into it and let it be a map for how to think, feel, speak, and act.
What do you need to do or say?

Do you have a strategy for doing or saying that?

What are the steps and stages in the process?

3. Use sensory awareness to calibrate and track your progress.
Is the film a good map that's actually working? Receive feedback and test it out. Step into the director and producer perspective to use the feedback to keep refining and updating your film.

Are you getting what you want?

Are you progressing step by step along the way?

What lets you know?

4. Receive the feedback and compare it with your original goal.
Given the feedback, what do you now need to do?

What adjustments or variations do you need to make?

Are you moving in the right direction?

Do you need other resources to assist you?

5. Repeat this process until you find a way to succeed.
If you are moving in the right direction, how much persistence do you need?

What do you need to keep up your motivation?
The elements in this basic neuro-linguistic system for creating and using your internal cinema as a training film include the following:

1. Clean sensory awareness. Skill at accessing an uptime state and using it to cleanly track from good models and learning experiences to your mental movie.
2. Awareness of cinematic features that allow you to use your senses fully. Discernment of your internal default settings and flexibility to shift and alter your internal movie as you map things.
3. Editorial ability to effectively use your soundtrack (the linguistic or meta-representation system of language and words) so that the movie you play inside has a good script to follow.
4. Ability to detect and direct the higher intentions, designs, motivations, and purposes so that the movie you live in has the right qualities and properties (meta-programs and meta-states).
5. Ability to step up a level and choose to produce the quality of life, behaviors, relationships, feelings, and so on that makes the movie a rewarding production (meta-states, gestalt states, well-formed outcomes, executive states for sustaining direction).
6. Openness and flexibility to detect and receive feedback as information to then use in editing and refining (mapping) new features into your movies.

Cinematography as a neuro-semantic system

Here is where we are in this analysis and overview: NLP as a communication model involves the input, processing, and output of *information*. Yet our *awareness* of such information occurs via the "languages" of the mind, our sensory representation systems. We experience these metaphorically "on the screen of our mind" as an internal movie where we see, hear, feel, smell, and taste the referents. This is not real, only phenomenological. But it is "real" to us—it is real inside our neurology. That's why it makes a difference *what* we represent and *how*.

Knowing this now puts into our hands the tools for "running our own brain." All we have to do is it take charge of the movie. This means rising up in our mind as our own editor, director, producer, and executive (see Figure 2.3). If the movies we are playing do not put us in the best states, if they do not provide us with a training film for how to perform with excellence, then we need some new audio-video tracks for our mind. There's nothing wrong with us: it's the cinemas we have been playing. If we get sick and tired of feeling scared, terrified, and timid, we have to stop playing the horror movies in our mind and replace them with some heroic adventure films.

Communing with another person, as in "communication" (words that suggest to us the word elements "co" and "union"), refers to the exchange of information and meaning so that we enter into a shared experience of meaning. This is not a linear process, but a nonlinear one. It goes round and round. It involves feedback and feed-forward loops.

In this cinema of the mind, the language model of NLP (the Meta-Model) gives us the tools for stepping back from language so that we can see its layers and structure and so that we can use questions to unveil the plot of the movie. Then we can see the hidden associative meanings and contextual meanings that make up the script.

Because Meta-Model *questions* focus primarily on structure ("How do you know that?"; "How do you do this?"), they let us understand the plot and narrative of the movie. When we ask it of someone with an impoverished movie, it exposes its weakness and invites the editor part of our mind to invent a new script.

Early descriptions of the Meta-Model used the term "challenge" as a synonym for "question" and this led to some unfortunate consequences. The term suggests to some people that the Meta-Model is combative, argumentative, and even aggressive. Yet it is not. Yes, certainly a person can use it in such ways. Yet the model itself is essentially *explorative*. And as a tool for exploring, we use it best when we come from an attitude of empathy, when we seek to build rapport: "Help me to understand what you're thinking and feeling. *How* do you do that or know that? What does that mean to you?"

Using the Meta-Model, we take the initiative to understand the movies playing in the minds of others. Rather than wait around for others to share, we proactively go first. So we enter the other's world. We model the other's models or internal movies. This allows us to discover the other's patterns and style for turning our information signals into movies. We can do this with the most extreme examples. What kind of movie does a paranoid schizophrenic play in his mind? Or someone who is a multiple personality, or a sociopath? Their sensory systems, words, language patterns, symbols, metaphors, strategies, meta-programs, meta-states, and so forth will give us that information. While we use language to model a person's language, we do that to discover what frames they have set about their movies. This moves us to the higher levels of mind.

Sometimes it's surprising, even shocking, to discover the movies some people play over and over in their minds. It always makes sense to them. And, when we know the patterns of how a person "makes sense" of things, we can use those very patterns to more effectively get through to that person. We call this *pacing*. It means that we match the other's model of the world. This makes our language especially powerful and effective. It enables us to understand, create rapport, build empathy, reduce misunderstandings, reduce conflicts, and so on. Lots of good things!

Why in the world are you watching that *movie?*

If we make sense of the world through the sensory representation systems that play like a movie in our mind with a soundtrack that contains words as well as other auditory components, and the movies we play signal our entire neuro-linguistic system about how to respond, then why in the world do some people watch some of the sick and disgusting movies that they do in their heads?

Why do they watch horror movies? Why do they watch fatalistic defeatist movies? Why do they create and repeatedly play videos of insult, humiliation, contempt? Why do others play movies of trauma, abuse, and rage?

Why? Because they are *trying* to make things better. They are *trying* to finish them, make them go away, or they think that they have no other choice and have to. Whatever the reason, we think that the system is attempting to do something positive and of value. It's just not working. It's just a wrong choice and understanding. This brings up a crucial principle about our neuro-semantic systems and an essential one to understand if we are ever to become masterful with NLP:
People are always doing the best they can with the resources that they have. They always have positive intentions behind even their most ugly and hurtful behavior.

The good intention behind the horrible movie

The phrase "positive intentions" has been misrepresented and misunderstood by many. And that's understandable if a person doesn't know about "logical levels". In fact, some in the NLP community have actually rejected this principle and tried to eliminate it from the model. Yet this is not only a valuable but an essential premise to NLP and especially to the very spirit of NLP.

To believe in positive intentions does not mean that we think all behavior is good and therefore there is no such thing as evil, and that we therefore condone everything. That is *not* its meaning nor how we use the phrase. Positive intention grows out of an understanding of the *systemic nature* of the mind-emotion-body-culture interaction. And, since it is the foundation for reframing, we have to be able to recognize levels and the differences of levels to understand it.

Positive intention means that our behaviors, talk, actions, and so on at the primary level are driven at a higher level by a positive intention of trying to make things better. Everything we do, at some higher level we do for a positive reason. It may not be positive for the person receiving the behavior, but it is positive for the one producing it. At least the person is *intending*, wanting, desiring, hoping, and believing it is. That may be a delusion. It often is. It may not only *not* serve any positive value, but may make things a hundred times worse. The "positive intention", then, may only have the most superficial semblance to anything "positive".

We do not use positive intention to validate ugly or hurtful behavior. Nor do we use positive intention to dismiss behavior or to let someone get away with murder. Instead we *use* it to help the person or ourselves *reframe* our thinking so that we do not confuse person and behavior.

Who we *are* as people is *not* defined *only* by what we do. We *are* much more than what we *do. Doing* and *being* refer to two very different experiences and concepts. Actions come out of *being*, but do not utter the last word about us. How we behaved at eighteen months, three years, at fourteen, as a young adult, in middle years, or whenever differs significantly. Behaviors are just *expressions* of a person, not the *heart and soul* of a person.

We do well to remember this. If we confuse person and behavior we fall into the trap of "unsanity" that Korzybski called *identification*. As you will discover in later chapters, this creates a complex equivalence that will only imprison us and lock us to our actions. And that prevents further growing and developing.

We use positive intention to discover (or to create) higher and more positive value frames so that we can see ourselves and others beyond a particular behavior. Typically, we find that even the worst behaviors are performed because a person is trying to protect himself or herself, to improve his or her life, to promote his or her ideas or causes, to avoid pain. The *intention* may be very well and good to the person.

But the person's map about *how* to do that may be very faulty and lacking—impoverished. The producer or director part of our higher mind *wants* to create a beautiful and successful movie, but the only films available are those that play out scenarios of hurt, ugliness, nastiness, evil, insult, revenge. At the higher level we mean well; at the lower level we don't have an appropriate strategy or map for how to make it happen.

How is it that the hurtful or obnoxious behaviors dominate? Mostly because some lower- or primary-level film gets activated and we get so caught up in it that we can't rise up to a higher level. This is especially true when the primary emotions of fear and anger, revenge or hurt are activated by some threat or danger. Then our first-level *attentions* are so strong and intense we cannot step out of that movie and consult with our executive-level mind to consider such matters as consequences, others, morality, ecology, and health. It's not that we are evil or demonic at the highest intentions, but that the more dramatic and vivid movies are really sick and toxic, and consuming.

Frequently, at the lower levels of mind, our *intentions* may be negative, ugly, hurtful, malicious, or wicked. We may want to hurt another, abuse, or murder. But why? Why do that? What will we get when we get that? By shifting to higher levels and discovering or creating the higher *positive intentions*, we move ourselves or another beyond the negative motives. This gives a person a chance to remap and to begin operating from a more positive intention.

Otherwise, we demonize ourselves or others and assume that "at the core" I, he, or people "are" evil, bad, or demonic. Assuming that we act to live, for example, or to survive, be safe, enjoy, connect, love, feel good about ourselves, contribute, self-actualize (Maslow's list of human needs and drives), this enables us to foster growth and to frame things so that it gives us new opportunities.

Effective communication with others (even with ourselves) and effective transformation of dysfunctional patterns begin as we assume the best and look for positive intentions. We cannot reframe behaviors if we don't. The reframing models operate from this premise and it is this that makes them powerful. Using them in therapy, in business, with loved ones, or in parenting represents a very different attitude and spirit than what most of us have learned in our culture. Very few of us grow up learning to run this film. This movie is a very proactive model compared with the reactive movie of rage, revenge, and playing the victim that most of us learn.

If you want to see the spirit and heart of NLP in action, look at it in these communication frames that the "looking for positive intentions" cinema demonstrates. These frames came originally from the heart of Virginia Satir and Milton Erickson—it's the heart of truly being human, caring, and respectful.

Be proactive. Take the time to enter into another's world, to calibrate to that person, and to pace the other's reality. Assume the best. Look for positive intentions. Use feedback when you don't get the response you want.

Some who train in NLP have not sufficiently emphasized this. Those who would use these powerful technologies to manipulate negatively, to take advantage of others, to pull the wool over others' eyes, and/or to seduce them will not be able to hide their motives. That's the nature of higher frames—they leak out into our words, gestures, and behaviors.

Those who have taken the powerful models, techniques, skills, and patterns of NLP and used them to misguide, manipulate, and use NLP for purely selfish motives have discovered this the hard way. They may get by with it for a while, but only for a while. And rightly so. As neuro-linguistic creatures, what we hold in our mind, especially in the highest levels of our mind (our meta-states), will percolate down the levels and come out.

The meta-domains in our cinemas

Have you noticed the four meta-domains of NLP in this description of the mental movies that we run to process information?
We use the Meta-Model to track information from words, whether precise or vague, into our mind-body systems to create our movies and to supply them with a language soundtrack. And, as we track from words to our internal movie, so we also process information from nonverbal features such as physiology, actions, tones, gestures, use of space, and volume and turn them into internal films.

We use meta-programs to track the frames for our movies. This gives us information at the editorial, director, and even producer level. Meta-programs inform us about how to color and filter the input.

We use the Meta-States model to establish the meta-frames of the cinema. They give us vital information about purpose, intention, motivation, design, and quality.

Via meta-states we input information about the value frames, belief frames, identification frames, decision frames, history frames, expectation frames, and so on.

This is why we have structured this mastering-of-NLP course to explore more fully these four meta-domains and to use them as redundant models for the structure of our experiences. This is the crucial thing. These meta-domains all describe the *same thing*. They give us four approaches or avenues for describing experience. One via the path of words and language; another the path of perception; the third via the layers of states; and the fourth by the cinematic features we edit into our movies. Together they provide a fourfold redundancy to our modeling the structure of experience.

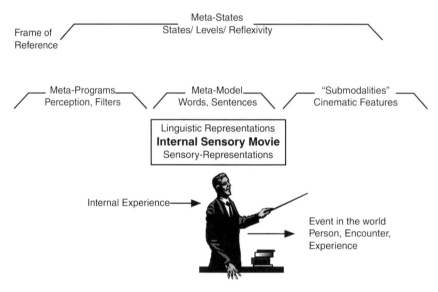

Figure 2.4

Summary

We have presented the NLP model as a one about using the sensory "languages" of the mind to create an internal mental movie. This allows us to simplify the jargon of NLP and to offer a more user-friendly metaphor. It enables us to think about information processing that affects such things as thinking, reasoning, emoting, feeling, psychosomatic processes, and skills in terms of cinematic features.

As a cognitive-behavioral model, NLP presents a systemic model of information inputs and processing. As we "sense" that we see, hear, and feel things as if watching a movie in our mind, it sends signals to our entire neurology. That's what makes it neuro-linguistic.

Yet the movies of our mind are also influenced by higher frames. These frames determine editorial features that we call "sub-modalities", the sorting patterns that we call meta-programs, the attitude and disposition frames that we call meta-states and the abstract and hypnotic language patterns that we call meta-model distinctions.

This now puts the four meta-domains of NLP into one unified model.

Chapter Three
The Pathway to Mastery

What is the pathway to NLP mastery? What is the *attitude* that jet-propels mastery? Which higher-level theoretical frames contribute to mastery?

The pathway to mastering NLP lies in developing the *right kind of attitude*. In the last chapter we talked about that attitude. How many of the secrets of mastery did you pick up there? Conversely, the pathway to NLP mastery does *not* involve merely the acquisition of technical precision. There are lots of people who have learned the model and learned it well. They can run the patterns. They can quote the steps. They can describe the theory. But, they don't have *the attitude*.

Mastery inherently and inescapably involves a certain *attitude*. There is a certain spirit or frame of mind that supports mastery and similarly there are attitudes that will undermine mastery. While we have presupposed this spirit and designed it into every chapter and exercise in this work, we also want to make it explicit. We want you to know what we believe and what we have sought to do in this book. There are far too many trying to present NLP unconsciously. This by pre-supposition denies the very heart of NLP, namely, getting people to "run their own brains".

Part I

The attitude that performs magic

The original *attitude or spirit* of NLP arose from the original three wizards that Richard Bandler and John Grinder modeled that initiated this adventure into the structure of subjectivity. Bandler and Grinder started out in search of a set of competencies—skills of excellence. One primary question drove their exploration:

How were these world-renowned therapists able to produce what seemed like "magic" in their communications with their clients?

They wanted to know *the structure* of such magical experiences. They were also interested in the structure of this therapeutic and communication magic because they happened upon it. Bandler was just listening to the audio recordings of Fritz Perls (the creator of Gestalt Therapy) and in mimicking his way of talking, accent and all, he discovered that he could perform the "magic" as well. For a 21-year-old college student, this was incredible. What was going on here? How could he do this?

John Grinder was brought in to find out. He worked with Bandler to help him pull apart the linguistic structures to see if they could discover the structure. Grinder brought to the table his linguistic skills and genius. He could break things down into structure using the latest linguistic tools available in the mid-1970s, transformational grammar. Bandler brought to the table his natural genius of mimicking— the foundations of his modeling skills. Bandler's genius also involved his ability 'to handle *patterns*, which undoubtedly explained his skills with music and mathematics and his interest in computers.

NLP began with the attitude of *curiosity, exploration, amazement, wonder, mimicking, modeling, adventure*, and *passion*.

Some of the NLP co-developers along with other trainers and thinkers have noted in various articles and presentations that NLP lost steam some years later owing to "the war of the magicians", when egos got in the way and attitudes of competition, scarcity, win/lose, suspicion, and turf conflicts caused many in the general public to become suspicious of the field.

Yet the *true spirit* of NLP is a spirit that flows from the initial presuppositions that Bandler and Grinder found and encoded from the wizards. Today we have those in what we call "the NLP presuppositions". These presuppositions refer to those assumptions, belief systems, principles, premises, and higher-level dispositions that we recognize as the governing *frames of mind* that empower the wizards in discovering and performing their magic.

This means that, above and beyond the mental movies that we make in our minds about NLP, the patterns for running our own brains, how to use NLP, and so forth, for mastery we need to develop the right kind of higher states or attitudes. We need the attitude of a neuro-linguistic magician. This means learning and adapting the attitudes that allow us to direct and produce our own mental movies in ways similar to Satir, Perls, and Erickson and to Bandler and Grinder.

An attitude of magic

In the first volume of *The User's Manual for the Brain*, we set forth those NLP presuppositions. These are critically important because they serve as the theoretical frameworks of NLP. Even though NLP presents itself as a "model" for communication and change, and prides itself on being a structural model for human subjectivity, NLP does have a theory and an ideology.

A model of science will have a theoretical explanation, testable hypothetical assumptions, working guidelines, a list of variables and elements, a syntax and a set of techniques that result. Regrettably, much of the earlier NLP trainings presented only the "techniques" of NLP. Though extremely powerful, NLP has more, much more, as a science. NLP offers these presuppositions as the theoretical understandings for its model.

As beginning practitioners, we learned and were introduced to the presuppositions in several ways. While we consciously introduce them, we mostly install them by using and demonstrating them. We do this by encouraging participants to spend time discovering the usefulness of these presuppositions for directing behavior toward excellence. Once installed as our unconscious frames, these presuppositions operate as our higher-level frames and so govern our thinking, perceiving, acting, speaking.

Doing this enables the presuppositions to work as neurological filters and beliefs. This makes it easy to see the world in terms of these understandings. Other mental "entities" also operate as mental filters. For example, what we deem important or not important (values) shape our perception. The meta-program filters also do the same. And, because beliefs function as meta-frames, we will want to install enhancing beliefs from the beginning. That's what the NLP presuppositions provide us.

Why is this important? So that we can "run our own brain" and facilitate others to do the same. We do that in order to model and replicate excellence in our lives. This is the passion of NLP. The early co-developers of NLP learned these principles as they modeled and used various disciplines: Gestalt therapy, family systems therapy, Ericksonian hypnotic-medical psychotherapy, general semantics, cybernetics, information systems, transformational grammar, cognitive-behavioral psychology, and Batesonian anthropology. In the process they discovered what enabled these people to create the excellence they did. They found out that the leaders in these fields produced excellence because they operated from the framework of certain beliefs and principles—the NLP presuppositions.

Having learned these principles at the practitioner level, we now shift to yet a higher use of them as we move into the master practitioner level. Our aim is to more fully install these premises as our frames of mind so we more fully understand and appreciate them. We will want to let them govern our thinking, direct our understanding, and to modulate our feelings and responses. When that happens, we step up to more excellence in what we do.

When these "core" beliefs function as meta-beliefs, they operate as "controller states" of mind that modulate and control our behaviors. They function as the meta-frames that give meaning to all of our lower-level beliefs, values, decisions, understandings, expectations, meta-programs, and so forth. This explains the profound influence they exercise over our thought-feelings and our behaviors. They govern how we function in the world and what we, in turn, receive from the world. So we will want to fully install these higher-level beliefs as frameworks for excellence, which will drive us toward our desired outcome.

Lakoff and Johnson (1999), in *Philosophy in the Flesh: The Embodied Mind and its Challenge to Western Thought*, describe the meta-stating effect of presuppositions in how they shape our thoughts and behaviors:

> We go around armed with a host of presuppositions about what is real, what counts as knowledge, how the mind works, who we are, and how we should act. [p. 9]

Cognitive science, however, does not allow us direct access to what the cognitive unconscious is doing as it is doing it. Conscious thought is the tip of an enormous iceberg. It is the rule of thumb among cognitive scientists that unconscious thought is 95 percent of all thought-and that may be a serious underestimate. Moreover, the 95 percent below the surface of conscious awareness shapes and structures all conscious thought. If the cognitive unconscious were not there doing this shaping, there could be no conscious thought. [p. 13, emphasis added]

The "shapes and structures" of the cognitive unconscious for Lakoff and Johnson shape our consciousness. This refers not only to the metaphorical structuring that arises from the kind of bodies we have (neurological embodiment) but also to our presuppositional premises. For Lakoff and Johnson, our reasoning arises from our bodies, our relationship to gravity and the world, and become the frames that we use.

Similarly, Bateson noted that our framing, or punctuating of events, enables us to build up the mental "contexts" that then direct, modulate, and self-organize our experience. We speak about these powerful meta-stating processes in meta-states as directionalizing our thinking-and-behaving system (e.g., our neuro-linguistic states). So, as beliefs, these presuppositions serve as *attractors*. They attract and organize both our internal and external environments. They attract forces from within and without that support the presuppositions. Conversely, they delete everything that does not fit the presuppositions. Once we install these presuppositions so that they are part of our higher frame of mind, they operate in the background of our mind, focusing our thought-behaviors.

Presuppositional attitudes

As a practitioner, you already know the NLP presuppositions. So, as we review them briefly, we will use them to suggest *the kind of attitude* or a meta-state frame that transforms us so that our practice of NLP moves to a higher level of mastery. With that in mind, read the following from the perspective of imagining fully taking on each presupposition as a frame of mind for directing your own mental movies of NLP. View each premise as:

- an empowering belief;
- an enhancing understanding about the world, people, and neuro-linguistic states;
- an enriching value of importance;
- an exciting way of being and functioning in the world.

Try each on, not so much as an understanding or *principle* (you should already have them installed at that level of mind) but as a *belief*, as an everyday *attitude*. Then examine each presuppositional principle in the following ways:

- If I used this as an attitude, what attitude would that be?
- Do I have permission to think and feel this way?

- Am I willing to give myself permission to make this my way of perceiving things?
- Will I give myself a chance to try this on as an empowering attitude?
- How will this affect the way I talk and act?
- What effect will this have on my relationships? My skills? My expertise?
- What adjustments, shifts, and changes will it entail concerning my way of being in the world?
- Am I willing to commit myself to this principle?
- What one thing could I do today that will begin to actualize this presupposition?

1. The map is not the territory

Originating from the work of Korzybski in *Science and Sanity* (1933/1994), this offers the foundational epistemology of NLP. The idea of constructionism is that we *construct* our model of the world. We put this first because it is primary in the NLP framework.

A map *is not* the territory it represents. It cannot be. We map a territory as we create a symbolic representation of it. So the words we use are not the events they represent. What goes on inside our head regarding an event is not the event, but only our perception of that event. Our internal representations are not the same as the event they represent.

Neurologically it is impossible for us to bring the world or events into our mind. It cannot be done. What exist "out there" are energy manifestations. The electromagnetic field that we call light is radiation and it has no color. It's not the kind of "thing" that can have color. Yet we see color. We do so because our nervous system *creates* color via our rods and cones. Bateson was fond of saying that such things as coconuts, monkeys, and mothers cannot enter the mind. Nor are our mappings exact or accurate replications of what's in the world. We map using symbols and representations to create our sensed cinema. We map our internal movies leaving lots of things out and distorting other things.

We are sure you know about and understand the map-territory distinction. That's the beginning. Yet the questions for mastery are:

- Do you feel it in your body?
- Is it part of your way of being in the world?

Conceptually we know that when we fail to use the map-is-not-the-territory principle it causes miscommunication and personal problems. This happens whenever we act as if others should operate from our maps, as if they should be the "same". Do you *feel* that intelligent people should see things the *same*? Do you feel that each person should and will have a unique mapping? Test yourself.

If you assume that others have (or ought to have) the same perceptions as you do and so don't first consult them, the map-territory distinction isn't in neurology.

Expect conflict. Expect mind reading. Of course, when we do, we operate from maps rather than learn about the maps of others.

In working with couples, we find that a major breakdown in communication occurs in the way people engage in mind-reading statements.
"I know you don't love me."

"You don't care about me."

"You are so jealous."

"I know how you feel."

As practitioners we learn how to effectively respond to such statements by asking:

"How do you know X?"

"What specifically am I doing to cause you to choose to believe Y?"

Yet now we care about something else. We care about *feeling* the map-territory difference so that mind reading *feels* ill formed and outside of the way that we move through the world.

Whenever we link one thing and equate it with another thing, *and do so without awareness*, we show the lack of having the map—territory distinction embodied.

"You don't love me because you're always late and keep me waiting."

"I don't think I'm doing well at work because my boss never tells me how much he appreciates me."

Again, we know how to meta-model such statements.

"How specifically does being late mean that I don't love you?"

As practitioners we learn how to ask questions that enable the speaker to sort out and to distinguish the levels involved in such statements. By way of contrast, as we become masterful with this, we learn to *feel* the map-territory distinction and to stay mindful of always operating from some map. As we restore the feeling sense that there is always a mapmaker, always a movie producer and director, we know that we always are dealing with maps *of* reality, and not with reality itself.

Giving other people and events mystical control over us is another sign. This is the cause-effect trap. Recognizing the great gulf between map and territory stops us from engaging in the foolishness of believing that other people and events actually "control" our mind. We master map-territory when we know and *feel* that no one can make us believe or feel anything against our will. What we think-and-feel is always our choice.

Thinking that our experiences are "real" in some ultimate or determinist way indicates that we have not yet incorporated the map-territory distinction. That we may have grown up in a dysfunctional family does not mean that we are, or have to remain, dysfunctional. It only means we learned some poor ways of thinking and acting. We can learn both to know and to *feel* that we are more than our experiences. And that's the magic.

Consider the situation of having long ago experienced some traumatic event. It could have been a war, imprisonment, terrorist attack, car accident, murder, rape, molestation, divorce, loss of a loved one. If it is *not* now occurring, then the only way that trauma can be "alive" to us is the movie we have of it. Past events are just that, *past*. No longer occurring.

So, if it feels as if it were still occurring, we are doing it. We are still playing the movie and stepping into the movie and cueing our neuro-semantic system to experience the movie. "It's all in our mind-body-emotion system." The traumatic feelings of today are functions of our mental horror movie, not of the trauma. That's why some people keep the trauma feelings alive for years, even decades, and some people do not. That's why some people recover quickly and get on with life and others play out a movie script of being "a victim for life".

What's the difference? The difference is in the scenarios they are playing out in the theater of their mind and how they have edited that movie, and the attitude they take as director of the movie, and the purposes and motivations they use as producer.

It is as simple as that. It is as profound as that. This explains why "the phobia cure" can work in moments to almost instantaneously and dramatically alter our neuro-semantic reality. The problem is never the person, never the experience, never *what* we have been through. The problem is always the frame, always the mental movie, always the higher frames running the movie. Change the movie and its frames—and life changes.

Feeling the difference between map and territory empowers us in the confidence that we can change our maps. This adds to our mental flexibility. It allows us to more easily shift perspectives, open our mind to new and different information, think in new ways. This, in turn, frees us to explore the maps we've been navigating by. Do they really serve us well? As we start by exploring our personal limitations, we stop blaming others and events. We stop identifying with events. And we start to explore and create empowering maps and movies that allow us to live in more resourceful ways.

2. *People respond according to their own internal maps*

Precisely because the map *is not* the territory, we hold *all* of our perceptions, understandings, beliefs, frames, and "truths" tentatively. And, as we hold them as *just a map*, this helps us to lighten up and to be more explorative. And, as this indicates that everybody else also operates from maps, we don't have to get mad at their maps: we can simply explore them. We can explore the mental movies playing in the theater of their minds and then understand their world.

This leads to another valuable insight: namely, that all of us respond according to our internal maps. What we think, feel, say, and do makes perfect sense given the shows that play in the cinema of our minds. So the responses that we don't understand, the behaviors of others that don't seem to make sense, do make sense and are rational. They are *psycho-logical* to the frames and movies playing in the individuals' minds.

Even the talk and behavior of schizophrenics make perfect sense—*given* their maps and the movies that guide their talk and actions. Meaning is an "inside" job. We do not respond according to what is "out there". We respond according to things, according to the movie playing "inside" a person's mental theater and the *meanings* it generates.

You respond to the world from your internal mapping. All of your responses make perfect sense according to *what* and *how* you map things to create your movie. Your partner also responds according to his or her map and its movie. But it is not your map. You can count on that. The same applies to your children, friends, colleagues, employer. We all respond from our own movie maps.

Is this your *attitude*? Do you now know intuitively to expect people to operate according to their maps? Do you know that, before you can change your response, your internal maps or movies have to change? Are you willing to let this become your attitude?

We master NLP as we develop the desire and the ability to map the very best internal cinemas. It means finding them, developing them, and then sharing them. If it all boils down to maps and movies, then its maps of excellence that enable us to produce excellence in any arena of life. Recognizing this plasticity of meaning expands our sense of what's possible. It expands our sense of what is possible for us and for others. When others talk and experience limitations and problems, we immediately know that it's their movies and so begin exploring that. Mastery of NLP involves always questioning maps, our own and those of others. We constantly ask ourselves:

● What are the probable meanings and maps that drive this or that behavior?
● How has this person mapped such things as causation, meaning, value, self?
● What frames empower and/or disempower the person?

3. Meaning is context-dependent
While Korzybski noted that all meaning is context-dependent, it was Bateson and his associates who truly showed what the *contextual nature* of meaning truly means. They did this in their revolutionary hypothesis about the psychotic state of

schizophrenia. In *Steps to an Ecology of Mind* (1972/2000), Bateson speaks about frames, framing, punctuating the events of life, and establishing levels of such things as learning, meaning, and thought. It was Bateson who introduced the understanding that events, words, and signals take on their significance or meaning via contexts and contexts-of-contexts. It's not only the movie but how we have framed the movie.

This means that we can transform meaning by simply changing contexts. How do we think about aiming for a goal? Which frame do we put around that? Do we use the success or failure frame? Do we use the practice-and-experiment-until-you-develop-your-skills frame? Do we use the exploration frame? Would there be a difference in significance between these frames?

If meaning is context-dependent, then any word, phrase, statement, event, behavior, or relationship can be rendered meaningless by a different frame and can be given new textures by other frames.

As practitioners we have learned to ask reframing questions such as:

- In what context would this problem be beneficial to myself or another?
- Where might I use this for some good?

Now we go further. We develop the attitude that *nothing inherently means anything* as an intuitive feeling. When we know that in our gut, then we will have the mental flexibility to not immediately and automatically buy into any "meaning". We will check its ecology. We will quality-control our thinking-feeling states:

- Does this way of thinking or feeling serve me well?
- Does it enhance my life?
- Does it empower me as a person?

Since meaning is context-dependent, and we change meaning by changing context, and since nothing means anything, we can step into the higher frame of mind and know that *we are the meaning maker*. We are the ones who attribute the meaning. Do you know that? Do you feel that? Is that your attitude? Say it and then affirm it with a "*Yes!*"

Nothing in itself has meaning. No thing, no person, no event has meaning until a meaning maker gives it meaning. Every meaning maker gives events different meanings. Every meaning maker, consciously or unconsciously, has choice regarding which meaning to give things.

4. Mind and body are systems that inevitably and inescapably affect each other
As practitioners, we discovered that mind and body function as one cybernetic system. They are not different things that function apart from each other. Where we perceive, think, reason, imagine, or remember (cognize) we feel, experience in our

neurology, in our body (soma), and so emote. That's why we write with hyphens and connecting dashes: mind-body, thinking-feeling, neuro-linguistic, neuro-semantic. We can only talk about "mind" and "body" as separate things linguistically. This linguistic mapping does not mean that such elements exist apart from each other. They do not.

This explains the "placebo effect". What we *think* is in a pill can affect our body as much as what is actually in the pill. Harmless sugar pills (placebos) can effect healing states. That's because "mind" affects and influences "body" for good or ill (think of psychosomatic illnesses).

Modern medical research has started to recognize this mind-body connection. Lakoff and Johnson (1999) say that we have roughly 100 billion neurons in our brain and these neurons form "100 trillion synaptic connections." This gives the phenomenon that we call "mind" lots of ways of signaling "body".

Mastering NLP involves incorporating this understanding as our attitude and intuitive feeling. We need the sense, "Of course, it's always mind-body; it's never 'mind' apart from 'body' or apart from 'emotion'; it's never 'emotion' apart from 'mind' ". This attitude then enables us to work holistically, to integrate the mind-body-emotion system, and to check the higher levels of the mind for congruency and ecology. It all works together. To do otherwise falls into the insanity of "elementalism" (Korzybski). That's why using punctuation to link words and prefixes to words reattaches the parts that we have elementalized to our detriment.

5. Individual skills are developed and operate as we enhance and sequence our representation systems

Our understandings began as we studied the sensory representation systems and the meta-representation systems of language. This was the stroke of genius that surprised Bateson, as he noted in his preface to *The Structure of Magic, Volume I*. Who would have thought to use our phenomenal "senses" as the foundation of "thought"? Yet it worked. NLP has become a field of study today because it worked.

We "think" by reproducing a sensed or phenomenal awareness of images, sounds, smells, and other sensations. Our internal mental movies are not literal. Inside the brain, there is no mental screen. We do not literally "see" or "hear" things in there. Yet it *seems* as if we did. The *appearance* of such "re-presentations" of sights, sounds, and sensations is our *phenomenal sense*. We know that we "abstract" (select, generalize, delete, and distort) from the outside world and create our mental movie of it. Yet what gets in is not the things themselves. What gets in is information, information *about* the outside world. "Knowledge" is entirely structural, said Korzybski. It is entirely form and structure, said Bandler and Grinder. And that's why form, structure, and context play a more crucial role in the structure of experience than content.

With this as our attitude, we know that every human skill has a representational structure. We know that we can track every skill as an internal movie on the screen of our mind. And this moves us to true mastery. We "run our brains" by receiving, storing, processing, and outputting information. We think about such as computational: input ➜ output. Stimulus ➜ Processing ➜ Output (the TOTE model). This is what we mean when we say that we now think in terms of strategies.

How does this experience, behavior, or skill operate? Which words and higher-level concepts do I need to encode a skill?

At the mastery level we immediately and automatically feel curious about every behavior, no matter how obnoxious. We wonder, "How do you do that? How do you split your mind in this way? How do you not recognize this feeling? How do you fly into an outrage and act stupidly?"

We think *structurally*.

Nor does the brain stop at just the first level of representational meaning. Our brains continually reflect. We have thoughts about thoughts. We classify, then we classify our classifications. We create conceptual categories, then put those in categories. This allows us to create higher neuro-semantic states and complex states such as resilience, proactivity, and wisdom.

Our move into mastery occurs as we know that it's all made out of the same stuff: representations. This allows us to develop skill in eliciting structure, utilizing form, and installing higher-level frames through the sequencing and coalescing of the representational systems as we design-engineer new and exciting states.

6. We pace another's sense of reality by respecting and matching the person's model of the world, creating rapport

Given that we all create unique and idiosyncratic models of the world (mental movies) informed by our unique way of representing and framing things, we learn to effectively pace by recognizing and respecting this. Then, with that attitude, we put ourselves in a position to effectively match or pace each person's style. Since the structure of rapport involves entering into another's movie world empathetically (going into second perceptual position), this allows us to create an environment for effective communication. This nonjudgmental approach involves an understanding attitude, an attitude that seeks first to understand. This gives us entrance into the depths and riches of others.

Building a gestalt meta-frame

These first six NLP presuppositions orient us to human nature-to the way we create movie maps and then operate by those cinematic representations, experience meaning by our mental contexts, and so on. Consider these now as a whole:

- The map is not the territory.
- People respond according to their internal maps.
- Meaning is context-dependent.
- Mind and body operate together as a holistic system.
- Skills emerge from developing and sequencing representation systems.
- Rapport arises form respecting and pacing another's model of the world.

Taken together, and used as a whole, what kind of gestalt state do these six presuppositions create for you? Layering mental frames one on top of another activates a system and often a new gestalt emerges. Then we create something that's "more than the sum of all the parts" and of all the frames.

As we recognize and believe that nothing "out there" runs our brain unless we default to it, we take ownership of our cognitive powers. This results in our knowing that we can change our perceptions as fitting for a given context. The resulting confident frame of mind then saturates our entire physiology-neurology system. We think in terms of structure, process, and strategies. We think in terms of systems, outcomes, and resources. We think in terms of respect, validation, and permission. Together, the six pre-suppositions coalesce to give us a flexibility of consciousness that empowers our mind for excellence, for becoming a master. And this is the spirit of NLP.

EXERCISE: Turning the NLP presuppositions into felt beliefs
Let's turn these first six premises into a felt belief or attitude.

1. Identify and verbally express the presupposition.
For example, say the words, "The map is not the territory."

Then play around with that expression to recode it in other words. Express it in synonyms.

2. As you express the presupposition, tease out the ideas that make up the concept at the primary level and at the meta-levels.
PS: Pointing to "the territory" out there beyond your skin.

MS: Not negation. My idea about what's out there is not what is actually out there.

"Whatever I say does not equal and comprise what's out there."

"Only a map, only a way of representing and thinking about what's out there."

3. Step into the expressions kinesthetically by letting your hands, arms, legs, stomach, breathing, and posture mime the expressions.
Playfully express the ideas and expressions until you feel a greater and greater clarity about how the expression maps out and creates an enhancing belief.

Playfully express the opposite for a contrastive analysis: "My map is the territory."

4. Put a label or term on the feelings, emotions, and meta-feelings that you evoke in this process.
What does it feel like when you fully and completely step into the idea that "The map is not the territory"?

It feels like a dis-identification, it feels like a key distinction, it feels like I'm witnessing external reality, like I'm a mapper.

Free-flow in the ways you describe and own the feelings.

5. Imagine moving out into tomorrow and the weeks and months to come with these feelings.
Future-pace this attitude so that you make a movie of taking it into your work, relationships, or home.

6. Check ecology, then amplify the feelings.
Let them double, triple, or more.

Part II

In moving toward mastery we are here making sure that we have fully incorporated the NLP presuppositions not only into our way of thinking but also into our way of being in the world. That's the key. Making them our felt reality. Let us continue the presuppositions.

7. We distinguish person from behavior because we are more than our behavior
Just as "the map is not the territory", so behavior is not the same as a person. We act and express ourselves through our behaviors, and yet at the same time we, as persons, are much more than our behaviors. No behavior fully expresses us. None of our behaviors at any given moment in our history fully expresses all of our thinking, feeling, valuing, or believing. Our behavior is not who we are, and it does not exhaustively define us.

Therefore, as we index our behaviors to the time, place, context, relationship, or purpose in which they arise and belong, we realize that every behavior is a *particular* behavior at a *particular* time, place, context. In other situations and times, we behave differently. This contextualizes behavior. In some contexts, our behavior drastically changes.

This leads to a complex attitude that can value, honor, and respect a *person* while recognizing that we often do not live up to our best behaviors. It enables us to avoid identifying with our behaviors and not identifying others merely with their behaviors. People are more than their behaviors. This attitude enables us to give them a chance to grow and change. Assuming that they are doing the best they can given their movie mapping, we cut them some slack.

This presupposition along with the others keeps altering our frame of mind to give us more enhancing beliefs about who we are, what we value as dear to us, how we define and sort for reality or create meanings. Is this presupposition your attitude? Do you always and clearly distinguish person and behavior? Do you know better than identifying yourself with some particular behavior? Do you know that no matter what you think you are, you are more than that? When you let this principle sink in, you'll master the principles about feedback because it is never about *you*, only about your behavior.

8. In some context every behavior is useful and has value; every behavior is driven by some positive intention

As practitioners, we already know that every behavior has a *positive intention* behind it. The challenge is to find the positive intentions. As we move to mastering NLP, our ability to separate person from behavior and to assume that people are trying to accomplish something of value is our automatic and default frame of mind. We edit and direct all of our movies from that perspective.

The positive frame of this presupposition empowers us to handle obnoxious behaviors. Without operating from the positive frame, it's easy to get put off by behaviors and to jump to the conclusion that some people are "evil". That belief, in turn, then blinds us to seeing and recognizing redeeming features. It invites us to demonize people, and to treat them as nonhumans. A more complex and yet accurate understanding is that even good people do bad things, evil things, but never for the *sake* of "evil": they do them to achieve something of value. What's missing is long-term thinking, checking ecology, considering the consequences for others.

How easily can you turn on this attitude? Do you have immediate, or even better, automatic access to this attitude? What do you need to believe or refuse that will allow you to make this assumption?

When we combine these ideas so that we distinguish people from behavior and frame people as doing the best they can given the resources they have available in a given context, this evokes several new gestalts. It evokes *forgiveness*, magnanimity, and graciousness. Together these also empower us to be able to create rapport with more ease and congruency.

9. Behavior and change should be evaluated in terms of context and ecology

As practitioners we discovered the importance of asking questions about context and ecology. We learned to "run an ecology check" on beliefs, decisions, states, or responses in order to make sure that we take our whole life system into account. We have learned to consider the contexts of our communicating and relating with others. We learned to note the systems within which we live (for example, individual, family, co-workers). This makes for health, balance, integrity.

Is this change congruent within all of our contexts? Is this change appropriate, empowering, or respectful? Is this change congruent with other people in the system?

What attitude does this presupposition elicit? It evokes and creates the attitudes of thinking holistically, thinking in larger terms, thinking long-term, and consequentially. Does this describe your frame of mind? Can you step into it easily? If not, what holds you back from thinking reflectively in this way rather than just reacting from a limited and narrow perspective?

How much is *thinking ecologically* part of your mindset? If the ecology check involves thinking *about* our thoughts and feelings, and questioning our states, then it inherently operates at a meta-level. As a self-referential state (or meta-state), it describes how we reflect back on our thoughts and feelings. (see "The Ecology Check as a Meta-State" at www.neuro semantics.com). Ask yourself:

- Does this thought, belief, value, attitude, emotion, behavior, or way of communicating serve me well?
- Does it enhance my life?
- Does it move me forward toward my desired outcomes?
- Does it limit me in any way?
- Does it empower or disempower?
- What effect does it have upon my relations with others?

Quality-control thinking enables these evaluations to question our experiences. When well installed it comes from a higher state of interest, curiosity, mindfulness, or observation. We move there to check the ecology of a certain piece of consciousness or behavior in relation to, say, our health, career, relationships, family, or culture.

To "run an ecology check" on our thinking, believing, valuing, emoting, behaving, or communicating, we first have to move (conceptually) to a position meta to the thought or belief and to then evaluate that evaluation. As you imagine this as your everyday attitude, realize that it is this attitude that contributes tomastery.

10. We cannot not communicate—even when we try not to communicate, we do
Communication is inevitable. And the way we communicate affects what and how people receive us. Everything we do signals ourselves and others about our state of mind, wants, desires, or beliefs. Appreciating this about the communicating process moves us closer to the attitude of mastery. We know that to *not* send or receive a letter also communicates. Because we can, at our higher frames, expect and look for certain responses, we can read their absence as conveying a message.

We cannot *not* communicate, because communication also involves the nonverbal messages that we send via such cues as gesture, tone, volume, movement, and breathing. A great portion of communication occurs nonverbally. How much? No one knows for sure. Different experts give different percentages and analysis. An old model based on *animal*-communication research of one-word commands came up with the classic 55 percent, 38 percent, and 7 percent: 55 percent was due to visual impressions (face, gestures, posture and the like), 38 percent was due to tone and volume, and 7 percent was due to words. And, when you are communicating one-word commands to dogs, this makes sense: the dog will look at your face and listen to your tone to get your meaning! These numbers undoubtedly do *not* hold when it comes to human communication (see the article on our website about the original research and its surprising origins: www.neurosemantics.com/Non verbal_Communication.htm).

Bateson noted that mammalian communication is significantly attuned to nonverbal signals that communicate messages about *relationship*. He also spoke about how animals (such as dogs, dolphins, cats) use the beginnings of a set of actions to communicate relationship. The meowing cat who rubs up against our leg says, "Dependency, dependency" in an effort to get you to "mother" it with milk. The cat is not using the gestures as a symbol that *stands* for "milk".

Here contextual cues, given nonverbally, make up a lot of communication.

In this, the very way we communicate affects what another sees and hears, and how another interprets our messages. *Congruence* between *what* we say in words and *how* we say it in physiology, tonality, or gesture communicates at a higher level whether we can be believed and trusted. Incongruence says that we should not be believed and trusted. It "communicates" this because we use congruence and incongruence to set such frames.

Adopting the attitude that making our verbal and non-verbal signals congruent should therefore be one of our top priorities if we want to be effective, elegant, and powerful in our communication. When choosing a meta-program, people tend to have preferences for verbal or nonverbal channels. Many will watch and read nonverbal signals and evaluate them as more real or important. Others will do the opposite. Realizing this enables us to make communicating congruently important.

Consider the stage hypnotist who asks you to form a circle with your thumb and index finger. He says, "Form a circle like this." He forms the circle and then says, "And touch your chin." He touches his cheek, not his chin.

What do most people do? The vast majority will form a circle with their fingers from his suggestions and follow his lead in touching their cheek in spite of the words "touch your chin".

I demonstrated this recently with a group. Of the fourteen present, only one participant placed his hand on his chin. One placed it on his cheek and then moved slightly toward his chin. The other twelve participants placed their hands on their right cheeks and were utterly amazed when I explained what I did. We do communicate with nonverbal signals and often the messages we send are subtly powerful in influencing responses.

11. *The meaning of communication is in the response we get*

As NLP practitioners, we entered into this field and discovered this wonderfully surprising idea. Typically, it takes a while to fully understand and appreciate this idea. Given our cultural frames, it tends to be a more challenging one to buy into and fully accept.

Violating, as it does, common cultural conventions about communication, this statement presupposes that our "communication" involves two people co-creating an understanding. That's why we never know what we have communicated. We know *what* we said, perhaps even *how* we said it, but not what we *communicated*, not what the other heard. It is in only in the other person's response that we can be informed about what the communication has done inside the cinema of the his or her mind.

When this becomes our attitude, when it becomes our frame of mind, the very nature of our communicating changes. And it changes radically. For one thing, we immediately drop all the blaming and accusing as we move into a nonfault, inter-active style and focus on finding out what was heard and then clarifying. Failing to get the response we want now enables us to keep searching and to stay motivated in that search. This new mindset involves accepting full responsibility in the exchanges.

We can express this presupposition by saying that the most important information about an exchange is *the response we get*—verbally and nonverbally. The response we get indicates to some extent what another has heard. We need to know that. This leads to a new frame of mind. It enables us to value the response of others as indicative of how close we are to mutual understanding. Thinking I have done a super job in explaining X precisely, while a listener thinks that I meant Y means that I have communicated Y to him or her.

A response of, say, dislike, contempt, refusal to communicate, or manipulation offers insight into the meaning of my communication. It probably means that there are not enough similarities or foundation for a healthy relationship. It does take two to communicate. So, when we're dealing with someone who doesn't want to communicate, we should recognize that reality.

We now know that we do not and cannot directly make another person see, hear, feel and experience the same mental movie as the one in our head. At best we can only provide the best cinematic cues possible and keep adjusting our words and nonverbals until we all agree that we are sharing a fairly similar movie in our sep-arate theaters. This changes the very purpose of communicating. It's like speaking (or writing) a screenplay for each other giving directions not only about what to represent in the film, but how to encode it. When the other has a similar coding, we then say that we have succeeded in communicating.

12. *Whoever sets the frame for a communication exchange governs things*

As we noted in the last chapter, every mental movie is framed in some way. There are no films, even snapshots, in our mind without some frame: some frame of reference, frame of meaning. And, because higher frames govern the lower as producers govern directors who govern editors who govern players, so the higher frames provide the most influence in our neuro-semantic system.

Not only that, but someone or something always sets these frames. And whoever sets the frame governs or controls the subsequent experiences or the movie. The resulting thoughts, ideas, concepts, beliefs, emotions, behaviors, language, problems, solutions, and experiences come from the higher frames. This invites us to explore the editor level of our mind, the director level, and the producer level. It invites us to ask who has created the map (thereby questioning the Lost Performative) or what frame is in charge of the movie.

Do you know this intuitively yet? Do you automatically *feel* it so that it governs your everyday attitude as you interact and communicate? If you did, how would that affect your attitude? What attitudes would begin to develop and grow if you did?

13. *"There is no failure, only feedback"*

When we act and our actions do not immediately or fully get the response or outcome that we want, what do we call that? Culturally, most of us have learned to call it "failure". To "not succeed" is to fail. That's our cultural equation. It leads to playing the "failure film". We see ourselves not succeeding and the editor zooms the movie in on what failed, colors it dark, plays foreboding music in the background, and frames it as, "Oh, how sad, how pitiful, this is the way life is!"

We typically think of a nonsuccess in this all-or-nothing way. Once we create the concept of "to fail", then its easy to invent the category of "failure". This is where the problem begins.

Problem?

Yes, the problem of perceptually seeing and sorting for "failure" as a life and "self" category. When we do that, then it leads to a nominalization of a nominalization summarized in the deceptively subtle phrase, "I am [first nominalization] a failure [second nominalization]." Then we become afraid of this category or the potentiality of that judgment (more nominalizations). You can only imagine the movies that we create in our minds from this mapping.

As NLP practitioners we know and recognize this nonsense, do we not? We have already learned that the term "failure" is not real, that it is a nominalized judgment, and that the term has deleted critically important information: when, where, how, in what way, by what criteria, and so forth? Recognizing it as a toxic frame, we also learned this new reframe for an "activity that does not succeed". It means feedback. It means learning. It means recognizing our humanity and adjusting what we do.

We know the movie that we should be playing in the cinema of our mind. The "feedback film".

Yet knowing that is not the same as *living* and *feeling* that, is it? This is the test of mastery. Do you feel the NLP premise that there's no failure, only feedback? Is there any failure for you? On the emotional level, do you ever experience "failure"? NLP mastery involves moving beyond the old movie of failure and playing the new one until our very neurology knows how to feel the excitement: *"It's feedback!"* And to feel fully curious: "What can I learn from this?"

What do you want to feel when an action fails to get the response you want? What emotions does the idea of "it's feedback" suggest to you? Pick a good one; pick an emotion that will help you when such occurs. Do you want to feel resilient? Motivated? What attitude do you want? What attitude do you admire and love in others who do not go to "failure," but maintain an optimistic attitude and use it to improve themselves?

Effective communicators, be they businesspeople, therapists, coaches, parents, or thinkers, operate from a free spirit. They have a program of personal efficiency and resilience even when things don't go right. They refuse to get down. They refuse to judge or condemn themselves. They do not begin to doubt themselves. They activate their intelligence to learn.

We begin our mastery of NLP on the day that we set the necessary frames that empower us to truly live by this tremendously freeing principle that "There is no failure, only feedback."

14. The person with the most flexibility exercises the most influence in the system
This "the Law of Requisite Variety" comes from systems theory and cybernetics and most immediately from Bateson, who mentioned it repeatedly in his works. As a master in training, you will find that this premise encourages flexibility as an attitude—the ability to adapt, change course, look at things in new ways.

Do you have that attitude? How often do you become rigid and stubborn? What triggers that?

Identify the triggers and then practice setting this presupposition as your new frame, telling yourself, "This gives me the chance to adapt. Having a stable objective and criteria and a flexible style for getting there is the secret of success."

Do you believe that? Are you ready to say yes to that? If so, then you are on your way to mastery. To become masterful, we have to become more flexible, more willing and able to shift our thinking, feeling, speaking, and behaving. This means thinking outside the box. This means the willingness to consider our previous hard-earned knowledge as possibly being wrong or at least outdated. Such thinking also encourages thinking systemically, which we will refer to repeatedly in this work.

15. *There is no resistance, only the lack of rapport*

When we communicate and push to achieve our goals it sometimes *seems* as if we get "resistance". Yet what we call "resistance" and classify as someone *resisting* our ideas, suggestions, desires, or goals is, according to Milton Erickson, not resistance, but a signal that we have not created sufficient connection. Now there's a reframe! Milton not only did not "believe" in resistance, but he refused to use that category as a map in his mental world. He simply did not play the "this person is a resistant client" movie in the theater of his mind.

So he didn't get very much resistance. He got messages and signals to spend more time pacing, empathizing, listening, and creating rapport. Rather than believe that there is such a thing as "resistance" and think that some people are "resistant clients", or that sometimes people may resist just for the hell of it, Erickson intro-duced into NLP this much more resourceful frame and premise. What we find when people seem not to be with us and even fight us is an emotional state of feeling unappreciated, invalidated, forced, or controlled.

When we turn this premise into a movie in our mind and play the video called *There Is No Resistance, Just the Lack of Rapport*, we then find it easy to recognize and accept responsibility for our part in the situation. When we meet what seems like resistance, we know that we have not made our interactions and communications safe enough for the other person. There's nothing to fight about. No one to blame. It is just a matter of gaining rapport, entering the other's reality.

This changes the meaning of what we have previously classified as "resistance". What does resistance mean? Just that we have not obtained sufficient rapport. It means that we have not paced enough. It means that we have not spent enough time truly seeking first to understand. What does this then suggest? Simply that we can do so. We can become active and proactive in seeking to understand. We become focused on making things safe.

This isn't absolute, of course. None of the NLP presuppositions are. They are all influenced and affected by contexts. Certainly there will be times when someone resists us and it will have nothing to do with the lack of rapport. It will instead have everything to do with that person's state. We will find people who don't care about safety, being understood or validated or appreciated, and who are more focused on refusing to accept our view of things or suggestions.

Yet, even in knowing that, we go to that position *only* after we have first sought to deal with things by empathy, rapport, and understanding. When we have sufficient evidence that the person does not want or care about being understood, then we can adopt another strategy. Prior to that, however, we will assume responsibility and creatively come up with many other responses so as to make nonresistance and cooperation a real option for the other person. Generally, most people cannot resist when they feel understood, validated, safe, respected, when they're given time and space.

As those seeking to master our practice of NLP, we start from the assumption that we will be the ones setting the frames. So we will take charge of *our* responses, pacing, communicating, seeking to understand, adjusting flexibly, and defusing. We go right in because we manage our states and we build rapport. We match and pace. We don't interpret the others as "resistant": we interpret things as an opportunity to use our skills in regaining rapport. We use that opportunity to stretch our abilities and to learn much more. That's the movie in our mind, and that's the role we play.

16. *People are not broken: they work perfectly well*

People have all the internal resources they need to succeed. Unless a person has brain damage or their nervous system is diseased or damaged, they will have all the necessary neurology, mental abilities, indeed, all the wherewithal, to achieve state management, healthy frames of mind, sanity, and effectiveness.

People are not broken. They are not doomed by previous problems. They are not victims. How different this is from the "victim" mentality of many models of human behavior! That's why we say, following Richard Bandler, "It is never too late to have a happy childhood."

We assume that people are not be broken but work perfectly well and don't need fixing, that they need coaching only regarding how to access their resources. This describes a very different movie in our mind. And with that movie we play a very different role from that of trying to fix people. We focus more on facilitating and coaching. Our attitude is that, since people are not broken, they must be running some poor and impoverished strategies and probably do it very efficiently.

That's why we are *not* into fixing people. That's why co-dependency as a coach, consultant, therapist, teacher, parent, or whatever does not *fit* the NLP model. This also influences what we mean by mastery in this field. Mastery does not mean knowing all the answers or being supercompetent in all areas. Not at all. Mastery means being able to think in terms of patterns and structures, being able to explore, gather high-quality information and playfully coach people into more effective uses of their own skills and resources. We simply trigger, stimulate, and even provoke people to access their own resources. Mastery means we give up advice giving and coach others to find the answers to their own questions and problems. We know that advice giving is not only *not* helpful, but that it evokes resistance. And resistance shows our lack of rapport and our ineffectiveness of matching and pacing.

Our attitude becomes a masterful one when we think along these lines: "I will assist others. I will provide coaching instructions so they can access and use their own skills."

17. People can learn quickly, sometimes with one experience

As NLP practitioners we know just how quickly brains learn and can learn. We know that brains learn very quickly. Anyone with a phobia demonstrates that. Typically one terrifying experience is all it takes for most people to learn: "Never do that again! Totally stay away from elevators, planes, criticism ..."

We know that if we or another attaches massive pain to anything, the human nervous system will typically learn very quickly about what to avoid. How does this translate in terms of an attitude that we can adopt that will assist us in mastering this field?

The attitude that people can learn quickly first of all teases us into finding and exploring the mechanisms that support accelerated learning patterns. It further shifts us from the old paradigm that learning, change, transformation, and success are "hard" and going to take a long time. We don't play that movie in our mind. We watch and edit a different movie.

Part of what accelerates learning so that it becomes faster and more *quickly* adopted in our mind-body-emotion system is the strength of emotional experience that drives the lesson or learning home. Strong emotions can accelerate learning. Of course, they have to be the right emotions and the intensity of the emotion also has to be appropriate.

Generally, an intense emotional state taps into the dynamics of a "mood set" or what we call "state dependency" in NLP. In state dependency the emotion of that state colors all of our learning, memory, imagination, communication, behavior, and perception. Knowing this cues us about how to use state dependency mindfully. It raises such questions in our mind as:

- What state could we use to accelerate learning X?
- How much intensity does Y state need to be for this person to activate state dependency?
- Does this person function best with aversion or attraction emotional states?

Knowing that people can learn quickly also enables us not to question or doubt someone's ability to learn even though they might entertain lots of self-doubts. We know better. We know about the brain's tremendous ability to learn things and to do so with a few repetitions and sometimes just one. We know about the power of the higher meta-levels for setting frames that completely alters the movies playing in the theater of our mind. We know about numerous meta-state structures that accelerate learning with fun, playfulness, ease, and pleasure.

We know that having the right pattern or strategy (or movie) makes all the difference in the world. What stops some people from learning something is that they are going about it all wrong. There is structure to experiences and sometimes, when we lack the right structure for a given experience, using the wrong structure will never get us there. It's not that we're stupid. It's not that we cannot learn. It's the case that *that strategy* will never do it. If you have the wrong recipe for baking a chocolate cake, if you have a recipe for roasting a turkey instead, all of your *learning* will not work. You can know the number to the president or prime minister of your country, but if you're using it to call your best friend next door it will not work.

Why is it that people can learn so quickly to resolve a phobia? Does that prove that they are really bright or smart? No. It's just that they use the right process for "running their own brains" about a phobia when they use the phobia cure. So with the allergy cure, the Swish Pattern, reframing, Time-Lining processes, or meta-states patterns. The acceleration in learning is that we are using a top-notch process that works.

People learn quickly when they have the proper pattern for changing, updating, or editing their internal movies. It is that simple. We can also get leverage with other higher frames that can change the whole production. So, with this new attitude, we ask:

- What context would get this person to act, learn, change-totally, right now?
- Is there any frame that's slowing down the learning?
- Which frames would facilitate and accelerate the ability to learn?

18. It's better to have choice than no choice, and, the more the choices, the more flexibility in handling the challenges of life

As NLP practitioners, we discover from the beginning that having one choice is not real choice at all. Even when we have *two* choices, that must mean that we are on "the horns of a dilemma". True choice does not actually begin until we have three or more options. It is then that we begin to truly have a sense of choice, options, and freedom.

While having choice creates other challenges, it is better to have choice than no choice. Having choices enhances life even if it calls upon us to be more conscious and more responsible. Having more choices gives us room for more behavioral possibilities, creativity, flexibility, options.

From a therapeutic perspective, we become "clients" precisely when we do not have a sense of choice. Without choice, we feel "stuck", forced, caused, determined, victimized, incapacitated, or controlled. Without a sense of choice we can play only one movie in our mind and we feel controlled by fate to play only that one, even if it is sick, toxic, and morbid. Even if we have one other choice, we may then still feel that we have no good choices and are therefore powerless to really affect our life or our destiny. This makes us less than human, less than what we can be.

In moving toward mastery as practitioners, we take on this empowering premise as our attitude. This changes the cinema of our mind and the quality of that internal movie. Now we believe something more empowering: "There's always something I can do. I can always find or create many other options and choices. And, if I can't change the outside world, I can always choose a better attitude, a more resourceful state. That's one freedom no one can take away from me."

Do you hear the *attitude* in that? That's the attitude of a person who has learned to master his or her own internal world and it is the essential attitude that we need to master our use of NLP.

With an attitude like that we never quit. We keep on going, keep on searching. We refuse to become stuck in *our* thinking. We believe in creativity, possibilities, and options. Options, in fact, increasingly become our meta-program. That means if we don't have the flexibility to shift from procedures to options, we will severely limit our ability to master NLP. That's because ultimately NLP is not a set of procedures: it is an art. It is an art that calls upon our creative intelligence. More often than not, we invent things as we go.

While there are many procedures for moving from a stuck state to a choice state, the most dynamic NLP and NS patterns have not yet been invented.

How much is this premise about choice in your attitude? Are you willing to let it become your spirit?

19. *People make the best choices available to them when they act*
Do we always make the best choice in what we do? Of course not. The choices we make are frequently poor choices. Yet, it is *the best we can do in that moment given our state*. And that's a crucial difference. It may not be our best, but being at our best and producing our most resourceful behaviors *depends* upon our states and upon the cinema that plays in our mind at any given moment.

The verbal and behavioral responses we generate are functions of our neuro-linguistic states and our model of the world in a given context. We do what we do and say what we do to achieve something of value and to fulfill some need at that moment. That's what this presupposition says. Given our state, learning, skills, and other conditions in a given context, we do the best we can. When we do very poorly, make horrible choices, it is the best option we have available. In those instances, the problem is not "us," but our poor and sick maps and mental movies. Somehow we thought we were going to make things better.

This attitude enables us as practitioners *not* to get put off by the ugly and hurtful behavior of people. It enables us to rise above the behavior and to see it as the best choice available in our model of the world at the time. We do this to pace the person and create rapport. In doing this, we again separate person from behavior, intent from action, so that we can validate the person, get the hurt and misunderstandings cleared out and then induce more resourceful states for the person, states where the person will have more resourceful choices.

This presupposition changes our attitude about hurtful actions and traumatic behaviors. It doesn't lower our standards or values. It simply keeps us focused on enabling the person to change. Wallowing in anger, guilt, pity, or victimhood about the evil behaviors does not change things, but makes things worse. We don't do that. People are not their behaviors, nor do their behaviors define them. A person who sexually abused someone once upon a time is not always that kind of person. So, where other fields blame, NLP offers hope.

As practitioners we know that we cannot solve a problem at the *level* of the problem. Behaviors occur at the primary level. So, to understand a given behavior, we rise above that level. We move up to intention, understanding, or resourcefulness and set frames that make the behavior irrelevant and impossible. We background the old behaviors as just stupid choices so that we foreground solutions for the future. We use our meta-mind to do that to activate the meta-mind of the other person.

20. We are responsible for "running our own brains" and thereby managing our own states

Knowing that we can "run our own brains", we learn as practitioners the specifics about how to do precisely that. In doing so, we develop a new attitude about taking charge of the movies that we run in our mind and the various cinematic features and frames that allow us to turn on the brightest and best. This gives us a new sense of power. It is not the power to control others or the world, but the power to control ourselves, to take charge of our mind, emotions, speech, actions, and choices. Robbins (1986) called this "personal power" the ability to take effective action.

All in all, it generates a larger sense of self-efficacy and so centers us in our own values, visions, beliefs, and mission. Doing this rescues us from playing the blame game. As we "run our own brain", we develop ego strength to face and accept reality on its own terms. We adopt an attitude of mastery over ourselves that says, "I am in charge of my mind and what it creates. The movies that I play in the theater of my mind are my movies. If they don't serve me well, I can edit them, retire them, find or create a new movie. My mind management may not be absolute or perfect, but it is mine."

Installing the presuppositions as enriched meta-states

EXERCISE

1. Tease out the structure of one of the NLP presuppositions as you express it in a succinct and vivid way.

- What are the thoughts-and-feelings of the presupposition at the primary level?
- What are the sensory-based components?
- What are the meta-level thoughts and feelings that set a frame, establish a category or classification for the primary state?
- For example, in "there is no failure, only feedback", we have "not seeing, hearing, or feeling ourselves experiencing the accomplishment of a goal and feeling frustrated, angry, upset, or curious at the primary level. Yet at the meta-level we have set a frame, "Just feedback", or "Just information", as we have said "No" (one level) to the idea that we should classify it as "failure" (the first meta-level).

2. Step into the primary state first.
- Accept, welcome, experience, and notice the primary state. Express it in words, feelings, movements, images, and sounds the best you can.
- What is the movie playing at the primary level?

3. Rise up in your mind to a meta-level to set a meta-state frame.
- What does this mean? "It means feedback." "It means there is a positive intention at some level trying to accomplish something of value for this person. I wonder what."
- What do you believe about this? "It's just a map."
- How is this valuable?

4. Rise up and confirm this frame.
- Would this frame enhance your life and in the long run bring empowerment, balance, or ecology?
- Would you like to have this, use this, keep this? (Elicit layers of "Yeses".)
- Perhaps I should take this away from you. (Elicit strong "Nos" as the person fights to keep the frame.)

5. Future-pace and install in your life.
- So will you keep this with you?
- How will you do that? When, where, how, with whom?

Testing and evaluating the spirit of mastery

EXERCISE
1. In pairs, explore the following questions to identify each person's integration pattern.

- Which of the NLP presuppositions seems already well integrated into your way of thinking, feeling, speaking, and acting?
- How is it that you have embodied that premise as your very attitude?
- How long did it take you to do that?

2. Explore the NLP presupposition that you find the most challenging.
- Which of the presuppositions do you find the most challenging?
- Which frames make it difficult to embody?
- Which ideas, beliefs, or feelings would have to change in order to let that pre-supposition just slide in?
- What would it have to change to? Describe as fully as possible.

3. Using the as-if frame, pretend that you have that presupposition in your way of life and fully step into it.
- As you access the as-if frame, what is it like visually, in the sounds you hear, the words you use, how you stand, walk, breathe, or look?

4. Check for objections.
- What stops you from keeping this?
- Take every objection and use it to reframe and restructure the infor-mation in the as-if frame. Continue until you can access the state comfortably and with no objections.

5. Check ecology and future pace.

Summary

As with every other experience, mastery has a structure. It doesn't just happen, without rhyme or reason. There is form and reason to the process of mastering a field. As we apply the principles and structure of mastery to mastering NLP, we tap into the magic and power of mastery itself.

The *attitude* that facilitates mastering this field lies in the presuppositions of NLP. The sooner and more thoroughly we integrate and *embody* these premises, the more quickly and thoroughly we will develop true mastery with NLP. This means incor-porating the very spirit of NLP so that it becomes the way we think, our frame of mind, and not just a technique.

Part Two

Mastering the Four Meta-Domains of NLP

Chapter Four
Mastering the States Our Movies Create

Where do our neuro-linguistic states come from? They come from our mental movies. Play a horror movie in your mind and guess what feeling states you will create.

The same goes for a movie full of rage and anger, joy and playfulness, a comedy, drama, meta-drama, or whatever. The movies we play in the theater of our minds cue our bodies about how to feel and what to do.

This means that *our mental movies are not neutral.* There's a price to pay for every movie you create and entertain in your mind. And you will pay the price for admittance to that audio-video experience in terms of your kinesthetic feelings, your emotions, your health and wellbeing, your sanity and adjustment to reality, and your responses. What price are you paying for the movies playing in your mind?

The relationship between what goes on in our minds in terms of the cinematic features and our mind-body states of consciousness describes a fundamental principle about our functioning. As a cognitive-behavioral model, NLP explains why we have to take charge of our own brain and "run our own brain" if we want to develop top-notch skills at *state management.*

Why? Because our mind-body-emotion states are functions of our movies.

Neuro-linguistic states

We need a crystal-clear understanding about what we mean by a *"state* of consciousness", or a neuro-linguistic state. The term "state" and these other terms describe a *dynamic mind-body state* that operates as a neurologically embodied state of mind-emotion-and-body. As such it initiates an energy field comprising our thoughts, emotions, and neurology.

This dynamic and systemic description replaces one of the original ideas proposed in NLP by Leslie Cameron-Bandler. She proposed a three-way division of a person into external behavior (EB), internal state (IS) and internal process (IP). While this had some usefulness, it also created an elementalistic division of these facets of personality that are false-to-fact. There can be no internal state without internal processing. These are not separate elements. They overlap and interlink in multiple ways. Even behavior can initiate a state and, of course, we express our states in terms of our behaviors.

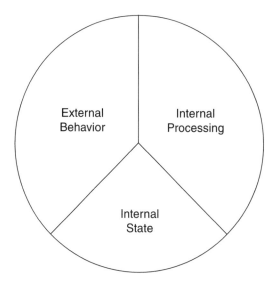

Figure 4.1: Three-fold division of personality

We experience life in specific mental and emotional *states*, which are made out of our *state* of mind (internal processing), *state* of body (behavior, physiology, neurology), and *state* of emotion (kinesthetic sensations informed by higher-level evaluations). All of these are interrelated. We cannot separate them. When we do separate them, we do so only linguistically, as a description, as a way of talking. The separation is not real. As we think, so we feel in our body and move and act, and this entire configuration (or gestalt) is what we mean by "experience". We live and move and have our being as mind-body persons—as a neuro-linguistic class of life.

As a neuro-linguistic class of life we *experience and map* the territory beyond our skin, the world "out there", so that we can effectively relate to it. This means that, most fundamentally, we operate as pattern detectors and mappers, and this gives us our unique ability to *program* ourselves. As we map things, so we become. It begins with our *neurology*, how we use our nervous system and sense receptors, and then it moves to our *linguistics*, how we use symbols, words, metaphors, and classifications to create mental and emotional programs.

In this way we discover how to take charge of these processes and *run our own brains* using NLP models and technologies. Taking charge of our "reality constructions" empowers us also in controlling our neurology. Building ever more accurate and enhancing models of the world increases our resourcefulness. This describes the heart of NLP-state-management excellence. NLP, as the study of "the structure of subjective experience", began as a search to understand how superior language skills create therapeutic magic.

Figure 4.2: The components of neuro-linguistic magic

Linguistics

*The sensory representation systems that make up the cinematic movie in our mind (the **VAK** for short)*

Visual: pictures, scenes, images

Auditory: sounds, noises, music

Kinesthetic: sensations, touches, tactile, proprioceptive, motor movements

Olfactory (smell), gustatory (taste), and vestibular (balance)

The language representation system (auditory-digital) that we use to fill in the conversation track in the mental movie.

Words, sentences, linguistic structures

Mathematics, music symbols, metaphors, stories

Neurology

The functioning of our nervous system as it interacts within our body and physiology of our central, peripheral, and autonomic nervous systems.

Pathways to state

We create our *states* of consciousness from our mental-emotional-somatic mapping, which we encode as our internal mental movie. What we experience as our "states", our neuro-linguistic states, are such things as our thinking, feeling-in-our-body, emoting, responding, speaking, and behaving. This gives us two royal roads to state:

1. The internal representations of our internal cinema

Internal representations specify the state of our "mind"–that is, the things that we internally map out visually, auditorially, and kinesthetically to make up our internal movie. It also includes the things that we say to ourselves at a higher logical level about the movie. Our meta-representation system of language encodes most of our understandings, learning experiences, beliefs, and values. These facets of mind make up either the soundtrack of our movie or the editorial frames. Because we always have a choice about *what* to represent and *how* to code that representation, we have "representational power".

2. The physiology of our body and neurology

Physiology and neurology describe the physical state, the state of our "body" (soma), and the things that we experience in our body: for instance, health, posture, breathing, biochemistry. This includes what we've been eating, how we have been sleeping, our state of health, and all of the activities that go on in our nervous systems, immune systems, autonomic system, and so on.

These two pathways or roads to state give us two avenues or processes by which we can elicit a state. We can use "mind" to think, represent, and encode information that calls forth a state. We can use "body" to move, breathe, and posture ourselves in such a way that it calls forth a state. While this is basic NLP 101, many practitioners do not seem to appreciate its importance. This is the foundation of state management, state control, and self-discipline. This establishes the practical skills for taking charge of our own lives.

Exercising state-management skills

How skilled are you at using the components and the royal roads to state control in order to manage your everyday states, to recognize your states, to nudge yourself out of unresourceful states and into resourceful ones, anchor the empowering ones, to interrupt the negative states, and to then use various NLP patterns to "run your own brain"? How often in a week or a month do your states "have" you rather than your having them?

EXERCISE
1. Identify your top five or ten resourceful states.
For example, you could list learning, playful, confident, determined, persistent, or whatever.

2. Identify and describe the state in sensory based terms.
What would you write if you were to present a screenplay description of the state?

3. Create a menu list of referent experiences.
● Identify at least five referent experiences that evoke the desired state in you.
● Rehearse those referent experiences in your mind to refresh them and to make them as sensory rich as possible. See them on the screen of your mind, then step into each of them to experience them.

4. Practice state induction and anchoring.
Pick one of the states and practice inducing it. When you get a strong representation of the state (a 6 or above on a scale of 0 to 10), then anchor it for yourself.

5. Test your anchor and state.
Break state. Then test the anchor as you think of a time in everyday life when you could use that particular resourceful state.

Use this procedure with all of the states, knowing that, as you practice eliciting states and getting your body and neurology to know how to re-experience the states upon cue, it provides you a richer repertoire of responses.

State management #101

Since skill in actually managing our states lies at the heart of NLP training and actually being a practitioner of this art, the more we know about states, what they are, how they work, the factors that influence them, the more skilled we will become in handling them. Here is a summary of the NLP basics about states.

State object
States have objects. When we are in a mind-body state, we reference certain objects. In primary states (e.g., fear, anger, joy, calmness, sadness) the object of our state is usually something *outside* of ourselves and beyond our nervous system. Ask, what your (or my) thoughts-and-feelings refer to.

At meta-levels, the object of the state changes from something "out there" to something inside. That is, to another thought, feeling, state, memory, imagination, or idea

State awareness
Awareness of our states and the factors that influence them gives us a basic recognition that begins the state-management process. Because all states *habituate*, count on your states to drop out of your conscious awareness. That's why we have to work at consciousness to become aware of our states.

EXERCISE
Practice noticing both *what* state you experience and its *quality*:

- What is the quality of the state?
- What are its properties, tone, intensity, other qualities?
- How pure is the state?
- How congruent or incongruent is the state?
- How complex and/or simple?
- What is the meaning or the semantics of the state?
- What pain or pleasure qualities make up the state?
- How is the state encoded and structured?

Identify the qualities, properties, features, distinctions in your internal cinema—the codings of the film that govern its intensity (for instance, vivid, sharp, quick, degree of movement).

State accessing and induction

Accessing and *induction* of state refers to how we put ourselves and others into states. What are the mechanisms that allow us to access or reaccess a state? We essentially have two primary methods, we can remember a state or imagine a state:

Memory: If we use memory, then we say something like, "Recall a time when you felt, thought, experienced, or whatever." Or, "Has there ever been a time when …?"
Imagination: If we use imagination, then we say something like, "What would confidence (or motivation, or playfulness) look, sound, and feel like if …" "If you were experiencing this state in its most intense way, how would you know it inside?"

State altering

Altering, changing, or transforming a state naturally follows from knowing how to access and induce a state. Actually, this is the ironic thing about states. They never stay the same—they cannot. They are always in flux. So, even though the term "state" sounds static, our neuro-linguistic states are dynamic and forever changing. Count on it. Our states are forever altering, shifting, and transforming. Developing an understanding and awareness about it can enable us to find and recognize those processes by which we naturally change our states. Do you know what methods you naturally use to *alter* your states?

Figure 4.3: State journaling

Instructions:
Draw a circle to represent the states that you have experienced today from the time that you first woke up to the present time. Inside the state: draw a smile or frown to indicate a positive (+) or negative (-) emotional quality of the state. Put a number (0 to 10) for intensity. Underneath the states identify the content of your internal representations and the factors of your physiology that play a role. You can use an asterisk to indicate things that triggered the state (the natural anchors in your world). Design: to highlight your awareness of state, state shifting, state composition, and so forth.

↑ **Intensely positive states** ↑

Comfort Zone

↓ **Intensely negative states** ↓

5	6	7	8	9	10	11	12	1	2	3	4	5	6	7	8	9	10 →
waking up						noon			afternoon			evening			late night		

State intensity and amplification

One of the ways that we can alter our states and thereby affect state management involves turning them up and/or down in intensity. We can begin by simply gauging our states in terms of intensity.

- How much do you experience the state of, say, confidence, motivation, self-esteem, resilience?
- What level of strength or weakness does the state convey?
- How much does it dominate your consciousness?
- Do you need more of that state? Do you need less?

If we need more or less we can crank up the intensity of a state by increasing or intensifying the cinematic features of our mental movie. Similarly, we can turn the state's intensity down. Typically, the more we make our internal movies closer, brighter, or bigger, the more we turn them up and the more we will experience that state. All states do not have the same level of intensity, so gauge for intensity level. For less intensity, we need only to shift our representations. Change the cinematic movie in the mind and the emotional intensity of the state changes:

- Do you need more "juice"?
- What processes do you rely on for amplifying your states?
- How do you crank them up?

State interrupts

As we can affect a state in terms of amount of neurological intensity, we can also completely interrupt a state so that it gets thrown off track and the mental and neurological processes that created it cannot continue. This gives us the ability to stop any and every mind-body-emotion state. We do not have to tolerate any state going into a runaway mode. All we have to do is use various jarring, interfering, and sabotaging thoughts, events, or behaviors to interrupt the state. When we can interrupt our state at will, this gives us mastery over our states, so that we "have" them, rather than let them "have" us. Knowing that you can always interrupt, stop, and/or prevent a state from running away also increases personal confidence in being able to handle situations.

State-dependency

The dependency of a state refers to the way our states can govern or rule our learning, memory, perception, behavior, or communication. State-dependency is a naturally occurring phenomenon. Whenever we get caught up in a strong and intense state, that state can seem to take on and have a life of its own. In various psychologies and fields this is called by a variety of terms, including "emotional expectation set", "conceptual expectation set", and "mood set". This means that, once in the state, for the most part the state will determine what we see and hear. It determines our memories, speech, behavior, communication, and feelings. Often, what's wrong with us or another person is the state we're in! In that *state*, the *state* governs the way we're thinking, feeling, talking, and acting.

State contrasts

Not all states are the same. State configurations come in all sizes and shapes. Just because we may have accessed a state of thoughts-and-emotions and physiology, we may not access a similar state to someone else doing the same. By stepping back from our states and comparing one with another, we can gain insightful understanding about the structure of a state and the differences in our mental movies and the frames that govern:

- What explains the difference?
- Is it just the way it is encoded in terms of the representation systems or language?
- Does it occur at a primary level or meta-level?

State anchoring

"Anchoring" a state in NLP is a user-friendly version of Pavlovian or classical conditioning. This means that we can set up a *trigger* so that we can more easily elicit or access a state. Pavlov did that with an autonomic-nervous-system state, the state of salivating. Using meat and meat powder, he would trigger the salivating response in dogs and, while they were in that state, he would ring a bell. With just a couple repetitions, the bell could trigger or access the salivating. It was as if he had "anchored" the state to the bell, hence the use of this terminology.

This means several things. It means that *conscious awareness* is not necessary to *anchor* a state. It means that we can even anchor unconscious states and do so apart from a person's awareness. It means that, when we have anchored a state, we can (to some extent) turn it "on" and "off" through using the anchor. In NLP, we say that an anchor allows us to transfer neuro-linguistic *states* across time, space, contexts, and behaviors. That's what makes them useful and "magical".

To set up a trigger or anchor we can use any sensory system (such as sight, sound, sensation, movement, gesture, word). It is as simple as *linking* another stimulus to the state in addition to whatever natural or internal triggers elicited the state. When we do this, we then have the ability to move that state around in time and space in order to build more resourceful states.

While *anchors*, then, are Pavlovian conditioning tools for state management and occur all the time, there is an art to setting them and using them. While they are simple in one sense, a masterful use of them does depend on both understanding and practice. The reason is because effective anchoring depends upon the uniqueness of the stimulus, the intensity of the emotional state, the timing of setting the anchor when the person reaches a peak feeling of intensity, and the purity of linking a particular stimulus with a particular state. Failing in any of these four facets of anchoring will cause "the anchor" to be weak or ineffective. That's why it's critical to calibrate to the person's state, to wait until the person reaches a *peak* of intensity in the experience, and to then link an *unique* trigger to it.

Once it is set, we can then test to see if the trigger works. When you "fire off" the trigger, does that reaccess the state? If it does, then you have set an anchor and can now use that anchor as a way to move that state (usually a resourceful one) to a new time, place, situation, or behavior.

Anchors are *not* buttons. They operate symbolically. The touch, tone, look, gesture, or volume does not mean anything in itself. It has meaning for that person only because that stimulus has been *linked* to some neurological response or feeling. When we anchor in multiple systems, the redundancy works to set up the linkage in a more stable and dependable way. That's why we not only touch, but use a specific word spoken in a unique tone with perhaps gestures and looks that also set it aside as having this special meaning.

State utilization

Ineffectiveness is often a case of simply being in the wrong state. For instance, we may have something to say but find that we can't speak up. Perhaps we're too fearful. This is where *using* another state, a more resourceful state, becomes valuable. In state utilization, we access and use a more resourceful thinking-feeling state than the one we're in.

- Where would I like to use this state?
- What would it look, sound, feel like to have this state in this or that situation?

State strategy

The "strategy" of a state refers to the sensory-based pieces of information in our mental movie, neurology, physiology, and so on that make up the step-by-step sequential composition of a state. In strategy work, we track down the representational sequence of the steps that go together to put ourselves into a state. And since every state has a structure, a strategy format, when we model the pieces of a strategy, we obtain a "recipe" as it were for how to create that given state. Similarly, every time we access a state or induce a state, we have employed a strategy. It's the strategy that initiates the state.

States and emotions—states as emotional states

Our states are *emotional states*. As they involve the thoughts and representations that play out in the theater of our mind, they are also emotions. So, what is an "emotion"?

An emotion is more than just a kinesthetic feeling. It is not merely a thought. Rather an emotion is a combination of both a kinesthetic state and a mental state.

An emotion is what we feel in our mind-body system that is made up of a combination of sensations and evaluations that we express in words *about* the kinesthetics.

As a meta-level phenomenon, our "emotions" are evaluative judgments, meanings, values, and beliefs that we hold and that show up in our body (soma) as feelings. As neuro-linguistic states, they provide a significant part of our messaging whereby we make evaluations regarding our experiences. That is, our emotions register the difference (the evaluative difference) between two things:

1. Our model of the world (our wants, expectations, shoulds, understandings, history, hopes, imaginations), and;
2. Our experience of the world (our present-moment sense of what we are getting).

The "emotions" we feel in our body as kinesthetic sensations are a very rich phenomenon that we automatically create. An evaluation creates an emotion. It is not merely the evaluation of our model of the world (all the rich nuances of our mental maps), but it is our evaluation of those evaluations in light of present-day experiences (our experience of the world). So, when map and territory meet, an "emotion" results.

To answer the question, "What emotions do you feel?" we have to ask two other sets of questions:

1. What are you thinking? How are you interpreting things? What do you expect? What do you want? What memories are you using? How have you mapped things?
2. What are you perceptually experiencing from the world? What are you seeing, hearing, feeling, and otherwise sensing?

The *difference* between your map and your experience of the territory registers in your body as an emotion.

In experiencing emotions, we experience signals and impulses in our body to *act*, to *do* something. That's why the stronger the emotion, the more the impulse to act and the more likely we will react to things. The term "emotions" tells part of this story. In "e-motions" we have *motion* and movement. When we experience an "emotion," the lower parts of the brain, among them the thalamus, limbic system, and the amygdala, activate the motor programs within our neurology to get us to take action. Sometimes this serves us very well; sometimes it does not. An emotion does not tell us that we should act: it just provides us the feeling and the energy to act.

Technically, we could even describe *primary* emotions as operating as a meta-level phenomenon. From the beginning, NLP has described emotions (including primary emotions) using the terminology of kinesthetic^{meta} (or K^{meta}). This highlights

Figure 4.4: Emotion scale

the fact that even with primary emotions we could *tease out* the cognitive evaluation about the actual sensation. In primary emotions a *level* has coalesced into and merged inside a state, so that the cognitive evaluative, or judgment, has become part and parcel of a set of the kinesthetic sensations.

In working with states and meta-states, this distinction has not led to any practical results, so we have not pursued it. We have rather relied on a more general distinction between primary states and meta-states. Yet it's valuable to know that, even in the primary emotions, we have meta-level cognitive evaluations that have already *coalesced* into a primary state. This is valuable in that it provides an illustration of how meta-levels do merge with primary states and can do so to such an extent that it can become nearly impossible to tease out the layers.

Cinematography and emotions

All of the above highlights the fact that we feel what we feel because of the movies playing in the theater of our minds. As we map out various screenplays and movie scripts, so we represent them. As we create the appropriate audiovisual tracks of the movies, along with the soundtrack with the words that we use to narrate the meaning of the movie, so we go into a state.

This gives rhyme and reason to all of our states. Yet we are mostly unconscious of our movies. What are we consciously aware of? Our emotions. Our somatic (bodily) sensations, feelings, responses, and what our motor programs are urging us to do. That's what we're aware of. Our consciousness goes to the *result* of our internal computations, map making, framing, and meaning making, not to the processes. Our attention goes to what our body is experiencing as we register the evaluative impact of the internal movie with our sense of the external world.

That's why *emotions*, emotional urges (drives, needs), and behaviors are much easier to notice and focus on than the internal processes that create them. Yet our emotions are but the results and symptoms of the internal processing. And that's why trying to change an emotion *directly* is usually next to impossible. That's why commanding our emotions is not an effective intervention.

To change our emotions and all of the bodily processes involved in an emotional state we have to go higher. We have to retrace our steps back to the mental movie that encodes our mapping and the frames of that movie. Transformation of our state occurs when we change the movie—when we change the screenplay, the script, how it is edited, or how it is framed. Play a different movie and our states change.

Using our mind's movie magic

Consider someone with a phobia. How does a person create or install a phobia so that by *just thinking* about a trigger (e.g. a snake, elevator, flying, speaking in public, confronting a boss) he or she can freak out and fill the body with fright? How does that work?

All a person has to do is simply entertain a really good horror movie in full "Sensorama" of appropriate sights, sounds, and sensations in the cinema of the mind and they will become filled with fright. Without an exception, we have found this true for every single person suffering from a phobia in the past twenty years. People who are phobic have a marvelous strategy for scaring the hell out of themselves.

If you wanted to model that, you would only need to ask lots of questions about the mental movie.

What are you seeing? How big is this picture? How close? Is it in color or black and white? Is it a snapshot, two-dimensional and flat, or is it a three-dimensional movie? Any soundtrack? What music or words? What is the tone, volume, tempo, and pitch of this soundtrack? Any smells or tastes? Are you inside the movie and experiencing it or are you sitting outside of it and watching it like a spectator? How far back in the theater of your mind are you sitting?

Those questions enable us to understand *what* the person is internally representing and *how*. By recognizing the cinematic structure of the experience, we also facilitate the person to be able to recognize the frames and the frameworks that govern the emotions. The emotions are not mysterious. They do not just come out of the blue or from nowhere. They make perfect sense *given* the movie. The questions also invite the person to learn how to become their own internal movie director.

The movie magic we perform with NLP is that of taking charge of the movie from the editor's, director's, or producer's position. Stepping up to that place enables one to begin to truly choose about how to encode the audio-video tracks.

How about pushing that picture back so that you have ten rows between you and the movie? What if you made it a black-and-white snapshot?

It's not that we refuse to look at the movie. It's that we learn to look at it *while staying resourceful and empowered*. Like the television programs and documentaries that reveal how the directors create "the movie magic" in the visual effects, we also can learn how to create internal visual effects, auditory effects, and other sensory effects that make our internal world more magical.

That's important. When we have a dramatic and exciting internal world, it affects and governs our external world of behaviors, emotions, speech, relationships, and the things that we externalize. Actually, our external world can be no more bright, positive, healthy, fun, loving, or successful than the movie playing in the cinema of our mind.

Now, on to the world of your neuro-semantics

Yet there is more. Not only do we *represent things* in our mind, but we also *frame* the movies in our minds with meaning. We can explore the horror movies of those people with phobias and find out not only about their *representations*, but also their meanings and references.

Okay, I have an idea of the terrible images and the horrible scenes that you are referring to, but what does that mean to you? What frame of reference are you using to view this? What do you think *about* that? What do you *feel* about that?

Beyond mind-body, we give things meaning and that creates our inner attitude or spirit. After all, some people *love* horror movies; they buy up the latest Stephen King novel to *enjoy* being scared and frightened. Other people *play with* the terror knowing that it's "just a movie." This enables them to see the terror without its bothering them. The way they frame it governs how they respond. Is it real or unreal? Is it serious or just for fun? Is it entertainment or a real danger?

Our frames of mind govern the meanings (or semantics, hence neuro-semantics) that we give to things. What's your *frame of mind* about health, happiness, self, success, relationships, work, career, exercise, or fitness? Your frame of mind determines the games that you can play. If you don't want to play the phobia game around some trigger, we could first change the movie that you play inside your head, but we could also simply go higher and change the frame of mind (the meanings) that you give to he movie. This is where we change the beliefs, assumptions, expectations, decisions, and other frames that make up the higher levels of your mind.

The magic of transforming our movies

As we master NLP and NS, we use the skills and patterns for directly changing our mental movies. This gives us a way to take charge of the commands we send to our body.

The first step in this is movie awareness. We can't edit the movie until we recognize it.

What are we seeing, hearing, and representing? Which movie is playing?

After that comes practicing movie editing skills and altering the movie's higher frames.

What *frames* are you using as you think *about* that movie?

Summary

We are a neuro-linguistic class of life in that, as we think, so we feel. Mind, body, and emotion are all interconnected in such a way that we can use either "mind" or "body" as a pathway to understanding and eliciting our states.

Our emotions and emotional states are not unsolvable mysteries. They operate according to a certain "psycho-logic" that has structure and form.

As we create internal movies of our thoughts, memories, and imaginations, and as we *frame* our movies so that we see and experience them in certain ways, so we go into states.

The art of state management is one that starts from understanding our states and then developing the necessary skills to become the editor, director, and producer of the cinematic productions that we entertain in the theater of our mind. This leads to emotional intelligence.

Mastering NLP means taking control of how we represent and reference. It means making the productions of our internal cinemas world-class features. Then, what we manifest on the outside in our behaviors, actions, gestures, emotions, and speech manifest the great movies playing in our minds.

Chapter Five
Mastering Meta-States

As we introduce the Meta-States model, we introduce it first as the third meta-domain of NLP. You will find, as thousands have, that this model will tremendously facilitate the process of mastering NLP. Yet this model will do much more than that. As you will discover, an understanding of meta-states will provide a unifying structure for the other models of NLP, such as the Meta-Model, Meta-Programs, "sub-modalities", and trance.

One of the first distinctions you will be able to make with meta-states is that between different kinds of states: primary states, meta-states, and gestalt states. You will also be able to tune your ears to hear the linguistic markers of the higher states, to move up and down the meta-levels (the "logical" levels), to flexibly take a meta-position with grace, and to use the meta-level principles to guide your use of NLP. On a personal level, meta-states mastery will take you upward until you take an intentional stance with regard to your highest intentions, so that they practically guide and direct you as you move through everyday life. Above and beyond all that, meta-states will give you a unifying link to all of the higher meta-level phenomena that prior to this model were unorganized domains or areas of NLP: beliefs, for example, and values, decisions, concepts, identifications.

Part I

Introducing the Meta-Domains

There are four meta-domains in NLP. Historically, NLP began with the first meta-domain of the Meta-Model. Richard Bandler and John Grinder (1973, 1975) identified and packaged the linguistic (or, more accurately, the neuro-linguistic) distinctions of the Meta-Model. They did that by using the linguistic model developed by Noam Chomsky (1965): transformational grammar. They utilized the language patterns they discovered in Perls and Satir. It was, in fact, the elegant use of language by both Perls and Satir that first captured their imagination about the "magical" use of language to effect incredible transformations in people. And both Perls and Satir talked and wrote much about the power of language in therapy. This is where they started. Also influencing their thinking was the Gregory Bateson model of logical levels. He and his associates of the Palo Alto Group (Jackson, Haley, Weakland, and Watlzawick) had been working on and developing reframing patterns for a number of years. This also entered into their calculations.

From this emerged the seminal NLP work by Bandler and Grinder, *The Structure of Magic*, Vols I and II (1975, 1976), which initiated the adventure. It provided the basic model regarding how we think about how language works (both the sensory representation systems and the linguistic system). This established the skeleton structure of neuro-linguistic reality. Thereafter Bateson encouraged them to model Milton Erickson and his style of nonauthoritarian hypnosis. Within a couple years this modeling of hypnotic language was encoded in writing in *Patterns I* and *II* (1975, 1976). With all of these tools, they were able to identify and model numerous patterns for "running your own brain" and transforming unresourceful experiences.

That was the first meta-domain, the domain of language as a meta-representational system.

The second meta-domain began to take shape around 1982, when Leslie Cameron-Bandler was doing "classical NLP" according to Wyatt Woodsmall. As she ran into some unexpected and inexplicable roadblocks that prevented some of the NLP patterns from working, she took that as a "rare and unprecedented opportunity." Thereafter she and Richard Bandler specified the first 14 meta-programs. These *perceptual filtering patterns* provided an explanatory model about how a thinking pattern can permit, amplify, sabotage, or nullify one of the NLP transformation patterns.

This opened up the second meta-domain in NLP, the Meta-Programs.

The first mention of the third meta-domain occurred when Wyatt Woodsmall (1988) included meta-states in a list of his meta-programs. He noted that "states" of consciousness can occur at both regular and "meta" levels. This corresponded to the "meta-part" Bandler and Grinder (1983) mentioned in *Reframing* (1985, pp. 71-2)–a part operating at a meta-level to assist one from getting caught in a loop. Andreas and Andreas (1991) also referred to the meta-function that created meta-states when they used meta-questions to identify the positive intention behind a behavior.

"And when you get this fully and completely, in just the way you want it, what do you get that's even more important?"

Repeating this meta-question eventually elicits a set of "core" states—each of these states is a meta position to the previous state and to the original primary state. However, it wasn't until 1994, while modeling and researching the structure of resilience, that I (MH) came upon the idea of a state-about-a-state. Thereafter, I more fully articulated the structure and processes involved in such meta-states by rearticulating Korzybski's work (*Science and Sanity*, 1933/1994) about second-order and third-order abstractions. It also involved rediscovering the extensive conceptual models of Gregory Bateson (1972, 1979) about meta-levels and his emphasis upon higher levels governing and modulating lower levels. This led me to write several works on this subject, *Meta-States* (1995), *Dragon Slaying* (1996), *NLP: Going Meta—Advance Modeling* (1997).

The fourth meta-domain was first described by David Gordon in *Therapeutic Metaphors* in 1978. It was called "sub-modalities" by Richard Bandler. He used "sub-modalities" as a term to replace the previous terminology which Todd Epstein had coined, "pragmagraphics". As a result, no one recognized or even thought about "sub-modalities" as being meta to anything. The word misled us all. Yet these distinctions, as we will show in Chapters Seven and Eight, operate at a level meta to the representational screen.

Beyond states to meta-states

In the last chapter we focused on developing a crystal-clear understanding about *states*, about neuro-linguistic states. That's crucial for state management. It's also crucial for understanding NLP systemically.

Why? Because rather than focus on thoughts, representations, logic, or treating the variables of experience as separate pieces that we tie together in a linear way, when we understand the systemic and dynamic nature of our neuro-linguistic and neuro-semantic states, we are given the key to understand modeling, transformation, change, communication, and much more in a systemic way.

This is one of the truly valuable contributions of meta-states. Based upon the fact that we always live and operate out of some mind-body-emotion state, the Meta-States model integrates some facets of how the brain works that traditional NLP had not. These facets include self-reflexiveness, recursive loops, psycho-logical levels, and multiordinality.

As the term implies, a *meta*-state refers to a higher-level state, a state that references a previous or a primary state. How does this happen? It happens as a wild and wonderful thing whenever we access one state and relate it to another. This is how we create a meta-state. We construct a *meta-relationship* between the facets, parts, or variables of our states. And, since our mind-body-emotional states are made up of the mental movies we play in our heads, our physiology, and our emotions, we can play with any of these variables, relate them to each other, and—hey presto!—a meta-state.

Meta-states are more complex states that arise from our self-reflexive consciousness. Just reflect back onto what you just thought, felt, or did with your physiology, and suddenly we are meta-thinking or meta-feeling. The technical term and field is meta-cognition. In these states, we no longer relate to the world, but we relate to ourselves, namely, to our thoughts, feelings, or to some abstract conceptual state.

In the process of meta-stating (relating one state to another) we access a state of thoughts-feelings (T-F) and apply it to, or bring it to bear upon, another state. Doing this layers one state upon another. For example, we feel upset about our anger; joyful about freedom; angry at our fear. The object of the state changes from an outside and external object to an internal, conceptual, and semantic object. We now think-and-feel about previous thoughts-and-feelings. Operationally, a meta-state involves a state of consciousness *above, beyond, and/or about* ("meta") any other state of consciousness, a state-about-a-state.

In a primary state, mind-and-emotions (as holistic neuro-linguistic processes) relate to some specific object. *Consciousness* goes out to the world and internally represents it, which then activates kinesthetic responses.

"I feel afraid of John and his anger when he doesn't get his way."

"I feel angry at Jill's handling of the meeting."

In a meta-state, consciousness *reflects* back onto itself to a former state of mind or state of body.

"I'm afraid of my fear."

"I'm disgusted with my anger."

"I feel angry at being afraid."

"And, when I realize that, I feel guilty."

In the primary state of anger, we feel angry *about* a thing, person, or event "out there", whereas in a meta-state, we move into a meta-level and, in our thoughts-emotions, reference another state.

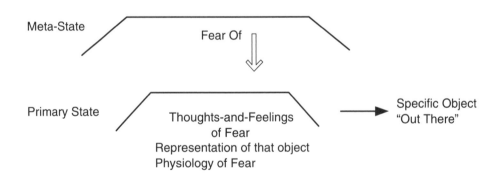

Figure 5.1

In self-contempt, we feel and think contemptuously *about* our self. In courage, we have a sense of risk taking, overwhelming passion, a so-what? state of mind about a primary state of apprehension, dread, or fear. In the meta-layered state of *courage*, we "*face* our fear". Our thoughts-feelings about some other thoughts- and-feelings put us into a position meta to the primary level. We have moved to a level of meaning about the previous experience.

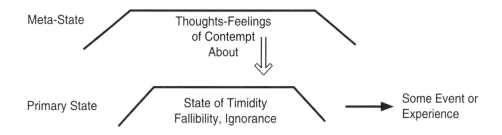

Figure 5.2

A meta-level references lower levels. It thereby affects, governs, modulates, and organizes the lower levels. Because it sets the *frame of reference* for the lower level, the higher meta-level *drives* the lower levels. This explains why a special kind of "magic" occurs at the meta-levels and why meta-modeling, and meta-programs have such pervasive influence. Accordingly, meta-states can amplify the primary state, reverse it, alter it or result in one of at least sixteen kinds of responses (Chapter Thirteen and Fourteen).

A meta-state involves several pieces, even multiple pieces, of consciousness. It may

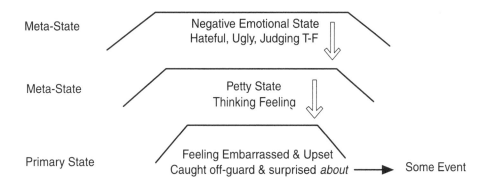

Figure 5.3

involve many layers of consciousness about consciousness. This explains the systemic nature of states and meta-states and how they can become layered and embedded in thoughts, beliefs, values, or understandings.

"I feel bad about feeling so petty about my embarrassment and upsetness over being caught off guard about the surprise party the other day."

Here the person first felt surprised and shocked about a social event that didn't go his way. Then he felt self-consciously embarrassed about that and upset, perhaps uncomfortable, and out of his comfort zone. Then some little petty thoughts bounced through the corridors of his mind. In that tunnel-vision state of mind he then made a big deal about his embarrassment, which only complicated matters. Then later he thought about things and judged his response as making him a "bad" person. In doing this, he effectively created a true meta-muddle.

Meta-states and the cinemas of the mind

Questions: How do our meta-states affect the mental movies that play on the screen of our mind? If our internal cinemas put us into states so that we feel fear or horror when we play fearful scenarios in our mind, joyful and playful when we play comedy routines, confident and courageous when we play heroic movies, what happens when we have a state about a state?

Answer: Our meta-states set the frames for our movies.

Are you running an old fear film in your mind about the danger of speaking up in public, asking your boss for a raise, or interviewing? That gives us clues about the movie. But what do you think about that experience? Do you *justify* your fear, *validate* it, *hate* it, treat yourself with *contempt* for the lack of courage, *feel stuck* as if you had no other choice? These states about your states describe and install the mental and emotional *tone* of your movie.

In terms of the movie metaphor, they describe *the attitude* that you have as the editor of your own movies. Our meta-states texture and qualify our movies, giving them their affective tone. They describe the attitude or frame of mind as we direct our lives. So, as we move up the levels—"What to you think or feel *about* that?"— we identify our higher frames of mind as editor, director, producer, and executive.

If I play an "enraged and outraged" film and do so with the higher frame or meta-states of shame or self-contempt about that, feeling out of control, or being "made" angry by someone else, then the mental movie has these qualities. This introduces the dynamic complexity of how states upon states interface with one another other. Sometimes they make the movie stronger: feeling justified about my anger intensifies my anger. Whereas calm relaxation about the anger reduces it and makes it more manageable. Respectfulness of others while angry adds yet another texture to the movie.

EXERCISE: Meta-stating your movie frames
1. Identify a movie that you've been playing in your mind that puts you in a not so resourceful state.
- What non-enhancing state or states do you sometimes experience?
- What movie initiates those states?

2. **Take a meta-position editing stance.**
- Suppose you had to continue playing this same movie, but could choose the attitude that you use in doing so. Which attitude would you pick?
- Access the state of that attitude and apply to the state of the movie.

3. **Experience and evaluate.**
- As you fully experience the higher state and apply it to the movie, how does it affect the movie? What happens?
- What other resource state or attitude would you want to use also?

4. **Quality-control the experience.**
- How well does this new attitude about the old movie serve you?
- Does it enhance your life?
- Is there any other awareness about other resources you could bring to bear upon the old movie?

Enhancing state management using meta-states

Meta-states enable us to enhance our state-management skills in numerous ways. Mostly we use the meta-stating process of *applying one state to another* in order to texture the first state with various resources (calm anger, joyful learning, confident excitement or fascination about using feedback) and to set frames for higher-level attitudes. Every time we meta-state, we set another frame for our state. This allows us to develop truly high-quality states as we texture and enrich them with all kinds of resources.

What is the central *mechanism* that makes meta-stating possible? Korzybski noted that it is the unique ability that we abstract about our abstractions. We call this *going meta* or using our self-reflexive consciousness. Practically, this means that we can always think about our thinking (meta thinking), talk about our talk (meta-communication), feel about our feelings (meta-emote), model our model (meta-model), and so on. Our meta-cognizing makes possible the multi-layering of our states. This meansthat what we first think (or feel) about something is just our firstthought. Our second thought will have more influence. Meta-thoughts or feelings operate as ahigher and more pervasive "logical level" of our awareness.

Meta-states represent highly complex pieces of awareness that we call self-reflexive consciousness. This ability to think about ourselves—our thinking, feeling, choos-ing, or behaving—enables us to transcend immediate time, space, being, values, experiences, and so forth and to bring other awarenesses to bear on our thoughts. This transcendental consciousness means we can transcend immediate sensory based reality.

Meta-state distinctions

Because we can always "go meta" to our current state, we can generate many meta-levels of states. We can speak about *simple* meta-states (those with one state upon state), *complex* meta-states (those that involve multiple states), and gestalt states (those from which emerge new systemic properties).

Korzybski described the power of self-reflexive consciousness to create both science and sanity as "consciousness of abstracting," which creates *levels of abstraction*. He sketched out these levels starting at the bottom and moving upward:

1. The world of energy manifestations outside the nervous system;
2. The sense receptors that abstract from that world;
3. Specific sense receptors with their structures of axons, neurons, dendrites, nerve impulses, and neurotransmitters that create patterns of nervous impulses;
4. The impulses and neurotransmitters stimulate the brain (thalamus, cortex, etc.), to create various internal representations (VAK);
5. Sensory-based words and descriptive language;
6. Evaluative language about the previous level of words.

And the list goes on. The more we abstract, the more we move into the land of abstractions. This leads to higher and higher understandings, schemas, models, theories, and hypotheses about the world (the scientific process). It takes us further away from experiential reality at the sensory level. We begin living by definitions, ideas, concepts, abstractions, beliefs, hallucinations (intentions, or word definitions in our heads) rather than by sights, sounds, sensations and smells (the world of sensory experience) (extensions—specific referents in the territory of the world).

Primary states and meta-states

As we have identified primary colors and primary emotions, we also experience primary *states*. These include the primary emotions expressed as making us afraid/angry, relaxed/tense, glad/sad (pleased/displeased), tired/energetic, distracted/focused, and averse (hating)/attracted (loving).

Korzybski conceptually played around with the adventure of transforming "first-order effects" into second-order effects:

> We then have curiosity of curiosity, attention of attention, analysis of analysis, reasoning about reasoning (which represents science, psycho-logics, epistemology, etc.); choice of choice (which represents freedom, lack of psycho-logical blockages, and shows, also the semantic mechanism of eliminating those blocks); consideration of consideration gives an important cultural achievement; knowing of knowing involves abstracting and structure, becomes "consciousness", at least in its limited aspects, take as consciousness of abstracting; evaluation of evaluation becomes a theory of sanity, etc.

He warned about some meta-states that "represent morbid semantic reactions." I (MH) described these as "dragon states" in *Dragon Slaying* (1996):

> Thus the first order worry, nervousness, fear, pity, etc. may be quite legitimate and comparatively harmless. But when these are of a higher order and identified with the first order as in worry about worry, fear of fear, they become morbid.

> Pity of pity is dangerously near to self-pity. Second order effects, such as belief in belief, makes fanaticism. To know that we know, to have conviction of conviction, ignorance of ignorance, etc. shows the mechanism of dogmatism; while such effects as free will of free will, or cause of cause, etc. often become delusions and illusions.

This analysis of meta-states indicates the complexity that can arise in experience and consciousness. But we have not finished with it. Korzybski spoke of another group (1933):

> A third group is represented by such first order effects as inhibition, hate, doubt, contempt, disgust, anger, and similar semantic states; the second order reverses and annuls the first order effects. Thus an inhibition of an inhibition becomes a positive excitation or release; hate of hate is close to "love"; doubt of doubt becomes scientific criticism and imparts the scientific tendency; the others obviously reverse or annul the first order undesirable semantic reaction.

A meta-state can *negate* the content emotions at the lower level and can *create a paradox* that shifts the experience to a higher level. This offers lots of possibilities for transformation. When we take a primary emotional state and feed it back onto itself, the *interface* of state-upon-state can generate more than a dozen different effects. When I doubt my doubt, I become more sure. When I procrastinate on my procrastination, I get busy. The meta-level of "putting off" negates the primary level of "putting off", so that we stop putting off.

Sometimes a state-upon-a-state generates confusion. At other times it amplifies the first state, distorts it, turns it into something wondrously useful or destructive (fear about fear = paranoia; belief in belief = fanaticism). The mixtures of meta-states provide truly wild and wonderful human experiences and generate what we have designated as gestalt states-states that are more than the sum of the parts.

Effectively distinguishing primary states and meta-states

1. Appropriateness
- Is this response appropriate to the stimuli offered?
- Is this response directly or indirectly connected to it?

2. Nature of the emotion
- What is the nature of the emotion involved, kinesthetic or conceptual?
- Is it an emotion of the body or of the mind?

Figure 5.4: Second-order abstractions or states-upon-states

curiosity of curiosity (intense curiosity leads to the study of curiosity!)

attention of attention (attending attention)

analysis of analysis (study the discipline of analysis)

reasoning about reasoning (science, psycho-logics, epistemology, etc.)

choice of choice (freedom, lack of psycho-logical blockages)

consideration of consideration (an important cultural achievement)

knowing of knowing (abstracting, consciousness)

evaluation of evaluation (a theory of sanity)

worry about worry (morbid state of worrisomeness)

fear of fear (paranoia)

pity of pity (self-pity)

belief in belief (fanaticism)

conviction of conviction (dogmatism)

ignorance of ignorance (innocence)

free will of free will (an empowering sense of choice)

anger at fear (self-anger)

joyful about anger (celebratory about a human power)

sad about anger (self-reflexive awareness of misuse of that power)

angry about sadness (awareness that sadness is inappropriate or not useful)

fearful about sadness (non-self-acceptance of feelings of sadness)

guilty about feeling angry (self-judgment for experience of a tabooed emotion)

inhibition of an inhibition (positive excitation, release)

hate of hate (love)

doubt of doubt (scientific criticism)

procrastination of procrastination (action)

interruption of interruption (confusion)

prohibition of ... anger (with taboo of a primary emotion)

3. *The object of the aboutness*
- What is the object of this state?
- Is it something external or internal?

4. The nature of the language
- What kind of language describes this?
- Is it sensory based language or evaluative based terms?

5. The perceptual position
- Which perceptual position seems to organize this state?

Meta-stating accelerated learning

Which meta-level resources would you like to access and apply to create a rich state of accelerated learning? Which frames do you need to set in order that you may automatically integrate and implement your learning experiences into your everyday activities and behaviors?

EXERCISE
1. Identify the resources.
- Brainstorm about how you want to refine and texture your learning state.
- What resourceful states do you want to bring to bear upon your basic learning state?
- What sequence do you need to put these states-upon-states in?

2. Playfully explore possible resources.
Menu list: Playfulness, experimentation, passion, a "Just do it!" attitude …

3. Access and apply the resources to the PS within which the learning occurs.

Part II

As we begin intentionally working with meta-states, it's inevitable that we will have questions about the *affective* nature of these higher states, how to anchor them, for instance, and how they affect the movies at the primary level. That's our focus in this second part of this chapter.

The feeling of meta-states

We know what a state feels like, but what does a meta-state feel like? In the state of fear or anger, joy or sadness, stress or relaxation, attraction or aversion—we know what these emotional states feel like. We feel them in our bodies.

But meta-states differ from primary states in several ways and this is one of the key differences. In primary states, our thoughts-and-emotions are strongly focused on the event, person, or situation that triggers the state and so feels more immediate.

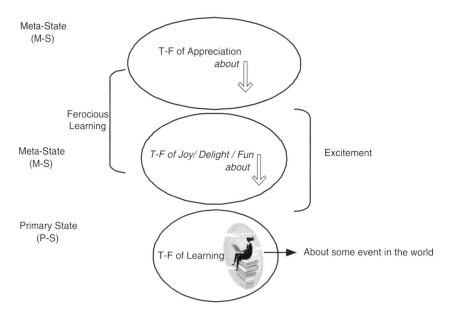

Figure 5.5

In a primary state we make a movie and experience ourselves as the player or actor of the movie. This gets all of our neurology directly involved.

But when we go *meta*, we step back from the movie just enough to notice the movie, to notice that we have a movie, and to notice other things about our movie. Doing this *feels* as if we were moving up in our "mind" and more *out of* the movie. This explains why we typically find it difficult to specify what meta-states *feel* like.

What does self-esteem, resilience, or proactivity feel like? What does feeling mischievous, protective, or stubborn feel like? What does being argumentative, forgiving, or assertive feel like? *Where* do you feel these states? What specific kinesthetics correspond to these states?

We typically experience meta-states in a different way from primary states precisely because they *seem* to be more in the head than in the body. This is typical, but not always true. Sometimes when we *step back* from the primary movie, we *step up and into* an even more powerful emotion *about* the movie and it makes the whole thing even more intense ... and so fills our body even more strongly. Becoming *terrified* of being embarrassed is like that. Being ecstatic with joy *about* falling in love can be like that.

What does this mean?

It means that meta-states are *not* "dissociated" states. "Dissociation" is the wrong word and *not* a synonym of "meta". As it is a psychiatric label of the DSM-IV, we would recommend eliminating the terms "association" and "dissociation" from our NLP vocabulary. Instead, think about *stepping into* and *stepping out* of different states. We are always in a state, always in our bodies. There is no such thing as being "out of the body". Disembodiment means death. It may *feel as if* we were numb, not feeling, weird, outside ourselves, yet those are "feelings"—meta feelings.

In meta-states the more layered nature of thought-and-feeling (note the hyphens holding these concepts together) upon thought and feeling creates a higher level of complexity. We now "feel" our evaluations and judgments. "I feel judged, dumped on, on top of the world, like taking a risk, and so forth." These are not kinesthetic sensations, but evaluations of the mind.

They are frames—frames of mind and attitudes. They describe the conceptual states that we are operating from. So, unlike the highly unstable and frequently changing primary states, meta-states describe more stable mental states that stay with us. Meta-states operate as the higher-level frames of reference and meaning that we give to things.

Typically our meta-states lack the strong kinesthetic sensations we experienced in primary states. We can easily identify where in our body we feel primary emotions. But this becomes more difficult in meta-states. Now meta-states can *coalesce* into the primary level and take on strong kinesthetic qualities. That can and does happen. We can transduce our meta-level concepts, evaluations, and frames and get them into neurology, into muscle. We call that meta-state *coalescing*. That's what happens when a meta-state becomes a meta-program.

It is language, along with other meta-representational systems, that enables us most effectively to layer many levels of meta-states together. With each additional state that we *step into* and *apply* to all of the previous ones, we set higher frames and more pervasive influence of the whole system. This can have all kinds of effects on the cinematic features of our mental movie. Depending on the meta-frames that we access and apply, we can become more or less emotional, more or less involved in our motor programs, more or less involved in values, beliefs, intentions, and so on. It all depends. To date, we have identified sixteen interfacing effects that can occur. Each creates a different *feel* to the meta-state structure (these will be detailed in Chapters Thirteen and Fourteen).

Meta-state anchoring

Can we anchor a meta-state? Given all this about the complex layering of the mind, what happens to the process of anchoring when we come to meta-states?

In brief, yes, we can anchor meta-states and, yes, we can anchor meta-states kinesthetically; yet meta-state *anchoring* also involves more finesse and more skill. Why? Because it is not as simple as merely *linking* stimulus to response. Because meta-states involve higher-level abstractions (evaluations, framing, believing) we have to use the meta-representation system of language and abstract symbols.

Have you ever tried to *kinesthetically anchor* a complex state such as high self-esteem, resilience, proactivity, seeing opportunities, or creativity and find that later the *touch* didn't seem to re-elicit the state very well?

That's because a meta-level structure, like a meta-state that involve meta-feelings, needs a more abstract symbol. The layered complexity of meta-states creates this. While there are exceptions, we typically need to find and use the right linguistics. That enables us to write the script, the screenplay, the higher-level meaning, and the frame of the experience. It is *language* that glues the states together. That's why most "beliefs" need a succinct expression in order to really stick. For ages people have intuitively known this. That's why they have naturally moved in the direction of "affirmations", somehow sensing that they need words, the *right* words, compelling words, hypnotic words, to hold and sustain the higher state.

Early in NLP, Bandler and Grinder designed language as secondary experience and as the meta-representation system. They said that words work as an anchoring system–in fact, the most extensive anchoring system available to the native speakers of a language. With language, we can glue our states together. In terms of the sensory-based movie playing in the theater of our mind, we use words at two levels: as the words that make up the soundtrack of the things that are said in the script, and as the meta-frames that define what's going on. Like the words that flash across a movie that name the movie, or that describe the next scene.

Sometimes one word will anchor a meta-state: "self-confidence", "mother", "resilience". If a non-sensory-based word evokes and calls forth a mental-emotional conceptual state, then it works as a trigger. We usually create such through lots of repetition. Once we have the conceptual state, redundantly anchoring in as many systems as possible, using repetition, using a strong emotional intensity, and finding the most compelling words, these are the things that can anchor the meta-state.

Typically, it takes more time and repetition to access, build up, and install a meta-state frame. Installing meta-levels of cognition, awareness, and experiencing means that we are setting in place not only the specific screenplay for ourselves, but also setting in place our editorial style and also our director motivation, intention, and attitude. That's why language is so important as we move up the "logical" levels. Language allows us to stabilize the higher levels and to sustain them over time. In anchoring meta-states, we can also use other higher-level symbols, nonpropositional symbols such as poetry, proverbs, icons, and music.

The psycho-logics of meta-states

As a model, that of Meta-States provides a new and different way to think about meta-level phenomena. Traditionally in NLP, we have left the common labels for meta-level phenomena as we find them in everyday language. We speak about such in the common parlance: beliefs, values, understandings, decisions, evaluations, judgments, intentions. Yet what are these things of the mind?

They are meta-states.

A "belief" differs from a "thought" in that it is a confirmation thought about another thought. That's why we can "think" about things without "believing" in them. We can just think about them. We can represent them. We can encode them. And we can do all of that without taking a stance about them. Do I believe that or not? Do I have any questions or doubts about that or not? We can think without feeling sure or convinced *about* whether a thought is true or not, real or not, valid or not, confirmed or not. But when we validate a thought and evaluate it as real, as confirmed, then we begin to "believe" it. This makes a belief a richer and fuller state than when we just think about the same referent.

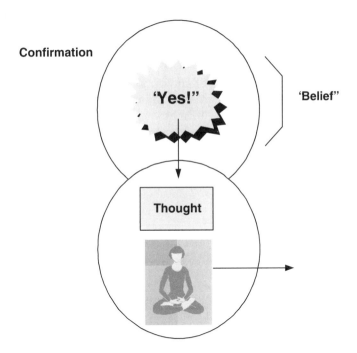

Figure 5.6: From "thought" to "belief"

Thinking that I can update my maps and develop a much more resourceful way of life radically differs from believing it. Thinking that I can handle criticism effectively and use it as just feedback, and so explore what the other person means and his or her positive intention, is not the same as believing that. The first involves a set of ideas and representations; the second is a confirmation that turns it into "a command to the nervous system" (Bandler, 1985).

In terms of meta-levels, all "logical" levels above the primary representations of our mental movies, are *beliefs*. We have beliefs about many things, these "beliefs" are encoded in all kinds of nominalizations. We hold belief frames about:

- What's important and valuable: values.
- How to define ourselves: identity, identification, self-definition.
- Origin and destiny: spirituality, mission, purpose.
- What we can and cannot do, or are capable of: capabilities.
- What to choose: decisions.
- What we can expect: expectation, anticipation, imagination.
- What previous experiences count: history, memory.
- What we know: knowledge, understanding, paradigms.

Every time we "abstract" to create one of these meta-phenomena, we create or elicit another "logical level", or meta-state. The abstraction induces us into a state—a neuro-semantic state of mind and body. As we move up the levels of abstractions and use more abstract forms of representation, we move into the realm of "mind". (We do have to remember, this is never disembodied "mind" but always an embodied mind. That's what makes all of our states *neurological experiences*.)

We can even do this to such an extent that we move *beyond* the ability of words and language to encode our thoughts. Our thinking and feeling can become *that* abstract. Consider the abstractions in mathematics and physics. Eventually we have to shift to using even higher-level abstract and nonpropositional language, such as metaphors, stories, poems. This also highlights the hypnotic nature of meta-states and that the direction of trance is *up* rather than down. It's going into higher and higher levels of abstraction, into the land of nominalizations, to quote John Grinder.

Movie glue

Creating a single shot or scenario of a movie is one thing, but how do we create and hold together all of the frames of a movie so that when it plays, it plays out a consistent and meaningful story? At the primary level, it's child's play to represent this and then that, and then this other. But how do we create a compelling and meaningful narrative?

To do that, we need language. Language is the *glue* that allows us to tie ideas together, experiences together, to create a plot, to develop a theme, to write a script that coheres over time. So, again, it is the meta-representation system of abstract symbols, notably language, that holds our meta-states structures together over time. Cinematically, they function as our ongoing screenplay or plot that narrates the story that we "hold in mind" and believe in.

That's why the frames of our mind are mostly made up of words, sentences, stories, explanations, and beliefs. This is also why the great majority of our beliefs are encoded linguistically rather than by a picture, sound, or sensation. Check it out for yourself. Think of something you believe in without using words, without telling a story, without the linguistics of explanation or reason.

Words, language, and all symbolic systems provide us with the meta-symbols above and beyond the sights, sounds, sensations, and smells of our movies. As such they operate as the conceptual glue that holds together our thoughts, meanings, concepts, and narratives. Words glue meta-states together, giving us the ability to hold linguistic structures, environments, syntax, and so forth together.

If we use linguistics to glue the separate frames of our movies together, then how do we unglue them or re-edit our movies?

We unglue the film plot that tells horror stories, that sketches scenarios of determinism, pessimism, and helplessness by indexing and modeling, asking questions of the language. This, of course, is the magic of the Meta-Model.

If we put our movie plots together with words, then we can pull them apart by pulling the words apart.

This is what we mean by meta-modeling. As practitioners, we already know that the Meta-Model identifies the processes by which we track the information of words into sensory information for the representation movie in the theater of our mind. Conversely, when we question the words, we challenge the tracking and this pulls the language narratives apart. It dehypnotizes. It deframes. It cuts and clips apart the old movie scenarios. It stops those B-rated movies in their tracks.

That's why we use the explicit questions of the Meta-Model to inquire about the form of the movie. As we "challenge the ill-formedness" of the impoverished screenplay, the movie stops, changes, and ceases to be as it was. This is the stroke of genius of the Meta-Model. We use words as anchors to cue us about *what* to represent in our movies. Yet many words leave out so much information. We generalize and distort so that the movies that run are based on the scantiest of outside information.

Questions about the poorly constructed cinema *unglues* the old editing so that it can no longer be maintained. The questions take the fluff and vagueness out of the old scripts. As we denominalize the frozen actions, we break up the frames (or meta-state) that govern the movie and we invite the movie maker to recover valuable sensory-based information that changes the movie. This is the movie "magic" that occurs inside our minds-hearts-bodies-and-emotions in response to the linguistic questions of the Meta-Model. All we have to do is ask questions about specificity. So in asking, "How do you know …?" a person rises up in his or her mind to a new space, to a place where they can operate as their own movie editor and director. They rise up to a place where they can run their own mental movies.

We can unglue the words that scripted limiting meta-states. As we question the linguistic connections that wrote the old screenplay, we can use complex equivalences, cause-effect relationships, presuppositions, mind-reading, and so forth to narrate a new movie plot.

Transforming the "failure" film

Consider "failure" as a state that some people experience and as a one-word induction that invites them to play a negative movie in their mind. Already, it is a meta-state and refers to a frame of mind about unsuccessful events.

Let's start by asking, "*Where* do you feel 'failure' in your body?" Typically, most people will not be able to tell you. Why? Because failure is not a feeling, but an evaluation and judgment. As a nominalization, it indicates that we have generalized from some events and evaluated those events. That's why most people do not experience "failure" as a kinesthetic sensation. When someone takes this nominalization and then identifies with it ("I am a failure"), they create with these words an even more complex meta-state structure.

Let's question the language to unglue the pain encoded inside:

- What did you fail at?
- When did you fail at this?
- What criteria and standards do you use in making this evaluation?
- How often did you fail at it?
- What have you learned that will now help you to succeed?
- What adjustments do you plan to make?

These modeling and indexing questions challenge a person's way of mapping an internal movie. It's like a film critic tearing apart the poor plot and structure of a movie script. It invites the actor to reread the lines with some critical thinking skills to see if the plot of the movie really makes any sense.

This slays or tames the dragon state encapsulated by the line, "I'm a failure". To create such a toxic state, a person has to take a nonsuccess experience and generalize from it to the idea of "failure". Then frame it as serious, dangerous, personal, predictive of the future. A person then has to identify with it and use it as his or her identity label, then close the mind to developing any new learning experiences and competencies, and use "failure" as a box to imprison one's hopes.

The reflexivity of Meta-States

At the heart of the Meta-States model we have a dynamic and fluid layering that gives us the *levels of mind*. The levels of thought provides a way to move easily from first-level thought to second-level, third-level, and so on. It gives us a way to *sort out* the confusion that so typically arises when we think about the layering of the

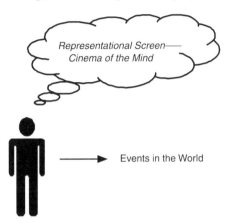

Model of the world (Frames of Frames):

It's Beliefs
all the way
UP

Frames-of-References (Paradigms of Paradigms)
Identifications (Identifying With Thoughts @ Rep.)
Paradigms (Beliefs Systems: Beliefs @ Beliefs)
Understanding (Formatting Thoughts @ Thoughts)
Decisions (choosing Thoughts @ Thoughts)
Valuing (Thoughts of Importance @ Thoughts)
Believing (Confirmed Thoughts @ Thoughts)

*Representational Screen—
Cinema of the Mind*

Events in the World

Figure 5.7: The levels of the mind

mind. Historically, philosophers have gone round and round in circles about this and gotten lost confusing the layering with some entity inside the "mind" (another of their nominalizations). So they went in search of "the ghost in the machine". Of course, there is no ghost in the machine of the mind.

What is there? There's *reflexivity*. There is the fact that we can *conceptually* step back from our thoughts and think a thought about that thought. It's still we who are doing it. It's still our brain doing it. We are *thinking* at Level One, "Should I take this new job? I don't know. If I do, this and this could happen, but, then again, I'd be giving up this and that benefit."

But then we don't leave it alone. We begin entertaining thoughts *about* that thought. It's these second thoughts that shift us to a higher logical level: "Why can't I make up my mind? I hate it that I get into these states of indecision."

There is no ghost, or entity, inside our mind thinking these thoughts: *it is still we who are doing the thinking*. But we are thinking about the first thoughts, and so *layering* the first thoughts with these second thoughts.

And on we go: "Yes, I've been through Meta-States training and I know that, if I *hate* my own states, I'm turning my energies against myself. This is really disgusting. I'm not only creating internal confusion, but I'm violating the very principles I've been studying— Oops! There I go again. Feeling disgust at how I'm thinking.

I'm going to create a terrible Dragon State out of all this. What's wrong with me that I can't run my own brain more effectively? ... Stop! I've got to stop this. I'm in the loop. I've got to get out of this loop ... and it's that damned indecision that started it. I'm afraid of where this is going."

Getting into a negative loop like this is part and parcel of the human experience. We all know it; we all have been there. It's an indication of how our *systemic* consciousness works. As there are loops and networks of loops (feedback and feed-forward loops) in the very biological structures of our brains, so there are networks of loops in our mind. In Meta-States we use the metaphor of a dragon and the negative loops "dragon states". It's just a metaphor. It refers to how going round and round and turning negative mental and emotional energy against ourselves puts ourselves into self-conflict. This leaves the energy nowhere to go except to *attack oneself*. That's not good. It creates such negative states as self-conflict, incongruence, limitations, and self-imposed prisons of the mind.

What's at work here is nothing more than reflexivity. We are simply *reflecting back onto ourselves* and to our thoughts and emotions. We do not have to posit entities, ghosts, or demons. We are simply layering our thoughts and emotions with thoughts and emotions—we are simply meta-stating ourselves. We are mentally reflecting back onto ourselves in a mindless way. The solution is to become mindful. It is to become aware of the layering, the looping, and to quality-control it so that it serves us well rather harmfully.

Early in NLP, Bandler and Grinder recognized that we can get into a loop and they thought that "being in the loop" was always and only a bad thing. But that was where they misperceived the nature of meta-states and so missed the true nature of "logical levels". There are good loops.

In fact, to manage the higher levels of the mind all we have to do is simply to become aware of the looping. As we accept it, we are able to take charge of it. This means enjoying the ride and just noticing what thoughts and feelings to default to and reflect back on ourselves. As we do, this will seem and feel counter- intuitive at first. "We just notice and accept?" Yes. We meta-state ourselves with acceptance, observation, witnessing. Once we do that, then we can quality-control the specific thoughts and emotions that we are reflecting back onto ourselves with. Then we can interrupt them, shift to more enhancing thoughts and emotions, and/or use a wide variety of NLP patterns.

The mapping that creates our movie meanings

The *levels of thinking and emoting* (the levels of thought) that we have in Meta-States offers a simplified and streamlined version of Korzybski's model. His Structural Differential contained a levels-of-abstraction model. You can find that model in his *Science and Sanity* (1933/1994). In Meta-States it enables us to make distinctions between the levels of mapping that we create.

1. Perceptual mapping

Our mapping begins with our neurology and sensory equipment of eyes, ears, nose, flesh, inner ear, and other organs abstracting from the world of energy manifestations out there and mapping them. This creates perception. As the energies strike, stimulate, and affect our sense receptors, we create our first unconscious mapping of the world. We experience this as seeing, hearing, feeling, smelling, and tasting. Our neurological mapping is preconscious, part of what Lakoff and Johnson (1999) called our "cognitive unconscious". Because we have pretty much similar nervous systems, we all experience and create very similar maps of the world.

2. Representational mapping

We see, hear, smell, and otherwise sense without consciousness of doing so. Awareness of our awareness is the next step in development. Little children experience primary awareness long before they become aware of that awareness. They see Mommy and Daddy. But, at first, we lack "representational constancy". We are not able to "hold" the images. Out of sight, out of mind. That's why babies and small children get such a kick playing peek-and-boo. The sight of a face suddenly dis-appearing and reappearing jars their awareness each time. Not so with older children and adults. Why? Because, even when they're out of sight, we *hold constant* our mental snapshots and movies.

Through this ability to *hold* our representations stable we are then able to manipulate them, to change, alter, and transform them. We call this "thinking". Yet it is really awareness of our thinking and creatively playing around with our mental movies. It is here that we begin to differ from each other. We experience the same event and perceptually see, hear, and feel it in very similar ways, but what we encode inside and what we focus on is unique to us.

Our representational mapping gives us our phenomenological "sense" of the world. We first map it over from our sensory experience onto our screen of consciousness, which makes up our internal theater of awareness, our personalized cinema. Then we use our sensory mappings to re-present the world to ourselves. We may make it close or far, in color or in black and white, big or small, we may have the soundtrack at various volumes, tones, or pitches. We may have other sounds in the soundtrack. This is representational mapping.

3. Conceptual mapping

When we shift to conceptual mapping, we move up the levels of the mind to layer onto our movies the ideas and concepts that we receive or invent. We use these as our frames of reference and frames of meaning about the movie. This creates our internal contexts for making meaning, defining what's real, what's important, and what affects our self-definition.

Our conceptual mapping involves the generalizations that we create and use for being, functioning, thinking, feeling, relating, believing, valuing. We learn a great deal of our conceptual mapping from the cultural frames that we grow up in and absorb outside of conscious awareness. Here we continue the differentiation from each other. Here we enter into the matrix of the frames of our mind—made up of all our belief frames, value frames, identity frames, decision frames, history frames, and so forth.

This level of mapping continues without end as we embed one concept within another and yet another. It includes the cultural mappings that we inherit from the communities in which we grow up.

Levels of meaning in our movies

What does "meaning" mean? The word itself refers to that which we "hold in mind". What we "hold in mind" is meaningful to us. If we don't hold something in mind, it can't mean anything to us. And, because we map things at different levels, we also construct different kinds of "meanings." There are two kinds of meanings that we then translate into our mental movies.

1. Primary-level meaning

All "meaning" starts out as mere *association*. What anything "means" at this level is simply a matter of what have we associated with it, which stimuli we have linked to which thought or feeling. Inasmuch as brains go places, we represent referents and link them up with other referents, with feelings, with emotions, with ideas. These associations, both external (uptime) and internal (downtime) create primary-level meaning as linkage. We link things together that are close together in time and space, or that occur in the same vicinity.

What "fire" means depends upon a person's experiences. So with "criticism", "learning", "self", or whichever concept you choose.

2. Meta-level meaning

After first-level association, we create higher-level forms of "meaning." These take the form of the mental frames that we attribute to our movies. As we conceptually put frames around things, we so frame our movies.

For example, consider what happens when we play the "beware of criticism" movie in our minds. We take the associations (positive or negative) that we have with "criticism" and what at first was a "point" of reference now becomes our "frame" of reference. It becomes the experience or association that we use to think about other things that we put in the same category.

If we had associated "criticism" with being insulted, feeling put down, physically spanked or troubled, we might generalize from that experience and use the idea of "hurt" or "distress" as our frame of reference for any communication that someone gives us that falls short of what we want to hear. This mapping of meaning is no longer simple association. It is something higher. It is classifying or categorizing an event (someone saying words, or someone using a certain tone of voice) inside of the frame of "hurt" or whatever.

This is contextual meaning. We are using *ideas* as a reference system. Now we are using a referent as *a way of thinking about* something else. We no longer treat it as an event. Now we treat it as a conceptual category. We meet a person in authority having a bad day and being gruff and we draw the conclusion that "authority figures are threatening and distressing". The person and the event are no longer treated as such. We have elevated such to a *category of the mind. Now we think in terms of the meaning of that event* and apply it to other things. This meta-stating process describes how we take references, use them as classes, categories, or frames of the mind. It doesn't make sense. It is not logical. But it does create "psycho-logical" sense.

Context, or frame, meaning creates a different kind of meaning from associative meaning. We call it contextual or structural meaning. Now we understand things, not because of what's linked to something but because of the category of ideas it lives within.

The basic meta-stating pattern

With all of that in mind, we are now ready to offer a simplified version of the meta-stating process. This is the basic pattern used in all meta-stating processes. This is the pattern involved every time we jump logical levels, access a logical level, or work with any meta-level phenomenon. The pattern is basically that of *accessing another state* (or some facet of a state, thought, emotion, physiology) and *applying* it to another state by arranging the pattern in terms of the following five terms (which, as it happens, all begin with the letter A).

1. Access a resource state
Which resource state do you want to bring to bear on or apply to the primary state (PS)?

A "resource" can be a thought, feeling, idea, belief, value, memory, imagination.

2. Amplify fully and anchor
Juice up the resource state and establish an anchor for it by touch, sight, sound, or word.

3. Apply to another state
Bring the resource to bear on the PS (this creates meta-level anchoring), or embed the PS inside a resource state.

4. Appropriate to your life by putting into your future ("future pacing")
Imagine having this layered consciousness in your mind as your frame as you move out into your future.

5. Analyze the quality, health, balance (ecology) of the system
Would it enhance your life to set this resource as your frame of reference for the PS experience? Would every facet of your mind-and-body align with this?

Developing skill with meta-states

EXERCISE: Meta-stating joyful learning

1. Identify a joyful referent experience.
Have you ever had a lot of fun and pleasure doing something?
Menu list: drawing, baking a cake, skiing, rollerblading, singing, playing games.

Imagine that delightful experience again fully so that you see, hear, and feel it.

Feel the strong feeling of joy, delight, and fun that you had then.

2. Amplify and apply.
As you feel all of those feelings, think about "learning …"

Think about the learning experience you are now undergoing and that you will undergo with NLP and NS.

Think about other learning experiences that you will engage in …

3. Notice the transformation.
As you feel those feelings of joy about some learning experience, notice how texturing your learning with joy … changes things, transforms things … Stay with those feelings for just a moment.

4. Confirm the transcending and including.
Do you like that?

Do you appreciate those thoughts and feelings of joy about your learning?

Would you like to keep this? Really?

EXERCISE: Meta-stating a sense of personal power
This is a pattern for recognizing and owning the very core "powers" or functions of our neuro-linguistic functioning. Doing this establishes the basis for *personal empowerment*, *responsibility*, *proactivity*.

1. Access a full experience of your four Central powers.
You have two private inner powers: (1) thinking (representing, believing, valuing, understanding, reasoning); and (2) emoting (feeling, somatizing, valuing).

You have two public and outer powers: (1) speaking (languaging, using and manipulating symbols, asserting,); (2) behaving (acting, responding, relating).

Notice these as you step into them fully. Access them so that you begin to feel these powers. Use your hands to mime out these powers in your own personal "space" to create your circle of power and influence and responsibility.

2. Access and amplify the resource state of ownership.
Has there ever been a time, maybe during childhood, when you said "Mine!' fully and completely? Think about such a time. Be there. Feel it when you strongly sense that something is yours, when every fiber in your being says, "Mine!" Keep it small and simple: "My hand!" "My eye." "My cat." "My toothbrush."

3. Access the states of acceptance and appreciation of "Mine!"
Imagine a reference that allows you to fully and completely feel a sense of acceptance … when you just welcomed and acknowledged something … a rainy day, the traffic. Now feel this acceptance about what you own as yours.

Recall a reference that enables you to feel a warm sense of appreciation for something, when you see value and delight in the value of something. Feel that appreciation about this sense of ownership.

4. Amplify these states until your neurology radiates.
Amplify your sense of ownership, then acceptance, then appreciation and apply them to your power zone.

Let your words emerge as you language it effectively. "This is my *zone* of power. I am totally responsible for my *responses* of mind, emotion, speech and behavior …"

5. Future-pace.
Imagine in the weeks and months to come moving through the world with this frame of mind about your zone of response … power …

The art of flushing out meta-levels

To become a master with NLP and Meta-States necessitates mastery of *going* meta. The movie playing in the theater of our mind is framed. It is framed repeatedly and is embedded in layers of thoughts, feelings, and meta-layers of concepts. Because these higher meta-frames comprise a tremendous portion of the structure of sub-jective experience, we need to be able to flush out the higher frames so that we deal with the entire matrix of the mind.

All meta-levels in our mind are made up of the same "stuff" that we have at the primary level. We *use* our see-hear-feel representations and words to build up meanings at the meta-levels, the matrices of our mind. The following set of questions in various categories offers lots of ways to explore and elicit the higher-level structures. As you use these, remember that the different categories are *not* different things—they are just *other ways* of expressing the same thing, the meta-frame.

This means that we can view a "meaning" as a belief, a value, an identity, an under-standing. Every frame has *every one of these categories within it*. Confused? This is precisely what confuses most of us about the higher levels of our minds. When we nominalize these categories, "beliefs", "values", and so forth they miscue our mind-body systems and we begin to think of them as "things." They are not. All of these words are but expressions of various *mental processes—the framings that we do* that create our neuro-semantic reality.

1. Meanings: the "ideas" that we keep holding in mind
- What does this mean to you?
- What else does it mean to you?
- How much meaning does it hold for you?

2. Beliefs: the "ideas" that we affirm, validate, and confirm
- What do you believe about that?
- How much do you value that belief?
- Do you have any beliefs about that belief?
- How have you confirmed that belief?
- How strong is that confirmation?

3. Values: the "ideas" that we value, treat as important and significant, esteem
- How is that important to you?
- What do you believe about that value?
- Why is that important or valuable to you?

4. Identity: the "ideas" we build up about our "self" and use in self-defining.
- Does this affect your self-definition or identity?
- How does it affect the way you think about yourself?
- What does this say about how you perceive yourself?

5. *Aboutness: the "ideas" we have about other ideas*
- What do you think about that?
- What do you feel about that?
- What comes to mind when you entertain that thought?

6. *Principles: the "ideas" that we treat as guidelines, laws, settled conclusions*
- What principles do you hold about that?
- I understand what about that?
- How does this idea work?

7. *Decisions: the "ideas" we separate and "cut off" (cision) from other ideas or choices allowing us to say yes to some and no to others*
- What decisions drive this?
- So what will you do?
- How do you complete the following sentence stems:
- "I will …" "I choose …" "From this day forward …"?

8. *Intentions: the "ideas" you have about your motive, intent, desire, wants*
- What is your purpose in this?
- What is your intent in this?
- What do you get from that?
- And, when you get that as you want it, what will that get for you?
- Why is that valuable to you?

9. *Outcome: the "ideas" we have about goals, outcomes, desired ends*
- How do you want to see this turn out?
- What do you want from this?
- What consequences do you hope will come from this?

10. *Understandings: the "ideas" you have that "stand" "under" you as mental support for your world*
- What do you understand about that?
- What knowledge do you have about this?

11. *Expectations: the "ideas" we have about what we anticipate will happen*
- So what are you expecting?
- Where did you learn to expect that?

12. Paradigms, models, schemas: the "ideas" we have that come together as more complex mappings about things
- What paradigm (model, schema) drives and informs this?
- What paradigm are you relying on in your understandings?

13. Metaphors, nonlinguistic symbols: the "ideas" that we form in nonlinguistic ways
These could be poetry or music or icons, for instance.
- What is this like?
- If this were a color, what color would it be?
- If this were an animal, what animal would it be?
- What would this sound like if you put it to music?
- If you made up a poem or story about this, what would you say.

14. Realizations: the ideas we suddenly develop as new insights, understandings, eureka! experiences
- How does it feel to realize this?
- When you realize this, what do you think?
- Now that you know, what do you want to do?
- Now that you're aware of this, what comes to mind?

15. Permissions: the ideas regarding allowance of an experience versus being taboo
- What happens when you give yourself permission to experience X?
- As you give yourself permission for this, notice what happens. How well does that settle?
- How many more times will you need to give yourself permission?

Summary

Not all neuro-linguistic "states" are the same. We have states at different levels. We create mind-body states about mind-body states and so have primary and meta-states. This introduces the third meta-level model in the field of NLP after the Meta-Model (language) and the Meta-Programs (perception).

Meta-States gives us a description of the levels or layering of the mind, of all meta-level phenomena, of how we create meta-programs in the first place, and of how we create rich and layered states of mind and emotions.

The four meta-domains speak about the same referent—*subjective human experiences*. One views them through the filter of *language*, another through the filter of *perception and thinking patterns*, another through the filter of *states of consciousness*, and yet another through the *cinematic features and distinctions* that we encode in the theater of our mind.

Meta-states are inevitable because of our mind's inherent reflexivity. We *reflect back onto* the thoughts, feelings, and physiology of our states. We never just think, we always think about our thinking. Meta-states refer to the reactions we have to our reactions.

Taking meta-states into account in our exploration of the structure of experience introduces a *different kind of thinking* into NLP. It is nonlinear and systemic through and through. This means including not only the linear step-by-step process of "strategies"—of tracking down the representations—but also of recognizing the meta-level frames governing the representations.

Meta-States means that in addition to the sensory movie playing in the theater of our mind—the movie that signals our body and works like a blueprint for how to think, feel, live, do and be—we also have frames around that movie influencing and controlling it.

Chapter Six
Meta-Stating Mastery

There are many reasons why Meta-States as a model offers a framework for *mastering NLP*. We suggested many in the previous chapter and will offer more in this chapter. Without understanding how the higher levels of the mind work, a person will not be able to fully grasp and work with meta-phenomena—such things as beliefs, values, negation, decisions, and domains of understanding.

There are those, of course, who master NLP without *explicitly* knowing Meta-States. Yet they have taken the long and more arduous road. When they eventually develop that mastery, it is a mastering of working with meta-levels. They intuitively know many of the meta-states principles. Yet there is a problem. It arises for the simple reason that they do not know the meta-level principles *explicitly*. Consequently, they cannot articulate the structure of their intuitive knowledge. This makes their competence unavailable to them. It also creates another limitation. Though one may have high-level skills and competencies in these domains, the person will lack a unified understanding of how all of these facets of NLP fit together.

While we often hear many positive comments and testimonies about Meta-States in our trainings, the ones we most often hear are comments about the *unifying effects* of Meta-States on the whole of NLP:

- "Meta-States puts all of the parts of NLP together."
- "It brings all of the separate elements together under a larger umbrella."
- "It has given me a larger perspective that informs me about what to do when, how to do things, and why it all works."

These descriptions highlight the fact that many find and use Meta-States as a unified field theory for NLP. So have we. In this chapter, we present more about the *meta-stating process* and how it leads to a unified field theory. This will set the stage for Chapters Thirteen and Fourteen, which will pull all of this together for a systemic model of NLP. In terms of mastering NLP, by developing skill in Meta-States you will:

- Learn what meta-programs are and how they are created.
- Quickly alter, transform, or work with meta-programs.
- Develop greater skill with beliefs: belief detection, change, deframing, and so on.
- Work effectively with belief *systems*—layers of embedded beliefs.
- Recognize the nature of trance as the layering of thoughts and become more skilled in working with trance phenomena.

- Recognize that the language of meta-states (meta-phenomena) involves the meta-representation system that the Meta-Model most elegantly identifies and questions.
- Appreciate the wide range of choices we have for conversationally reframing ideas and creating lines for changing minds.
- Tie together all facets and domains of NLP from presuppositions to domains of understanding (knowledge) to concepts, and so forth.
- Model excellence and pathology to create new models for advancing the field of NLP.
- Use the four meta-domains for advanced modeling, since they give you a four-fold redundancy for the same thing.
- Empower you to model even cultural phenomena and realities.

Appreciating the meta-connection

Bateson (1972) wrote extensively about meta-communication and meta-relationships. It was he who introduced and popularized the prefix "meta" in this context:

> Within the field of pure communication theory, the steps of an hierarchic series may be constructed by successive use of the word "about", or "meta". Our hierarchic series will then consist of message, meta-message, meta-meta-message, and so on … Further complications are added … by noting that messages may be about (or "meta" to) the relationship between messages of different levels … in human relations another sort of complexity may be generated; e.g., messages may be emitted forbidding the subject to make the meta connection. [p. 248]

The meta-connection refers to the near-magical ability to "go meta" in our mind. It involves the ability to rise up in our mind and to connect things from a meta-perspective. Developing awareness of this skill enables us to catch, understand, and work with the meta-connection. If we fail to do this, we are left in the dark and then the meta-level patterns will play and dominate us. Bateson described this as the structure of schizophrenia.

Applying the function of going meta so that we make the meta-connection between neuro-linguistic states gives us meta-states. When we step up into a state of mind-and-body-and-emotion about another state, we have accessed a higher state of consciousness. It is a state above, beyond, and/or about (meta) the previous state. This gives us a new and more complex experience. In terms of how to analyze the structure of experience, a meta-state moves us into a second- or third-order abstraction (Korzybski). It moves us into an executive state of mind from where we can run, govern, modulate, and organize our everyday states. In common parlance we speak about meta-states as our frames of reference, moods, predispositions, attitudes, and so on.

The nature of reflexivity involves an infinite regress, a never-ending process. This means that our ability to "go meta", to abstract about our abstraction, explains how it is that we can create meta-states upon meta-states in an unending process. No matter what we think, feel, or experience at one level, that never has to be the end of the process. After such we can yet:

- Think about our thinking (meta-thinking)
- Feel about our feelings (meta-emoting)
- Think about our feelings (meta-thinking)
- Feel about our thinking (meta-emoting)
- Talk about our talk (meta-communicating)
- Model our modeling (meta-modeling)

… and so on.

The relational structure of level upon level creates an "aboutness" that also enables us to distinguish levels. The "aboutness" in primary states refers to external content: "I'm afraid of John".

But in meta-states, the aboutness refers to another state, or internal content. In meta-stating, we shift "logical levels" as we move to a state that recursively refers back to a previous state: "I'm afraid of my fear", "I'm disgusted with my anger", "I worry about my anxiety over how angry I get".

From meta-states to gestalt states

The meta-function and meta-connection elicit an emergent property in the mind-body system. In the process of meta-stating we find that more complex states emerge. These are states that involve more than just the sum of the parts. So we call them appropriately, gestalt states.

A "gestalt" is a larger configuration that's "more than the sum of the parts". Gestalting refers to using the systemic processes of the mind-body-emotion system. When we have an interactive system (our mind-body neuro-linguistics) we have a context within which *systemic* phenomena can arise—*emergent properties* or "gestalts". This means we need to *strategically think through* the effect of level upon level in order to check the ecological value of a particular form of meta- stating.

Meta-stating involves the operation of *system processes* due to the feedback nature of reflexivity. *Emergence* occurs. New qualities emerge in a nonsummary, nonaddi-tive way. A gestalt-like structure-forming, summarizing, and integrating activity emerges from the overall experience. This creates a "structure-as-a-whole" feeling or "gestalt".

This highlights the systemic consciousness that emerges. As the processing of con-sciousness *reflects back onto* the products and processes, it feeds itself back into itself. *Feedback* from a state and set of interactions thereby re-enters the system and becomes part of the next stage of development of the state. The *feedback loop* creates the next level up, which operates as the higher-level frame and classifier. Because of this, the feedback process creates a *self-organizing system* with the thinking-feeling of the feedback as *the attractor* for the meta-state. The content of our internal representations becomes the attractor of the higher state or frame. This, in turn, stabilizes in the meta-level formulation. It creates what we commonly call a "self-fulfilling prophecy". In this way, the meta-state generates an unconscious frame and stability.

Meta-States adds a holistic or systemic frame to the linear TOTE model. This infusion of meta-levels allows us to create *a fuller model of modeling* that takes reflexive consciousness into account. A person's thoughts and feelings feed back onto previous states. The somatic embodiment of the mind plus emotional state generates a "field" of forces or energies and, as the feedback process continues, it generates a systemic organization that continually elaborates upon itself, making it more layered and rich. In the field of cognitive psychology, Norman Holland has applied meta-cognitive processes by describing this process in terms of "feedback loops governing feedback loops".

We see the power and pervasiveness of meta-levels in how meta-states govern, modify, modulate, control, drive, and organize primary states. This means that primary states do *not* play the *most important* role in our lives. Meta-states play that role. Gregory Bateson (1972) specified this principle in noting that meta-messages modify lower-level messages.

When we make the meta-connection inside our neuro-semantic system, we generate a sense of ourselves as not only actors in our movies, but as the camera person, editor, director, producer, and executive. These higher-level states are meta and gestalt states that emerge and, as they do, we experience a higher-level awareness and an expanded sense of control over our own processes.

Meta-state modulating and coalescing

By the process of *repetition and habituation*, higher frames or states eventually *coalesce into* the lower states. In this way, as meta-states coalesce they become perceptual filters or meta-programs. Where do meta-programs come from? Originally we engaged in a way of thinking like global perceiving or focusing in on details (specific), like matching or mismatching, like wanting to specify a procedure or keeping options open for alternatives, and we bring this thinking style to reflect back on our thinking. Eventually the *thinking format* becomes so habitual, so regular, so well developed, that we constantly default to it. We come to value that way of thinking. We believe in it. We start to identify ourselves as "that kind of person". With time, this becomes our style of perceiving things. This describes what we mean by a "meta-program".

We mostly *construct* and *learn* our meta-programs. They emerge from the meta-stating process of bringing a sorting style, thinking style, or perceptual style to our regular everyday thinking. We then solidify this thinking style through other meta-stating frames. We bring frames of reality, confirmation, importance, and so on to the thinking style.

So, while there are undoubtedly neurological and genetic preferences and predispositions about some of the meta-programs, these are only tendencies. They do not fate us to a thinking style. What makes our meta-programs seem so real, so solid, and so stable are the meta-stating processes that we embed the meta-program into.

How does all of this affect our mental movies? All meta-level frames color, texture, give a tint and feel and attitude to our movies. What we *experience* inside the movie as the actors in the films is tremendously influenced by those producing, directing, and editing the movie. Their attitudes and intentions and motivations penetrate the movie.

Multiordinality: the language of meta-stating at many levels

We have many terms to describe *mental phenomena*. We also have a way to sort through them to understand more specifically their structure. As *multiordinal* terms, they mean nothing apart from their level of abstraction. We have to specify the level in order to determine their meaning. "Multi-ordinal" refers to a distinction Korzybski introduced and extended to the Meta-Model in *Communication Magic* (2001). We will review it more thoroughly in Chapter Twelve.

These conceptual powers enable us to build thoughts at many different levels. Not to notice the levels, to confuse the levels, and/or to wish the levels would just go away creates confusion, "paradox", contradiction, and all sorts of category errors. Not all thoughts are equal. They do not occur at the same level. "Thought" occurs at many different levels and we label such by different terms. This generates differences in emotions— there's primary-level emotion (driven, determined, encoded, and structured by primary-level thinking). Then there are meta-feelings (determined and controlled by meta-level thinking). We can also discover and sort out meta-meta-feelings.

Primary-state "love" differs from loving the feeling or state of love. We call that infatuation. Yet we can also "love" infatuation (the love of love). This love of love of love now gives us romanticism *and* it begins to challenge our ability to track the levels. What about love of love of love of love? What's that? Have you ever imagined or could you imagine someone loving the experience of romanticism? And above that? This is multiordinality in action.

We know the experience of trusting or believing in someone. Can you believe in your belief? That creates a strong sense of conviction and tends to close the mind. Can you believe in your con- viction (belief of belief)? Now we have fanaticism. Can you believe in your belief of your belief of your belief (believe in your fanaticism)?

All of this means that in running our own brain and in assisting (coaching) someone else in running his or her brain, we need to take into consideration both mind and meta-mind levels. They differ. And they operate by different sets of principles.

Let's apply this to the internal cinema that we run in our mind as we represent things and map understandings and strategies. Take the word "action". At the primary level, as we play our movies we are *inside them as the actors*. We don't play the movies just for entertainment: we play them and *step into them* and use them as a way to map the world and navigate through life. "Action" at the primary level describes what we are doing, saying, gesturing, or behaving.

Yet when we *step back* in our mind to the director's or editor's role and think *about* our film and edit it a bit here, add in this resource, zoom in on this or that idea or understanding, foreground an area of concern—when we do that, what we are doing then involves very different kinds of "actions". Then, as director, when we say as it were, "Lights, camera, *action!*" The actions of these higher levels end as we then *implement* them at the primary level.

The same applies with the "actions" we take as producer of our movies and as the chief executive. What we do at these levels is set policy, decide on direction, establish agenda, motivation, reason, and tie it all into our reason for living. Very different kinds of "actions"—yet vital. This is multiordinality at work.

Meta-stating cultural realities

The use of multiordinality, along with the levels of mind, enables us to appreciate how we create so many cultural realities. There are so many hundreds of thousands of nonsensory "things" that exist as part of our culture that do not exist at the brute-fact or sensory-based level. NLP has scantily touched upon this area. Yet with the Meta-States model we can now give precise descriptions of how we construct the cultural realities inside which we live our everyday lives. These are the cultural realities that we cannot videotape or capture through any sensory-based technology—and yet they are "real" to us neuro-semantically.

The same basic meta-stating process that empowers us to create the matrices of our mind in terms of beliefs, values, and so forth also enables us to create and set *cultural frames* in our mind. This creates the mental and conceptual contexts in our minds about cultural or social facts. In this way we construct our social realities and then begin to relate to them as "real".

Taking cue from John Searle in *The Construction of Social Reality* (1995), I have used his formula for modeling a more precise way to think about how cultures (that is, groups of people) construct higher-level "realities". This now gives us a way to specify the neuro-linguistic environments that we live in and deal with. It further enables us to model social realities. Searle offered this deceptively simple formula: X counts as Y in C.

X in this formula refers to the "brute facts" of the world. X is the sensory-based world that we can empirically see, hear, feel, smell, and taste.

"X counts as Y" identifies a new way of seeing and reckoning and dealing with X. We no longer treat X as just X: it is now Y.

Y is the higher-level abstract classification. It is the meta-term that we use to classify, categorize, and frame the X. Y is the evaluation.

C refers to the context, environment, situation, or culture in which we make the classification.

This formula allows us to take a brute sensory-based fact of the world (X) and to categorize it in such a way that we classify X as being a Y in a given social context. When we do this we construct a social reality that didn't exist before and call into existence a social, cultural, or institutionalized "fact".

For example, we can take a piece of paper (X) and turn it into "money" (Y). As we print on that paper designations and symbols of various denominations of money, we start the process of creating a cultural "fact". "This piece of paper stands for a hundred dollars." Of course, if "we" who do this have not been properly empowered with the right to do so, then it is "counterfeit money". If the US government does it, then it counts. It is "real US currency." Then the piece (X) truly counts as money (Y) in the context of a given country.

It is this meta-level structure that allows us to take brute facts of the world, such as coins, paper, plastic, and numbers, and use them *as if* they were something else. It all happens through a symbolic process. The paper is still paper. But symbolically the brute sensory-based X-fact is transformed into a meta-level-meaning Y-fact through numerous contexts of contexts.

Running across a white line of chalk marked out on a field of grass (X) in certain contexts can now *count as* "making a point" (Y) in a football game (C) if that game is "official" (and not just "practice") and is played according to the rules of the governing body (C of C). What *is* "running across a line"? At the primary level it is just a set of actions of a person. But at a higher level it can be a social fact, a cultural fact, and an institutional fact. Constructing it as such, however, involves several meta-levels.

We have to designate *who* can run across the line. If a cheerleader or fan grabs the ball and runs across the line, it is not a "point". We have to designate when and how a *real* game starts and stops, which distinguishes it from practice, playing around, or just demonstrating.

We have to designate the rules that govern the event. We have to designate and commission the governing body who oversees games and declare them official or not.

In the construction of social "realities" and "facts" there are layers upon layers. We create multiple meta-levels of symbolic reality and "hold it in our mind" in such a way that it becomes cultural frames, social frames, institutional frames.

In this way we can do much more than merely make meaning and appraise the meanings of things. We can also assign status to things, can create social and cultural roles, assign functions: for instance, performance and operations (speech acts) and status functions (obligations, responsibilities, privileges). The meta-connection gives us the ability to call new cultural realities into existence. It allows us the ability to take other realities out of cultural existence. A minister might perform the first: "I pronounce you man and wife." A judge might do the second: "I pronounce this marriage null and void. I pronounce you divorced." Similarly: "I pronounce this corporation no longer existing."

What went on in your mind as you read this section? How did these words affect your mental movies and their frames?

We begin with our primary movies and track onto the film in our mind the brute facts of the world. Then we rise up in our mind to create an editorial comment, definition, or description as to what that X means or counts for. We set a frame so that we know how to interpret the piece of paper that reads "$100" or the man running with a ball across a white line.

There are hardly any frames in our minds more outside of our awareness than our cultural, social, and institutional frames. Yet these are some of the meta-phenomena and "logical levels" in our minds. When and where did we construct them? We mostly constructed them by absorbing the cultural assumptions, rules, and way of life as we grew up. We learned them informally and implicitly rather than explicitly.

They mostly operate *unconsciously* until we step out of that universe and into another culture. It can be a national and racial culture, a business or family culture, a religious, educational, or corporate culture. Yet when we do, we then tend to become aware that suddenly the rules and way of life that we have known do not work here. The Xs here count for other Ys here.

Meta-state design engineering

To become masterful with meta-states and meta-stating, we *bring a desired state of mind-and-emotion to bear on another state* so that we apply one to another. We do this to create more resourcefulness and to establish a higher frame of mind about the primary experience. This gives us the ability to create some marvelously powerful, enhancing, and resourceful states.

EXERCISE: Design engineering with meta-states

1. Identify a primary state to work with.
Which primary state do I need or want to enrich with some meta-level frames?

2. Select high quality resources.
Which qualities do I want to bring to bear on the primary state?
Menu list: calmness, distance, meditation, contemplation, height, professional attitude, acceptance, appreciation, playfulness …

3. Consider the effect of the resource on the primary state.
Which resources in thought or emotion would effectively temper and texture the primary state?

4. Chose your style of meta-stating.
How do I want to bring the resource to bear upon the primary state?

How do you apply the resource?

5. Add other tempering resources.
What else would enrich the primary state? Centeredness, good boundaries, clarity of my desired outcomes?

6. Solidify the experience.
What meta-levels would support and solidify the meta-state? For instance, appreciation of negative emotions such as fear, anger, grief, upsetness, stress? Acknowledgment and acceptance of our fallibility, tenderness, spirituality? Evaluate the ecology.

Meta-stating negative emotions

Given the nature and structure of reflexivity, of our mind-body-emotional states reflecting back onto themselves and so creating the meta-connection, we now can realize and reckon with one of the most fundamental systemic principles of the "holoarchy" of meta-levels—namely that, whenever we bring negative emotional energies (negative thinking and feeling) back onto or against ourselves (or against any conceptual facet of ourselves), we put ourselves at odds with ourselves.

To do this is to turn our psychological energies *against* ourselves in useless, unproductive, and typically toxic ways. When we become afraid of our anger, when we shame ourselves for being fallible and making a mistake, when we experience guilt or despise ourselves, we put ourselves into a spin, and out of that negative looping will come what we call "dragon states". While there are some exceptions to this, they are as the exceptions, not the rule. This is the rule.

If you turn *negative* thoughts, feelings, ideas, physiology, and so forth *back onto* yourself or any facet of yourself, you misuse the "negative" emotion and will more than likely create a dragon state.

Given that, the dragon-slaying and -taming processes in Meta-States give us a way to use our reflexivity more appropriately and healthily. The following process offers a general patterning for handling "negative" emotions and thoughts.

1. Identify an emotional state you have difficulty handling or managing.
Menu list: anger, fear, disgust, a sexual situation, something religious.

Which negative emotional state of thought-or-emotion do you not like, can't stand, hate, wish you didn't experience? Which negative states do you feel as "taboo"?

How is this a problem to you? What do you think-and-feel *about* this?

2. Check your permission level.
Go inside, quiet yourself and say, "I give myself permission to feel X." Now, notice any internal responses that might arise as you say this.

How well does that settle inside? What objections, if any, may arise to this? What resources would you need to access in order to more fully accept this?

3. Design-engineer a new meta-stating structure.
Go inside and give yourself permission congruently with a strong and resourceful voice that reframes the objections and notice how that settles.

- "I give myself permission to feel anger because it allows me to recognize things that violate my values and to take appropriate action early."
- "I give myself permission to feel the tender emotions because it makes me more fully human."

4. Meta-state the negative emotion with a powerful out-framing resource.
What for you would be a resource to use in tempering your experience? Access each one that you identify and amplify it fully. When you have a strong state, apply it to the negative emotion.

Menu list: Acceptance, appreciation, calmness, thoughtfulness, fallibility, playfulness.

5. Quality-control the permission and add needed reframes.
Imagine fully and completely moving into your tomorrows with this outframe on the negative emotion. Does any part of you object to letting this operate as your orientation or attitude? If so, recycle back to Step 3.

6. Put into your future and install.
Would you like this to be how you move through the world? Your orientation?

Dragon slaying and/or taming

Sometimes we cannot proceed or succeed until we take care of some internal "dragons". As long as we have internal conflicts that tear us up, sabotage our best efforts, turn our energies against ourselves, or prevent us from becoming congruent and aligned, we can't move on. We all know this experientially. We already well know that every program of *internal conflict* inside us puts the brakes on our efforts or undermines those efforts.

In using the term "dragon", of course, we use a metaphor. What does it stand for? It stands for nonenhancing, nonproductive, problematic, useless, and toxic states. It stands for all of those states that make life a living hell. Some of these states simply feel like "dragon" state full of fire and poison and destructiveness. Others turn us into dragons! Effective state-management skills enable us to shrink down the dragons, tame them (put their energies to positive uses), or to slay them. The idea of "slaying" means eliminating, getting rid of, and destroying. It's sending the limiting belief to the museum of old beliefs. It is meta-modeling the linguistic structure so that it can no longer operate as a false-to-fact map about something. Sometimes we "slay" our dragons through acceptance, appreciation, even love. Adler believed we must love our neuroses to get over them.

EXERCISE
Step 1: Flush out the dragons by naming them.
We begin by throwing our linguistic net over the dragon and naming it. Name your dragon. It could be an emotion, an experience, an idea, a concept. What states do you experience as morbid and toxic that you don't have permission to accept? (Disgust, hate, fear, anger, embarrassment, shame, guilt, religious feelings, awe, optimism, hope, love, sexuality, need for revenge, need to be grand and glorious, need to hurt someone?)

Are there any areas of life in which you have turned your psychic energy against yourself? Any things you experience as taboo? What states, feelings, and experiences do you become intolerant about? What states do you not allow yourself to experience? What states do you forbid yourself or others? What impulses do you condemn as not acceptable?

Self-expectancies give us a particular avenue for flushing out dragons. Pick an area (an emotion, event, experience, idea) and complete a sentence stem about it. Generate five to twelve statements. Just begin writing. Do not censor whatever comes to mind. Let whatever thoughts come and intrude ... just to find out what comes up for you in regard to the following experiences.

- When disappointments occur, I can expect myself to think or feel ...
- When someone rejects me, I can expect myself to think or feel ...

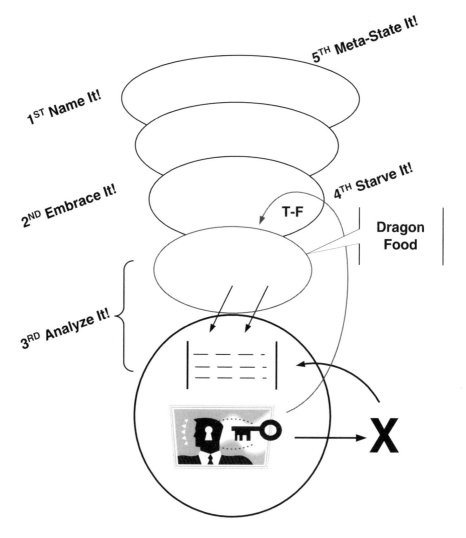

Figure 6.1: Dragon slaying

Step 2: Welcome and embrace your dragons.
To do this we will meta-state the dragon with the state of *acceptance*.

a) *Identify something you accept.*
Think of something small and simple that you accept that you may not particularly *like*. It might be a rainy day, lots of traffic on the road, paying your bills, cleaning the bathroom.

b) *Access that state of simple, matter-of-fact acceptance.*
Feel it … fully … let it fill your body.

c) *Apply to the dragon.*
As you feel that acceptance, apply it to your "dragon" ... and just notice what happens when you do.

Welcome the dragon in knowing that it is *just an emotion, just an experience, just a facet of life or of being human ...*

d) *Give yourself permission.*
Do you have permission to experience this emotion, thought, awareness, or experience? Go inside and give yourself permission in a calm and resourceful voice.

- "I give myself permission to experience this emotion because it is just an emotion ... and I am so much more than my emotions ..."
- "I give myself permission to experience this activity or event because it is just an event and it doesn't define me any more than I let it ..."

e) *Test.*
How does that settle? Do you need to give yourself more permission? How many more times do you need to give yourself permission before it will begin to settle more?

Who took permission away from you? Does the taboo really enhance your life? Or does it simply turn your psychic (mind-body) energies against yourself?

Step 3: Slay the dragon by tearing it apart.
Language drives and encodes most of our meta-states. We create language frames *about* our emotions and experiences and thereby construct *meaning*. Too often we construct *disempowering meaning* as we overgeneralize, delete important understandings, or use cognitive distortions in our thinking. We end up with dragon meta-states made up of *painful meanings* that undermine our resourcefulness.

If language creates the mess, by "de-languaging" (deframing) we can pull the "dragons" apart and remap in much more effective ways. Use the Meta-Model to question, challenge, and index specifics to test the language for being well formed. Use the questions of the Meta-Model to unglue the disempowering meanings.

The questions enable us to discover how we meta-stated ourselves into the painful meaning states and that can inform us about how we can stop the nonsense. If a meaning is sick and toxic and you ask enough questions about how it works, you will be able to slay the dragons. You will be able to pull apart the morbid states of negativity and pessimism.

What do you call this dragon? How does it operate as a dragon to you? When did you learn to think-feel this way? Who taught you to experience X in this way?

Does this enhance your life or empower you as a person? Does it always work this way? Every time? For everybody? How do you know to call it by this term or phrase?

What specifically "causes" this? How do you *have to* feel or think when this happens? What are you presupposing in order for this to work in this way?

Step 4: Starve and/or interrupt the dragon.
Dragons have to be fed to be sustained, so kick away the food tray and watch the dragon begin to quickly shrivel up. What fuels dragon meta-bolism? The very components that make up a mind-body state: internal representations, beliefs, ideas, ill-formed language, symbolizing, and physiology. Eliminate the old self-talk and the dragon evaporates.

What specifically would help you starve your dragon? Are you willing to stubbornly refuse to allow the old ways of thinking, talking, imagining, and remembering? What referents will you have to say "Hell, no!" to?

Interrupt the dragon. Pattern interrupts can spoil dragons so that they no longer function in the way that they have. Stand on your head. Stick out your tongue. Take a hundred long, deep breaths while trying very hard to not imagine Elvis Presley dancing a jig.

What would interrupt your dragon? What behaviors, thoughts, imaginations, and so forth would make your dragon flee?

Step 5: Create a meta-state induction for the dragon.
Bring a resourceful state to bear on the dragon state. Begin with such resourceful states as the following: acceptance, appreciation, calmness, quality-controlling, not-me, not-forever, not-about everything, positive intention and value, originally useful. Use the pattern of *access*, *amplify*, and *apply*.

As you recall a time of personal empowerment, clarity, or relaxation and *feel this* fully about *that* (the dragon), how does it begin to transform things?

Meta-state your dragon with refusal. Are you willing to utter a strong and definitive 'Hell, *no!*' to your dragon? Are you going to say, 'I'm not going to let you ruin my life!'?

Cast a meta-state spell to bring forth your inner prince or princess. Once you have slain or tamed the dragon, use your power of self-reflexive consciousness to become even more resourceful as you build up some positive meta-states that leave you fully integrated, centered, congruent, and empowered. With self-reflexiveness build, create, and install empowering meta-states such as self-esteeming, resilience, proactivity, forgiveness, uninsultability, inner serenity, and magnanimity.

Meta-stating "self" with acceptance, appreciation, and esteem

Using the meta-state process enables us to create a solid sense of self-appreciation and self-esteem. Doing so allows us to establish a solid core for centering ourselves, for setting a frame of high value and worth for oneself, and for operating with high self-esteem even in the face of dignity-denying or threatening experiences. We will access three states that lie across a continuum of "liking':

Figure 6.2: Continuum of welcoming

Acceptance	Appreciation	Esteem
Welcoming-inviting in	Gentle openness	Highly valuing as important, significant, worthwhile
Non-judgment	Welcome warmly with attraction/love	
W/o endorsement		Welcome with awe, honor

EXERCISE

1. Access the resourceful states of acceptance, appreciation, and awe.
Access each state by using a small and simple referent so that you can access the feeling of the state fully and discreetly.

2. Amplify each state and apply to self.
Amplify each state until you have a robust enough state to then *apply* to your sense of self. Bring each resource to bear upon self (or concept of self) so that you set each as your frame.

3. Apply self-esteeming to a needed context
Is there any context, situation, or event wherein you feel tempted toward self-contempt, self-questioning, self-doubt, and/or self-dislike? In what context would you prefer a more resourceful response?

4. Apply self-esteem to the old self-contempt context.
Apply and notice how it transforms the old context. Are you ready to respect yourself, no matter what?

5. Imaginatively put into your future.
Imagine moving through life in the weeks and months to come with this frame of mind ... Do you like this? Notice how this would transform things for you ... Does every aspect of the higher parts of your mind fully agree with this?

Mind-to-muscle pattern

The following meta-stating pattern enables us to turn informed and valued principles into the muscle memory of neurological patterns. This happens when we learn to type on a keyboard. The original learning may take a considerable amount of time and trouble in order to get the muscle patterns and coordination deeply imprinted into one's muscles. Yet by practicing and training, the learning experiences become incor-porated into the *very fabric of the muscles themselves*. We then lose conscious awareness of the learning experiences as we let our neurology and muscles run the program. At that point, we have translated *principle* into *muscle*.

The same holds true for expertise, excellence, and mastery in all other fields, be they sports, mathematics, teaching, surgery, selling, or public relations. We begin with *a principle*—a concept, understanding, awareness, belief—and then we translate it into *muscle*. I have found this especially true in our modeling projects regarding such things as resilience, leadership, wealth building, selling excellence, and learning. This pattern creates transformation by moving up and down the various levels of mind sothat we map from our understandings about something from the lowest descriptive levels to the highest conceptual levels and back down again.

EXERCISE

1. Identify a principle or concept you want incorporated in your muscles.
- Which concept or principle do you want to put into your neurology?
- Describe your conceptual understanding.
- What do you know or understand or believe about this that you want to set as a frame in your mind? State it in a clear, succinct, and compelling way.
- Okay, now state it by finishing the statement, "I understand …"

2. Describe the principle as a belief.
- Would you like to believe that?
- If you really, really believed that, would that make a big difference in your life?
- State the concept by putting it as a belief. Say, "I believe …"
- Now state it as if you *really did believe it*. Notice what you're feeling as you say that again.

3. Reformat the belief as a decision.
- Would you like to live by that belief? (Yes.) You would? (Yes.) Really? (Yes.)
- Will you act on this and make it your program for acting?
- State it as a decision by restating the belief as you say, "I will …" "I want …" It is time to …" Or, "From this day forward I will … because I believe …"

4. Rephrase the belief and decision as an emotional state or experience.
- State the belief decision again noticing what you feel.
- What do you feel as you imagine living your life with this empowering belief and decision?
- Be with those emotions … let them grow and extend.
- Put your feelings into words: "I feel … I experience … because I will … because I believe …"

5. Turn the emotions into actions to expression the belief/decision.
- "The one thing that I will do today as an expression of these feelings, to make this belief decision real in my life is …"
- And what one thing will you do tomorrow? And the day after that?

6. Step into the Action and let the higher levels of your mind spiral.

- As you fully imagine carrying out that one thing you will do today—seeing, hearing, and feeling it—you are doing this because you believe what? Because you've decided what? Because you feel what?
- And you will do what other thing? Because you understand what? Because you feel what? Because you've decided what? Because you believe what?
- And what other thing will you do?

Meta-stating "intentions"

When it comes to our thoughts, every "thought" has two levels or dimensions. First, we have the level of thinking *about* something. This gives us the *content*, of the thought. At this primary level we have something "on" our mind. We have something "before" us that we are seeing, hearing, feeling, or noticing in some way.

Second, we have yet another thought, this time, a "thought in the back of our mind" *about* the first thought. At this level we have higher- level thoughts that classify and categorize the first. These higher thoughts tell us how to interpret the first thoughts. They represent our higher frame of mind or frame of reference that we use in processing the first thought.

So the complex task of *thinking* involves thoughts in the front of the mind (our *attentions*) and thoughts *in the back of the mind* (our *higher-level intentions*).

Actually, we have layers upon layers of thoughts behind, or above, our thoughts. This means that all of our thoughts have agendas, motivations, or intentions. We can discern this *two-layered nature* of thought in terms of intention and attention. Rollo May (1969) noted this in *Love and Will*, saying that this allows us to distinguish attention from intention.

Thought's *attentional* content is what gives us our primary-level focus. It answers such questions as:

- What's on your mind?
- What are you thinking about?
- What are you representing? How? In what way?

Thought's *intentional* drive gives us our teleological outcome, or intentionality. In doing so it moves us up into the meta-levels of awareness, into the higher frames of our mind. It answers other questions:

- Why are you thinking that?
- What's your motivation, agenda, or intention behind that thought?
- What thought lurks back there in the shadows of your mind about X?

This means that every thought-feeling state actually moves us forward by two dynamics, or two psychic powers: intention and attention. *Attention* directs us to the primary-state content while intention directs us to the meta-level frame and desired outcome—or positive intention. We experience the attention as *overt* and the intention as *covert*.

When the attended concept, construction, or set of representations of your mental map does *not* work in terms of inducing you into a resourceful state so that it allows you to move on in life, then you truly need to strengthen your intentions and then align with your attentions with those highest intentions.

How? By making a meta-move to your higher intentions or outcomes. Doing that allows us to take an *intention stance* in life, a stance that will serve us well to enhance our lives with more choices. To do this we will begin by giving ourselves permission to create and live in the new attention, to get out of our comfort zone, and to let the new intention become a higher-level attractor. As we do, we give it an opportunity to become a self-organizing attractor in our mind-body-emotion system. And we do this because "energy flows where attention goes as determined by intention."

EXERCISE: Meta-stating an intentional stance

1. Identify an important work-related activity.
What are some of the tasks that you engage in as part of your everyday life or career? What do you need to do in order to succeed?

Good, let's use that activity as a reference point to explore your higher Intentions.

2. How is that activity important to you?
We take it that that activity is significant, right? *How* is it significant? How is it valuable? Meaningful?
In what way? What else is important about that? How many other answers can you identify about this activity?

3. Move up the meta-levels—one at a time.
So this activity is important to you because of these things. And how is this important to you? What's important by having this?

What's important about that outcome? And what's even more important than that? And, when you get that fully and completely and in just the way you want it, what's even more important?

(Continue this until you flush out and detect all of the higher values.)

4. Step into the higher-value states of importance so that you feel them fully.
That must be important to you? (Yes.) So just welcome in the good feelings that these meanings and significances invite, and just be with those higher level feelings for a bit.

Do you like that? (Yes.)

Let those feelings grow and intensify as you recognize that this is your *highest intentional stance*, this is what you are all about—isn't it? Enjoy this awareness.

5. Bring the higher states/frames of mind down and out.
Having these higher feelings in mind … fully … imagine this intentional stance getting into your eyes, into your body, into your way of being in the world and imagine moving out into life tomorrow with them … and as you do … and as you engage in that work-related activity that's part of your life, health, wealth-building plan notice how the higher frames transform it … And take all of this into tomorrow and into all of your tomorrows …

6. Commission your executive mind to take ownership of this.
There's a part of your mind that makes decisions, that chooses the pathway that you want to go. Will that highest executive part of your mind take full responsibility to "be of this mind" about this activity and to remind you to see the world this way?
Imagine using this as *the basis of your inner life*, your way of being in the world. Do you like that?

7. Invite other resources.
Would you like to bring any other resource to this intentional stance?

Would playfulness enrich it? Or persistence? Or passion? Or …?

EXERCISE: Meta-stating "strength" through embedding
This meta-stating pattern offers a way to embed experiences into a representation of strength and vitality.

1. Access a strength state.
Access a full 3-D movie of a time when you felt very strong. Fully recall or imagine being in a place where you feel absolutely strong and capable. As you do, see what you saw, hear what you heard, and totally feel what you felt. As you access this resourceful state, amplify it until you reach a peak with it—then make sure that you have it fully stabilized and anchored kinesthetically so that you can step into:

- the body of strength;
- the arms and hands and body posture of strength;
- the eyes and facial expression of strength;
- the breathing and voice of strength.

2. Set this state as your frame of reference for the next few minutes.
Continue to see and hear what you see and hear that elicits your *strength state* and as you do we're going to ask you a series of confirmation questions about this wonderful state:

- Do you like this experience? (Yes!)
- Would you like to have lots of access to this state? (Yes!)
- Would it serve you well to be able to "fly into this state" at will? (Yes!)
- So you do like it and want it? (Yes!) Really? (*Yes!*)
- No, you don't! (*Yes, I do!*)

(Continue to confirm and validate and get a *Yes!*—a meta-yes!, to this state.)

Do you have permission to feel strong and capable like this? If there are any objections, answer them and keep reframing the permission request until you get a strong and "definitive *Yes!*"

3. Embed as you hold your strength state.
Now, holding on fully to the intensity of this state in a constant way, and only to the extent that you can feel this fully, where in life or to what trigger would you really like to feel this?

Is there anything that can evoke in you a feeling of weakness, fear, wimping out, hesitation?

Think of that thing as a tiny, tiny little picture—the size of a dot in the middle of what you see and hear while you're in your strength state.

As you think about *where* and *toward what* you want to have more strength, open up the picture of that trigger *only at the rate and speed* that you can continue to hold the feeling of strength constant ... or as you notice it increasing ... as you open up that picture.

As you continue to see those times, places, events, people, words, tones, and whatever it *was* that *used to* rob you of this resource of strength, open up that movie as a submovie to your *much larger and bigger movie of strength* ... and notice what happens to the old movie as you *embed it in this resource* ... Notice how it transforms and begins to yield to the higher governing influence of your state of strength and capability. And stay with those good feelings until you have programmed your brain to go here every time that old trigger occurs and to *feel all of the power and resourcefulness of this higher and bigger movie.*

4. Confirm the embedding of the difficulty in a higher frame.
- Do you like this? (Yes!)
- Does every part of you like this way of responding to those events? (Yes!)
- So you'd like to keep this resource with you for the rest of your life? (Yes!)
- Okay, so as you imagine yourself taking this frame of your strength state into tomorrow at work and in other contexts ... see it, hear it, feel it ... and do you still like this? (Yes!)
- And do you fully know that you can embed all kinds of problematic feelings and states inside of higher resources? (Yes!)

Summary

Working with mind not only involves representationally tracking the mental movie playing in the theater of our mind, but being able to *go meta* at all the higher levels so as to recognize all of the embedded frames we have layered upon our movie that influence the movie.

As the third meta-domain of NLP, Meta-States plays a key role in truly mastering this field because it offers such a unifying framework for all of the component elements of NLP.

The usefulness of Meta-States shows up in how it enables us to sort and separate the levels of mind, to understand the structure and origin of meta-programs, "sub-modalities", and many other facets of NLP. This will become increasingly clear in the coming chapters. First we will re-examine "sub-modalities" as the most misunderstood domain in NLP.

Chapter Seven
"Sub-Modalities" as Editorial Meta-Levels
The Fourth Meta-Domain

Our mastery of NLP of necessity involves developing a knowledgeable understanding of *the editorial distinctions* for our internal movies so that we are able to use them skillfully. As we now turn to the domain known as "sub-modalities", we do so to do two things. First, to fully acknowledge and honor all the work that's gone before in this area. Second, to build upon this domain of knowledge and to transform it. As already suggested, the term "sub-modality" is an unfortunate and mistaken one. It misdirects our focus. The distinctions that we use in this domain are not "sub" to our representational screen, they are *meta*.

The domain of "sub-modalities" actually functions as a fourth NLP meta-domain. If we had known this, we would have designated it as the second or third domain because, chronologically, it arose prior to the discovery of Meta-States. But we did not know this. We did not even realize this in our work on "sub-modalities" that first challenged the idea of the distinctions as "sub". So here we will speak about it as being the fourth meta-domain.

We also made another mistaken when we wrote *The Structure of Excellence* (1999). We said in that work that "sub-modalities" were discovered or made explicit in NLP about 1985. We thought that was true, but it was not, although we had received charts during our original trainings in the mid- to late 1980s regarding "the history of NLP" that set the date of the discovery of "sub-modalities" at 1985. Yet that was a mistake. "Sub-modalities" were known in NLP almost from the very beginning.

How do we know that? What leads us to that conclusion? David Gordon's 1978 book, *Therapeutic Metaphors*, that's what. He has in that work an entire section on "Sub-Modalities". And, by the way, because he always spelled "sub-modalities" with the hyphen, we have opted for that in this book.

Apparently, however, very few people paid any attention to "sub-modalities" at first. What suggests this? Primarily the fact that after Gordon's 1978 work, the next reference in the literature of NLP to "sub-modalities" does not occur until 1984-85.

Consider that for a moment. Book after book was published from 1978 to 1984 *without* any mention of "sub-modalities". Then in 1985 Richard Bandler began exploring this area and using "sub-modalities" in some new ways. You can see this in

Magic in Action (1984) and *Using Your Brain for a Change* (1985). In fact, these works highly focused on "sub-modalities", as if they were a new discovery.

What are "sub-modalities"?

The term seems to indicate that "sub-modalities" are a lower "logical level" to the representation systems, yet is that right? The literature says that it is in these "sub-modalities" that we will find "the difference that makes a difference."

Yet is that what Bateson meant by that phrase? Would Bateson approve of applying his phrase to "sub-modalities"? Why is it that many of the "sub-modality" mapping-across patterns do not always work? What *mechanism* actually explains how "sub-modalities" work? Why "sub-modalities"?

You may have noticed that we have not only been using the hyphenated term, but we have always put it in quote marks. Why?

The reason is, as we shall soon argue, that these distinctions are not truly "sub" to modalities, that the model is simply mistaken about that, and that the term is an unfortunate and misleading one. "Sub-modalities" do refer to distinctions in the modalities. That much is true. But the distinctions are meta-frames and operate semantically rather than as a lower "logical level" to modalities.

At the time when NLP first developed, the general thinking in the field viewed these distinctions as smaller or finer facets of the sensory representations. Therefore it was natural to think of them as "sub" to the modalities. From that perspective, the term made perfect sense. The idea was that "sub-modalities" were *sub*units of the modalities, a lower logical level, as members of the class of the visual system, the auditory system, or the kinesthetic system. The governing metaphor at the time was that "sub-modalities" were the molecular structure, the subatomic level of the mind's representations.

Running with that metaphor, Bandler, McDonald, Andreas, and others, including myself (MH), began writing and exploring "sub-modalities" as if we would find inside them the atomic structure of subjective experience. Those were exciting days. And, in spite of the theoretical mistakes in it, produced many useful patterns.

Later, Bandler would push this approach to its extreme in his search to find the borders or edges of what "sub-modalities" would develop. In designing DHE (Design Human Engineering), he thought that he could go beyond mere modeling to designing features for human evolution using "sub-modalities" and then "stick the new program into the human brain as we would into a cyborg." As intriguing as this is for those of us who love sci-fi flicks, this approach went nowhere. After the first ten years of DHE, there was not one pattern or model that the folk in that area could point to that even began moving in that direction. We even wrote a critical review of DHE, "Ten Years and Still No Beef", which you can find on the website: www.learninstitute.com/DHECritique.htm

There is a reason why "sub-modalities" did not open new doors of discovery or create new patterns or models. When we first began our exploration and research on "sub-modalities" for a book, we did not know that we would be discovering that reason. Yet as we began the exploration and research into "sub-modalities" we found that we had to entirely rethink the domain of "sub-modalities" and where they fit into NLP. What resulted for us was a new and fuller understanding of "sub-moda-lities"—what they are, how they work, and the difference this makes. (See *The Structure of Excellence: Unmasking the Meta-Levels of Sub-Modalities*, 1999.)

The term "sub-modalities"

The term "sub-modalities" was introduced into NLP by Bandler. Prior to that, Todd Epstein called them "pragmagraphics". Originally, they viewed these quali-ties, features, and distinctions of the modalities as a lower logical level. Metaphors were used by numerous people about these finer or smaller distinctions operating as if they were the molecules that make up the elemental nature of thought.

As a term, "sub-modalities" is a false and misleading one. They are actually meta-frames, hence, meta-state structures, and so *meta-modalities*. Yes, we know that the term has been used too long in NLP to change it now, and our intention here is not to eliminate the term, but to understand it more accurately. Then we can become more masterful in using these "sub-modalities" distinctions.

Actually, things would have gone along much better for NLP if we had kept the term "pragmagraphics". This term would have focused attention on two facets of these distinctions:

1. These distinctions are graphic features of our internal movies. They govern the video, audio, and sensory tracks in the cinemas that play in the theater of our minds.
2. These distinctions have tremendous pragmatic effect upon our states and meta-states.

The structure and level of "sub-modalities"

Here is the scope of this chapter: the *features* of the modalities that we have called "sub-modalities" do not actually operate at a "sub" level, but at a meta-level as the higher frames, the editorial frames that we bring to the content of our movies. This may take some explaining and demonstrating.

To follow our line of reasoning, suspend your final judgment. Our aim is not that you necessarily agree or disagree with this analysis. More important is that we all develop increased ability to *effectively discern and use* "sub-modalities" to run our own brain, model excellence, and facilitate greater resourcefulness in others.

Seeing "sub-modalities" as meta-frames (as meta-modalities) explains why some of the so-called "sub-modalities" are also meta-programs.

Consider that. Some of the very distinctions that we call "sub-modalities" at other times we call meta-programs. How could the same feature or property at the same time be a "sub-modality" and a meta-program? How could that be? A meta-program suggests something at a higher level; a "sub-modality" suggests something at a lower level.

Which is it? Do these features operate at a meta-level or at a "sub-modality" level?

Here are a few examples:

1. The distinction that we call "associated" and "dissociated"

If you examine the lists of NLP meta-programs and "sub-modalities," you will find "associated" and "dissociated" in both lists. This distinction refers to being "inside" an experience (associated) or "stepping aside" from an experience in every sensory system: in the visual, auditory, and kinesthetic systems. We can see, hear, and feel from *inside* and from *outside* our bodies, from *inside* and *outside* our eyes, our ears, our skin. Yet associated and dissociated are also classified as a meta-program. How is a person sorting for things, inside or outside? Either as a driver or critical meta-program, some people can't think of any experience without being in it or out of it.

So which is it? When you *step inside* your internal movie in your mind, have you just made a "sub-modality" shift or have you used a meta-program? If it is meta, how can it be sub? If it is sub, how can it be meta?

2. The distinction we call global versus specific-zooming in or out

Here's another puzzle. When we create a mental movie in our mind of an experience, we can see the forest rather than the trees. We can construct a movie that gives us the big picture or we can focus in on the details and notice things more specifically. However large or small a "chunk" of information we process as we watch on the cinema in our mental theater, we nonetheless either move up or down the level of abstraction. We call this a meta-program.

Yet in terms of "sub-modalities", this description is what we also call "zooming in" to the details of an image, sound, or feeling or "zooming out" to get a larger picture, a more global image. When we describe our activity as zooming in and out we use "sub-modalities"; when we speak about it as a point of view on an up-or-down scale of deduction to induction, we call it a meta- program (global/specific).

So, which is it, sub or meta? Or, could it be both?

3. The distinction we call matching versus mismatching

The meta-program of matching versus mismatching sorts for whether we are conceptually noticing whether the relationship between two things is "the same" or "different". Whenever we notice two things—my job this year and last year, the car I now drive versus the one I drove when I first began driving, last year's holiday and this year's, this book and some other NLP book—we compare things. As we compare, how do we engage in the comparison? Are we looking for similarities or differences? And to what degree? In what sequence?

How does this occur at the representational level? What occurs in our mental screen? Do we compare and contrast by seeing two pictures and foregrounding (a "sub-modality" distinction) the similarities or the differences? Perhaps we hear two sounds, voices, tones, melodies and we foreground how they are similar first (matching), then how they are different (mismatching).

4. *The distinction we call options versus procedures*

The meta-program of sorting for, paying attention to, and thinking in terms of options involves looking for alternatives, choices, whereas thinking in terms of procedures means looking for sequence, order, the right way to do something. Here we have a continuum along the concept of our style of action. On one end of the pole we want options and at the other end we want a procedure. One comes from the state of choice and freedom, the other from the state of safety, rightness, properness, or order. These are the meta-states that drive these sorting styles.

So what is occurring at the level of the sensory information playing out on the mental movie of the mind? In the meta-program of "options", there will probably be images of multiple lines, doors, or pictures that represent choices. It could be multiple voices that encode the choices. In "procedures" there will probably be one motion picture showing, or possibly a series of still pictures, each focusing clearly and precisely in a step-by-step process. There could be a voice sequencing the steps, even using ordinals, "first, second, third" and so on. So, at the "sub-modality" level, multiple images, voices, sensations, and so forth that are somewhat dim and fuzzy could stand for options; and a clear, in-focus, single movie, voice, or sensation could stand for the right procedure.

When "sub" is actually "meta"

What does all of this mean? What are we to conclude from these puzzles? We could conclude that we have made a diagnostic mistake in NLP and that these distinctions are really a "sub-modality" or a meta-program. Or, we could conclude that we have simply been using a wrong word and metaphor, that there really are no such things as "sub-modalities", that the distinctions, features, and properties that we are actually referring to are ways of framing or editing our mental movies.

So this is our conclusion. Somehow, what we call meta-programs and "sub-modalities" are two facets of the same thing. Both occur at meta-levels and indicate the way we frame the images in our mind.

As a result, this way of viewing these domains offers us new latitude as we use NLP. Using the point of view of "sub-modalities" is sometimes more useful. Similarly, sometimes using the perspective of meta-programs is more useful. At other times, neither term really works all that well, so we simply talk about the distinction as meta-levels, meta-frames, or meta-states.

So, as we continue to use the term "sub-modalities" to refer to the perceptual organization of thoughts and the qualities of thought in each representation system that make up our internal movies, we do so with fuller awareness of their meta-level structures. This is important. It's important because it enables us to think more productively about how "sub-modalities" work and how to work with them.

"Sub-modalities" refer to the *qualities and characteristics* of the modes of representation that we use in creating and editing our movies. We actually do this from a meta-level because you have to go meta to even notice a "sub-modality". When we are at the representation level of our movies, how we see, hear, feel, smell, taste, and say things is simply one of the built-in features of the movie. We have to *step outside of the movie* (go meta) in order to notice—is it in color or not, close or far, loud or quiet, fuzzy or clear, warm or cold? What are the cinematic features that we have edited into and encoded in our movie?

Then, after we notice and recognize the *structure* of the encoding of the movie, we have to go meta also to shift the coding.

"Make the picture black-and-white. Good. Now push it away from you. That's right. Now how do you feel?"

That's fancy editing and it does *not* occur while you are in the movie. You have to make a meta-move to do that kind of "running your own brain."

And there's another thing. What does black and white stand for? What does color stand for? Bright? Dim? Loud? Close? What do these structural facets of the movie stand for?

You see, just because we use these features, these properties, and these distinctions, they in themselves do not carry the meaning. Meaning occurs at even yet another higher level up. Meaning, as always being context-dependent, depends on the frame it is embedded in.

That's why merely restructuring these features does not always work, and does not always work for everyone. Typically "close" means more real, more compelling, more convincing. But it depends. Bring a picture so close that you see the dots and then what? More real? Bring the picture so close that you see into the pores of the skin-more compelling or desirable? We don't think so.

Typically, "bright" also means more, more desirable, stronger in emotion, and so on. We make our pictures of our goals and outcomes brighter and we feel more compelled, more motivated. We have a *bright* future. Makes sense. But make a picture of a romantic candlelight dinner brighter. Does that increase the feelings of romance? Not for most people.

What does all of this mean? It means that the structural features and distinctions of a movie, which we call "sub-modalities", are the structural coding that we bring to, and apply to, the mental movie, and so occur at a meta-level as our framing and the distinctions are dependent upon a yet higher level for *their* meaning. They are semantically governed by yet higher frames.

There you have it, the truth about "sub-modalities". They are not sub at all: they are meta. They are not smaller or finer distinctions: they are the structural code that we bring to and incorporate into our movies as we edit various qualities and properties into them. That's why when you ask people "sub-modalities" questions you see them sit back. They lean back to take a look at the structure. And structure, as we all know, is above content.

Back to the basis of our representation systems

One of Bandler and Grinder's strokes of genius in NLP was in formatting "thought" in terms of the representational systems. That move was so obvious and yet so profound. It was so profound that Bateson commented on it in his Foreword to *The Structure of Magic*.

From there, they described the tremendous richness of sensory information that we have available via our neurology. At every moment in time we have a wealth of input in all systems. In fact, our sensory input is easily overloaded. That's why our nervous system constantly filters things out, only selectively attends other things, generalizes what we're dealing with, and distorts other things. In this way our neurology is our first line of defense against the overly rich territory "out there". Our sense receptors and neurology function as filtering mechanisms to screen input via these systematic modeling operations. In this way we map the territory.

But how to map, what to map, how to encode, how to store, how to frame? These are the questions we unconsciously answer as we create our maps. The result? Our mental movies. On the screen of our mind, we re-present things. Primitively, we have general pictures, sounds, and sensations. But as infants we don't know how to make very refined distinctions. The artwork of babies, then young children, then older children, up to adults, shows how we progress in this. As we mature, we develop more refined ways to *structure* and to *frame* our representational movie. We move from primary colors to those with finer distinctions. This represents a higher and more developed framing.

This means that the finer distinctions are not "smaller" pieces, sub-pieces, but higher pieces. As a way to structure our mental movie screen, they are structural in nature.

Cinematic features of our mental movies

Using the cinema metaphor gives us the ability to sort out the *levels* of awareness and representation in how we construct the cinemas that we entertain in our minds.

1. Representational level
This level describes *what* we see, hear, feel, and otherwise per-ceive as our internal movie plays. Here we are typically *inside* the movie and experiencing things as an actor or player in our thoughts.

2. Editorial level
This level describes *how* we structure, encode, and frame our movie. From the editorial position, we decide on where we put the camera and what perspective we use (the perceptual positions). From this level we edit the movie with certain cinematic features ("sub-modalities").

3. Director level
At this level we direct the movie and ourselves and others as players inside it. By giving the actors their motivations and intentions, we establish the general attitude and disposition to be conveyed. We also direct the editor in the editing.

4. Producer level
At this higher level, we establish and operate from the value and identity frames that we have meta-stated into existence. At these levels we are focused on what we are producing and our sense of mission and destiny.

5. Executive level
This is the highest meta-state level. Here we have a mindful sense of having a choice about the decisions we make that influence everything below it: production, directing, editing, and experiencing.

Testing the old NLP Belief Change Pattern

One of the first things that cued us that there was something awry in the "sub-modality" model was Bandler's Belief Change Pattern using "sub-modalities". Do you remember that pattern? In brief, it involves these key features. If you have not played with this pattern, stop right now and try it for yourself:

1. Identify the critical "sub-modalities" of a strong belief.
2. Identify the critical "sub-modalities" of a doubt.

3. What strong but *limiting* belief would you like to change? If you did, what would you prefer to believe?
4. Exchange the "sub-modalities" of the limiting belief for those of a doubt. Turn the images and sounds on and off from belief to doubt, then turn the belief all the way down (white out), then turn back on as the new empowering belief. Stop. Hold. Amplify the critical "sub-modalities" of a strong belief.

The problem with this pattern is that theoretically, if it works, it should work for any belief, strong, weak, limiting, or empowering. So try that out.

1. This time think of a strong empowering belief. See if you can turn it into doubt and then all the way down so that you don't believe it any longer. For example, "People can learn to run their own brains". "What we call 'failure' is just information and we have the choice about how to interpret it as failure or as feedback."

Now let's do the opposite.

2. Think of something that you doubt, that you are not sure of, that you are back and forth about, and see if you can turn it into a strong belief. Example, "Criticism can't hurt me".

What we found, and what literally hundreds of NLP practitioners, including internationally known trainers, told us is that this "Sub-Modality" Belief Change Pattern seldom works. Bob found that he couldn't get it to work for himself and only seldom with participants and clients. Michael found that he could force it to work in trainings, but only if he set enough expectancy frames, and, even at that, it was not dependable. When it does work, it's because the critical "sub-modalities" involved setting validation frames at a higher level.

Using the validation frame for new beliefs

For us, this raised several crucial questions:

- What is the difference between a "thought" and a "belief"?
- Can you "think" things that you do not "believe"?
- When you "believe" things, are there always "thoughts"?
- What turns a mere "thought" into a more dynamic "belief"?

As we chased down the answers to these questions, it became clear that we can indeed think all kinds of "thoughts" without believing them. We can read books and editorials, and listen to people, and, though we can fully and completely represent the thoughts and create a vivid and dramatic and even compelling internal movie of such, we can still doubt, question, or not believe the thoughts. When we do "believe" we feel sure and convinced that the idea is true, real, and valid. This is the difference. "Thought" that we represent without thinking as true, real, or valid is just a thought, a mere representation. This gives us mental space for considering without committing ourselves to it as true, real, or valid. It's these second thoughts, these thoughts about the primary thoughts, that transform the thought into a belief. Framing a thought as "real, true, accurate, valid" meta-states the thought so that it becomes more than just a thought, a new gestalt, a "belief".

It is the validating process that creates beliefs. Then, when we "believe" we don't just think something, at a higher level of mind we give our assent to it: "Yes, that's right. That's true. That's real. That's important. That's been proven. That's the way it is."

It is this meta-state of a *validated* thought that we call a "belief". When we doubt, we oscillate back and forth, "Yes, that's true ... Well, but maybe not. Maybe that's not true." The shortcut expression of validation and invalidation, affirmation and disaffirmation, are the words "yes" and "no". Therefore, when we access a "yes" state we have the power to validate a thought into existence as a belief. When we access a "no" state, we have the power to deconstruct or deframe a belief so that it becomes just a thought.

This describes the structure of how we all develop and grow into beliefs and how childhood beliefs deconstruct into mere thoughts in adult life. We represented fully Father Christmas, had delightful and vivid mental movies of him, and we had lots of validation from parents, television, culture, media, stores, and peers. The validation made it not just a thought, but a belief. Later, as we grew and matured, we began to question and doubt the movie. We began saying, "No, I don't think so. But maybe it is. I've got it on the best word. They wouldn't lie to me!"

This has led us to design the "Meta-Yes-ing" and "Meta-No-ing" pattern for belief change. Does this eliminate "sub-modalities"? No, there are still "sub-modalities" within strong utterances of "Yes".

EXERCISE: The "sub-modalities" of a Meta-Yes and Meta-No
1. Identify a strong and powerful belief.

2. Notice how you validate it.
State the belief and notice what higher-level thoughts you have about that statement. Notice how you say "Yes" or "Of course". Notice the "sub-modalities" of this "Yes".

3. Contrast this with a strong disbelief.
What do you definitely *not* believe? State what you do not believe as a belief and notice what higher level thoughts you entertain *about* that statement. Notice how you say, "No", "No way", "Nonsense!" "Stupid!" How do you invalidate? Notice the "sub-modalities" qualities of your "No".

What are the features and distinctions in your voice, tone, gestures, or pictures that enable you to say a "yes" or a "no"—that is, to validate and to invalidate—that set

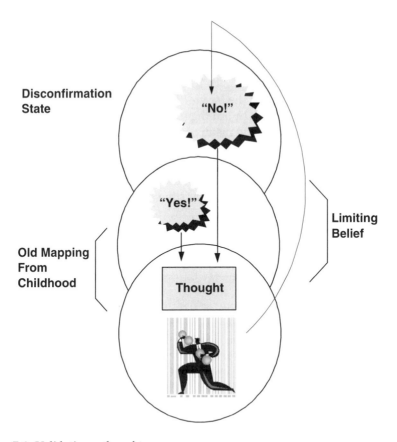

Figure 7.1: Validating a thought

a frame that transforms a thought into a belief and vise versa? It is not that we don't have or need or use these "sub-modalities" distinctions: it is that they operate as meta-frames and are semantically driven.

Structural framing using information distinctions

"Sub-modalities"—as the qualities that distinguish the sensory representations that work at a meta-level to set semantic frames—provide our brains specific structural information. This information tells us how to respond and how to feel. At the meta-level of formatting, "the difference that makes the difference" is the frame. If this is what we mean by "sub-modalities", then we could say "sub-modalities" comprise that difference. But, if we think that "sub-modalities" exist at some lower "logical level", then we have left the structural level, the meta-level. That was what Bateson meant by that phrase. If we could reinvent the term, "meta-modalities" would be far more accurate.

This means that such distinctions as close/far, bright/dim, color or not, loud/quiet, and so on structurally format our mental movies and allow us to edit our movies in new ways. In the phobia cure, we float back to the projection booth and edit the trauma movie so that we can watch it. The *concepts* of such things as distance, faded color, and fuzziness typically work *semantically* to give us "psychological distance" from the content thoughts of the movie.

Is "distance" or "fuzziness" *inside* the movie? No. These are the conceptual frames that we apply to (or bring to bear upon) the movie. They are the structural coding or recoding that allows the movie to mean something different to us.

What about the *concept* of feeling comfort or pleasure and rewinding a movie in fast speed? Is that the content of the movie or our framing? Run your brain that way and your neuro-semantics change. That's the magic.

These features (distance, fast rewind, fuzziness) are distinctions we bring to our thoughts and give us a way to *symbolically* alter the contextual frames within which the content plays out. So what we have labeled "sub-modalities" are actually meta-frames. To recode, we engage in the meta-stating process that brings different editing features to our movies.

In this, "sub-modalities" give us *a symbolic or semantic* way to encode higher concepts that are nominalizations and not things that we can see, hear, feel, smell, or taste like "real", "unreal", "past", or "future" As you recognize all of this about "sub-modalities", you can begin to feel a growing confidence that these new understandings are only going to increase your ability to work with and handle the distinctions that we use in framing our thoughts—and, of course, that then enables us to use "sub-modalities" as leverage points in change techniques. So, given that we all mentally structure our experiences using what we call "sub-modalities", we now know how to listen for and utilize these brain-encoding distinctions.

The structural change that we use in such magical patterns such as the phobia cure involve using "sub-modalities" for encoding and recoding the frames that we have been using. Now we can simultaneously listen for the *emblems* that we use in the movie—that is, all of the cinematic features (the "sub-modalities") and the *semantic meanings* that we give to such symbols.

The symbolic nature of "sub-modalities"

We have noted that "sub-modalities" work symbolically or semantically. We have designed Figure 7.2 to illustrate this. This indicates that how a given "sub-modality" works depends entirely on the meanings that a given person or culture gives to that sensory symbol. We are the ones who bring and apply our interpretative frames to the images.

When we find a difference that makes the difference in an experience, we can then use it to change the experience. Yet because every culture will use "sub-modalities" in its own particular symbolic way, that culture will be the governing meta-frame

Figure 7.2

Concept	Emblem	Semantics
Meta-level frame *Ideas, abstract* *knowledge*	*See-hear-feel symbol* *"Sub-modalities"*	*Meaning* *Neuro-semantic reality*
"Belief"	Tone of "Yes"	Reality strategy, command to the nervous system
"Disbelief"	Tone of "No"	Unreal, stupid
"Doubt"	Oscillating between "Yes" & "No"	Maybe state, indecision
"Time"	Line, circle, or spiral	Measuring between the occurrence of events
"Past"	Left of self, behind	No longer occurring, relevant
"Present"	12 inches of space immediately around front of self	Now, here, today, present
"Future"		
"The real"		
"Imagined"		
"Importance" "value"		
"Unimportance" "trivial"		

for what "sub-modalities" mean. And, inasmuch as the members of that culture will share a symbolic semantic reality, they will typically share a similar attribution of meaning to "sub-modalities". The meaning is not in the "sub-modalities": it is in the meaning attributed to them. For most people, making our movie brighter will intensify our feelings. Yet this isn't always true. Every person will have his or her own idiosyncratic coding system and so will various cultural groups.

"Sub-modalities" are actually meta-level structures.

Summary

The story of "sub-modalities" in NLP is the story of how the language tricked and misled a community that prides itself on linguistic accuracy and precision. The term seemed to have made sense originally, but then problems and puzzles arose that made it questionable.

Today we know that the cinematic features that we have mislabeled are actually *meta-modalities* and operate as an editorial meta-frame. Recognizing this provides us new insights about how these distinctions work in our internal mapping of our movies and what we can do with them.

Now also we know that "sub-modalities", as a domain of knowledge and exploration in the structure of subjectivity, give us our fourth meta-domain.

Figure 7.3: "Sub-modalities": The cinematic symbols of sensory representations

Visual	Auditory	Kinesthetic
● Brightness	● Pitch (low/high)	● Pressure
(from dull to bright)	● Location of sounds	● What sensations
● Focus	● Continuous/interrupted	● Location
● Color (degree)	● Tone	● Extent
● Color/black & white	● Number of sources	● Moisture
● Size	● Associated/dissociated	● Shape
● Distance	● Tempo	● Texture
● Contrast	● Volume (low/high)	● Temperature
● Movement	● Rhythm	● Movement
(Still/moving)		
● Direction	● Duration	● Duration
● Foreground/background	● Distance	● Intensity
● Location	● Clarity	● Frequency
● Snapshot-movie	● Whose voice	● Rhythm
(Still-moving)	● Music, noise, voice	
● Number of images	● Clarity, intelligibility	
● Bordered/panoramic	● Melody	
● Shape, form		
● Horizontal & vertical		
perspective		
● Associated/dissociated		
● 3-D or flat (2-D)		

Language (or the auditory digital) system
- Location of words
- Sensory-based/evaluative
- Simple/complex
- Self/others
- Current/dated

Other systems
- Smells
- Tastes
- Balance (vestibular: dizzy, disoriented, etc.)

Chapter Eight
Meta-Modalities
Using the Cinematic Features Frame

In the previous chapter we discovered the truth about the so-called domain of "sub-modality". They are not sub at all, but meta. They are the meta-frames that we meta-state into existence and use to edit the movies of our mind.

If "sub-modalities" are the *symbols* of sensory images that stand for various concepts by which we frame our movies with various properties and elements, then when we learn to listen for them in everyday talk we will be able to recognize how they affect the editing of our movies. NLP has long emphasized listening to linguistic predicates (what we predicate or assert about things) and assuming they are *literal* descriptions (emblems). What we have added here is to then inquire as to what these literal emblems stand for *semantically*. You already probably hear "sub-modalities" in the following statements:

- "This project just seems dull today."
- "I hear you loud and clear."
- "Something smells fishy about his proposal."
- "My future has become really bright."

"Sub-modalities" are easy to recognize in such statements. How do we do recognize them? By simply focusing on the *sensory-based* statements: dull, loud and clear, fishy, bright. Sensory-based terms provide editorial instruction to our inner editor about how to frame the sights, sounds, sensations, and so on in our movie. This also now leads us to the next step in exploration and modeling, meaning, and the neuro-semantics of those images.

What do these symbols stand for? How is the person using them as a conceptual frame of meaning? What do these literal images semantically represent?

Asking these questions takes us to the *evaluative* level—to the meta-state level. We really don't understand a person's model of the world by just hearing the "sub-modalities". We also have to know how their conceptual meta-stating works.

Secrets of "sub-modalities"

The following summarizes the key *secrets* of "sub-modalities" so that we can consciously and intentionally use them to work more effectively with experiences and with modeling experiences.

1. You have to go meta to detect and work with "sub-modalities".
Detecting and working with "sub-modalities" necessitates the ability to make a meta-move. This means moving above content to structure. You've heard this before. While we emphasize the structure-content distinction in practitioner training, it becomes even more important at the master practitioner level. Identifying "sub-modalities" means developing an *awareness* of the structure of our experiences, which we can't do while inside the move. From inside the picture, we can't see the frame. We can only see the frame when we "step aside". This conceptual step is something we do *in our minds*. It is not the same as dissociation. It is rising up and accessing or stepping into another state, a state at a higher level.

Why is this so important? If we don't access a higher level, we will get caught up in *content* and never see the code, the form, the process, the structure. Yet that's what gives us the leverage or magic of transformation.

2. "Sub-modalities" work and transform experience via the editorial frames.
In working with "sub-modalities", we do *not* deal with the subatomic or molecular structure of the basic building blocks of representational thought. We rather work with "logical types"—the levels that create neurocognitive framing of meaning.

So we not only *detect* "sub-modalities" at meta-levels, but also *change* and *shift* these symbols in our movies from the editor's position outside the movie at the higher levels of conceptual frames. Once we move to where we can recognize the *structure* of an experience, then we can restructure, reformat, and recode it.

This means that "sub-modality" work is another form of reframing. Consider that. When you change "sub-modalities", you recode the movie playing in your mind. As the editor of the film, you make it brighter or dimmer, you bring in a humorous soundtrack or turn the volume all the way down. This is framing with "sub-modalities". You are changing the frame—and frames do not occur inside pictures or movies or sounds, but outside.

With the Meta-Yes Belief Change Pattern in NS, we reframe a thought from a doubt frame, a disbelief frame, an I-don't-know frame, to a validation frame. What specific tones of voice for your words ("Yes", "Of course", "That's it", and so forth) or kinesthetic gestures simply describe the "sub-modality" symbol? This, by the way, is why, in the pattern, we ask people to gesture, move, breathe, and to use their full physiology. In doing that, we access the kinesthetic "sub-modalities" for validation. We say, "Give me the eyes of *Yes!*" "Give me the walk." Nor do we explain that these are "sub-modalities" in the trainings. We say this is the *state* of "yes" and we are setting this state in a meta-position to the thought. Does this now fascinate you as to how the four meta-domains work together systemically? If it did, how would you be breathing, talking, or moving? See!

3. The difference that makes a difference is the meta-level symbol for the new semantic frame.
In January 1970 Gregory Bateson introduced the phrase, "the difference that makes

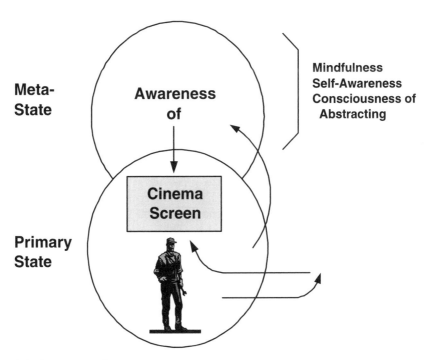

Figure 8.1: Awareness of awareness

a difference." He introduced it at the nineteenth annual Korzybski Memorial Lecture, when he chose to explore anew the classic Korzybski statement, "The map is not the territory." It was then and there that he posed the question, "What gets onto a map?" In answering that, he said differences. "Differences," he said, "are the things that get onto a map." (p. 451)

He then posed yet another question, a more important one: "What is a difference?"

In answering that, he said it involves "an abstract matter" and that's because, when it comes to maps, we "enter into the world of communication, organization" (p. 452)—the world of mind. This means that we have left the world of forces, impacts, and energy exchanges—the outside world of the territory. One is the world of Newton and his laws. The other is the psychological world of communication and "information" or "news of difference". He described all of this in *Steps to an Ecology of Mind* (1972):

"... the elementary unit of information—*is a difference which makes a difference*, and is able to make a difference because the neural pathways are themselves provided with energy ..." (p. 453)

"The territory never gets in at all. The territory is *Ding an sich* [thing in itself] and you can't do anything with it. Always the process of representation will filter it out so that the mental world is only maps of maps of maps, ad infinitum. All 'phenomena' are literally 'appearances' ." (pp. 454-55)

What Bateson described as "appearances" we have been describing as the mental movie that plays out on "the screen of our mind" (another Bateson phrase). All we have inside are maps, and maps of maps (i.e. the meta-levels).

So what is the difference that makes a difference? Information. It is the coding, encoding, or structural framing that we do that creates "news of difference". Question. When we pull a picture closer to us, is that "news of difference"? It may be. And, it may not be. Does making a picture fuzzy always change things, create difference? No. Not always. Yet sometimes it does.

Again, it is not the symbol that carries the meaning: it is the *frame* from which we interpret the symbol. The frame provides the interpretative key. The symbol in itself means nothing. Listen to any language that you don't know. Watch any foreign film. Is there meaning in those sounds? The sounds mean nothing *apart from* the semantic frame of a given linguistic community. Figure 8.3 at the end of this chapter sketches out the relationship between a sensory-based item that we use as a cinematic quality in our movie, the meta-program that it corresponds to, and how it carries a neuro-semantic significance as a meta-state.

The differences in mind that create, make, and cause differences in feeling, neurology, response, or skill are the higher meta-states or frames. Bateson demonstrated this again and again as he noted how higher levels, higher logical types, govern and modulate lower levels. This, in fact, is the definition of a "logical" level.

And, to let you in on more of the secret, this is the structure of magic. Again, Bateson (1972): "All communication has this characteristic-it can be *magically modified* by accompanying communication." (p. 230, emphasis added.)

We have described this dynamic as the mechanism that governs "logical" levels and one of the key principles of meta-states. Not surprisingly, then, it is one of the secrets of the sensory symbols that we call "sub-modalities". Of course, this really changes and challenges the received knowledge about "sub-modalities" passed down from Bandler.

"The difference that makes a difference" involves at meta-levels the frames of reference that we use to make meaning. That's why a person's belief frames, value frames, and presuppositional frames can make a given "sub-modality" work in one instance and fail in another. This is why understanding frames, knowledge frames, intentional frames, history frames, decision frames, and many more govern "sub-modalities". So, if all you are using are "sub-modality" shifts, you will be very limited in what you can do in coaching, therapy, and change work.

How frames govern the cinematic features of our movies

If "sub-modalities" are but the symbols that stand for higher-level frames, then we can reason inductively ("chunk up") from "sub-modalities" to the meta-state frames that determine their meaning (or semantics) and we can reason deductively ("chunk down") from meta-states, meta frames (beliefs, values, decisions, understandings, identifications) to "sub-modalities".

One practical result of this is that it offers us more flexibility in shifting up and down the levels of abstraction when working with someone. This provides us with more choices in how to respond and it gives us a double track for where to enter someone's model of the world. If they process information more abstractly (globally), we start up and come down; if they do so more specifically (details), we start down and move up. Yet, in doing so, we operate from the neuro-semantic principle that it's the higher levels that govern and modulate the lower levels. That allows us to always outframe any symptom or problem.

Consider how this applies to an experience of hurt or trauma. Imagine a person who has come to believe in the meta-level belief about himself, "time", and coping with problems using the following: "Whatever has happened, no matter how unpleasant and distressful, it no longer exists."

Now invite this man to recall a memory of a very unpleasant situation. Ask him to "recall it fully and completely. And as you do, step in there … and be there … seeing what you saw … hearing what you heard … and feeling what you heard …"

Will this reintroduce trauma? It is, after all, an invitation to trauma. Therapists who believe that "to get over pain you have to refeel the pain" utter this induction on a daily basis. But will it retraumatize this fellow? Will he go back into the state?

No. He will not.

Why not? His meta-frame will not let him. It will actively prevent him so that he will typically *not* make his pictures so close, vivid, and three-dimensional or his sounds so lifelike and vivid; will not let his sensations to retraumatize him. The meta-frame will protect him from encoding the symbols like that. In the "back of his mind" he will have, consciously or unconsciously, a presuppositional reality that will *not* permit it. And, even if we make the induction more specific—"… and I want you to zoom up really close, even closer, to the screen so that you see the blood …"—even that will not traumatize because he will *interpret* the symbols in a nontraumatizing way. After all, he "knows" that it's done and over and no longer influencing him.

Conversely, suppose another man operates from a very different meta-frame: "Whatever pain and distress you have experienced in your life will always be with you, you can never get away from it, and it will determine your identity and future. It's about who you are and what you can look forward to, namely more of the same. That's the way it is."

Now invite this man to step *out of* a memory of pain. Ask him to "put it up in the theater of your mind … that's right and now just observe it from a distance." Put him through the entire phobia-cure pattern and he will probably complain that he can't do it, or that it's too hard, or that he can make pictures, or can see it well, or something. He will probably find himself stepping back into the memory even when he tries not to.

What's happening in that? What's going on?

You've got it. *His frames.* His higher neuro-semantic frameworks that govern how he interprets things, believes, values, identifies. It's his frames that are driving these responses.

Ask him to step out from the movie theater where he watches the old movie and to move back to the projection booth (the double-dissociation structure). Again, he has even more difficulty doing this. Why? Running his brain in this way violates his higher frames. He has to fight against the higher levels of his mind, and typically we know who is going to win.

And even if you do coach and nudge and encourage him so that he begins to watch the old B-rated movie, even two steps removed and behind the Plexiglas, he may still experience traumatic feelings *way back there* as he watches the movie.

There have been numerous reported cases where something as powerful as the phobia cure has not worked. I remember the first time I saw and heard a person experience a panic attack while in the projection booth. At the time I figured I had not adequately set up the induction. But when I checked, I had, and she was still panicking. Why? She was afraid of her anticipations of watching the movie and going into state again. Talk about a meta-level fear, fear of her becoming freaked out by fear!

Again, what is going on here? The meta-frame. The person has the ability to feel bad and traumatized *about* the trauma.

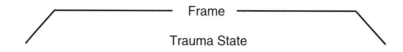

Figure 8.2

The most important thing for us is the realization that it is not the images, symbols, or specific movie that's playing that actually performs the magic of NLP. The magic lies not in the content of *what* we have the person see, but in the *structure*. That's why the *process* at the primary level can be NLP-perfect to some pattern and still not work. Above and beyond the content of any given process are the higher meta-level processes at work.

So what do we do in such cases? We explore the *meanings* (frames of meaning) that the person gives to the "sub-modality" details.

Sometimes in doing that we have to interrupt the person's state and invite them also into a meta-awareness of their own structure. "So let me get this right. You have this belief that the past determines the future?" Frequently flushing out such frames (we call this "naming the dragon" in dragon slaying) is a sufficient move that blows it out. If not, we can get leverage by using the quality-control frame. "Does this belief really serve you well, enhance your life, make you resourceful, and bring lots of joy and fun to life?" When you get a "no" that's the time to amplify it through the roof so you get a strong "*Hell, no!*" With that you are then ready to invite the person to an executive level of mind, to the level of decision:

"Are you ready to stubbornly refuse to take counsel of that old belief and to install a more empowering belief like, 'The past is just that, past learning experiences; the future is wide open to my dreams, plans, actions, and decisions.' Would you like that?"

Knowing "sub-modality" work by the higher semantic frames that govern them, the skill of coaching, psychotherapy, negotiating, and leading is like jumping logical levels faster than the client or customer. That's another Meta-States principle. Whoever sets the frame controls the game.

When the man sets frames about himself and his life using such notions as pity, shame, guilt, being a terrible person, hopelessness, we outframe by jumping to a higher level faster than he does.

"And as you look at that sad pitiful wreck of a man *for the last time in your life* knowing that change has begun to occur, and will continue to occur even when you are not noticing it consciously, you can begin to wonder, really wonder, about how you can also step back into comfort, relaxation, self-appreciation and all kinds of resourceful states and format your future according to your values and decisions, unless it's more of a party to play the victim role ... or you could learn from the old B-rated movie so that you never have to repeat those patterns that didn't work then and ... as you do, this just allows you to turn around now and face a brighter future than you could have even imaging before ..."

When we encounter a person with such rigid, limiting, disempowering, insulting, and traumatizing meta-frames, the problem is always the frames, never the person, and never even a particular pattern.

Our experiences result from our frames. Meta-frames identify our more abstract and conceptual maps of reality by which we create our meanings and that we use for interpreting the details in the movies as well as our typical attitude and orientation. So it is in changing these that the highest magic occurs.

When "sub-modality" patterns fail

While there are many NLP patterns that involve mapping one set of "sub-modali-ties" over to another set, such "sub-modality" shifting to recode the inner movie does not always work. We now know why.

In the description of trauma the internal representations of the movie give us the content of our thoughts. Above and beyond that, we have the structural facets or *the cinematic features* of the movie. And above that we have the semantic frames that govern the interpretative meanings. Together all of these elements of the system combine to create the overall gestalt of the experience. And from that gestalt we respond. When we encode a painful memory as associated, having a close-up image and sound, bright, three-dimensional, loud, or whatever, that struc-ture typically means, "Enter into this experience again and fully feel distressed, angry, fearful, upset ..."

But these "sub-modalities" do not *inherently* have these meanings. *We* use them to format such meanings. There are people who can alter their cinema so that they watch their younger self, at a distance, in black-and-white images, with little sound, in dim light, and on a flat two-dimensional screen and *still* feel panic, terror, and anguish. How could they do that? All they need is a semantic frame such as, "It's the content that counts. Changing how it looks or sounds is only trying to trick my mind."

4. The symbols we call "sub-modalities" are meta-modalities.
This is a key secret about "sub-modalities". The term has misled us to look "under-neath" the images or "inside" the movie rather than recognize the importance of frames and meta-states. This explains why DHE has been so unproductive. Mostly, DHE is lots of NLP "sub-modality" exploration in the context of trance. To that extent it can be fun, playful, or useful for loosening old frames. But, to the extent that people think that the "sub-modalities" will create new realities without deal-ing with meta-level frames, it offers nothing new. That's why it has *not* led to designing new human realities.

What we have here is the legacy of a misleading metaphor. The cinematic features are not sub to the movie, but meta. The distinctions we work with in our movies are not smaller units and so are not "*sub*-modalities".
How could the *quality* of a picture—such as having movement like a movie or still-ness like a snapshot, or having color or being in black and white, close or far, fuzzy or clear—exist as a "smaller part" of the whole?

How could the *quality* of a sound—such as the volume (quiet to loud)—exist as a "smaller part" of the sound?

(See the critique on DHE on the Neuro-Semantics website.)

5. To work effectively with "sub-modalities", set semantic frames to empower the sensory elements.

When we set higher semantic frames, there will be a modulating effect that will shift the features or distinctions in our movies. That is, the distinctions we work with in our movies are not smaller units and so are not "*sub*-modalities". These distinctions will shift and change when we set higher meta-frames as the critical semantic states. You can see that this describes the actual processes and mechanisms in the most magical interventions in NLP (e.g., the phobia cure, reframing, the swish pattern, grief pattern, allergy cure, re-imprinting, Time-Lines). It's the meta-level frames that make these patterns work.

All of this means that "sub-modalities" actually work and operate *under the governance* of meta-levels. To work effectively with these cinematic distinctions in our movies, which are not smaller units or "sub-modalities," we will set and use higher-level frames.

Frequently, "sub-modality" chunking down and mapping across consumes lots of time and never enables us to actually get to the structure of the experience. Imagine attempting to demolish a building by pulling it apart brick by brick, only to discover that it has an overarching structure. You've just been dealing with the façade and not the structure. You've dealt with the symptom rather than the framework. In the human domain, this can leave us feeling frustrated, powerless, even hopeless. Breaking down a structure into small chunks *without paying attention* to its larger structures uses up precious energy that could better be devoted to the meta-levels.

Here's another problem. Sometimes making changes at the "sub-modality" level may only create a temporary shift. Many have experienced a shift in a belief, understanding, or decision during a training or session, but then find the old pattern reasserting itself later. The intervention worked temporarily, but did not last.

What explains this? Why would it not endure?

Because there are a higher meta-state and semantic frames that are operating as a *self-organizing attractor in a neuro-semantic system*. The "sub-modality" changes dealt only with symptoms, not the cause. That's why attempting to change beliefs only with "sub-modalities" will typically not work. Nor does the confusion-to-understanding pattern. How many people learn to "understand" things by mapping the "sub-modalities" of understanding across to their confusions?

Clearing up your pictures, making them closer, using one voice at a time, feeling calm and relaxed *will* help. But, if you don't have a meta-level structure formatting your data, you will not understand. What we call " 'sub-modality' magic" works by activating the appropriate meta-frames.

Summary

With the discovery that "sub-modalities" are really a meta-domain and that they govern how we edit our movies, we now understand that what those "sub-modalities" as symbols stand for governs how to interpret them. We can also now see how they relate to meta-states, to the linguistic distinctions of the Meta-Model, and the meta-program distinctions.

"Sub-modalities", as the editorial meta-frames that we use for encoding our movies and framing them, give us clue as to how we use them *semantically* and why the mere distinction will have different meanings and therefore different effects with different people and cultures.

Magic lies not in the content of what we personally see, but in the *structure*. That's why the *process* at the primary level can be NLP-perfect to some pattern and still not work. Above and beyond the content of any given process are the higher meta-level processes at work.

"Sub-modalities" do not *inherently* contain meanings. *We* use them to format meanings. There are people who can alter their cinema so that they watch their younger self, at a distance, in dim, 2-D, black-and-white images with little sound and *still* feel panic, terror, and anguish.

"Sub-modalities" actually work and operate *under the governance* of meta-levels. Our movies are not small parts of larger units and so are not "sub-modalities". To work effectively with this distinction we use the modulation of the higher levels.

Figure 8.3

"Sub-modalities" enable us to discern the features, qualities, and properties within the cinemas of our mind. They provide the symbols for encoding information. However, they are not sub, but meta. When we consider these distinctions of "location", "intensity", "distance", or "volume", these are nominalizations and so exist at higher levels of the mind. That's why we use "sub-modalities" to encode meaning and why they work symbolically and semantically. And that's why we have to ask the questions of meaning. "What does it mean to you when you encode your images as close? Or, as far away? As three-dimensional or two-dimensional? With a serious tone or a humorous one?"

"Sub-modalities"→ (Sensory codings)	to meta-programs → (Meta-frames for seeing)	to meta-states (frames) Neuro-semantic states
Cinematic quality	**Meta-programs**	**Meta-states Conceptual states**
Representational systems Sensor-based descriptions The form & structure of thought	Thinking patterns @ RS Evaluations Higher meanings @ thought	Semantic states Higher level Evaluations

Visual →	**Representation system: VAK**	
● Brightness		
● Focus/defocused		
● Color/black & white	→	**Real, current**
● Size		**Old, past**
● Distance: close or far '	→ *Chunk size: general/specific*	
		Impactful
● Contrast	— **Global/detail**	**Compelling**
● Movement	Options/procedures	
● Direction	Sensor/intuitor-uptime-downtime	
● Foreground/background	Judger/perceiver-controlling/perceiving	
● Location	Self- referencing—other-referencing/	
● Associated/dissociated	External ref.	
● Changing/steady		
● Framed/panoramic		
● 2D (flat), 3D (holographic)	→	→ **Real/unreal**
● Speed: fast, slow, normal	Match- Mismatch/Same-Difference	

Auditory		
● Pitch	Toward/away from values	**Motivation**
● Continuous or interrupted	Associated/dissociated	**Associated/ dissociated**
	Goal sort: optimizing/perfectionism	
● Skepticism		
● Tempo: fast/slow	Value buying: cost, time, convenience	
● Volume: loud/soft	Time tenses: past/present/future	**"Time"**
● Rhythm	In time /through time	

157

- Duration
- Cadence
- Foreground/background
- Distance
- Location
- Clarity

Affiliation: independent/dependent/team/
Manager
Extrovert/introvert /amivert

Convincer/believability-VAK or words   **Proof**

Kinesthetic
- Pressure

MO: impossibility-possibility
MO: necessity-desire

- Location & extent
- Shape
- Texture
- Temperature
- Movement
- Rhythm
- Duration
- Foreground/background
- **Associated/dissociated** → **Thinker/feeler**
- Intensity
- Frequency
- Weight

Chapter Nine
Mastering Programs of Perception
The Meta-Domain of Meta-Programs

The second meta-domain of NLP is the domain of Meta-Programs. It is this domain that we use to profile people and to "read" personality patterns. This domain enables us to begin to "figure people out" in terms of the thinking patterns that drive their way of reasoning and computing. As a practitioner you already have a general sense about the model of Meta-Programs as the perceptual filters that govern:

- Attention: What we pay attention to
- Sorting: What we sort for
- Information processing: How we process information and emotion

In this chapter we describe meta-programs in terms of:

- what they are
- how they work
- the effect they have upon us and our states
- where they come from
- how we create them
- how we can change them
- how we can detect them in language and behaviors
- how we can use them in communicating
- how we can use them in profiling neuro-linguistic programs

Doing this will allow us to present the theoretical framework of understanding about these "programs" and how they operate in human personality. In the next chapter, we set forth more than fifty of the meta-programs that have been identified in NLP. You can find a more exhaustive presentation of this material in Michael Hall's *Figuring Out People* (1997).

Overview of the meta-programs

By definition, meta-programs are those programs in our minds and eyes by which we have learned to perceptually filter or color what we see. As perceptual filters, meta-programs identify what we sort for, pay attention to, look for, and "see".

Where do these ways of seeing things come from? They mostly come from how we have learned to see and perceive. They come from habituated meta-states. Meta-programs are solidified or coalesced meta-states. As such they involve ways of thinking and conceptualizing that have gotten "in our eyes", that is, they are meta-states that have coalesced into our neurology.

What are the sources of our meta-programs? Meta-Programs arise from both nature and nurture—from natural dispositions and tendencies and from learning experiences. Meta-programs, as we experience them, also arise from the solidification of meta-states. They begin as a learned, taught, and/or coached way to think, sort, and perceive, and eventually become our mental program for such.

For example, suppose you grew up hearing messages like, "pay attention to the details", "your head is always in the air", "the devil is in the details". With such instructions, we would probably learn to focus our attention on specifics, or details.

Conversely, what if we received the following injunctions? "Can't you see the forest for the trees?" "What's wrong with you, don't you see what's happening?" These statements invite us to sort for the bigger picture and to get a global view of things. In each case, the injunctions and/or prohibitions set up meta-frames for how to think and will induce corresponding states. The detail state will involve leaning forward, caring about specifics, thinking inductively, whereas the global state will involve leaning back, caring and valuing gestalts, and thinking deductively from principles.

When this habituates so that we regularly and systematically apply either the detail state or the global state to our everyday processing and experiencing, we access and apply a meta-state structure to our perceiving. At first this creates a fluid state-about-a-state experience. But over time as we value it, believe in it, and identify with it, the meta-state becomes more firmly established and solidified. That, in turn, allows the state to coalesce so that it textures and qualifies all of our primary states and experiences. The higher state begins to operate as a canopy of consciousness, or as a meta-frame, over all of our perceiving and sorting. This describes the process of how our meta-states transform into meta-programs. It structures our very sense of who we are, ourselves as a person, and what we call our "personality".

Sorting choices on a continuum

Most meta-programs represent a continuum of responses and choices. Thinking about them in this way allows us to plot the majority of meta-programs along a continuum. When there are choices on either end of the pole, this can lead to extreme versions of the particular meta-program and the creation of a driver meta-program. In this case, the meta-state has been solidified, confirmed, validated, and even identified with and so takes on a "solid" feel as if it were a permanent structure of personality. When this happens, the meta-sorting "program" drives our way of perceiving. We feel as if driven to sort and think that way, and unable to think in any other way. When this happens we experience a loss of flexibility.

Conversely, when we can easily move back and forth along the continuum, we say we have a high degree of flexibility of consciousness. This gives us more choices and power of response in different contexts. We can just as easily shift back and forth between sorting globally and sorting for details, matching and mismatching, operating in a procedural way and operating more loosely, looking for options. This necessitates practice and the right attitude.

Contextual frames of mind

Do our meta-programs operate in all contexts, or are they sensitive to contexts? If we have and use meta-programs in one area of life, will that pervade all other areas and contexts of life?

Meta-programs can operate in this way, yet typically they do not. For the most part, meta-programs are context-dependent. They shift and change depending on the given context. At work, we may operate with a different sorting style than we do at home, in relationships, when on vacation, or whatever. Meta-programs are not personality types.

These programs do not work as a typing of "personalities" but as a description of how people think, sort, and operate in given contexts, at given times, in this or that situation. So while we have been using (and will use) the nominalizations, "meta-programs", "personality", "perception", "perceptual filter", and so forth, these are not actual or real "things". They refer to processes.

The context-dependency of meta-programs gives us the ability to operate with different meta-programs in different contexts, environments, or situations. We can shift and change. We can adopt different sorting, perceiving, and filtering. This offers an explanation as to why we should not use or confuse meta-programs with "personality traits" and try to define what a person "is". These patterns (or, more accurately, patternings) are not written in stone. They are descriptions of how we behave, mentally and perceptually, in a given context at a given time within a given relationship. They are descriptions of how we have learned to sort and process information. Rather than solidified personal "traits", these are ways of functioning, ways of "running our brain".

Changing meta-programs

Can we change our meta-programs? You bet! Meta-programs are quite changeable.

Of course, the degree of changeability that we experience in the meta-programs that we have developed and solidified over the years depends on several factors. It depends on such things as our beliefs about changing them, our desire and motivation, our willingness to give change processes a chance, the skill of the person working with us, the patterns used in bringing about a change. Any and every meta-program can be changed if we desire a change and have the skills to make it happen. If, however, we believe that they are real, that they are things, that they are unchangeable, such beliefs will prevent us from effecting much change. If we believe that the map is not the territory, that the processing style is a sorting behavior, that they arise from our history of meta-stating, then changing them will be fairly easy.

Profiling with meta-programs

From the beginning, NLP has been known as a model for "reading people". Daniel Goldman introduced the readers of *Psychology Today* in 1979 to NLP as "The People Who Read People". In that original piece, Goldman described eye accessing cues and sensory-specific linguistic terms as ways that the NLP model enables us to read people. Yet meta-programs provide an even more profound way to "read", or, as we say today, "profile", people.

However, meta-programs are not a form of personality typing. Unlike the old Greek tradition of identifying the type of person, meta-programs do not describe what we are but how we function. Meta-programs describe how we sort information, process emotion, the style we use in communicating. These are but the "programs" of mind, emotion, speech, behavior, and meaning that we have used until they have become our habitual way of operating. And that's why we can use them for profiling.

Profiling means that we can use meta-programs to match up people with tasks.` For instance, someone who has a strongly developed program for details will be much better suited for a task, job, and profession that allows that way of sorting to be utilized. Conversely, the person who naturally or habitually sorts globally will experience a better fit with a task that calls for such. So one kind of profiling involves matching up the prerequisite operational style of a job with a person.

Profiling can also be extended to fitting into a group or team. Here people who naturally and habitually match will find it much easier to fit into a team. Mismatchers can do so but only if they are running their own brains (in this case, their meta-brains) so that they can turn the mismatching on and off. Paying attention to differences and how things do not fit (the mismatching style) can seem "negative" and "conflicting" to people who don't understand. Conversely, consciously inviting the mismatcher to mismatch and reality-test a new plan or project once the plan is ready for that kind of testing can put that person's highly developed skills to good use.

We can therefore use meta-programs profiling for relationship analysis, whether between couples, business partners, groups, team members, new employees in a business, or marketing to a particular audience. We can use meta-program profiling as part of our strategic thinking for planning a presentation, training, writing an article or book, or planning a party.

Profiling with meta-programs works not because of typology, but because neuro-linguistic patterns habituate. We use a way of thinking, emoting, semanticizing (making meaning), speaking, behaving, and relating repeatedly and the pattern becomes a "program." It drops out of conscious awareness. It becomes one of the unquestioned assumed frames of reference of our mind. We live within it as if it were part of the canopy of our consciousness. As a solidified meta-state, the meta-program coalesces into our neurology. Thinking patterns coalesce into neurology, as do our motor programs for driving a car, dressing, typing on a keyboard, and other mental or emotional programs for how, for example, to cope with criticism, deal with an unhappy child, or deal with deadlines. They become part of muscle memory.

With meta-programs we say that they "get in our eye" and become part of our perceptual filters. The way of seeing the world that began as an intentional effort to consciously look for or pay attention to sameness or difference, options or procedures, black-and-white distinctions or continua, now becomes our default choice for how to perceive things.

This means that, if we learn to listen for these meta-programs, we will begin to hear these distinctions as people talk. We will even be able to see some of them in how people move, gesture, posture, and act. There will be both linguistic markers of the meta-programs and audio-visual markers in analogue behaviors. It doesn't really take much more than acute sensory awareness to notice that, when a person talks about the big picture and the need to get a larger perspective of things, he will lean back and gesture upwards as if trying to see or draw a big picture. Similarly, just watch a person talk about details, about minute facets of a project. Watch her move closer and maybe hunch over a bit and lower the voice and gesture in smaller movements. Watch a person talk about steps, stages, and sequences of a task versus the person who talks about wanting many options, many choices. If you have eyes to see and ears to hear-you will see and hear the person demonstrate the meta-program.

This gives an entirely new twist and understanding to the so-called dimension of body language, does it not? The language of the body is unique and idiosyncratic to each individual and does not *mean* a specific thing that we can catalog in a dictionary of body language. Rather, as we calibrate to each person's special way of manifesting (embodying) his or her own meta- programs, we will be able to recognize their idiosyncrasy.

Profiling meta-programs involves watching for the key or driving (critical) meta-programs that govern the way a person sorts for things. We have divided the meta-programs into five basic areas corresponding to five of the most basic responses we use as we engage the world—our thinking, emoting, choosing, communicating, and semanticizing responses.

Typically look for one or two driving meta-programs in each area for a particular task, activity, or context. Our meta-programs will change in different contexts. Again, that's why they do not provide a personality typing, but describe a way of behaving or operating. To profile a person, ask:

- In this context, this person seems to mostly be sorting for ...
- His thinking style is mostly characterized by ...
- Her emoting style is mostly characterized by ...
- The style of choosing is mostly dominated by ...
- The communicational or relational pattern seems mostly driven by ...

EXERCISE: Profiling practice

In this and the following exercises, use the chart of meta-programs at the end of this chapter. For details about the meta-programs, see Chapter 10.

1. Identify a person and a context.
What context would you like to play with as you practice meta-program profiling—business, personal, hobby, with friends, at home, with children?

2. Identify a specific instance.
Which occasion or situation would offer a typical expression of this person? When was that? Where? Other details?

3. Sit back as an observer.
Access an observer state. Run through the five categories of meta-programs. (Use the list of meta-programs at the end of this chapter.)

- Mentally:
- Emotionally:
- Volitionally:
- Communicationally:
- Behaviorally:

4. Check in with the person.
Do not make the mistake of thinking that your assumptions or mind reading is automatically correct. Instead, assume that you are just guessing, then present your best guess to the person to check out if it fits for the person. (Do not argue with them. Grant them the grace to have the last word about their meta-programs! Be especially aware if they mismatch you on most everything you say!)

Meta-level analysis of meta-programs

To become aware of our own meta-programs, we have to step aside as it were to take a meta-position to them. We have to do that precisely because meta-programs operate at a meta-level to the content of our thinking, emoting, and perceiving of things. Doing so allows us to sort and separate the primary states wherein the content occurs. Then we can notice our perceptual style.

In conceptualizing the structure of meta-programs, we have used the traditional categorizes of consciousness (such as cognition, emotion, choosing). Using these meta-distinctions gives us the following way of diagramming the meta-programs.

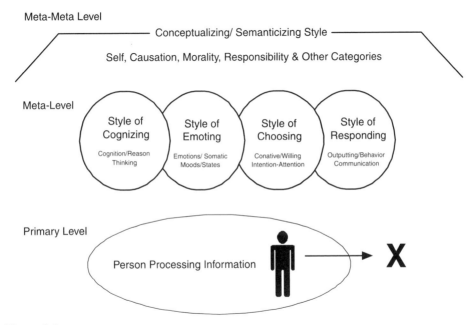

Figure 9.1

NLP Mastery and the Meta-Programs

The very story of how the original Meta-Programs arose tells the account of why knowledge and skill with these distinctions separate practitioner level from master-practitioner level. The myth goes like this. Leslie Cameron-Bandler was practicing "classical NLP" when she began to find that she could not get some of the patterns to work. "Why?" she asked herself. "What's different? What prevents reframing or the swish pattern or collapsing visual anchors from working in this context with this person?"

It was from such experiences that she and Richard Bandler began identifying some "programs" that particular individuals were running at a higher or meta-level, hence meta-programs. If a person was sorting for others in an other-referent way, that might interfere with swishing to the "resourceful me" for whom the problem is "no problem". A detailed, oriented person may have trouble getting the big picture of a reframe that's too global. Meta-Programs were invented to explain why the change technologies (patterns for "running your own brain") frequently may be interfered with or sabotaged.

Meta-programs are not only the programs that are running, but those that have been so habituated that we use them as our frame of reference. The program as a state, belief, understanding has gotten into our neurology—into our eyes. Now we see the world in terms of matching or mismatching, in terms of what options are available and how many or what procedure is the right one to perform. The state of going toward the things of importance may make it hard for us to hear or provide data about the aversions that we no longer want. The state of moving *away from* may make it difficult for us to identify a well-formed outcome that we could set as a goal.

This description also highlights the relation between meta-states and meta-programs. Meta-programs are simply the end-product of meta-states. When meta-states become habitualized and stabilized, they become meta-programs.

EXERCISE: Exploring your own meta-programs
1. Identify key meta-programs.
Identify three or four of your primary meta-programs, those that may be "drivers" or "critical" meta-programs.

2. Explore their sources.
Where and when did you develop your meta-programs? To what degree do you feel they were inherent in your temperament and to what degree do you feel that you learned to function in that way of sorting things?

3. Explore change possibilities.
How would you change your meta-programs if you wanted to? Which patterns would you use?

Learning to detect patterns of perception

If our meta-programs are typically and mostly outside our conscious awareness, how then do we bring these "programs" back into awareness? How can we become more aware of them? How can we learn to see the effect they have on the way we process information and interact with others?

Your self-preparation
1. Turn up your reasons for paying attention.
If you had a way to detect, sort out, and pay attention to these meta-level patterns, if you could consciously detect and track how any given person attends the

world, you would have a way to understand more effectively and even predict that person's style of hearing and responding to things. This would give you an awareness of that person's model of reality.

2. Access your best NLP state of sensory awareness.
Access your uptime state.

3. Access your best NLP state of flexibility.
Knowing another's model of the world and having the flexibility to alter your own behaviors and communications empowers you to meet that person where they are. This way of connecting and matching creates rapport, which reduces resistance, conflict, and misunderstandings.

What to do as a practitioner
1. Assist the person into a more fully associated state.
The more the person is in an experience, the cleaner the in- formation we'll gather. Amplify that state when necessary and appropriate.

2. Switch references.
Use the temporary-employment frame: "If I were you for a day, how would I have to do that?" "Teach me how to do that."

3. Anchor the experience.
Do it without using the kinesthetic system.

4. Slow the experience down and keep recycling.
Most subjective experiences go by too fast to catch all of the embedded patterns within it the first time. We see and hear much more when we see a fast-paced movie the second and third times.

Recycle through the experience with the person to gather more information.

5. Invite the person to step into and out of the experience.
Watch the difference between associated & dissociated experiences.

Developing mastery with meta-programs

1. Practice one meta-program at a time.
Take each meta-program at a time and practice it until you develop proficiency in recognizing it and in using it while speaking. As you do this, be sure to refuse to overwhelm yourself with the entire list. Consider the meta-program you are using if you keep sending your brain to thinking about how you have more than fifty to learn.

2. Mindfully choose to move from content to structure.
Do you have permission to step out of content? We have to go meta in order to lis-

ten for processing patterns. Does this make you self-conscious? When you begin paying attention to structure (to the meta-programs), are you afraid that you won't be able to remember what the other person is saying? Don't worry. We speak at only 100 to 150 words a minute, while we can think in thousands of words a minute.

3. Develop elicitation flexibility.
Use open-ended questions to elicit meta-programs:

- "Would you tell me about one of your favorite holiday experiences?"
- "What do you think about developing more effectiveness in communication skills?"

Try out some close-ended questions, sometimes they will work: "Is this glass half empty or half full? What does it look like to you?"

Elicit meta-programs by using downtime questions. Any question that requires a person to "go inside" to access the information they need in order to respond is a "downtime" question. Learn to ask these types of questions. If the person doesn't have the information on the tip of the tongue, that person will typically begin to also demonstrate the meta-program. And the person will act out the meta-programs in a variety of ways. So to elicit meta-programs, simply ask a person to fully and completely recall something and have them then step into that experience and feel it fully as if there.

4. Remember, not all meta-programs carry an equal weight of importance.
Meta-programs differ according to how a person uses and values them in a given task or area. Identify context, and then prioritize them in terms of importance to that person in a given context.

Which meta-program is most important and impactful for this person? Which meta-program exercises the most significance in this person's experiencing?

5. Use the sorting grid (template) to track meta-programs.
Think about the list of meta-programs in the five categories as a sorting grid that you can use to help organize the meta-programs in your own thinking and memory. Use it as a tool for profiling yourself first, then those you know well.

6. Practice writing pacing statements.
As you gather information about a person's meta-programs, aim to use that information as soon as possible. You can practice writing matching statements or even begin pacing the person verbally on the spot. Doing this will greatly increase your communication skills.

For example, if a person operates as a strong "self" sorter (self-referencing) who mismatches with counterexamples (or with polarity responses), that person will tend to feel inclined to challenge people with "Prove it to me!" type of statements.

This can spiral into a pointless matching of wits if you don't watch out. Yet, knowing this, we can now counter this internal formatting with a pacing statement like, "You seem so good at knowing your needs that only you can truly decide what you deem as ultimately right. No question about that. And I don't know if what I have to say will make any difference anyway. But anyway here it is."

EXERCISE: *Discovering the structure of liking*

1. Ask your partner to think about a time when he or she liked someone upon first meeting that person.
How did you decide that you liked that person?

2. Collect meta-programs.
Use the meta-program sorting list and elicit as much information as possible about your partner.

3. Repeat.
Repeat this same process for when your partner disliked another person (a stranger, or now friend) upon first meeting him or her.

How did you decide that you disliked that person?

4. Debrief.
Invite a meta-person to this process. Feed back what he or she saw and heard in terms of meta-programs. Especially, feed back how the questioner displayed his or her own meta-programs in the process.

EXERCISE: *Identifying someone's agreement/disagreement signs*

1. In groups of three persons, begin a discussion about something of interest with one person who will share an experience.

2. Calibration for yes and no.
Watch for the person's autonomic nervous system's signals indicating "yes/no" and "agree/disagree". Elicit "yes" and "no" responses while calibrating to the subtle cues that indicate it even when they have no verbalization.

3. Challenge your calibration.
When you feel that you are calibrated to the person, ask him or her to intentionally not respond verbally or demonstrate a response in any obvious way.

Now verbally pace for two minutes to maintain rapport; then for one minute totally break rapport to get disagreement; and then for two minutes re-establish rapport. Watch for the signs of "Yes, we're together" and "No, you have it

all wrong."
The master art of changing meta-programs

Earlier in this chapter we noted that we can change meta-programs. Actually we have lots of ways and technologies for changing meta-programs. Robbins[AA8] (1987) says that one way to change a meta-program involves "consciously deciding to do so". That gives us our first way to transform or change a meta- program.

EXERCISE: Consciously changing a meta-program
1. Become aware of the meta-program.

2. Identify contexts and check the ecology and value of that meta-program in those contexts.

3. Give yourself permission to try that meta-program on for a day.

4. Shift your consciousness to the other side of the continuum to try on the other side of that meta-program.

5. Set multiple frames that will support using the preferred meta-program.

If meta-programs inform our brain regarding what to delete, then if we move toward values, we are thereby deleting our awareness about what we are moving away from. And if we sort for the details, we are deleting the global picture. This means that, as we redirect our awareness to what we normally delete, and value that information, and practice looking for it, this will enable us to practice sending our brain in a new direction. This too will eventually habituate so that we can do both patterns.

EXERCISE: Practicing the reprogramming of a new meta-program
The following process offers a more elaborate way to consciously try on a new meta-program.

1. Identify and ecology-check the meta-program.
Specifically identify when, where, and how you use this meta-program in a way that does not serve you well and identify how it undermines your effectiveness in some way.

2. Describe the preferred meta-program.
What meta-level processing would you prefer to "run your perceiving and valuing"? Specify when, where, and how you want this meta-program to govern your consciousness.

3. Try it out.
Imaginatively adopt the new meta-program, pretend to use it in sorting, perceiv-

ing, or attending. Notice how it seems, feels, and works in some contexts where you think it would serve you better. Even if it seems a little "weird" and strange owing to your unfamiliarity with looking at the world with that particular perceptual filter, notice what other feelings, besides discomfort, may arise with it.

4. Model it.
If you know someone who uses this meta-program, explore with them their experience until you can fully step into their position. When you can, then step into second perception so that you can see the world out of that person's meta-program eyes, hearing what he or she hears, self-talking as he or she engages in self-dialogue, and feeling what that person feels.

5. Run a quality-control (ecology) check on it.
Go meta to an even higher level and consider what this meta-program will do to you and for you in terms of perception, valuing, believing, and behaving.

What kind of a person would it begin to make you? What effect would it have on various aspects of your life?

6. Give yourself permission to install it for a period of time.
Grant yourself permission to use it for a time. Check for objections. Future-pace.

For example, what if you have typically operated using the Other-Referencing meta-program (#14) and you give yourself permission to shift to Self-Referencing, yet, when you do, you hear an internal voice that sounds like your mother's in tone and tempo saying, "It's selfish to think about yourself—don't be so selfish: you will lose all of your friends"?

This voice objects on two counts: selfishness and disapproval that leads to loneliness. So rephrase your permission to take these objections into account. "I give myself permission to see the world referencing centrally from myself—my values, beliefs, wants—knowing that my values include loving, caring, and respecting others, and that this will keep me balanced by considering the effect of my choices on others."

7. Future pace the meta-program.
Practice, in your imagination, using the meta-program and do so until it begins to feel comfortable and familiar.

"If you knew when you originally made the choice to operate from the other referent [name the meta-program you want to change], would that have been before, after, or during birth?"

Use one of the time-line processes to neutralize the old emotions, thoughts, beliefs, or decisions (the visual-kinesthetic dissociation technique, for example, or the decision-destroyer pattern). Once you have cleared out the old pattern, you can install

the new meta-program.
Changing meta-programs in and with "time"

Because our meta-programs refer to our strategies for filtering information and our strategies for seeing, it makes sense to update any strategy that's sluggish, inappropriate, and maladjusted. We know that the concept of "time" affects our meta-programs, but why and how?

As events come and go over a period of months or years, they create new learning contexts—contexts within which we learn to pay attention, sort, and perceive in different ways. So when we do pseudo-time orientation using various time-line patterns, we use a meta-level structure that alters our thinking contexts. Additionally, we use an inherently hypnotic process when we "go inside", access our time-line, and then float above it back to our "past". By doing this we access a highly eceptive and suggestible state, which amplifies our responsiveness to change.

The effect of meta-programs on "sub-modalities"

If meta-programs and "sub-modalities" are two meta-level domains and models that we use for finding and working with the structure of experience, and if many of the distinctions in each model overlap as they describe the same thing, we should be able to translate between meta-programs and the cinematic features of our movies, should we not?

EXERCISE
1. Think of one of your top ten NLP resource states.
Elicit a time and place where you were fully in that state. Recall it: is it a snapshot or a movie? Turn it into a movie. Fully notice your representations as you refresh this state and the drivingrepresentations.

2. Check the meta-programs of your resource state.
Use the meta-program list and check for the structuring of your representations in terms of the thinking patterns or meta-programs.

Shift back and forth between the meta-programs noticing how it affects the "sub-modality" distinctions that you use in editing your mental movies.

3. Solidify your learning experiences.
As you find more resourceful and empowering ways to structure your representations for the resource state, shift to those. Check the ecology as you future-pace.

Solidify through validating beliefs, values, identities, decisions.

Summary

The way we learn to perceptually see the world and the thinking patterns we use in processing information and sorting for things are called meta-programs. When habitualized, these operate in such stable ways that they seem like our mental software "programs".
This second meta-domain provides a model for how to think about, recognize, and use these thinking/perceptual patterns. Knowing and using such provides a tremendous jet propulsion for our ability to communicate, gain rapport, and influence.

Meta-programs arise from meta-states and the meta-stating process. Understanding this gives us greater flexibility and control over them in ourselves and others.

Template of meta-programs

The "mental" meta-programs

#1. Chunk size:
General/specific; global/detail;
  Deductive, inductive, abductive

#2. Relationship sort:
Matching/mismatching;
  Sameness or difference/opposite;
  Agree/disagree

#3. Representational system sort:
  Visual/auditory/kinesthetic/
  language

#4. Information-gathering style:
  Uptime/downtime

#5. Epistemology sort:
  Sensors/intuitors

#6. Perceptual categories sort:
  Black-and-white versus continuum

#7. Scenario thinking style:
  Best versus worst scenario
  Thinking; optimists/pessimists

#8. Perceptual durability sort:
  Permeable/impermeable

#9. Focus sort:
  Screeners/non-screeners

#10. Philosophical direction:
  Why/how; origins/solution
  Process

#11. Reality structure sort:
  Aristotelian/non-ARISTOTELIAN
  (Static/process)

#12. Communication channel preference:
  Verbal (digital)/nonverbal
  (analogue), balanced

The emotional meta-programs

#13. Emotional coping or stress response pattern:
 Passivity/aggression/dissociated

#14. Frame-of-reference or authority sort:
 Internal/external;
 Self-referent/other-referent

#15. Emotional state sort:
 Associated/dissociated; feeling/ thinking
 Stepping in/Stepping out

#16. Somatic response sort:
 Active/reflective/inactive

#17. The convincer or believability sort:
 Looks, sounds, or feels right; makes sense

#18. Emotional direction sort:
 Unidirectional/multidirectional

#19. Emotional intensity/
exuberance sort:
 Desurgency/surgency

The volitional meta-programs

#20. Direction sort:
 Toward/away from, past Assurance/future possibilities; approach/avoidance

#21. Connation choice in adapting:
 Options/procedures

#22. Adaptation sort:
 Judging/perceiving, Controlling/floating

#23. Reason sort of modal operators:
 Necessity/possibility/desire; stick-carrot

#24. Preference sort:
 Primary interest: people/place/ Things/activity/information

#25. Goal sort: adapting to expectations:
 Perfection/optimization/Skepticism

#26. Value buying sort:
 Cost/convenience/quality/time

#27. Responsibility sort:
 Overresponsible/underresponsible

#28. People-convincer sort:
 Distrusting/trusting

External-response meta-programs

#29. Rejuvenation-of-battery sort:
 Extrovert, ambivert, introvert

#30. Affiliation & management sort:
 Independent/team player/manager

#31. Communication-stance sort:
 Communication modes

#32. General response:
 Congruent/incongruent/ competitive/cooperative/polarity meta

#33. Somatic response style:
 Active/reflective/both/inactive

#34. Work preference sort:
 Things/systems/people/ information

#35. Comparison sort:
 Quantitative/qualitative

#36. Knowledge sort:
 Modeling/conceptualizing/ demonstrating/experiencing/ authorizing

#37. Completion/closure sort:
Closure/nonclosure

#38. Social presentation:
Shrewd & artful/genuine & artless

#39. Hierarchical dominance sort:
Power/affiliation/achievement

The conceptual meta-programs

#40. Value sort:
Emotional "needs," beliefs

#41. Temper-to-instruction sort:
Strong-willed/compliant

#42. Self-esteem sort:
Conditional/unconditional

#43. Self-confidence sort:
High/low

#44. Self-experience sort:
Mind/emotion/body/role

#45. Self-integrity:
Conflicted incongruity/harmonious integration

#46. "Time" tenses sort:
Past/present/future

#47. "Time" experience:
In time/through time; sequential versus random sorting

#48. "Time" access sort:
Random/sequential

#49. Ego-strength sort:
Unstable/stable

#50. Morality sort:
Weak/strong superego

#51. Causational sort:
Causeless, linear CE, multi-CE, Personal CS, external CE, Magical, correlational

Chapter Ten
An Advance Listing of Meta-Programs
Detailing the Meta-Programs Domain

Having described meta-programs as a domain and model in the last chapter, we have a basic theoretical framework for understanding these structures. We briefly related facts and factors that govern their origin, source, and nature. Every model of human psychology has a theoretical framework along with basic governing principles. Models also involve lists of distinctions or variables that make up the content details of the model. That's what this chapter is about.

Here we briefly summarize the more than fifty meta-programs that we presented more fully in *Figuring Out People* (1997). Each distinction usually involves a continuum that formats a range of responses. This is not always true. Under each category we have given a general description of the concept, the variables, and some eliciting questions. This overview is designed to be suggestive rather than exhaustive.

Listing of meta-programs

Lists of meta-programs began early in NLP with Leslie Cameron-Bandler and have expanded from 9 to 14 to 21 over the years. The following list contains 51 meta-programs.

The mental-processing meta-programs

1. Global versus specific: specificity/abstraction continuum
Concept: These terms refer to the size of the "chunks" (computer-programming language) of information that we need in order to understanding something. *Chunk size* can range from very small details to very large general understandings. On a scale from specificity to generality, people think in terms of the small supporting details and specifics that make something up to the big picture, globally, looking for the gestalt. This leads from inductive thinking (moving up the scale) to deductive thinking (moving down the scale).

- What size of information do you tend to prefer when you are learning, discovering, or seeking to understand something?

Five categories of meta-programs and the higher semantic meta-programs

Processing
Cognitive/Perceptual

#1 Chunk size
General/specific
Detail/global

#2 Relationship
Matching/mismatching
Same/difference

#3 Representation system
VAKO A$_d$

#4 Information gathering
Uptime/downtime

#5 Epistemology Sort
Sensors/intuitors

#6 Perceptual category
Black-white/continuum

#7 Scenario thinking
Best/worst
Optimists/pessimists

#8 Durability
Permeable/impermeable

#9 Focus quality
Screeners/non-screeners

#10 Philosophical direction
Why/How Origins/Solutions

#11 Reality structure sort
Aristotelian/Non-Aristotelial

Feeling
Emotional/Somatic

#12 Communication channel
sort
*Verbal-Digital/Non-Verbal-Analogue/Balanc*ed

#13 Emotional coping
*Passivity/aggression/
dissociated*

#14 Frame of reference
Internal/external
Self-Referent/Other-Referent

#15 Emotional state
Associated/dissociated
Feeling/thinking

#16 Somatic responses
Active/reflective/inactive
Stick/Carrot

#17 Convincer/believability
Looks, sounds, feels right
Makes Sense

#18 Emotional direction
*Uni-directional/
multi-directional*

#19 Emotional exuberance
Desurgency/surgency

#20 Motivation direction
Toward/away from
Approach/avoidance

Choosing
Conative/Willing

#21 Conation adaptation
Options procedures

#22 Adaptation
Judging/perceiving
Controlling/floating

#23 Modal operators
Necessity/possibility/desire

#24 Preference
People/place/things
Activity/information

#25 Adapting to
expectations
*Perfection/optimizing
skepticism*

#26 Value buying
*Cost.convenience/
quality/time*

#27 Responsibility
Over-responsible
Under-responsible
Balanced

#28 People convincer
Sort
Distrusting/trusting

Responding
Outputting-Behaving

#29 Battery Rejuvenation
Extraovert/ambivert/introvert

#30 Affiliation/management
Independent/team player/manager

#31 Communication stance
Blamer/Placater/Distracter/
Computer/Leveler

Conceptualizing/semanticizing
Kantian categories

#32 General response
Congruent/Inconfruent
Competitive/Cooperative; polarity.meta

#33 Somatic response
Active/reflective/both/inactive

#34 Work preference
Things/systems/people/information

#35 Comparison
Quantitative/qualitative

#36 Knowledge source
Modeling/conceptualizing

#37 Completion/closure
Closure/nonclosure

#38 Social pressentation
Shrewd-artful-genuine-artless

#39 Hierarchical dominance sort
Power/affiliation/achievement

#40 Values
List of values

#41 Temper to instruction
Strong-willed/compliant

#42 Self-esteem
High SE/low SE

#43 Self-confidence
Specific Skills
Low/high self-confidence

#44 Self-experience
Body/mind/emotions/roles/choices

#45 Self-integrity
Conflicted incongruity/integrated harmony

#46 "Time" tenses
Past/present/future

#47 "Time" experience
In time/through time

#48 "Time" access
Sequential/random

#49 Ego strength
Stable/unstable

#50 Morality
Strong/weak Superego

#51 Causational sort
Causeless/linear CE/multi-CE/personal CE/external

Figure 10.1: Levels of thought and language

High-level abstractions
↑↓
What does that meaning mean to you?
What idea, example describes this?
For what purpose ...?
What intention do you have in this ...?
What does this mean to you?

↑↓
What are some examples of this?
What are some referent experiences?
What do you mean specifically?
When? Where? Who? In what way?

The smallest details

We move up using hypnotic language.

We move up the scale by asking about meaning and significance ... by asking about various meta-levels: decisions, identifications, intentions, outcomes, etc.
When we move up, we get into the higher meta-model distinctions: nominalizations, complex equivalences, cause-effects, presuppositions, etc.
When we move up and down we elicit *the structures of intuition.*
Deductive intuition involves taking a general principle and applying or relating it to specific situations.
Inductive intuition involves taking lots of details and generalizing upward to new conclusions, meanings, and connections.

- Which direction of reasoning do you feel more comfortable with, inductive or deductive?
- Which do you want first when you hear something new, the big picture or the details?

2. Sameness (matching) versus difference (mismatching): relational continuum
Concept: Sameness or matching seeks to understand how something matches or fits with what one already knows. This may come out of and may lead to the state of wanting things to remain pretty much the same, to keep the status quo, to maintain the routine, or to avoid change. "Being the same, in common, similar, not changed."

Difference or mismatching seeks to understand something in terms of how it differs from what one already knows. This may come from and may lead to the state of wanting change, enjoying it, seeking it, resisting sameness, or routine. "Different, new, change, switch, transform, unique."

- What is the relationship between X and Y?
- How do you compare X and Y?
- How do you go about understanding something new? Do you look first for similarities and match up the new with what you already know? Or do you first check out the differences? Or do you first do one pattern and then immediately do the other?

Figure 10.2

Matching	Matching	Balanced	Mismatching	Mismatching
Sameness	with Exception	← Equally →	with Exceptions	Differences

3. Representational system processing
Concept: This meta-program refers to the system of information processing (sensory-based or language-based) that we prefer, favor, or trust and so makes up our preferred learning system.

Visual refers to activities such as seeing pictures, entertaining an internal movie.
Auditory refers to such things as hearing sounds, tones, volumes, and pitches, and talking to self.

Kinesthetic refers to body sensations, motor responses, and leads to such things as experiential learning, needing to get a feel for something, getting one's hands on it.

Language (auditory digital) refers to the linguistic and symbolic systems such as math, music, abstractions.

Elicitation:
- When you think about something or learn something new, which sensory channel do you prefer?
- Which channel do you use most commonly?

4. Sensor (uptime) versus intuitor (downtime)

5. Epistemology sort: sensors/intuitors

Concept: These meta-programs refer to where we look for the source of the information that we process-outside in the external world (sensor) or internal to our internal processing (intuitor). We have here combined two meta-programs that we originally separated in *Figuring Out People*.

Sensors prefer to operate with their see-hear-feel senses and so to operate in an uptime model of sensory awareness. They get information in see-hear-feel ways. This gives them a preference for empirical data, details, and the like.

Intuitors prefer to operate with their meanings (beliefs, values, experiences, history, skills, gut feelings) and so tend to operate from the downtime state—that is, inside in their "intuiting" ("in-knowings"). This gives them a preference for feelings, guesses, hunches.

Elicitation:
- When you listen to a speech or conversation, do you tend to hear the specific sensory-based data or do you go inside (downtime) and listen for what the speaker means?
- Do you want to hear proof and evidence from the outside or do you take more interest in your internal thoughts about it?

6. Perceptual-categories sort: black-and-white versus continuum

Concept: Some minds operate more skillfully in discerning broad categories while others operate with more sophisticated discernment recognizing gray areas and things in between the polar ends of a continuum.

Elicitation:
- When you think about things or make decisions, do you tend to operate in black and white categories or does your mind go to the stages that lie in between?
- Which do you value most?

7. Attribution sort: best-versus-worst-scenario thinking: optimists/pessimists-helpless/empowered

Concept: Sorting for the best-case scenario orients one in an optimistic, hopeful, goal-oriented, and empowered way. Sorting for the worst-case scenario orients one in a pessimistic, negative, and problem-focused way. When overdone, pessimistic thinking generates feelings of hopelessness. Seligman (1975, 1990) researched attribution styles and invented "learned helplessness" and "learned optimism".

Elicitation:
- When something happens, do you look first for problems, dangers, difficulties or do you think in terms of solutions, opportunities, or exciting possibilities?
- When you look at a problem, do you tend first to consider the worst-case scenario or the best? Does your mind go to problems and difficulties or to opportunities and positive challenges?

Figure 10.3

Worst case	Best case
Pessimistic	Optimistic
Helpless/deterministic	Empowered
Personal	
Pervasive	
Permanent	

8. Perceptual durability sort: permeable/impermeable
Concept: Our internal constructions can have different qualities. They can be permeable or impermeable. *Permeable:* difficulty in keeping an idea front and center in the mind. Impermeable: concepts strong and stable.

Elicitation:
- As you begin to think about some of your mental constructs, your ideas of success and failure, of love and forgiveness, of relationships and work, of your personal qualities, are your representations permanent or unstable?

9. Focus sort: screeners/non-screeners
Concept: Stimulus screening refers to how much of the environment we bring in and/or keep out.

Non-screeners: Highly distracted by the environment and stimuli around. Less selectivity in focusing, more arousal to distractions.

Screeners: More focused, have an easier time concentrating, less distracted. Can become inattentive, zoned out.

Elicitation:
- When you think about the kinds of places where you can study or read, can you do this everywhere or do you find that some places seem too noisy or have too much of other stimuli that prevent concentration?
- Describe your favorite environment for concentrating on something?

10. Philosophical direction: why/how; origins/solutions; philosophical/practical
Concept: This meta-program relates to how our minds think in terms of philosophy. Do we care more about source, origins, and "why"? Or, do we care more about solution, process, and "how" to get on with things?

Why?: Sorting for the past, source of things, origins, where it comes from.

How?: Sorting for use, purpose, practical concerns.

Elicitation:
- When you think about a subject (whether a problem or not), do you first think about causation, source, and origins (why), or do you think about use, function, direction, destiny (how)?

11. Reality Structure Sort: Aristotelian-non-Aristotelian; static-process
Concept: This meta-program relates to how we think about external reality itself.
Aristotelian: Sorts in terms of things being static, permanent, solid at the micro-level. World of objects, things, people. Nouns, nominalizations, use of "to be" verbs, identifications.

Non-Aristotelian: Sorts in terms of process, movement, change, flux, movement, non-things, nonlinear reasoning, systems.

Elicitation:
- How do you think about reality? Do you think about it as something permanent and solid made up of things? Do you think of it as a dance of electrons, fluid, ever-changing, made up of processes?

12. Communication-channel preference: verbal-nonverbal; digital-analogue
Concept: We have two primary channels, dimensions, modalities for sending/ receiving information.

Verbal and digital: Sorts for words, language, terms, content of message.

Nonverbal and analogue: Sorts for body expressions: breathing, posture, muscle tone, gestures, eye scanning, tone and volume.

Elicitation:
- When you think about communicating with somebody, what do you typically give more importance to, what they say or how they say it? Do you pay more attention to the words and phrases that you use or to such things as your tone, tempo, volume, eye contact?

EXERCISE: Positive-experience elicitation
1. Elicit a positive experience from a person.
What has been a positive experience for you in the last couple weeks or month?

2. In a group of three persons, invite a person to talk about a positive event.
Tell us about an experience wherein you felt enthused. Or successful. Or brilliant, creative, decisive, or a winner. (Make sure the experience is a positive one.)

3. Spend time coaching the person to provide increasingly more information.
And what else happened that you really liked? And how did you respond to that? I bet you liked that. Tell me more.

4. Summarize the meta-programs.
Stop after about five minutes, and present to the person a summary of how you have "read" his or her meta-programs. As you do, check with the person to determine the degree to which the person thinks your reading is accurate.

The emotional sorting meta-programs

The following describes the meta-programs that we use as we primarily experience the emotional affect of our processing.

13. Passive (flight) versus fight (aggressive)
Concept: This meta-program refers to how one's nervous system at the neurological level moves toward or away from stressors, threats, dangers, and a sense of over-load. Some take such on and go at it, others instinctively move away from it. Some have nervous systems that are highly sensitive to danger and others are highly insensitive to such.

Passive or the go-away flight response refers to moving away from dangers, stres-sors, or threats. Those with this meta-program typically use the Type-B stress response.

Aggressive or the go-at fight response refers to the process of moving toward, and going at, threats, dangers, and stressors. Those who use this meta-program typically use the Type-A stress response.

Assertive or mindful response refers to the learned response, the Type-C stress response, that arises from training in thinking and talking out stresses and deciding on fight/flight responses as appropriate.

Elicitation:
● When you feel threatened, or challenged, by some stress, do you immediately respond, on the emotional level, by wanting to get away from it, or to go at it?

14. Other Referent (external) versus Self-Referent (internal)

Concept: This meta-program relates to our sense or locus (location) of "control". Where do we posit it? Do we posit it inside or outside of ourselves?

Other or external Referent describes the view, perspective, and orientation of one who looks outward. This meta-program sorts for and pays attention to the views and opinions of others, to the authorities out there.

Self- or internal referent describes the view that one's own thoughts, values, and choice matter most. This creates the orientation of referencing ultimately from oneself, although a person may first gather lots of information from others.

Elicitation:
- Where do you put most of your attention or reference, on yourself or on others (or something external to yourself)?
- What do you rely on for your authority?

15. Associated versus dissociated: stepping in versus stepping out

Concept: This meta-program refers to our perceptual style. If we take a perceptual position of second or third rather than first we move to a dissociation of the information (and into other information). This shows up emotionally and somatically (in our body) as neutral feeling or dulled feelings. As meta-programs, these relative terms describe our position (mentally and emotionally) to a set of representations, whether we have stepped into or out of a particular state.

Associated refers to viewing and feeling things from the first-person position, being very much into the thoughts and emotions, and having lots of corresponding somatic and kinesthetic sensations.

Dissociated refers to viewing and feeling the world from second- or third-person position and so feeling not into the experience, but standing back and watching it as if a spectator.

Elicitation:

- Think about an event in a work situation that once gave you trouble.
- What experience surrounding work would you say has given you the most pleasure or delight?
- How do you normally feel while at work?
- When you make a decision, do you rely more on reason and logic or personal values or something else?

16. Somatic-response sort: active/reflective/inactive

Concept: Some people process information in a very active, quick, immediate, and impulsive way-the active style. Others engage in the handling of information much more reflectively, thoughtfully, and slowly-the reflective style. Others do not seem to engage in information processing much at all, or do so with much reluctance-the inactive style.

Elicitation:
- When you come into a new situation, do you usually act quickly after sizing it up or do you do a detailed study of all the consequences before acting?
- When you come into a social situation (a group, class, team, family reunion, or whatever), do you usually act quickly after sizing it up or do you engage in a detailed study of all of the consequences, and then act? How do you typically respond?

17. Convincer sort: sensory (VAK) and language

Concept: This meta-program refers to the state of feeling convinced about some-thing. What convinces you? How do you make your choices and decisions? Which sensory system do you use? What do you rely upon?

Visual convincer: You have to see it, imagine it, view it. You have to see it in color, close up, clearly. Seeing convinces.

Auditory convincer: You have to hear it, experience the sound qualities of it.

Kinesthetic convincer: You have to feel it, get a sense of how it feels, experience it.

Language convincer: You have to have the right words that properly describe it, that make the right and appropriate reasons, arguments; you have to have verbal proof, statistics, that kind of thing.

Repetition convincer: How many times do you have to be convinced in order for you to access the state of feeling convinced? Once, three times, fifteen times, never?

The never convinced always disbelieve and never are sure. They stay perpetually unconvinced and always entertain doubts.

The automatically convinced begin by giving others the benefit of all doubts. They are convinced from the start. They need no convincing. They are ready to believe.

The convinced by repetition are most people. They need so many times, from three to seven to forty. Repetition drives the knowledge, convictions, beliefs, and values home.

Elicitation:
Ask questions that presuppose decision-making:
- Why did you decide on your present choice of car?
- What helps you decide where to vacation?

- As you make a decision about where to go on vacation, how do you think about such? Do you see, hear, or create feelings about it?
- What lets you know that you can believe that a product feels right for you?

18. Emotional-direction sort: unidirectional-multidirectional

Concept: This relates to the focus and diffusion of emotions, emotional style in emoting, focus and spread of emotions over experience.

Multidirectional: Experiences emotions as spreading all over and contaminating other facets of life. Uncontained.

Unidirectional: Experiences emotions as staying contextualized to referent object and frames.

Elicitation:
- When you think about a time when you experienced an emotional state (positive or negative), does that bleed over and affect some or all of your other emotional states, or does it stay pretty focused so that it relates to its object?

19. Emotional-intensity or exuberance sort: desurgency-surgency; timidity-boldness

Concept: How much emotional exuberance or lack of it does one experience in emoting, especially in relation to others and to tasks.

Surgency: Experiences emotions with lots of intensity, very strongly, feels throughout body. Can lead to hysteria. Supported by frames that value emotions.

Desurgency: Experiences low level of emotional intensity; typically does not trust emotions, may not want them. Values certainty, predictability, stability. May have anti-emotion frames.

Elicitation:
- When you think about a situation at work or in your personal affairs that seems risky or involving the public's eye, what thoughts-and-feelings immediately come to mind?

EXERCISE: The sales encounter

1. Refusal to buy.
Get into groups of four persons, and one person identifies something that you would "never, but never buy". What would you never buy? What would you never put down any money for? (Pick something small, ridiculous, inane.)

2. Ask the person to the right of the refuser to attempt to sell that very item to him or her.
As the seller attempts this sell, the sales-resistant person should essentially consistently respond with a gentle refusal, just saying, "No, not interested". Play the role of being hard to get.

3. Forging on against resistance.
As the sales-resistant person refuses and doesn't seem even interested in buying, the seller should just forge ahead anyway regardless of the verbal and nonverbal resistance. Give it everything you have to win over the person.

4. Observers of the no-sell event.
While all of this is going on, two persons will simply be observing and writing down all of the meta-programs they can detect in both the seller and the sell-resistant person. Pay special attention in detecting the linguistic markers within the language patterns of the persons.

5. Debrief.
Blow the whistle on the game after four minutes or so. Then debrief by having the two meta-persons share the meta-programs that they saw or heard activated in the process. Those in the selling game can share how accurate, on target or off target the reading is and share about how it felt.

6. Round two.
The seller or one of the meta-persons, now equipped with the buyer's meta-programs, uses them to pace and lead the buyer into buying the thing that he or she will not buy. Notice the difference.

The volitional meta-programs

The following meta-programs highlight the volitional, choosing, and deciding part of mental processing as we sort for things.

20. Away from (past assurance/avoidance) versus toward (future possibilities /approach)
Concept: Our motivational sort describes our orientation in the world in terms of how we take action and make choices of value and importance. Do we move away from dangers or toward possibilities?

Away from describes thinking first about dangers, threats, apprehensions. This typically leads a person to prefer to first make choices about such matters as safety, avoidance of problems.

Toward describes thinking first about what a person wants: goals, dreams, outcomes, hopes, possibilities. This tends to lead one to develop a moving-toward values-and-objectives orientation in the world.

Elicitation:
- What do you want from, say, a relationship or a job?
- What will having this do for you?
- What do you value of importance about ...?

21. Procedures versus options

Concept: This meta-program relates to our adaptation style in the world, whether we move through it seeking to establish procedures, rules, and organized ways for how to do things, the right way to do things, or for whether we move through the world looking for options, choices, new ways to do things.

Procedure refers to seeing the world in terms of specific procedures for how to do things, and so sorts for processes, structures, and organization. This leads to such states as caring about finding and using the right way to do something, rules.

Options refers to seeing the world in terms of options and choices, inventing new ways to try things, exploring alternatives. This leads to such states as trailblazing, inventing, discovering.

Elicitation:
Ask *why* questions.

- Why did you choose your car (or job, town, bank ...)?

22. Judger (adapter) versus perceiver (floater)

Concept: This meta-program refers to how we adapt ourselves as we move through the world. Do we use a style of navigating life by adapting ourselves to it (perceiver) or by working to make the world adapt to us (judger)?

Judger or **adapter** views the world (and so makes choices) by seeking to exercise control or management over the world. This leads to the state of taking charge, acting, innovating, being a mover and shaker. Very characteristic of the Western way of life.

Perceiver or **floater** views the world as whole and something mostly to observe, notice, and experience rather than manage or control. This leads to the states of fiting in, finding the natural rhythms of the world, being passive, enjoying the observation, being a spectator.

Elicitation:
- Do you like to live life spontaneously as the spirit moves you or according to a plan?

- Do you find it easy or difficult to make up your mind?
- If we did a project together, would you prefer we first outline and plan it in an orderly fashion or would you prefer to just begin to move into it and flexibly adjust to things as we go?
- Do you have a daytimer-type of calendar? Do you use it? Do you enjoy using it?

23. *Necessity versus desire: impossibility versus possibility*

Concept: These terms are *modal operators* in linguistics from the Meta-Model and reflect our modus operandi or style of operating with regard to such things as events, tasks, people, information, Do we *have to, must we, should we,* do we *get to,* do we say *can't,* do we say *can?*

Necessity refers to the meta-frame that establishes a world of shoulds, musts, have-tos—necessities, rules, compulsions, laws.

Desire refers to a world of wants, desires, hopes, get-tos. This invites one to live in a world of desires, dreams, goals.

Impossibility refers to viewing the world in terms of "can't", impossibilities, "it won't work". This invites one to live in a world of limitations, inhibitions, prohibitions.

Possibility refers to viewing the world in terms of, for example, possibilities, cans, competencies. It invites one into the world of hope and dreams.
Elicitation:
- How did you motivate yourself to go to work today?
- What did you say to yourself that helped to get you moving?

24. *Preference or value choice: people, things, activity, information, location*

Concept: This meta-program refers to what we prefer as most important or significant in our choices.

People sort refers to the value and importance we place upon people and people issues: such as emotions.

Thing sort refers to the value and importance we put upon things, objects, technology, toys, and the like.

Activity sort refers to the value and importance we place upon activities such as tasks, projects, jobs, challenges.

Location sort refers to the value and importance we put upon places, surroundings, location, geography, environment.

Information sort refers to the value and importance we place upon information, data, researching, learning, reading, talking, seeing.

Time sort refers to the value and importance we put upon the time element, when we do things.

Elicitation:
- What would you find as really important in how you choose to spend your next two-week vacation?
- What kinds of things, people, or activities would you want present for you to evaluate it as really great?
- Tell me about your favorite restaurant.

25. Goal Striving Sort: perfectionism-optimization-skepticism

Concept: People differ in how they think-and-feel-and-choose to go after their goals. This meta-program relates to how we adapt and respond to expectations, goals, outcomes, striving.

Perfectionism: Going for flawless perfection, focus on end product, fearful of what could be wrong, miss the mark, never good enough.

Optimizing: Moving forward aiming to enjoy process and achieve aims, but taking numerous constraints into account.

Defeatist/skepticism: Negatively anchored to concept; refuse to set goals, refuse to compete.

Elicitation:
- Tell me about a goal that you have set and how you went about making it come true. If you set a goal today to accomplish something of significance, how would you begin to work on it?

EXERCISE: The ideal evening game (or, the dating game)

1. In pairs or in threes, take turns as a coach asking a practitioner open-ended questions that inquire about what makes for a great night out.

What would you want to know about a person before you ask him or her out? What would you need to know to have an evening out with a good friend? What would you evaluate as a delightful evening out with someone?

2. Free-flow in your responses.

Freely respond to the questions about what would make for an ideal evening out for you.

3. Debrief.

Create a list of all the meta-programs that you detected in the other person's responses.

EXERCISE: Asking for favor

1. Set a frame or context so that one person will aim to persuade another to do him or her a favor.
Ask an employee to do something—part of job or something extra. Ask someone in your business for a favor.

2. Ask ten questions.
The persuader begins by asking ten questions of the other person to identify his or her basic meta-programs.

Ask general, conversational questions to gather this information. Ask anything that you want to ask.

3. Use the meta-program profile.
After gathering meta-program information, frame your request (your desired outcome) in words that will reflect the other person's most compelling meta-programs.

4. Feedback for refining.
Afterwards, invite the other person to gauge the effectiveness of the request and to offer feedback about how it could be made even more personally compelling for him or her. Then use that information to provide an even more persuasive request.

The conceptual and higher-level meta-programs

Not all meta-programs occur at the first meta-level above content. As we have multiple levels of meta-states, we have multiple levels of meta-programs. We can have meta-programs about meta-programs. These higher meta-programs relate to how we relate to ideas and concepts and so are conceptual meta- programs.

26. Value buying: cost-convenience-quality-time
Concept: When purchasing, what do you sort for in the process? Imagine a diamond with each of the four choices on a corner. Put a check mark on diamond line for what you most want. This meta-program refers to how we think, perceive, pay attention, and sort for when it comes to purchasing and deciding to purchase. People differ in preferring to focus on cost, convenience, quality, and time in different ways.

Elicitation:
- What do you primarily concern yourself with when you consider making a purchase—the price, convenience, time, quality, or some combination of these?
- Put a mark on the diagram at the place that represents where you feel that you put most of your concern in the double-triangle. This foregrounds awareness of the trade-offs between the values.

27. Responsibility sort: underresponsible-responsible-overresponsible
Concept: A higher meta-program that addresses the concept of personal power—that is, the ability to respond and to be held accountable by others.

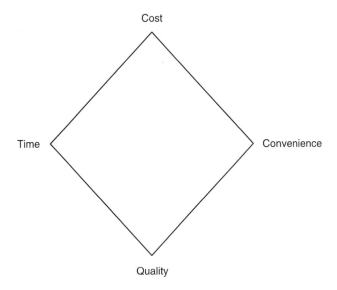

Figure 10.4

Underresponsible: Responds with lack of acceptance of owning or wanting responsibility. Blame, entitlement, dependency, victimhood, irresponsibility.

Responsible: Appropriately balancing ownership of responses for self and to others.

Overresponsible: Takes on too much ownership, leading to care-taking, intrusion, overinvolvement, stress.

Elicitation:
- When you think about having and owning responsibility for something in a work situation or personal relationship, what thoughts and emotions occur to you?
- Has someone ever held you responsible for something that went wrong that felt very negative to you?
- What positive experiences can you remember about someone holding you responsible for something and/or validating you as "response-able"?

28. People-convincer sort: distrusting-trusting; paranoid-naïve
Concept: This meta-program relates to how we feel "convinced" in general and how we sort for and respond to relating to others.

Distrusting, paranoid: Immediately, automatically, and pervasively assume the worst of others, distrust: leads to jealousy, envy, guardedness, defensiveness, shallow relationships.

Trusting, naïve: Immediately responds to others assuming trust, similarity, connections: leads to openness, warmth, friendliness, outgoing, can lead to being duped easily.

Elicitation:
- When you think about meeting someone new, do you immediately have a sense of trust and openness to the person, or thoughts and feelings of distrust, doubt, questions, jealousy, or insecurity?
- How do you typically choose to relate to a person, or a group of people, before you know them very well? Do you do so with trust or with caution?

External-response meta-programs

The following meta-programs focus on how and what we sort for as we *respond* to people and events. These concern how we interact with things and people and what we sort for as we do so.

29. *Rejuvenation-of-battery sort: extrovert—ambivert—introvert*
Concept: This meta-program relates to how we interact with and need or avoid people when we are feeling low or discouraged.

Extrovert: One turns outward to others, desires companionship, encouragement, and support.

Introvert: One turns inward to self, wants privacy, time by self.

Ambivert: One uses both in a more balanced way with a sense of choice.

Elicitation:
- When you feel the need to recharge your batteries, do you prefer to do it alone or with others?

30. *Affiliation: no-team, team and self, or team*
Concept: This meta-program refers to how one processes and handles working with others in task-oriented situations. How do we experience ourselves vis-à-vis the group? People generally process this question in terms of staying independent, team playing, or managing.

No-team refers to preferring to work alone and assuming sole responsibility for a job or task. People with this meta-program work best when in control of the part they contribute to a project. Language: I, on my own, prefer to do it myself.

Team and self refers to preferring to work with others and keeping responsibility for a task in one's own hands. Those with this meta-program understand working with others in a hierarchy and may at times assume control and subordination to superiors. Language: I motivate people, I get others to do things.

Team refers to preferring to work and share responsibilities for an assignment with others and believing in the synergism of people working together. People with this meta-program prefer working as a joint effort and participating with others. Language: on my own and with others, team, teamwork.

Elicitation:
- Tell me about one of your favorite working experiences. What did you like about it?

31. *Placator, blamer, distractor, computer, leveler*
This meta-program identifies the five basic communication stances known as the Satir Categories. These are the way people communicate under stress.

Placator refers to the perspective of desperately wanting to please, and so illustrates a high-level Other-Referent.

Blamer refers to taking charge by finding and putting blame on someone. A blamer operates as an extreme Self-Referent.

Distractor refers to wanting to *not* be known, to have to take a stance, and so constantly changes position.

Computer refers to wanting to operate exclusive from the intellect and to show no emotion, a kind of Mr. Spock response.

Leveler refers to wanting to be straightforward and to simply disclose thoughts and emotions in an assertive way.

Elicitation:
- How do you typically communicate in terms of placating, blaming, computing, and distracting, or leveling?
- How do you tend to act when you are under stress?

32. *General response: congruent/incongruent-competitive/cooperative-polarity/meta*
Concept: When we respond to people, things, information, and events we do so in

various ways. We can do so congruently or incongruently, competitively or cooperatively, with polarity, or a meta response.

Elicitation:
• When you come into a situation, how do you usually respond? (1) Do you respond with a sense of feeling and acting congruently and harmoniously with your thoughts-and-feelings or, do you respond with a sense of not feeling or acting congruently and harmoniously with your thoughts and feelings? (2) Do you respond with a sense of cooperation with the subject matter, or a feeling of disagreement? (3) Or do you prefer to go above the immediate context and have thoughts about the situation?

33. Response style: active, inactive, reactive
Concept: This meta-program refers to how we act out our thoughts, emotions, and choices.

Inactive style refers to a response style that generates little action. We think about things, meditate upon them, delay responding. In the end, we are fairly inactive.

Active style refers to a response style of quickly or immediately taking action on our thoughts and feelings and doing something. When it is well tempered, it will generate proactivity and taking initiative.

Reactive style refers to a response style of unthinking acting, operating from a reactive, even a fight/flight sense of danger or threat.

Elicitation:
• When you come into a new situation, do you usually act quickly after sizing it up or do you do a detailed study of all the consequences before acting?
• When you come into a social situation (a group, class, team, or family re-union), do you usually act quickly after sizing it up or do you engage in a detailed study of all of the consequences, and then act? How do you typically respond?

35. Comparison sort: quantitative-qualitative
Concept: This meta-program relates to how we compare things and what we use, whether quantitative or qualitative standards.

Quantitative: Perceives things through quanta: numbers, ranks, orders, measurements, standards.

Qualitative: perceives things through "quala": quality of an experience, person, or event.

Elicitation:
- How would you evaluate your work? How would you evaluate things in your relationship? How do you know the quality of your work? Upon what basis do you say that?

36. *Knowledge-source sort: modeling, conceptualizing, demonstrating, experiencing, authorizing*

Concept: This meta-program focuses on how we decide to learn something and where we gather data from. This program focuses on where we turn to as a source for information.

Elicitation:
- What source of knowledge do you consider authoritative and most reliable? From where would you gather reliable information that you can trust? When you decide that you will do something, where do you get the information to do it from?

37. *Completion or closure sort: closure—nonclosure*

Concept: This meta-program sorts for the fullness or lack of closure when we gather information.

Closure: Sorts for completeness, fullness of information, closure, story finished, loop ended.

Nonclosure: Doesn't make this sort, nice, but not necessary. Rests easily with ambiguity, confusion, open-ended processes.

Elicitation:
- If, in the process of studying something, you had to break off your study and leave it, would you feel okay about this or would you feel it as disconcerting?
- When someone begins a story but doesn't complete it, how do you feel about that?
- When you get involved in a project, do you find yourself more interested in the beginning, middle, or end of the project?
- What part of a project do you enjoy most?

38. *Social presentation: shrewd and artful—genuine and artless*

Concept: This one relates to how we focus when relating to and interacting with others in a social context.

Shrewd and artful: Filters for the social impression that we make, our presentation to others, carefully manages impression, fearful of negative impressions and judgments.

Genuine and artless: Filters for being real, not being a fake, being one's own person, saying and thinking what one truly does, devalues judgments of others.

Elicitation:
● When you think about going out into a social group or in public, how do you generally handle yourself? Do you really care about your social image and want to avoid any negative impact on others so that they recognize your tact, politeness, or social graces? Or do you not really care about any of that and just want to be yourself, natural, forthright, direct, transparent?

39. Hierarchical-dominance sort: power—affiliation—achievement
Concept: This one was developed by David McClelland about human interacting in work contexts and structures.

Power: Sorts for the power of choosing, having control, competing, dominating; politically minded; win/lose mentality common.
Affiliation: Sorts for connection, relationship, courtesy, getting along, win/win or even lose/win. Fears conflict and criticism.

Achievement: Sorts for accomplishing things, getting things done, end products.

Elicitation:
● Evaluate your motives in interacting with others in terms of your motivational preferences between power (dominance, competition, politics), affiliation (relationship, courtesy, cooperation), and achievement (results, goals, objectives) and using a hundred points as your scale, distribute those hundred points among these three styles of handling power.
  ● Power (dominance, competition, politics)
  ● Affiliation (relationship, courtesy, cooperation)
  ● Achievement (results, goals, objectives)

EXERCISE: Asking for a personal favor
1. Set a frame for a role-playing situation in which you will persuade another person to do a favor for you.
I want you to go to the store for me to buy some milk. I want you to come over and watch my kids. I need $10.

2. Playing nonresponsive.
As you do your best to persuade the other person, he or she will remain unpersuaded and just say no. Be unpersuadable, but pleasant.

3. Meta-person detector.
A third person will play the meta-person in order to detect the meta-programs of the two players in the role playing situation.

4. Debrief.
At the completion, use the information gathered about each other's meta-program to frame the request so that it's more influential.

Conceptual meta-programs

The following offer yet more conceptual or higher-level meta-programs that influence and affect our everyday perceptions.

40. Value sort
Concept: When we use the nominalization "value", it sounds like a thing, like something real and tangle and external. It is not. The process involves *valuing*. And we *value* by how we treat something as *important*, significant, and/or meaningful. Our "values" are the objects of this way of thinking-and-feeling.

By means of our valuing in our thinking, feeling, focusing, talking, and acting, we appraise things, people, experiences, qualities, and ideas as important. Accordingly, we build mental maps and movies about how something holds value to us. Our "values" then operate as our meta-frames and meta-states all at the same time and we use them to perceive the world. In this way they function as our meta-programs as well.

Structurally, a "value" contains a two-level phenomenon. To the primary-level thought, we first have it in some meta-program format (global/specific, match/mismatch, for instance). Then to the meta-program format we have a thought of importance and significance *about* it.

Every meta-program we use habitually, we value. Anticipate discovering that they actually have many reasons and motivations for engaging in such thinking! Our values arise, in part, from our meta-programs themselves, especially our driver meta-programs.

Elicitation:
• What do you think is valuable, important, or significant about this (e.g., job, relationship, idea)?

Self meta-programs: Sense of self in various dimensions

Concept: Our sense of self has many facets and domains of experiences.

41. Compliant versus self-willing
Concept: This meta-program refers to our relationship to choice, instruction, command, authority, power, control. Some people comply and others resist these experiences and so develop a different meta-program.

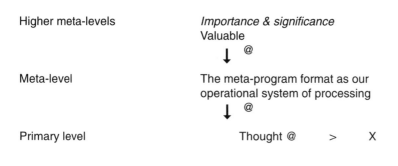

Higher meta-levels	*Importance & significance*
	Valuable

Meta-level	The meta-program format as our operational system of processing

Primary level	Thought @ > X

Figure 10.5

Compliance refers to those who take orders, information, and demands well, who comply with instructions. They may do so in an unhealthy way (fear of taking personal responsibility, cowering before everybody else), or they may do so in a healthy way (recognition of authority structures and willingness to receive instruction).

Strong-willed refers either to those who so define themselves in terms of their will and freedom of choice or to those so traumatized by obnoxious authority figures that they have set a frame for perceiving any instruction (even their own) as a violation of their freedom of will.

Elicitation:
- Can someone "tell" you something?
- How do you think and feel when you receive "instructions"?
- How well can you "tell" yourself to do something and carry it out without a lot of internal resistance?

42. *Conditional versus unconditional self-esteem*
Concept: This meta-program refers to the higher-level belief frames we operate from with regard to our conceptual understandings about the value and dignity of "self", what we believe about human beings.

Conditional self-esteem refers to viewing and feeling self-esteem as conditional and based upon any number of things as determined in a person's culture or belief systems: looks, money, strength, intelligence, degrees, status, and the like. People who prefer and use this as a meta-program are forever thinking, feeling, and concerned about how they are doing on the self-esteem scale. Their ego concerns are always "on the line".

Unconditional self-esteem refers to viewing and feeling self-esteem as un-con-ditionally given and therefore full, complete, and unassailable. People who prefer and use this meta-program operate with few ego concerns since they are centered.

Elicitation:

- Do you think of your value as a person as conditional or unconditional?
- When you esteem yourself as, say, valuable, worthwhile, having dignity, do you base it upon something you do, have, or possess, or do you base it upon a given (e.g., your inherent humanity or that you feel yourself to have been made in God's image and likeness)?

43. *Low versus high self-confidence*

Concept: This meta-program refers to one's feelings of confidence, trust, or faith in one's skills and abilities. It refers to how much faith in particular skills in a given context that a person operates from. It can also refer to a generalized sense of confidence in self to learn, develop, and grow.

Low self-confidence describes those who lack confidence to do a particular thing, and those who distrust their ability to learn.

High self-confidence describes those who have confidence in a particular activity, and it can refer to those who generally trust that they can learn and develop new skills.

Elicitation:

- As you think about some of the things that you can do well, and that you know, without a doubt, you can do well and may even take pride in your ability to do them skillfully, make a list of those items.
- How confident do you feel about your skills in doing these things? How have you generalized from these specific self-confidences to your overall sense of self-confidence?

44. *Self-experience definitions*

Concept: This meta-program refers to the beliefs and understandings that we use and operate from in defining ourselves, and so in how we experience ourselves. We can base our self-definitions on a wide variety of things: for instance, thought, body, status, emotion, roles, degrees, choice, experiences.

Elicitation:

- As you think about your thoughts, emotions, will, body, roles, and positions that you experience in life, which facets of yourself seem the most important, real, or valid?
- Do you think of yourself primarily as a thinker, emotional person, chooser, in terms of your physical looks or body, in terms of your roles and positions, or what?

45. Self-Integrity: conflicted incongruity-harmonious integration
Concept: The meta-program relates to how well you live up to your values, rules, and beliefs. It relates to the degree of your personal integrity.

Elicitation:
- When you think about how well or how poorly you live up to your ideals and in actualizing your ideal self, do you feel integrated, congruous, doing a good job in living true to your values and visions? Or do you feel torn, conflicted, not integrated, incongruous?

46. Time processing: past, present, future
Concept: Our processing of "time" in terms of the time zones of awareness refers to which time zone we prefer to sort for, pay attention to, and use in our calculating things.

Past-time processing refers to the preference to use the past, past events, past learning experiences, and so on. When overdone this can lead to your living in the past, to your wanting the security of past references.

Present-time processing refers to the preference for using the present, the now, and to valuing current experiences and feelings.

Future-time processing refers to the preference for using future possibilities as one's point of reference. This can lead to visionary thinking, possibilities, dreaming, or fearfully worrying about dangers and terrible things that might happen.

Elicitation:
- Where do you put most of your attention-on the past, present, or future?
- Or have you developed an atemporal attitude so that you don't attend to "time" at all?

47. In-time versus through-time
Concept: This meta-program has reference to how we code and process our time-lines. As a meta-frame about the concept of "time" it relates to whether we live in it or out of it, associatedly or dissociatedly.

In-time refers to processing "time" in such a way that the "line" goes through us (through our body) so that we live and perceive "inside of time" so to speak. This generates an experience of living in the eternal now, and easily getting lost in time. We live in a primary state of "time" and have little awareness of "time" as such. This makes us spontaneous, systemic, and random in our orientations and behaviors.

Through-time refers to processing "time" from a higher or meta-level, and so being out of time in such a way that our "line" occurs outside of us. It does not go through our body. This gives us more perception and awareness of "time" and makes us more sequential, linear and "on time".

Elicitation:
- As you take a moment to relax, and to feel inwardly calm, allow yourself to recall a memory of something that occurred sometime in your past ... And something else from long ago ...
- Now think of some event that occurred today ... and another ...
- Now think of an event that will occur, one of these days ... and another future event ...
- As you now stand back or above those "time" places in your mind, point to the direction of your future, and point to the direction of your past ...

48. "Time"-access sort: random/sequential
Concept: This meta-program relates to how we access our memories of the past and functions as a sub-category of how we store or code "time" itself. Two overall patterns prevail: those who use a random accessing style and those who use a sequential accessing style.

Elicitation:
- Use the "time"-accessing questions as in #47.

49. Ego strength: unstable-stable; reactive-proactive
Concept: This meta-frame relates to how well we face the world, reality, facts with mind, degree of adjustment. "Ego" refers to our cognitive and perceptual mind in facing what exists.

Elicitation:
- When you think about some difficulty arising in everyday life, a disappointment, problem, frustration that will block your progress, what usually comes to your mind? How do you feel about such events? How do you typically respond to internal needs or external hardships? Where do your mind-and- emotions go when you face a problem?

50. Morality sort: weak superego-strong superego
Concept: This one relates to our sense of conscience, to following moral and ethical principles.

Elicitation:
- When you think about some misbehavior that you engaged in, what thoughts-and-feelings arise when you realize that you have acted in an inappropriate way that violated legitimate values?

- When you think about messing up, doing something embarrassing, stupid, socially inept, what thoughts-and-feelings flood your consciousness along with that realization?

51. *Causation sort*

Concept: This one relates to how we sort for "cause". What makes things happen? Is it inexplicable magic, direct linear cause-effect as in mathe- matics and physics? Is it a whole range of contributing factors? Or does nothing actually cause other things, or, at best, do effects exist only in correlation with other events?

Causeless: No causes, all is by chance, random.

Linear cause-effect: Simplistic stimulus-response world.
Multi-cause-effect: Many contributing influences, systemic.

Personal cause-effect: I cause whatever happens, at cause for everything.

External cause-effect: I cause nothing, it all comes from without—blame!

Magical cause-effect: Superstitious beliefs about entities and forces in the univer-sal causing things.

Correlational: Recognizing things can happen simultaneously without a causa-tional relationship.

Elicitation:
- When you think about what caused you to work at the job that you work at, how do you explain that?
- What brought the current situation of your life to exist as it does?
- What makes people behave as they do?
- How did their relationship get into that state?
- Why did you get divorced?

Summary

There are a great many meta-programs that we can identify as thinking or sorting patterns. These give us a way to recognize the meta-frames at work governing the processing orientation and style.
Structurally, the more flexibility we have with our own meta-programs, the more responses we can generate and therefore the more influence we can exercise within our own system and within any communication or relationship system.

There is a contextual relativity to meta-programs. Because we frequently use different meta-programs in different contexts, it's important to take context into consideration.

Chapter Eleven
The Meta-Representation System
The Linguistic Domain of the Meta-Model

It all began with the Meta-Model. That was the first NLP model developed. John Grinder had been on the verge of creating the Meta-Model for several years, but it wasn't until he and Richard Bandler saw and heard the "magic" in Satir, Perls, and Erickson that they made the connection. It was then that they first tied the language distinctions of transformational grammar to the idea of transformational magic.

It is language, and the encoding of language as the sensory representation systems and in the meta-representation system that, initiated the NLP adventure. That's why we introduce practitioners to this first explanatory model of the Meta-Model at the beginning of training. Together with the Milton Model, these linguistic models were the first models of NLP. They established the foundational work in modeling and understanding how we communicate, make sense of verbal and nonverbal signals, and how to "run our own brains".

These linguistic models enable us to do two primary things: first, gather information with precision and accuracy; second, induce trance states in ourselves and others. In the first instance, we "dehypnotize" ourselves from previous trances generated by ill-formed linguistic structures. In the second, we learn how to induce resourcefully ecological trances.

The Meta-Model and the Milton Model are not so much different models, but models of linguistic distinctions used in inverse ways. Most of the linguistic distinctions found in one are found in the other. What differentiates them are not the distinctions, but *how* we use them and *what* we do with them. When we *question* the linguistic distinctions we invite and even provoke precision and specificity (whether from ourselves or others). We call that engagement meta-modeling. By contrast, to *employ and use* the distinctions (e.g., speaking in artfully vague ways), we induce and create trance states. This induction of trance is what we call *hypnosis*.

In these two uses of language, the NLP Meta-Model and Milton Model empower us to induce uptime states and downtime states. The first state, uptime, is what we mean by sensory awareness or sensory acuity. In this state, we have "lost the higher levels of our mind" (that is, all of our ideas, concepts, preconceptions) and have come to our senses. We have come back to a more innocent primary state. The second state, downtime, is what we mean by "going inside" to make meaning out of the vague words, sentences, and expressions given so that we can construct a wide range of idiosyncratic states. Downtime uses the depth metaphor. Perhaps we could say "in-time" or "inside-time" to designate the internally focused state where we are entranced by the internal movie.

We could use the word "trance" for both states. Trance simply refers to the transition from one state to another. Generally, however, we use "trance" for the states wherein we go "inside" (whether up or down) and so seem to be "asleep" to the world, hence the original use of the term, "hypnosis".

Revisiting the structure of magic

NLP began with the Meta-Model—a linguistic model of twelve distinctions that provides "the structure of magic". Bandler and Grinder picked up this phrase probably from Bateson's description of "the world of communication, information, and organization," which works in such a strange and "magical" way when compared with "the world of energy, physics, and effects".

When confronted with the "magic-like" effects that Virginia Satir, Fritz Perls, and Milton Erickson had upon the minds, hearts, emotions, bodies, behaviors, and relationships of people, their analysis of that "magic" identified how the magic worked. In building a model of that structure, they identified twelve linguistic distinctions. The names of most of these distinctions have their origin in linguistics, specifically in transformational grammar. This means that, to learn the structure of the magic and to perform the magic, we have to develop an intuition about these twelve linguistic distinctions. Doing that then allows us to replicate the verbal skills of the "three therapeutic wizards".

What is the Meta-Model? It is a set of linguistic distinctions along with a set of questions. The model is also recursive. That is, it has no end point. It was designed originally to track how Satir, Perls, and Erickson used language and to offer a way for anyone wanting to help another person to use language similarly. The model sets forth a theory of how language works in our neuro-linguistic mind-body system. It identifies the structural components, a set of guidelines to use, and offers a set of predictions as to what a speaker will obtain in asking the questions.

As such, this makes the model easy to learn and use. Figure 11.5 summarizes the Meta-Model in the chart at the end of this chapter. We have formatted it as it is typically formatted in NLP trainings around three categories:

1. The patterns or distinctions.
2. The questions or challenges as ways to respond to the distinctions.
3. The predictions about typical results.

In Figures 11.1, 11.4 and 11.5 we have sorted out the basic Meta-Model distinctions into the three modeling classifications that Bandler and Grinder originally used: deletions, generalizations, and distortions. This breaks the twelve distinctions into smaller groups, making learning and memory easier.

After that we have listed the linguistic distinctions. If you look at these and experience a semantic reaction, "Oh, no, not grammar!" then we recommend that you collapse that old anchor and set some new frames about these particular linguistic distinctions. Tell yourself, "This gives me the *structure of magic*." Do you know how they do that? Do you know what's so magical about these? You will never master NLP unless you learn this and develop that attitude and spirit of playfulness, curiosity, wonder, and fun with these distinctions.

Starting from simple to more complex, the Meta-Model identifies linguistic distinctions that you can actually hear as people talk with their language and see in writing. That means that these distinctions are *linguistic markers of magic*. Think of them that way. And, yes, we know that some of them sound bookish and academic. Just remember that they were created in this format by an academician (John Grinder). Also, these are not absolute categories. Even in the original NLP books, *The Structure of Magic*, Grinder put nominalizations in both the category of generalizations and deletions.

As you now look at that list, we want you to wonder and marvel … really wonder that within these seemingly simple linguistic distinctions are the possibilities both for creating all kinds of hellish black magic that can poison a mind, toxify a heart, generate personality disorders and pathologies, *and* for creating all kinds of wonder-filled heavens in human minds, genius, the highest of states, and new levels of expertise yet not experienced by humans. "The webs we tie and untie are at our command", wrote Bandler and Grinder, if only we know what we have (these linguistic distinctions) and discover how to use them as "incantations for growth".

Figure 11.1

The category of deletions:
> Simple deletions
> Comparative deletions
> Unspecified verbs
> Lack of referential index

The category of generalizations:
> Universal quantifiers
> Modal operators
> Lost performative

The category of distortions:
> Nominalizations
> Mind reading
> Cause-effect
> Complex equivalence
> Presuppositions

Mastering the first meta-domain

In NLP training, we typically introduce the Meta-Model without going into a lot of detail or providing extensive training in it. As we now move on to mastery, it is time to engage in more extensive training so that we can tune our ears in order to become intuitive about these distinctions. This means using them, practicing them, and developing the right attitude in using them. In fact, the wrong attitude with these linguistic distinctions can turn a person into a meta-monster, either drilling people like a district attorney or casting spells that create havoc in minds-and-emotions.

As you very well imagine, there are specific attitudes that will propel you into mastery of this domain as there are counterattitudes that will prevent you from ever becoming skilled.

The heart of the Meta-Model

What is the heart of the Meta-Model? What does a person just have to know about this model in order to do magic with it?

The heart of the model is the *representational tracking* idea. Do you remember that? We covered it in *The User's Manual for the Brain, Volume I* and in the early chapters of this work. The idea goes like this. We use words as *symbols*. These symbols *stand for* referents not present, which we can use to re-present to ourselves. We do so on what seems like an internal movie screen in our mind. To the extent that we can take a word and *track it over* to our mental screen and represent it, that word works well as a symbol. It's well formed. It provides sufficient information so that we can map a cinematic representation. To the extent that we can't directly track it over, that term or phrase is fuzzy and vague as a symbol and lacks the necessary details of the screenplay information for our movie. We either have to fill in a lot of the details or we are left with an impoverished movie.

A good representational tracking question is the Meta-Model test for a nominalization: "Can you put that X [the word] in a wheelbarrow?" Sensory-based nouns are the easiest of all words to track over.

- "He began to cry and large teardrops fell slowly down his red cheeks."
- "It was Johnny's fourth birthday when he received his dog, Spot, who had a white coat with black spots scattered around and one on his right eye."

Another good representational tracking question concerns the verbs, the actions. After all, who wants a mental movie where the *things* just stand still? We want teardrops *falling* and dogs *running across* a yard to fetch a yellow ball.

"Can you see, hear, feel, smell, or taste the things in the movie acting, moving, changing, or doing something? What do they do? Where do they start? Where do they end? What is the trajectory of the action? What is the quality of these actions?"

Meta-Model questions enable us to more precisely direct and edit our internal movies. This, in fact, is how we know when to ask questions and when we have enough information. By only tracking what we can see, hear, feel, smell, and taste, we ask questions to get more specific information so that we can continue our editing. This identifies perhaps the most crucial Meta-Model skill, being able to distinguish between sensory-based and abstract information.

EXERCISE: The most crucial meta-model
1. In groups of four or five, grab a newspaper, editorial, book, or some piece of literature.
Read a paragraph or two of whatever you are using while each person listens for the difference between sensory-based and non-sensory-based or evaluative information.

2. Review line by line.
Use different-colored highlighters for sensory-based and non-sensory-based information. Use the Meta-Model representational tracking questions and talk through until you have consensus about the words.

3. Read the section again.
As you do, notice your own representational tracking.

4. Brainstorm.
Use a list of questions that you would like to ask to gather more precise information so that you can complete editing your internal movie.

Questioning for editing purposes

In meta-modeling we use indexing *questions*, questions that index sensory information so that we can more fully and completely edit a mental movie. When we succeed at this, we end up with a well-formed and complete movie. Mapping from words as if they were a screenplay to the movie of our mind creates a richer, more detailed, and more accurate film.

As such, it provides one of the most important neuro-linguistic resources possible. It is the resource of an enriched and enhancing *map*. This saves us from the unresourcefulness of having an impoverished map of the world. Impoverished maps do just that—they *impoverish*. They impoverish our minds-and-emotions and therefore our entire response system.

Because the indexing questions of the Meta-Model enrich our map of the world, our mental movies become more alive, full, informative, compelling, and accurate. This is the "magic" that we speak of. What seems so *magical* in the lives of experts? They just seem to know what and how to do things. Their responses seem to be so intuitively right. That's what Bandler and Grinder noticed in Satir, Perls, and Erickson.

What explains such "magic"? The *structure* of that magic is the structure of their mapping. They operated by a different map of things. They sorted for different things. Accordingly, NLP arose first as a description or model of that structure, that magic.

One of the first things that Bandler and Grinder noticed in the three magicians was their *questions*. They asked what we now call "meta-modeling questions." And what was so magical about these questions? What magic do these questions perform inside us? These questions actually have the power to facilitate our ability to remodel our experiences and to create more resourceful maps and movies. When we simply ask ourselves or others these questions, we and they go inside, remap or re-edit the films in our heads in more useful ways. Now imagine that!

Yet there's more to the magic. As we linguistically question people, they mentally travel back and forward in time, reviewing and re-editing their movies. They go "back to the experience" from which they made their current map and they create a fuller linguistic map. And, while they become entranced with the content, at a higher level in their own mind, they are being coached to edit a movie they can live with and use to navigate their future more successfully. Stephen Spielberg, eat your heart out! Talk about magic! Ah, yes, the webs we weave with our words! The movies we edit in our minds by just listening to questions and responding!

As a theory, NLP proposes that human problems are mostly due to ill-formed maps. We have just been running some B-rated movies that made us feel bad and that took all the spirit out of us. When we create a better movie, a film worth watching again and again, we spring back to life and live more productively. It's something like the old cognitive proverb, "As a man thinks in his heart, so he is."

This cognitive-behavioral approach to human functioning of course springs from Korzybski's engineering idea that "The map is not the territory." We don't deal with the territory. We deal only with maps, with mental movies that play out on the screen of our consciousness. When we update and enrich that movie, it affects how we feel and act. It opens up new and more choices.

Formatting and structuring the Meta-Model

The very first formatting of the Meta-Model occurred in 1976 with the second volume of *The Structure of Magic*. In that volume, Bandler and Grinder suggested the following three categories as "useful in organizing our experience both in therapy" and in training seminars. These three categories summarized the Meta-Model:

1. Gathering information
2. Identifying the limits of the client's model
3. Specifying the techniques to be used for change (p. 165).

These categories also identify three purposes of the Meta-Model. Dilts has suggested the following three categories as natural groupings of the Meta-Model violations. He put specific language patterns under each category.

Figure 11.2

---

1. Information gathering
   a. Deletions (Del)
   b. Unspecified referential index (URI)
   c. Unspecified verbs (UV)
   d. Nominalizations (Nom)

2. Setting and identifying limits
   a. Universal quantifiers (UQ)
   b. Modal operators (MO)

3. Semantic ill-formedness
   a. Complex equivalence (CEq)
   b. Presuppositions (Ps)
   c. Cause-effect (C-E)
   d. Mind-reading (MR)
   e. Lost performative (LP)

In organizing the Meta-Model this way, Dilts emphasized its value for gathering high-quality information through questions, for setting and identifying the limits to one's model of the world, and for working with, identifying, and expanding the meanings that we give to things. Dilts (1983a) wrote:

> For me, this is what the Meta Model is all about: being able to increase your efficiency in anything by finding out that kind of specific information. Knowing anchoring, knowing strategies, or any technique by itself isn't going to get you anywhere unless you know *how* and *when* to use them … The Meta Model is all about asking these kinds of questions. What do you need? What would happen if you did? [p. 5]

It makes perfect sense to use the Meta-Model as an information-gathering technology. After all, it grew out of the questions that the therapeutic wizards asked their clients. Such questioning explicates how a given *model of the world* works, what elements make up that mapping, its linguistic structure, and how a person "knows" what he or she knows. It allows us to make explicit the magic spells that people live in. Of course, when we do that, our questioning can simultaneously have the effect of breaking the spells that are ill formed.

From this we can identify the most basic and essential questions in the communication magic model:

- What do you know?
- How do you know that?

The "logical levels" of the Meta-Model

By the mid-1980s, most charts organized the Meta-Model in terms of the three modeling categories (deletions, generalizations, and distortions). At first, they organized these lists from simplest to more complex (deletions to distortions). By the late 1980s many had turned this around to present the higher levels, as reflected in Figure 11.3.

Ordering the distinctions as a "logical level" system reveals that we have deletions in every linguistic distinction. Deletion, as a modeling process, occurs in the processes of generalization and distortion. It represents a smaller unit or *lower* level.

In cause-effect statements, we have deleted the connection. In mind-reading, we have deleted the process of how we know or how we have made our guess about another person's mind, intentions, and motives. In complex equivalence, we have deleted how we created the equation between the items existing on different logical levels.

Similarly, we have *generalizations* in most of the linguistic distinctions of the Meta-Model. We generalize how things work in causing or leading from one thing to another (cause-effect). We generalize the basic pattern of meaning (complex equivalences) as we specify that an external behavior (EB) equals an internal state (IS).

We generalize about the basic thoughts, emotions, and intentions in others (mind-reading). But, conversely, we may have no generalization when we simply delete the specifics of who, how, when, where.

Historically, the next step in the process of mastering the Meta-Model occurred when numerous people (Bandler, Lankton, and others) began *inverting* the order of the Meta-Model. Doing so led to the realization that we operate much more efficiently when typically we begin at the top with the largest-level distinctions and move downward.

The Meta-Model is a system of "logical levels" in that the higher modeling processes (presuppositions) *drive* (or organize) the levels below it, and the next highest process (distortion) drives generalizations and deletions below them. (For more about the "logical levels" of the Meta-Model, see *NLP: Going Meta—Advanced*

Figure 11.3

Distortions
Mind-reading (MR)
Lost performative (LP)
Cause-effect (C-E)
Complex equivalence (CEq)
Presuppositions (Ps)

Generalizations
Universal quantifiers (UQ)
Modal operators (MO)

Deletions
Nominalizations (Nom)
Unspecified verbs (UV)
Simple deletions (Del)

Modeling Using Meta-Levels.)

The magic of the higher levels

What significance does this restructuring of the logical-level system inherent in the Meta-Model have? There are several.

First, it highlights the fact that *higher levels organize and modulate the lower levels*. This partly explains the power of Meta-Model questions and how they challenge and shift things at a higher level of mind. Changing things at a higher level generates a pervasive effect, an effect that governs, controls, and organizes the transformations at lower levels. This means that at the lowest level in the system (the linguistic distinctions of *deletions*), we will get the smallest "chunk" of information. At this level, indexing and asking for specifics provide details of great precision. While these many details fill in the missing pieces, they may address only trivial concerns rather than crucial ones.

As we move up to the distinctions under the category of generalizations, we begin to get larger chunks of information-"beliefs". This gives us information about how a person has structured his or her world in terms of action style (*modus operandi*) and "rules" for living (lost performative).

When we get to the distortions category of linguistic distinctions, we have access to a person's internal world, which deals with causation (cause-effect), meanings and associations (complex equivalence), values and states (nominalizations), and beliefs about the states of others and what causes those states (mind-reading). Yet the largest level of all flows from a person's presuppositions-those unspoken assumptions in beliefs about such things as knowledge, meaning, self, destiny (presuppositions).

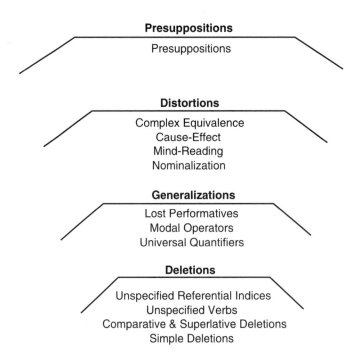

Figure 11.4

What does this mean in terms of learning to use the Meta-Model effectively? By recognizing the logical levels in this model, we can ask logical-level questions:
- What "chunk" size of information do I need?
- At what level does the person's difficulty exist?
- At what level will I get the most useful and valuable information?
- At what level can I intervene to get the most pervasive impact?

Summary

Originally it was the Meta-Model that began the NLP adventure as it discovered the "magic" that lies at our command in the words that we use. Theoretically, the Meta-Model explains this "magic" by formulating the structure of how we take linguistic symbols and translate them to the movies of our mind. Representational tracking is the Meta-Model tool that resulted from that.

The actual model consists of twelve distinctions along with twelve questions. These focus our attention on twelve different kinds of linguistic mapping that we can question to create more precision or use to induce more hypnotic states.

The Meta-Model teaches us that the "magic" lies in the structure, that what we do in creating a model of the world is to model language and thereby call movies and frames into existence.

Figure 11.5: The Meta-Model

Patterns Distinctions	Responses Challenges	Predictions Results
1. Simple Deletions		
"They don't listen to me."	Who specifically doesn't listen to you?	Recover the Deletion
"People push me around."	Who specifically pushes you?	Recover the Ref. Index
2. Comparative & Superlative Deletions (Unspecified Relations)		
"She's a better person."	Better than whom? Better at what? Compared to whom, what? Given what criteria?	Recover the deleted standard, criteria, or belief
3. Unspecified Referential Indices (Unspecified Nouns & Verbs)		
"I am uncomfortable."	Uncomfortable in what way? Uncomfortable when?	Recover specific qualities of the verb
"They don't listen to me."	Who specifically doesn't listen to you?	Recover the nouns of the persons involved
"He said that she was mean."	Who specifically said that? Whom did he say that you call mean? What did he mean by 'mean'?	Recover the individual meaning of the term Add details to the map
"People push me around."	Who specifically pushes you?	
"I felt really manipulated."	Manipulated in what way and how?	
4. Unspecific Processes—Adverbs Modifying Verbs		
"Surprisingly, my father lied about his drinking."	How did you feel surprised about that? What surprised you about that?	Recovers the process of the person's emotional state
"She slowly started to cry."	What indicated to you that her starting to cry occured in a slow manner?	Enriches with details the person's referent
5. Unspecified Processes—Adjectives Modifying Nouns		
"I don't like unclear people."	Unclear about what and in what way?	Recovers the projection
"The unhappy letter surprised me."	How, and in what way, did you feel unhappy about the letter?	speaker's sense of feeling "unclear" or "unhappy".
6. Universal Quantifiers		
"She never listens to me."	Never? She has never so much as listened to you even a little bit?	Recovers details about the extent of a process and counter-examples.

7. Modal Operators
(Operational modes of being)

"I have to take care of her."	What would happen if you did?	Recovers details of the process,
"I can't tell him the truth."	What wouldn't happen if you didn't? "You have to or else what?"	also causes, effects, and outcomes.

8. Lost Performatives
(Evaluative statement/s with the speaker deleted or unowned)

"It's bad to be inconsistent."	Who evaluates it as bad? According to what standard? How do you determine this label?	Recovers the source of the idea or belief— the map-maker, standards used, of "badness?" etc.

9. Nominalizations
(Pseudo-nouns that hide processes and actions)

"Let's improve our communication."	Whose communicating do you mean? How would you like to communicate?	Recovers the process and the characteristics left out
"What state did you wake up in this morning?"	How specifically did you feel, think, etc.? What behaviors, physiology, and internal representations make up this "state?"	Specifies the verb and actions

10. Mind-Reading
(Attributing knowledge of another's internal thoughts, feelings, motives)

"You don't like me."..	How do you know I don't like you? What evidence leads you to how a person knows?	Recovers the source of the information— specifies conclusion?

11. Cause-Effect
(Causational statements of relations between events, stimulus-response beliefs)

"You make me sad."	How does my behaviour cause you to respond with sad feelings? Counter example: Do you always feel sad when I do this? How specifically does this work?	Recovers understanding of how a person views causation, sources, and origins—specifies beliefs about how world works

12. Complex Equivalences
(Phenomena that differ which someone equates as the same)

"She's always yelling at me, she doesn't like me."	How do you equate her yelling as meaning she doesn't like you? Can you recall a time when you yelled at someone that you liked?	Recovers how the person equates or associates one thing with another. Ask for counter-examples to the meaning equation.

"He's a loser when it comes to business; he just lacks business sense."	How do you know to equate his lack of success in business with his lack of sense about it?	Could other factors play a role in this?

13. Presuppositions

(Silent assumptions, unspoken paradigms)

"If my husband knew how much I suffered, he would not do that."	How do you suffer? In what way? About what? How do you know that your husband doesn't know this? Why do you assume that his intentions would shift if he knew? Does your husband always use your emotional state to determine his responses?	Recovers the person's assumptions, beliefs, and values that he or she just doesn't question. Specifies processes, nouns, verbs, etc. left out.

Chapter Twelve
Meta-Magic and Extended Meta-Model
The New Meta-Model Linguistic Distinctions

The distinctions of the Meta-Model give us linguistic features that relate to modeling, map making, and well-formed structures for our internal movies. When NLP began with the eleven or twelve linguistic distinctions of the Meta-Model (the lists varied from eight to twelve distinctions), Bandler and Grinder did *not* claim that they had exhaustively identified every linguistic distinction. They, in fact, anticipated that additional distinctions would be added to the Meta-Model. They noted this at the beginning of *The Structure of Magic* (1975, 1976): "... our Meta-Model covers only a portion of the verbal communication which is possible ..." (p. 107) And, "... we suspect that some of the research currently being conducted in Generative Semantics ... will be particularly useful in expanding the Meta-Model further." (p. 109)

Given this, what *additional* distinctions can we find, identify, and develop to *expand* the Meta-Model? What other typical linguistic distinctions occur in our everyday expressions of thought and ideas that can also cue us to ill-formed structures of deletions, generalizations, distortions, and presuppositions?

I (MH) began my own search for missing Meta-Model distinctions in 1990 by engaging in an in-depth exploration of the foundational work of neuro-linguistics in the classic work of Alfred Korzybski, *Science and Sanity: An Introduction to Non-Aristotelian Systems and General Semantics* (1933/1994). I published these as a series of articles in *Anchor Point* as "The Missing Meta-Model Distinctions" (1992). These were later published in German (*Multimind-NLP Aktuell* magazine), then translated into Russian, Spanish and other languages and finally they were published as *The Secrets of Magic* (1998), which is now *Communication Magic* (2001).

Today if we ask, "Is there anything new to learn about the linguistic distinctions in NLP?" we delightfully tell you, "Yes, there is." In fact, numerous people have been exploring other linguistic distinctions that deserve a place in an extended Meta-Model.

Here we will briefly survey these new developments—the seven linguistic distinctions from Korzybski and two from the field of cognitive linguistics. The fact is, there have been a lot of new developments in the field of linguistics since 1975. In fact, just as The *Structure of Magic* was first being published (1975, 1976), Noam Chomsky, developer of transformational grammar, denounced the deep-structure part of the model. And that was only the beginning. In the following years, the whole field of linguistics went through tremendous upheaval, eventually moving on from transformational grammar entirely. Harris describes all of this in *The Linguistic Wars* (1993). Today, cognitive linguistics has taken the leading role and we personally think that it fits the NLP and NS models in a far better way. But our concern here is not for linguistics, but *neuro*-linguistics.

The value of the Meta-Model

The Meta-Model enables us to openly examine our maps and the movies that they elicit allowing us to make sure they are *semantically well formed*. We can examine them in terms of their construction, form, and usefulness. We can quality control our maps to make sure that they really will help us navigate various facets of life. If "the menu is not the meal", and we have an abbreviated menu, we can expand the menu choices. If we have a really old menu, we can update it. If the menu has become folded, smeared, or dirtied so we cannot even read it, we can replace it.

The Meta-Model entirely avoids the epistemological questions about the "truth conditions" of the map. Rather than evaluate whether we have "true" or "false" maps, it focuses more pragmatically on other concerns:

- Will our maps guide us to the places we want to go (e.g., bring us healthy relationships and success at work, give us the ability to achieve important goals, help us to achieve personal health and vitality, create bonding, help with conflict resolution)?
- Do our maps have a structure that basically accords with the territory? (Korzybski said that "structure and structure only" comprises the essence of "knowledge".)
- Do we have enough flexibility and openness in our maps to keep updating them as circumstances and events change? (Rigid maps carved in stone will eventually become dated and useless. In a process universe, we need flexible maps that allow us to keep adding to knowledge and to take feedback into account.)
- Will our maps allow us to navigate effectively in the territory that we want to move in? (We need to run an "ecology check" on the effectiveness of our map. This quality-controls the map for ecological balance. As we do this, we add "effectiveness" as a criterion to "accuracy of structure".)
- Do our maps allow us to look reflexively at the maps themselves? (Do we even recognize our thoughts, emotions, values, and beliefs as maps so that we can evaluate our maps, deconstruct maps, and remap as needed? To do so keeps our mapping processes as an open system rather than a closed one.)

Extending the Meta-Model

The first seven distinctions that follow come from the key linguistic distinctions that Alfred Korzybski identified in his General Semantics model. As linguistic markers, they cue us about different ways that our language can be ill formed and hinder us in mapping and engineering our neuro-linguistics and in communicating effectively.

To expand the Meta-Model with these distinctions for more productive map making, we have reformulated seven Korzybskian distinctions using the Meta-Model format. We have packaged them in terms of neuro-linguistic *distinctions* and *questions*. First come the distinctions for detecting the structure of the mapping. Then come the questions to explore the poor map construction or ill-formed structures. This makes these distinctions explicit in a way that Korzybski did not.

Figure 12.1

---

    1. Over-/underdefined terms (O/U)
    2. Delusional verbal splits (DVS)
    3. Either/or phrases (E/O)
    4. Multiordinality (M)
    5. Static or signal words (SW)
    6. Pseudo-words (PW)
    7. Identification (Id)
    8. Personalizing (Per)
    9. Metaphors (Mp)

The *distinctions* refer to the *language patterns* that indicate structures of mapping. These appear as the surface expressions or statements that we use as we communicate. Yet these forms often create conceptual limitations that impoverish our world.

To address this impoverishment, we question or challenge the linguistic structure. As we *meta-model*, we invite a person to reconnect to his or her *experiences* out of which the map arose and to remap it more fully, appropriately, and usefully. We do this specifically by offering a question, response, or challenge that elicits more specificity in indexing the referents or in constructing a more enhancing map. As meta-modeling engages our mapping processes, it activates our processes of encoding our movies in ways that are usually outside of our awareness. While the transformational grammar labeled this the "deep structure", cognitive linguistics describe it as the overarching hierarchies of "cognitive domains" and "matrixes of domains"—the meta-levels of our frames.

What the new extensions describe

1. Over-/underdefined terms

These terms refer to how we overdefine some terms at meta-levels and underdefine them in sensory-based terms. We talk about "marriage" and define it in abstract terms that exclude specific behavioral referents. This leaves us using lots of abstract terms that are not operationalized and so encourage vagueness, imprecision, hallucination, and ill-formed structures.

"This is a *beautifully* decorated room." What do you mean by beautiful? What features in this room meet your criteria for beautiful?

2. Delusional verbal splits

This refers to words that have verbally and linguistically cut apart processes and that treat the elements as if they could stand alone. "Mind" and "body" and "emotion" illustrate this. Where there is "mind" there is "body" and "emotion". So we use punctuation to indicate the full system of interactive parts that cannot actually be split, mind-body-emotion, time-space, neuro-linguistic.

"Well, in my mind I do know better but emotionally I feel like doing it."

"So tell me about the part of your thinking-and-feeling system that knows better and then tell me about the other facet of your thoughts-and-feelings that is activated to do otherwise."

3. Either/or phrases

Either/or phrases posit an Aristotelian worldview that assumes a simple black-and-white view of the world so that things are either this or that with nothing in between. Yet the great majority of things in the world are grays, in between, to some degree. "Either you love your job or you hate it." "Either you are a failure or a success." Filling in the excluded middle enables us to map things with more accuracy.

So there's nothing between failure and success? You couldn't succeed in some things and fail in others? You couldn't be on the verge of success but need to deal with a few things getting in the way?

4. Multiordinality

Multiordinality refers to the nominalizations that can refer to themselves. The meaning of the term depends on what level of abstraction is used. At each level, the term will mean something different. For example, at the first level, we experience love as attraction and affection. Then at the next level love of love becomes infatuation, then love of love of love becomes romanticism, and so on.

"My fear of disapproval is just eating me up and sabotaging everything I do."

"So this fear that you're speaking about, is it fear of Jim or Jane's disapproval if you do that project without their okay, or is it fear of the *idea* that they will disapprove? At what level is this fear?"

5. Static or signal words

Static words are those multiordinal terms that we have limited to a single, rigid, absolute, and static meaning. It may start as our way of specifying a multiordinal term, but then we fail to keep it flexible. Having specified how the term is used in one place, we freeze it so that it becomes static and universally true for all uses. This creates limitations and rigidity in thinking.

"I'm just afraid of being shamed and embarrassed if I fail."

"This 'fear' sounds like it is almost like a solid thing rather than a process. When you experience this fear about the *idea* of someone 'shaming' you, do they actually say, 'Shame on you!' in the tone of the childish curse, 'Nay, nay, nay, nay, nay'? Or is it that they look at you and roll their eyes? How do they do this shaming act and what is so fearful about it?"

6. Pseudo-words

Pseudo-words are those spell marks or noises that look and sound like words, and that we use as if they were truly symbols that stood for something that had actual or logical reality, but do not. They stand for nothing. They are pseudo-terms. "Unicorn" in the field of zoology is a pseudo-term. In the field of mythology, it does have a referent and so stands for a referent. "Heat" in physics sounds like a noun, a substantive, and therefore a real thing. It is not. This misguided physicists for centuries. It wasn't until scientists re-languaged the referent describing thermo-dynamic relations that the actual referent was mapped.

"Failure is just the worst thing. I just can't stand it. That's why I work so hard, to avoid failure at all costs."

"I'm fascinated by what you are referring to when you use the word 'failure', it almost sounds like a thing, like a wild beast trying to devour you. Where is this thing you call 'failure'? What does it look like? Is it always full grown or could there be a little mini-version of it? Would you be as fearful of it as the full-size version?

7. Identification

Identification refers to identifying with something and making it part of one's self-definition. It refers to the next logical development of complex equivalences. The equivalence is taken between one's definition of self and some external behavior, experience, or role, or some internal concept, belief, or emotion. There is no "same-ness" in the world: there are only differences. Identification starts insanity by ignoring that.

"You don't understand, I have been a failure all my life, and I'm afraid I always will be."

"Yes, you're right: I don't understand. I didn't know that you had been inducted into the Failure Hall of Fame as one of the great pioneers and leaders of Failurehood or that you had built it so thoroughly into your résumé. Does that identity have some perks that I'm not aware of? If it does perhaps I should identify with some of my failures and become one also.

8. Personalizing

Personalizing refers to both a thinking pattern (a meta-program) and a way of languaging events, experiences, things, feelings, or ideas as "mine" or "about me". In this way we mentally map problems into ourselves, thereby creating more limitations and unresourcefulness, or, conversely, personalize resources to fill up our neuro-linguistic world with resourcefulness.

"It seems that you're making fun of me and my pain. It's not funny. Losing that job was the worst thing ever."

"Well, yes I can see that you are nothing more than your job and that you *are* nothing more than what anyone says to you, and that taking everything anyone ever says to you *personally* is not only your style, but who you *are*."

9. Metaphors

Metaphors refer to one thing through another. While all language is metaphorical, when metaphors are alive and vital, we notice them and use them to set a frame as a way to think about one thing in terms of another. "Communication is a dance" radically differs from the idea that "communication is war".

Mastering the Meta-Model

Because our intention and focus here involve *mastering* the Meta-Model, what do we mean by this? What are the signs or indicators of such *mastery*?

Mastery means moving beyond using this list of distinctions and questions in an unthinking or rote way. When we first learn the Meta-Model, we focus on the *specificity* questions.

- Specifically who?
- Specifically when?
- Specifically how?
- With whom, specifically?

It makes perfect sense that we first learn to stop hallucinating from people's words and *representationally track* from the words to the sensory-based referents they elicit and that we track to our internal cinema. When we cannot do so, then we ask for more information.

"Who are you specifically talking about?"

As the person fills in the map details, then we can map it on the mental screen of our mind. Representationally tracking from the symbol used cleanly enables us to accurately hear and encode what the other person actually says. This, however, is a rare art and one not easily developed. It takes time, patience, and lots of practice to accurately hear what a person is saying and use the symbols without supplying more meaning. Representationally tracking enables us to avoid being hypnotized by the words of our clients, customers, and friends.

"That humiliation really sent me into a deep depression."

There is a high fog factor in those words. The nominalizations "humiliation" and "depression" have frozen some sets of actions and behaviors and encoded them as if they were things. The causation structure of the one nominalization causing ("sent me into") the other nominalization represents yet another ill-formed facet of the mapping. We meta-model such fog when we inquire about the see-hear-feel referents of these terms.

"Who was humiliated by whom, in what way, when, how do you know …?"

"How did the humiliating activities demand, force, or cause you to depress yourself?"

"What specifically did you depress yourself about? How did you do that, specifically?"

While meta-modeling begins here, it does not end here. First we get the missing pieces, the referent experience that has not been fully mapped. NLP mastery at this level involves understanding *why* we do this and *why* this is important.

Why?

Ah yes, the forbidden NLP question—at the practitioner level. But now, at the master practitioner level, we ask it and explore it. How is it that we can search out the why now, but not earlier? Earlier the *why* questions would contribute to the vagueness and ill-formedness of mapping. "Why are you that way?" "Why did you do that?"

Such questions would not have first flushed out the details of what happened: they would have invited the one questioned to provide reasons, explanations and rationalizations. That would not make anything clearer. It would have increased the fog. Yet once we have the details, once we have filled in the specifics of the map so that the mapping represents a fuller expression of the neuro-linguistic mapping, now we can explore the higher frame of reasons, understandings, even excuses and rationalizations. If we ask why at the practitioner level, we lack awareness of what the *answers* do, and so can easily get caught up in content and miss the very structure of the experience. Yet asking *why* at the master level means we are now able to listen for the supporting frames and being able to explore them *as structure*.

For example, someone says, "Criticism really hurts me. I feel crushed when I'm criticized unfairly." We meta-model by asking, "What do you mean by criticism [nominalization]?"

"Well, negative comments, you know."

"And how do you know that comments are 'negative'?"

"Well, ah, if the words insult me ..."

"Has that happened recently?"

"Yes, just yesterday. My boss said that I had messed up the report."

"And those words were an 'insult' and 'negative' and therefore the 'criticism' that hurts you?"

"Well, it's not the words: it was the tone. You know, that sarcastic and harsh tone of voice that he used."

"So a negative criticism that you experience as an insult involves a sarcastic and harsh tone?"

"Yes, exactly."

"So if he had said these words matter-of-factly, they would not have been a criticism?"

"Right. I would have heard it as his understanding and evaluation about the report."

"And you could have felt resourceful to have dealt with that?"

"Sure."

"What if he had said with the harsh and sarcastic voice, 'You really did a good job here!'? Would that have been criticism?"
"Of course."

This meta-modeling flushes out the details of the structure of the experience that goes under the classification of "criticism." Imagine if the person had started off asking a *why* question.

"Why are you so sensitive to being criticized?"

"Well, because of the way my dad treated me when ..."

Then the person would have taken off into history as if it were the history and the experience that caused that state, rather than the mapping. It would have then been so easy to have gotten lost in details of the historical memory and to reinforce the map and the state. How different indeed is meta-modeling. And how different when we ask the why question from the master practitioner level. After obtaining the structural details of *how* the person formats and frames "criticism", then we can ask why.

"Why do you think you connected the sarcastic and harsh tonality to the category of 'criticism'? What would have been the positive value of originally doing that?"

The *why of intention* is really a very different question than the *why of source*. So also with the *why of value and outcome*. "Why do you want that?" "Why is that important to you?" These why questions elicit very different information. They elicit the governing frames that structurally support the experience. So Meta-Model mastery involves knowing what why questions to ask, when to ask them, and what to listen for.

EXERCISE: Exercising your "why" options
1. Get a notebook and notice all of the why questions that you and others ask in a day's time. Write the why questions down and then discern the kind of "why" being inquired about.

2. Develop a set of why questions that enable you to explore significant meta-levels.

Mastering the presuppositions of the Meta-Model

The highest logical level in the Meta-Model alerts us to the structural framework of numerous presuppositions—presuppositions of, for instance, existence, time, and space. Tuning our ears to hear such presuppositions means learning to listen at a meta-level for the assumed framework above and beyond the words. To do this we have to step back, so to speak, from the words and in wonder about the presuppositions within the words.

We do this with other Meta-Model distinctions. For example, with modal operators of necessity, we learn to hear that a world of rules and laws (necessities) is presupposed.

"You have to get your act together."

"Have to? And what will happen if I don't?"

"Boys shouldn't cry."

"They *shouldn't*? Why *shouldn't* they? What's the rule that forbids it? Who forbids it? What will happen if they do? What will that mean?"

In Chapters Twenty-One and Twenty-Two we will delve into the presuppositions of language that explore the assumptive framework of such language.

Summary

The distinctions of the Meta-Model are those linguistic ones that identify styles of mapping in language. These linguistic features cue us about how we have edited, directed, and produced our mental movies.

That's why we can use them to unpack the screenplay information within them and more clearly understand the internal movies that play in the theater of our mind. By questioning the "how do you know?" and "what does that mean?" structure of the language, we discover how a movie works in terms of both content and structure.

The linguistic distinctions of the Meta-Model began with the original twelve and have now been extended to another nine to give us more ways to enter into a structure of experience and to identify its magic.

Figure 12.2: The extended meta-model

Patterns Distinctions	Responses Questions	Predictions Results
1. Over-under-defined terms (O/U) "I married him because I thought he would make a good husband."	What behaviors and respones make a "good" husband for you? What reference facts do you have for "husband?"	Recover the extensional facts about the terms used.
2. Delusional Verbal Splits (DVS) "My mind has nothing to do with this depression."	How can you have "mind" apart from "body" or "body" apart from "mind?"	Recovers the split that someone has created verbally in language.
3. Either-or Phrases (E-O) 'If I don't make this relationship work, it proves my incompetence."	So you have no other alternative except total success or failure? You can't imagine any intermediate steps or stages?	Recovers the continuum deleted by the statement. Either-Or structure.

Patterns Distinctions	Responses Questions	Predictions Results
4. Multiordinality (M) "What do you think of yourself?"	What do you mean when you refer to "self"?	Recovers the level of "Self" which can have many different meanings, depending on context and usage which speaker operates from.
5. Static Words (SW) "Science says that."..	What science specifically? Science according to whose model or theory? Science at what time?	Recovers the deleted details.
6. Pseudo-words (PW) "And that makes him a failure".	What do you mean by "failure" as a word that modifies no real referent.	Challenges a map that uses words which define.
7. Identification (Id) "He is a democrat." "She is a jerk."	How specifically does he identify with "democrat"? In what way? Upon what basis do you evaluate her using the term "jerk"?	Recovers the process of identification. Invites one to create new generalizations.
8. Personalizing (Per) "He does that just to irritate me."	How do you know his intentions? How do you know to take these actions personally?	Challenges the process of personalizing.
9. Metaphors (Mp) "That reminds me of the time when Uncle John."..	How does this story relate to the point you want to make?	Recovers isomorphic relationship between the story and the person's concepts.

Part Three

Systemic NLP

Chapter Thirteen
Systemic NLP
Thinking Systemically about the Cinematography of our Minds

There's a tremendous difference between knowing a lot about the great many distinctions in NLP and knowing how they fit together as a system. It is one thing to know lots of things about the finer distinctions regarding representation systems, meta-programs, value hierarchies, patterns for making changes. It is yet another thing to know how these domains of knowledge relate to each other systemically.

Knowing a lot of things about lots of NLP does not necessarily make for mastery. It only creates detail complexity. And, while that will give a person a richer and more detailed knowledge of a given area, it will not provide a more comprehensive and systemic understanding of the entire model.

Mastery comes when we have used the meta-connection to tie the detail complexity together into a unified system. That's where Meta-States as a model comes in. It comes in not only as the third meta-domain, but as a model for thinking systemically about unifying the various domains of NLP.

Unlike the other meta-domains, Meta-States is inherently systemic. This means that to know and work with meta-states, we shift to a different kind of thinking, we shift to thinking systemically. That's why the meta-thinking and feeling processes in Meta-States inherently facilitate systemic thinking regarding our neuro-linguistic and neuro-semantic states.

As a model, Meta-States provides insight into how we create the matrix "realities" of our frames and embedded frames. It enables us to think more systemically because it allows us to see the full circuit of the interactive parts and how reflexivity works. It allows us to think about our neuro-semantics as a system and to consider the role that iteration plays over "time" within the mind-body system. This allows us now to recognize and work with systemic relationships and interactions in our mind-body- emotion system. This allows us to work more effectively with the system quality of "betweenness". It allows us to recognize system properties such as emergence, gestalts, and paradoxes. O'Connor and McDermott (1997) have written an excellent work on the subject of thinking systemically using NLP.

Systemic thinking and valuing in meta-states

If it is self-reflective consciousness that enables us to go meta to our thoughts, feelings, experiences, and states. This is the mechanism that allows us to *layer* thoughts, feelings, sensations, upon one another. This mechanism also endows our consciousness or mind with a rich complexity and allows us to continually embed our states in various meta-level frames of reference to create a whole array of meta-phenomena (such as values, beliefs, understandings, and decisions). These are the "logical levels" of the mind, and emergent human states such as consciousness itself and spirituality.

This is why we have to shift from thinking of "logical" or meta-levels in a hierarchical way and adopt the systemic thinking of a "holoarchy." We'll explore more about a holoarchy in Chapter Fourteen. The prefix "holon" means that the parts contain the whole and the whole contains the parts. This creates a very different kind of *system* for the neuro-semantic system. Being able to think this way means seeing, thinking, and feeling them as dynamic, fluid, moving, and a process.

Many systemic values arise from this. For one thing, it generates our unique sense of our self-aware mind, a mind aware of itself *as* mind. Recognizing this, Meta-States enable us to understand ourselves more completely. This increases our EQ— emotional intelligence quotient. Because we have the kind of mind that can go meta to think of itself, we can reflect on our reflections. This self-reflexivity enables us to catch and work effectively with meta-muddles.

The systemic nature of mind and our neuro-linguistic states challenge our ability to effectively manage our states and develop personal mastery as well as provide us the skills for doing that. By going meta, we have a self-reflexive context for examining our thoughts-and-feelings and our models of the world. This puts us at a *choice point* about our maps. It gives us the ability to skillfully handle meta-phenomena. At meta-levels we experience such things as meta-programs, beliefs, values, decisions, time, identity, and mission. Every day we "leap logical levels in a single bound" into these phenomena. Now we can do it with our eyes open as we set new frames. Now we can *identify contexts and contexts-of-contexts* in which our experiences lie embedded within and we do that to understand the meanings, reasons, and whys that drive our experiences.

As the NLP Strategy Model expanded and developed the TOTE model, it enabled us to track down linearly neuro-linguistic reality. Meta-States enables us to add the meta-level distinctions and tease out the higher logical levels governing those experiences that involved embedded and layered levels of consciousness. Making *meta-level distinctions* allows us to explore and discover the principles that govern our unique psycho-logics.

Out of the mix of state upon state arises higher-level neuro-semantic or conceptual states. These higher semantic states encode our highest level of meanings and specify the frames of reference we use in navigating life. Recognizing them enables us to reframe, deframe, and outframe in ways to generate "magical" transformations—to do word magic (the Mind-Line patterns, Chapters Twenty and Twenty-One). Skill at that level transforms us into full-fledged neuro-linguistic magicians. Now we can track consciousness as it makes meta-moves. In terms of modeling, we can now tease out the meta-level structures inside and behind the more complex and layered experiences, and track with others as they communicate.

We move up and set a higher frame and that in turn, governs and controls experience and enables us to modulate the higher messages that organize things. This allows us to take charge over our own conceptual categories, contexts, and frames that govern the meanings that we experience. It answers the question, "Which organizing structure do I use ...?"

It allows us to qualify, temper, and texture states. We can now qualify, temper, and texture the properties (or qualities) of the state experiences that we want. This enables us to temper, balance, and synergize our states.

It allows us to avoid logical-level "category errors". We become skilled in recognizing the difference between description and evaluation so we do not confuse levels. We become skilled in recognizing and using multiordinal terms. This allows us to work with holoarchical reality.

Meta-stating as systemic thinking

Every "system" is made up of numerous interactive parts in which we input something and then output a result. A "system" *processes* input to transform it into an output. Typically, a system inputs information or data and outputs a response to that data. As such a system will have feedback and feed-forward loops. These can be open or closed depending on the nature of the system.

Given this basic definition of a "system", what then does it mean to "think" systemically? How does Meta-States facilitate our learning to think systemically?

The answer is that because *self-reflexive awareness*, or reflexivity, primarily describes the meta-stating process, it also describes nonlinear thinking. This is precisely why learning Meta-States involves *a different kind of thinking*. It is nonlinear rather than linear, it is both/and rather than either/or. It is simultaneous rather than sequential. It is meta-detailing rather than either global or specific. It is layered reflexiveness within a chaotic process rather than a set procedure.

This description offers many distinctions and we will sort them out in the rest of this chapter in several ways. First we will present a set of basic principles that govern the meta-levels; then we will identify sixteen of the state-upon-state interfaces that occur in the neuro-semantic mind-body system; and then we will translate that in terms of systems thinking.

Principles for thinking systemically

Similar to the NLP presuppositions that establish the theoretical and epistemological assumptions in NLP, we also have a set of presuppositions that we use as the basic premises or principles that we use to think about the logic of the meta-levels. The following principles both summarize and point to the different kinds of thinking that we use in Meta-States.

1. Higher "logical levels" drive, modulate, organize, and control lower levels

Gregory Bateson (1972) formulated this fundamental principle about "logical levels". Taking his cue from Russell and Whitehead and their theory of logical types, Bateson applied it to learning, schizophrenia, art, communication, and wisdom. A meta-level always serves as a frame of reference that classifies and categorizes its members. In doing so, it sets the frame of meaning for the members and therefore the filter and interpretative key for how to think about its members. As the higher frame it "in-forms" what its members mean and how we should respond to such. It is in this way that the higher level or frame governs the lower frames. Because of this, higher or meta-levels operate as "attractors" in a self-organizing system.

Practically, this means that whenever we set a higher-level frame of reference, we thereby empower that frame to dominate and permeate the lower levels. How will it specifically interface with the lower levels? That depends. In the next section we will detail a whole list of possible effects. These include the higher intensifying the lower states, defusing them, negating them, multiplying them, creating trance, creating paradox.

2. Someone or something will always set the frame of reference

If our very "thinking" is reflexive by nature, and we are forever meta-stating our thinking-and-feeling with more thoughts-and-feelings, then we or someone else or something else is always setting frames. This now raises a critical question for every experience and every mind-body system, "Who set the frame?" "What set the frame?"

Sometimes our frames are set through "osmosis" as it were. We simply breathe it in and live in it as the cultural, linguistic, familial, and professional frames in the mental-emotional atmosphere. About *contexts*, Marshal McLuhen once humorously noted that he didn't know who first noticed and specified "water" as such, but he knew it wasn't the fish. They live *in it*. That's why it is so much easier for us to notice each other's frames than our own. We live so much in our own frames and matrix of frames that they function like the *un*conscious or *outside* of conscious atmosphere like a canopy of consciousness.

Don't expect meta-levels and frames to be explicit, overt, or obvious. They typically are not. Because they exist *above* our everyday conscious awareness, we take them for granted and just assume them. Count on your meta-states operating as your unconscious frames—your "way of being in the world", your *attitude*.

Who has set the frames for you? What cultural frames have you just picked up and learned? Who was the map maker who suggested you play the mental movies that you do in the theater of your mind? Asking these questions flushes out the "lost performative" of our frames so that we can more mindfully choose our frames.

3. Whoever sets the frame will govern the experience (or run the game)

Since higher frames govern, and since somebody also sets them, the person who sets the frame thereby governs the subsequent experiences. This gives us perhaps a new understanding of leadership. Who is a leader but the person who establishes the meaning frames, the vision frames, the inter-pretative frames? A leader is a leader precisely because he or she gives people a new way to see things. Leaders primarily work with symbols. And whoever is in charge of constructing and marketing the neuro-semantic symbols governs our mind-body states.

All of the resulting thoughts, ideas, concepts, beliefs, emotions, behaviors, language, problems, solutions, and experiences are derived from whatever frames are set. These frames govern our individual neuro-linguistic systems and our cultural systems.

4. The whole gestalt determines the parts and from the parts, the whole emerges

This principle describes the systemic nature of our mind-body system as it speaks about the *gestalt* nature of our neuro-linguistics processes. Our mind-body-emotion "system" emerges from all of the interactive parts. It emerges from the interface effects of the meta-levels on the lower levels and so generates an overall gestalt or configuration of interactive parts. This, in turn, defines the character of the whole neuro-semantic system that we call "personality."

Thinking systemically using meta-states directs our attention to thinking not just about individual parts but about what happens dynamically and interactively. It moves us to think in terms of the whole. We experience the meta-stating of our internal experiences as holographic and can therefore see redundancy throughout the system.

5. We outframe to set up a higher-level frame of reference that will govern the whole

With this description, now it becomes obvious why there is meta-magic in stepping outside of the entire system and framing the whole. We call this "outframing". Even conceptually, stepping aside from a frame and reflexively thinking-and-feeling new and more resourceful thoughts about it allows us to be the master of our frames, the master of our matrix, rather than its servant.

We can, in one fell swoop, set an entirely new frame over the whole system and thereby completely change the nature, functioning, and gestalt of the system. This is part of the systemic thinking inherent in meta-stating. It means that we do not have to change every lower-level state, idea, belief, or frame. We can leverage the entire system by rising up in our minds, stepping aside from the system, and tweaking one small frame and thereby transforming everything.

In this way, the process of outframing can sometimes perform meta-level "magic" as it installs a new self-organizing attractor at the top of the neuro-semantic system. If you look for this to be "logical" in a linear way, you will be disappointed. It is *psycho-* logical. It makes sense from the use of the nonlinear mechanism of reflexivity.

6. Nominalizations and other meta-level terms radically change at each level

What does any particular nominalization mean at any given level of abstraction? It all depends. It depends upon the level and the interface effect of nominalization upon nominalization.

To describe this Korzybski invented the linguistic distinction *multiordinality*. This means that because we *abstract* at different levels, what something means depends upon the level at which it occurs. Korzybski described the different experiences in terms of levels, hence he talked about "second-order abstractions", "third-order abstractions", and so on. He noted that the majority of our most important terms are multiordinal, and that they really don't mean anything in particular until we find out at which level we use them.

In the extended Meta-Model (Hall, 1998, 2001), we noted that multiordinal terms are nominalizations that fit the reflexivity test. That is, "Can you apply the term to itself?" If you can, then the term is multiordinal and lacks a specific meaning. We can only figure out what we or another means by it by specifying the level at which we use it.

For example, consider the nominalization of "love". At the primary level "love" of an object refers to attraction and desire for something or someone "out there". I love Brenda. I love to ski. Can we love our love?

Yes. When we experience *love* of our love, our higher-level love is no longer for the object out there, but for our state of love. We love the experience of being in love. "Love" now does not mean that we are caring about and extending ourselves for some loved one. "Love" now refers to *loving* and desiring our state of being in love. We call this new gestalt, "infatuation". Love of love is infatuation. And that's a very different experience than the first-level "love".

Can we love our love of love? Can we love infatuation? Yes. We can *love* our experience of infatuation (our love of love). "Love" now at this third level means something yet different and so takes on yet another feel or tenure. Now we have "romanticism". And can one love romanticism (love of love of love)? And so it goes on.

Such multiordinality, however, is just the beginning. Take any other nominalization, especially one used to describe emotional states, and apply the first multiordinal term to yet another: we can fear our love of our love, we can love our fear of our fear, we can feel anger at our love of our fear, and so on. This is part of the different kind of thinking involved in Meta-States and identifies a nonlinear, systemic way of thinking.

7. *Reflexivity endows consciousness with systemic processes and characteristics*

With these examples of reflexivity, we can now see how this mechanism drives the levels of abstraction and so creates all kinds and qualities of meta-level experiences. Reflexivity simply refers to our consciousness *reflecting back* onto itself or its products (thoughts, emotions, beliefs, values, decisions, specific concepts). As it does, it sets up feedback and feed-forward processes and thereby creates a circular system. It is via reflexivity that we go in loops, go in circles, and spiral around ideas, thoughts, and feelings. As such, reflexivity is not a good or bad thing, although it is the very mechanism by which we create both the most glorious and the most demonic states possible.

8. *Meta-level disorientation and conflict create living hells*

Generally whenever we bring *negative* thoughts-and-feelings (states) against ourselves, or any facet of ourselves, we put ourselves at odds with ourselves. We create an inner-conflict gestalt. We attack ourselves with negative ideas, feelings, or physiology. And, when our self-relationship (relation to ourselves) becomes disturbed, we begin to loop around in vicious, downward, self-reinforcing cycles. This describes how we can misuse our systemic thinking. The mental mapping creates internal horror movies or fatalistic movies.

Whenever we fail to use our reflexivity in a healthy way, we turn our energies against ourselves and so create self-disturbing patterns. This includes those gestalts that we know all too well such as self-condemning, self-contempting, self-repressing, self-hating. This is the structure of pathology. It is what allows us to create the mental-emotional hells of neurosis, psychosis, personality disorders, and character disorders. Of course, once we turn on ourselves in such ways, it also creates a disturbance in how we relate to others. That's because if we have a pattern of turning negative thoughts-and-feelings *against* ourselves, we will tend to do the same to others.

9. *Undoing the meta-muddles and meta-messes frequently involves "paradox"*

The motivation by which we create many of our dragon-like states is often very good and noble. We want to avoid being ugly and hurtful to others, so we hate, despise, fear, or reject our anger. It makes sense. Or so it seems.

Yet in terms of reflexivity, when we despise, hate, fear, or reject our anger, we turn these very states against ourselves—against a basic emotion that we need. It's not that "anger" is bad at all. *How* we express our anger, that's where "good" and "bad" come in. We can do so in unhealthy, hurtful, and immoral ways that violate people, *and* we can do so in healthy ways that value and respect people. In itself, "anger" just means that we are registering a sense of threat and violation to our values. And we need that knowledge. We need that information. That is the kind of feedback information that we need inside our neuro-semantic system.

If we reject and make taboo our basic emotions, even the negative ones, we create a meta-muddle that will not and cannot be resolved until we do something that seems so counterintuitive and paradoxical. Namely, accept, welcome and even celebrate our anger.

Did we mention that this was counterintuitive?

Some therapies describe this as "paradoxical". Paradoxical intervention involves asking the person so afraid of his fear to intentionally become angry. It involves asking the person being ashamed of, feeling guilty for, and experiencing anger at her fear to intentionally show us what fear and panic is like when she experiences it fully. It involves asking the person who feels shameful and angry regarding his stuttering to have fun playing with stuttering and doing it on purpose.

It seems counterintuitive. The prescriptions seem paradoxical. Yet, from the inside, the person who has spent so much time and energy doing the very opposite by trying to avoid the experience is now invited to consciously experience the anger, the fear, the lack of fluency in speech, and it seems contradictory.

And so it is to the kind of thinking that created the problem.

Yet it is "psycho-logical" in that, when we accept, welcome, understand, observe, play with, exercise control over, appreciate, and validate the experience, we develop control over it. Now we have the experience instead of letting it have us. The solution to the system error that we experienced as the meta-muddle is resolved by what seems (from the inside) yet another system error.

So the very meta-level solution for health, integration, balance, and empowerment involves the counterintuitive responses of accepting rather than rejecting, welcoming rather than making taboo, and learning to appreciate instead of hating. The way to rid ourselves of unwanted thoughts, emotions, behaviors, and habits *paradoxically* involves welcoming, accepting, appreciating, and celebrating that very thought, emotion, and behavior. As we then welcome it into consciousness we can learn to receive the primary-level "information value" of the thought or emotion. Then we can choose whether we want to take counsel of it or not. We can then run a reality check on it, decide what to learn from it, opt to say yes or no to it. It is when we are *not* reckoning with our neuro-linguistic experience as just experience that we are led to repression, self-rejection, and all kinds of pathologies.

10. *We set a frame by using lots of neuro-linguistic energy and repetition*

How do we set a frame? How do we meta-state ourselves so that we consciously "run our meta-mind"? Why is it that we can "think" and entertain all kinds of great ideas in our mind but they don't seem to be running the show or making a real difference? If the higher levels govern the lower and we have some higher-level thoughts that are wonderfully resourceful, how come they are not self-organizing our system?

The reason is that mere "thinking" or mild "feeling" will not do in terms of setting a frame. This explains one of the chief occupational hazards of humans—we can "know" much more than we do. We can even torture ourselves with knowing so much "intellectually," but feel stifled and limited from making real through our actual behavior or feelings.

It is *not* enough to just know. We have to take our mental-and-emotional states and make them intense enough, compelling enough, and habitual enough so that they become our "frame of mind". Just as there is an art to anchoring, and merely touching, using a tone, shifting a gesture may very well *not* set an anchor, so with the meta-anchoring that we do with our meta-states. To meta-state effectively, we have to elicit sufficient energy so that it registers strongly in the mind-body system. That's why we amplify a state. We aim to create compelling movies with the cinematic features that activate our system, compelling validation that installs and locks it in, and the mental-emotional space that allows this to occur. To achieve this we use such patterns as Excuse Blow-Out, Meta-No-ing, Mind-to-Muscle, Meta-Yes-ing, Intentional Stance.

We can think, know, and feel and still not establish a higher frame or meta-state. We can "think" without believing, valuing, and deciding. All thoughts and emotional states do not immediately or automatically set a frame. That's good. We would not want that. We do need to know how to utilize the natural processes of how our systemic and reflexive brain works so that we can put the drama of cinematography, the energy of intensive states, the repetition that leads to habituation to work for us.

11. *Altering higher-level frames alters identity and destiny*

Typically, we cannot change what we do so that it lasts in a pervasive and generative way, without also changing who we are. This offers yet another explanation as to why we cannot at times set a new meta-state frame. Old identity frames frequently get in the way. We can leverage that by asking, "Who would you have to be in order to make this change?" "When you make this change so that it lasts, who will you become?"

Others in NLP sometimes refer to these sabotaging frames as "unconscious parts". These so-called "parts" are simply meta-level frames, typically identity frames. As identity frames, they block a change because it would violate our self-definition and who we would be. For the change to occur, we have to tease out these frames and outframe with a new meta-level identity frame.

241

Does our higher frame of our self-definition support the transformations that we seek or not? Do you have permission to become this kind of person? Or do you have some old limiting maps that keep you stuck in the old pattern, such as "That's just who I am!"? If we think of our behavior as a printout of our operating programs, then what are the operating programs that create a particular behavior? As a process, meta-stating almost always effects our self-definition and our sense of self. Frequently, by our first changing that frame, the other frames and experiences will self-organize our entire system. Imagine what would happen if you set a self-definition frame that you are the kind of person who is always learning, becoming more resourceful, who can always use feedback positively, who doesn't take offense easily.

12. Meta-levels inevitably coalesce into the primary state

Our reflexive awareness enables us to "step back" in our mind and think and feel about our experiences. We do this conceptually and yet if we keep doing it, the meta-state experience will inevitably merge and interpenetrate our everyday state. Meta-levels do not stay meta for long if we keep using them. The layering of thought or feeling upon other thoughts and feelings brings a coalescing of these energies. Repetition habituates them. Constant use makes them more and more stable, more and more our everyday frame of mind and so brings them back down into the primary state and so into our flesh, muscles, and eyes. This explains how meta-states become our meta-programs and how the features of our movies (the "sub-modalities") seem to eventually merge into the picture.

The only way to keep the "meta" level conceptual and just "in the mind" so that they don't get into neurology is to *not* use them or to forget to use them. Nonuse will make them less and less available. Or we could set some frames: "It's a great idea, but impractical"; "It's a wonderful resource, but not for me." Or we could fear using the higher-level frame because of anxiety about where it would lead to.

13. The sequencing of the meta-levels make all the difference in the world

Because there is a structure to the higher levels of our consciousness, the order and sequencing plays a critical role. If we sequence fear of anger, the fear will set a meta-state frame of dread about anger. Then we are prevented from developing any competence with anger. But, if we become afraid of being afraid of our emotions, that sequence may blow out the fear of anger so that we become open to learning how to more effectively manage our anger.

Being serious in our playfulness as many professional athletes are can cause them to forget that ultimately it is just a game. Conversely, being playful in our seriousness creates a very different dynamic. When we are playfully serious, we texture our earnestness and commitment with a larger-level sense of fun, joy, and play. Then the game is just that, a game. We give it our all, but we keep perspective about what it is and why we are playing. Here the meta-stating sequence makes all the difference in the world regarding the *quality* and *nature* of the experience.

14. *The quality of our states is textured by the higher levels*
Given the fact that the higher levels of our states, thoughts, and feelings percolate down into the lower levels, the very *quality* of any and every state is determined by the higher-level frames.

What is the quality of your anger? Your fear? Your confidence? Your sexuality? Your professionalism? Your commitment?

To ask this question is to explore the systemic nature of how your higher-level states influence the lower ones. If your "anger" is qualified and textured by fear, dread, anxiety, or taboo, there will not be much flexibility to it, much mindfulness about it, or much control over it. How different when your "anger" is textured by calmness, respect for others, flexibility to turn it on and off, willingness to learn from it, appreciation for it as a neurological signal.

Premises of the mind's matrix

Those fourteen principles describe most of the basic processes involved in working with meta-levels as a system. They help us to understand the dynamic, fluid, and nonlinear nature of our reflexivity as a system of feedback and feed-forward loops.

EXERCISE: *Playing with the matrices of Your mind*
1. Identify one of your frames of mind.
Which frame of mind governs your states and neuro-linguistic system that you'd like to explore for the purposes of this exercise? It can be positive or negative. Name one.

2. Engage in a meta-exploration of the frame.
What is that frame? How do you define and describe it? When do you use it? About what? What elicits it? (Identify primary-level triggers and cues.)

What is the value of the frame? How does it serve you? How does it not serve you? What problems does it create for you? What do you think or feel about it? (Repeat four or five times.)

3. Play with a new meta-frame.
What would you prefer as your frame of mind? Describe fully. When would you use it? Where? With whom? In what way?
Why? Why would this be valuable to you? How?

4. Play around with installing the new frame.
Would you really like to have this as your frame of mind? What would be five reasons why this would enrich or enhance your life?

Would you let anything take this away from you? How could you maintain it and install it? Describe the new movie this frame would trigger.

Meta-stating frames for a self-organizing system

In thinking systemically about the higher levels of the mind and what the meta-stating process does in terms of using our reflexivity, we have mentioned that, when we set up a higher frame, it organizes and modulates everything else in the system. In systems theory we describe this as *self-organizing*.

What does this mean? It means that *the system organizes itself to fulfill its programming*. It means that everything it feeds forward through itself and then out into the world via thought, speech, feelings, and behaviors will be in terms of that higher frame. It also means that what it receives as feedback from the world will be in terms of that frame. It sees and experiences the world in terms of the frame. The frame has become a *systemic attractor*.

Robert Dilts has written about the nature of self-organizing processes in his series called *Strategies of Genius*. The following succinctly summarizes the heart of what we mean by a self-organizing attractor:

> *Self-organization theory* is a branch of systems theory that relates to the process of order formation in complex dynamic systems. Paradoxically, it arose from the study of chaos. Scientists studying chaos (the absence of order) noticed that when enough complexly interacting elements were brought together, rather than create chaos, order seemed to "spontaneously" form as a result of the interaction.
>
> According to "self-organization" theory, order in an interconnected system of elements arises around what are called *"attractors"*, which help to create and hold stable patterns within the system. [p. 255]

We call something an *attractor* if it operates in such a way that it creates and holds a stable pattern together within a system. In the mental-emotional system of a human being, our meta-states as higher frames of mind do precisely this. The neuro-linguistic and neuro-semantic system involving thoughts operates in such a way that it evolves a structured framework. It does this as the higher frames emerge from the activity of the entire system.

When we think about something as simple as *perceptual* mapping, the descriptions in gestalt psychology show us how an attractor is some focal point in a phenomenon around which our perceptions become organized. The dot, line, outline, color, or something captures our attention and so brings a larger configuration together. As a result, we see a pattern. Actually, we construct the pattern.

The classic example is the old hag/beautiful woman gestalt. Here are a series of lines and curves. As we use various facets of the image, we come to see either an old hag or a beautiful young woman.

Figure 13.1: Old hag/beautiful woman

What specific features in the drawing pulls your awareness? What do you need to notice that allows the gestalt to shift so that you see the other image?

At the level of perception, a line, dot, shadow, or focus becomes that which attracts us to construct one image or the other.

When we move to higher-level information processing, to representational and conceptual mapping, the very *content* of ideas is what pulls on us to see things in a certain way. Now ideas, beliefs, and concepts function as the attractor. As such they attract to us the supporting ideas and thoughts-and-feelings that give us a gestalt at that level. In this, ideas energize our human neuro-semantic system.

How do conceptual attractors work to hold a pattern together? Several processes are at work. They *configure* the images and representations within a frame so that they attract a certain way of seeing, hearing, feeling, languaging, or responding. They structure the *foregrounding and backgrounding* of our perceptions so that we see things in terms of that pattern. They organize our *computations* by which we construct our model of the world including our belief formulas about causation, equivalence, and identifications.

Once we have set an attractor, the ideas magnetize and organize pieces of data so that it forms to fit the ideas, beliefs, and values in the frame. Once installed, it governs, informs and modu- lates experiences—as a kind of meta-filter, a self-fulfilling prophecy. It operates by feedback loops. It generates our "resonant signature" for how we move through the world and operate upon it.

EXERCISE: An attractor
What have you been, or are now, attracted to? What are the attractors in your neuro-semantic system?

1. List the ideas, beliefs, understandings, values, experiences, references, and so forth that tend to keep pulling on you.

2. What drives them? What empowers them?

3. Have you ever had an attractor but it has become nonoperational?

4. How has it been decommissioned? What destabilized the attractor? How did it become destabilized?

Meta-stating effects

Thinking systemically using Meta-States involves learning to think about the *effects* that arise when we bring one state to bear upon another. Applying one energy state of thinking and feeling to another creates various sequences and structures. From this we can expect some really wild and crazy interactions to result.

Creating state-upon-state structures from dynamic, fluid, and nonlinear energy invites all kinds of things to happen. The very same process of meta-stating can have an entirely different effect in another person's neuro-semantic system. That's why we cannot turn these system processes into step-by-step patterns that will work for everybody at all times in all cultures. Surprising consequences frequently arise from the mixture of these systemic interfaces. The following sixteen effects of the interface of one state upon another state describes some of the relational things that can happen.

1. Reduction of the emotional intensity
Some meta-states will reduce the primary state, such as when we become calm about our anger, when we become playfully belligerent, when we doubt about our doubt, when we link pleasantness to our tensions.

2. Intensification or magnification of the state's intensity
Some meta-states amplify and intensify the primary state by turning up the feelings. This happens when we worry about our worrying, when we love learning, when we develop an unruffled resolution about something, when we become anxious about our anxiety (hyperanxiety), when we love the experience of being in love, when we become calm about being calm, become belligerently playful, feel passionate about learning, or compulsive about being compulsive, appreciate appreciation, or experience boundless joy.

3. Exaggeration and distortion of the subsequent experience
This describes another interface between one state and another. Sometimes the construction increases the intensity so much that it distorts things. Generally, when

we bring a negative state of thoughts-and-feelings to bear on another primary state, we *turn our psychic energies against ourselves*.

Our anger becomes distorted into rage and reactiveness when we become angry about our anger. Or consider: defiant courage, loving the hatred of something, being afraid about fear, hesitating to speak nonfluently (thereby creating the gestalt of stuttering), feeling sad about sadness (create depression), and when we mistrust our accurate and appropriate mistrusting we mess up our ability to use our mind and emotions appropriately and effectively.

4. Negation or neutralization of a state
With state-upon-state structuring, we can collapse one level into another and make the lower level vanish. This can make a state go away or neutralize it. This happens when we doubt our doubt. Doing so usually enables us to feel more sure. So with resisting our resistance, the more we resist that resistance, the less there is. Consider developing a flexible compulsiveness. How much compulsiveness would be left?

When we procrastinate on our procrastination, and say that we will get around to the procrastinating later, we take action and put off the putting off. So when we mistrust our distorted and inaccurate mistrust, such mistrusting at the higher level enables us to trust more. Consider becoming really ashamed of feeling shame. "Shame on you! You should be ashamed of yourself for feeling shame about *that!*" What happens when you become impervious to confusion? What happens to the confused state?

5. Interruption of states
Sometimes the state-upon-state structure so jars and shifts our primary state that it totally interrupts us and arrests our current "psycho-logic". This happens when we feel humorous about being serious, when we intentionally panic, when we feel anxious about feeling calmness, when we feel calm about our anxiety.

6. Confusions of states
Some meta-state interfaces create confusion as various thoughts-and-feelings collide and *fuse with* (con-fusion) other thoughts-and-feelings and leave us experiencing the mixture in ways that we do not comprehend. It can happen when we experience a sense of being ridiculous when trying to be serious or when you first try on gentle loving anger, or frugal luxury, or bold timidity.

7. Contradiction of states at different levels creating "paradox"
What seems like a "contradiction" of two things at the same level is actually "paradox" and the failure to distinguish levels. This happens when we ask someone to intentionally panic. We typically think of panic and panic attacks as unpredictable

and uncontrollable events. So the very idea of purposefully doing it seems contradictory.

"I want to be sure that you haven't already solved this problem. So I want you to do your best, so really try hard to just panic right now … Just think of what it's like and reaccess that state. Because, sometimes problems just vanish or we forget how to do them."

This meta-stating suggestion sets several frames above the problem of panic (problems sometimes just vanish, maybe you have forgotten) and asks the person to access several states (such as purpose, intentionality). Suggestively it accesses several other frames by implication: failure ("try"), "vanish" or "forget" (never know when a problem leaves, surprise).

Shifting experience to a higher and different level explains such powerful techniques as "paradoxical intention". "Show me how you hold yourself and how you breathe when you depress yourself" Watzlawick (1984):

> Kant recognized that every error of this kind [map-territory confusion error] consists in our taking the way we determine, divide, or deduce concepts for qualities of the things in and of themselves. [p. 215]

Bateson defined *paradox* as a contradiction in conclusions that one correctly argued from consistent premises. Meta-state interfaces that create paradox include: "be spontaneous now!"; "try really hard to relax"; "never say never".

Or consider, "Never and always are two words one should always remember never to use" or "I'm absolutely certain that nothing is absolutely certain"; or the title of a book: *This Book Needs No Title*.

8. Dissociation from strong-feeling states

Not only can we reduce strong feelings, we can *step out* of an overly intense emotional state, "dissociate" from it. We do this when we *step out* from a strong negative state and *associate* (or step into) another state (intense or calm). "Dissociation" is a metaphor and does not mean that we are "out of our bodies". We are never *stateless* because we are always *in the body* and therefore feeling. We experience a sense of "dissociation" in the sense of feeling as if we were *not* in our body, when we are watching ourselves, objectively witnessing, noticing, being a spectator to our own experiences. When this happens we feel numb, apart, strange, and weird. If we dissociate dramatically enough, we can experience amnesia. Switching states rapidly and without a reference bridge so that we can track back produces amnesia and other trance phenomena.

Meta-stating interfaces that create dissociation include: the sense of pain being "over there"; feeling like a spectator to your anxiety by watching your movie of anxiety on the screen of your mind; observing an old trauma as if in a movie theater; stepping into a state of checking the ecological value of feeling resentment against someone; having the ringing in our ear and tuning it down until we don't quite hear it any more.

9. The creating of response potential by seeding of a new process

When a person isn't ready for a state or experience, when they find a resourceful state too far outside their normal ranges of states, it would be not be useful to evoke the state directly. It would be more useful to generate it indirectly. It is at such times that we might want to get a person to step into a state that gets them ready for the final state. We can access a meta-state about that primary state so that it *initiates* the process or begins the first step of the new experience so that it creates response potential for the person.

For the person too fearful, timid, hesitant, or unresourceful to just become courageous, we may invite him to have the courage to have courage, or to be willing to try on the courage to temporarily experience courage. We could have a person become playfully uncertain in order to consider something new. Or, of the person who says she just can't learn something, we can ask whether she might like to learn about how to learn a given subject. Willingness to become willing can set one on the pathway to willingness. Gentle anger can begin the process of accepting and appreciating anger so as to handle it more appropriately.

10. The grabbing and focusing of attention to swish the brain in a new direction

Those in the previous category are also good examples of how to grab someone's attention and to focus awareness in a new way. The juxtaposition of state upon state sometimes *swishes the brain* to a new awareness. We do this to provoke thoughtfulness and to send someone in a different direction. As such, meta-stating can arrest attention, overload consciousness, stimulate new thinking, and question axioms, beliefs, reasoning, or memory. All of this can have a deframing influence on the old frames.

So being really calm and respectful about anger was the meta-state line I (MH) used when I conducted anger-control classes for the Department of Corrections in Colorado. I also asked the men if they were yet appreciative about their anger or would like to be in order to really take control of how they experience and use their anger so that "you have your anger, rather than let it have you." And, what would it be like if you were actually lovingly gentle about the expression of your anger because you are the master of it? "Resist these suggestions, eh? You're good at resistance, but not that good, if you can't resist your own resistance. Go ahead, try in vain to resist it fully."

11. The entrancing or hypnotizing into a higher state

These last examples also show how meta-stating and interfacing state-upon-state involve hypnotic languaging. How often has such juxtaposition of states tranced

249

you out and sent you inside on a search for meaning? All you have to do for most people is take them up three levels in abstracting from state to state and they will "go inside." If that doesn't do it, take them up seven levels.

Why would meta-stating be so trancy? Because to make sense of wondering about just how curious we feel about learning about NLP and Meta-States, we are to go inside, and, with our inward focus, really explore our wondering, and wonder whether that wonder of the curiosity of the learning is sufficient, or whether we should learn to love the wondering; or wonder whether appreciating it would be better, since our intention is to become more resourceful.

We especially experience meta-stating trance when we shift logical types *and* set up benevolent double-binds.

"I want you to rebel against thinking about just how comfortable you can feel right now if you don't close your eyes before you're ready to relax deeper than you ever have before ... now as you do that you shouldn't wonder if you will only become more resourceful ... because then you'd be cooperating in the rebellion that you need to become truly masterful."

"I wonder if you're going to fail to succeed at not going into the mastery state whether you use trance or some other NLP process and to do so at exactly your own rate and speed or whether you won't do that just now, because the ability to just relax into the sense of confidence will double that mastery without you knowing it."

12. The gestalting of new emergent states and meta-phenomena

As we have noted before about states-about-states structures, these will frequently cause something "more than the sum of the parts" to emerge as an emergent process of the system itself. We call these experiences a "gestalt" to indicate that something new has emerged, something that we cannot explain as a summation of the parts. That's because it partakes of the systemic quality called non-additivity. This means we cannot just add things together.

Fritz Perls worked predominantly with the gestalt of "anxiety", which he believed was suppressed excitement. What others call "free-floating fear" he thought of in terms of some primary state of *excitement* that the person has become afraid of and has pushed down and suppressed. That's why he would ask, "What excitement are you suppressing? Just let it rise up."

The gestalt of existential concern arises often when we worry about what some thing or experience will "mean". It is a fear of meaning, of potential meaning, a worry about the significance of something. Even self-awareness as we humans experience it is actually not merely consciousness, but consciousness of our consciousness.

13. *The jarring of consciousness that explodes in humor or laughter*

The jolt and jar of state upon state often results in the gestalt of "humor", which Plato said is whatever we experience that seems "out of place in time and space without danger". So, when a juxtaposition of states tickles our fancy, delights our consciousness, surprises us, amazes us, or shocks us, it creates humor. And humor is a very powerful resource for lightening up, creativity, flexibility, perspective, and distance.

14. *The qualifying, tempering, and texturing of states*

It is the nature of the higher levels to *qualify* the experiences that are below. They do so because the higher levels set the frame for the lower states and for the primary experience.

You can see this in *joyful* learning and *boring* learning in *accomplished* liar and *devious* negotiation, in *charming* lie and *ruthless* compassion, in *cleverly* courageous and *courageously* clever, in *unspeakable* peace and *flexible* compulsiveness. In these, the qualifying or modifying terms as adjectives and adverbs indicate the higher level. You certainly see that, don't you? And you *undoubtedly* wonder, *really* wonder about all of the *mischievous*, *playful*, and *therapeutic* uses you can apply this to, can you not?

15. *Solidification of a state and frame*

If the higher levels govern and modulate when we set a frame and it creates an attractor that invites the system to self-organize around it, then, when we set higher meta-states of validation and confirmation, these will solidify and make the underlying experience more permanent and solid. This occurs when we access a state of belief in or value in something. Now that you trust this pattern to work so powerfully, you can take pride yourself in this pattern. Your belief in this belief about X, however, leads to a closed-minded fanatic approach. There can be a pride in a depression because it seems to make the loss mean so much. Some are proud of being jealous of another. And whatever we identify with we make our identity.

16. *The loosening of states and frames*

Conversely, when we set higher states of doubt, question, or skepticism *about* a lower experience, that doubting of X, questioning of Y, and being teasingly playful about Z loosens the reality. Be careful in the juxtaposing of doubt or questions about experiences that you want to endow with the strength of confidence, the confidence of conviction. Such doubting, teasing, laughing, not taking serious, and discounting can undermine and weaken the experience. Many do this to NLP patterns when they first encounter them and then wonder, "How come it doesn't work for me?"

Summary

Meta-States as a model is inherently systemic and nonlinear and so involves a different kind of thinking from the linear thinking typical of NLP.

Systemic NLP inevitably means moving to a nonlinear way of thinking about all of the interactive parts, domains, and models in such a way that we find the higher governing principles and the mechanisms that drive the system.

The mechanism of reflexivity primarily drives the nonlinear nature of our meta-state structures and so creates our ability to "go meta" and create meta-connections between things. Mastering the reflexivity of our mind-body-emotion system enables us to ride the feedback and feed-forward loops and to recognize the many kinds of effects that can result.

Chapter Fourteen
Meta-States as a Unifying Field Theory

From the beginning, Bandler and Grinder described NLP as a *meta-field*. NLP is not about psychology, although it modeled human functioning. It is not about psychotherapy although it began by modeling three therapists. It is not about hypnosis, although they created a model of hypnotic language and processes.

NLP is a meta-perspective in that it is about the structure of experience itself. It is about how to think and work with experience from a strictly structural point of view.

The term "meta" in this context and the idea of "going meta" came from Gregory Bateson and his work in the structural analysis of such experiences as cultures and schizophrenia. The unique contribution of Bateson powerfully influenced the development of NLP. He introduced the terminology of "meta" as a way to describe how to step back from the content of things and describe things from a "formal" or structural point of view. This began when he was a young anthropologist attempting to understand some cultures, to create an explanatory model of those cultures, and to operationalize his terms.

Bandler and Grinder brought many of Bateson's uses of "meta" to NLP. They brought in the idea of stepping back from a thought, emotion, or learning, and stepping up to a higher level of thought, a higher "logical type". When we do this, we can then classify and categorize the first experience. We gain perspective and awareness about it. We set frames about it. Bateson described meta-connection as a higher function of the mind that creates the systemic nature of consciousness.

Bateson explored *meta-connection* in relation to such things as communication, learning, grace, beauty, mind, pathology, schizophrenia, and alcoholism. Bandler and Grinder adopted the *function* of meta-connection in several ways. They created a *meta-position*, which they used for exploring experiences. They used *meta-parts* for working with limitations and for designing new parts. They built *meta* as an implied meta-state into the Strategy Model, the Phobia Cure pattern, Time-Lines, and Swish. I (MH) have devoted an entire chapter to description of the early use of implied meta-states in NLP (*Meta-States*, 1996/2000), which suggests that meta-states were there from the very beginning. They were simply not recognized as such, nor was there an explicit description of Meta-States as a model.

Today as a meta-domain in NLP, Meta-States offers not only a third avenue to identifying and working with the structure of subjectivity, but also provides an overall framework and theory for how NLP patterns work and why. We can now use meta-states systemically as an explanatory scheme to unify the separate parts, patterns, and domains. We can use meta-states for the personal resourcefulness that allows us to detect the higher levels while maintaining a higher-level perspective.

Meta-states as meta-frames

With your knowledge and experience of meta-states in the earlier chapters, you applied it to such matters as learning, anger and fear, and confidence. You know that when you access a state and *apply* it to another state so that it takes a *meta-position* to the second, you layer one state with another. Perhaps you have layered curiosity and exploration to learning. Doing that *textures* your learning state and gives it a particular feel, a particular quality.

It also creates a new "psycho-logics" within your neuro-linguistic system. You have made "learning" a member of the class of curiosity and exploration. It isn't this way for everyone. It is not something that we can count on as a "natural" consequence to schooling. But it can and does happen. When it does, the higher state of mind-emotion-body functions as *the frame of reference* for the lower state, in this case learning.

Meta-states operate as the *frames* for their lower states. This means that a *frame* is a meta-state and that the embedding of frames within frames creates a meta-state matrix of frames.

What's your *frame* for anger? What's your frame of mind *about* anger? What's your frame of reference about being angry, expressing anger, dealing with someone's anger?

Your answers to these questions will flush out your concepts, ideas, beliefs, principles, memories, and history about anger. They are belief states *about* ideas, concepts, history, expectations, and intentions. While these meta-phenomena go by many names, they are all meta-state structures. As we recognize that these nominalizations do not refer to different things, but different perspectives of the same layering of the mind, this meta-state structure gives us a whole list of frames that we can use in modeling the structure of experience, such as:

- conceptual frames of ideas, principles, understandings
- historical and memory frames as reference experiences
- domains-of-knowledge frames
- cultural frames
- family and personal frames
- belief frames
- value frames
- expectation frames

And what are "frames"?

The nominalization, and the metaphor, "frame" refers to how we mentally-emotionally *framed*, *structured*, *formatted*, or *punctuated* an experience, idea, thought, or mental movie.

Again, a "frame" is not a thing, but a process. *Framing*. The important thing here is that we frame when we *meta-state*. When we frame one state or experience in terms of another, we set a frame that defines the previous experience. We set a frame as a mind-body state about something else.

Consider the significance of this structure. Suppose you access a state of pressure and encode it in words like, "You have to study. Terrible things will happen if you don't!" What have you done? You have meta-stated, or framed, the learning state with a state of pressure or necessity. In Meta-Model and Meta-Program terms, you have used a *modal operator of necessity* linguistically to outframe learning with "necessity." If you do that often enough and access some really strong feelings of pressure, force, or control, what will your frame of mind be about learning? What state will that frame of mind create?

Suppose as a young child you are left out when the kids picked those they wanted on their ball team? It could have happened because you were two years younger and not as skilled. Suppose you felt so left out, so alone, and so unwanted that you took those strong feelings and applied them to all sports? What then? What will be your frame of mind about sports in the coming years? It could be *dislike* of sports, *disgust* of sports, sense of *inadequacy* about group activities. Yet the psycho-logics of human nature doesn't limit you to applying it only to sports: you could bring those feelings to bear about other conceptual categories and experiences, such as teams, society, self, or rejection.

Every meta-state sets a frame. In that frame, we have "beliefs", "values", "understandings", "expectations", "identifications", "intentions". This is the tricky thing about the meta or "logical" levels: while we use these nominalizations and we treat the "things" of the mind as entities, as static, unmoving entities, these are all processes. The problem is how to think about them, conceptualize them, and talk about them as *dynamic fluid processes*.

This means that if I meta-state learning with necessity and pressure, then I will probably:

- *Believe* that learning is hard, unpleasant, a necessary evil, not fun.
- *Value* getting away from learning rather than moving toward learning.
- *Understand* learning as undesirable, but what others or the world will force me to do.
- *Expect* to find learning hard.
- *Intend* to avoid it when I can, but "crack down" and "force" myself to do it when I have to.

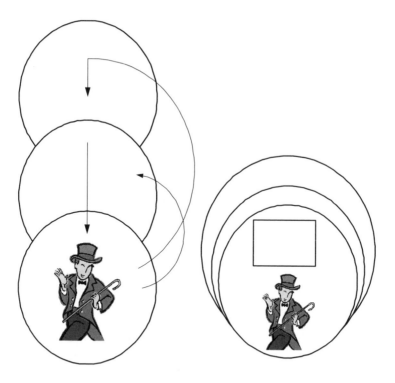

Figure 14.1

- Identify myself as "not good at learning", but the kind of person who likes to do other things.

This means that if I meta-state sports and athletic events with feeling unwanted, a sense of threat in being left out, and undesired, then I will undoubtedly also:

- *Believe* that team sports are stupid and not worth bothering with, that they make people feel terrible.
- *Value* staying away from group sports or situations where being left out may occur, or value individual sports.
- *Understand* that people can be cruel when it comes to competitive sports or activities.
- *Expect* that rejection could occur at any time.
- *Identify* myself with not being much of a sports person.

Think systemically to unify the field of NLP

With the four meta-domains of NLP, we can take four different *meta-perspectives* with regard to any experience. Even to move to each of these knowledge domains, we have to go *meta*. The *meta-move* supports us in the process of becoming effectively masterful in handling these domains.

If mastery depends on the meta-move, how do we learn to go meta? What can we do to practice this skill?

We learn to create and experience the meta-connection by distinguishing *content* from *structure*. We do so by moving above *content* to deal with the structure, context, and process of the experience. We do so with language, with perception, with state, and with logical levels.

1. Meta-Model

In learning and using the Meta-Model, we learn how to step aside from the *content* of words and sentences from the context of the movie playing in our mind. As we do so, we can then recognize *how* the words work in providing data for how we frame our internal movies. We make the meta-move outside the content of language to consider the words, sentences, and phrases in terms of *representational tracking*.

"When I take just these words, what sights, sounds, sensations, smells, or tastes am I able to construct in my mental movie?"

Asking this question facilitates "going meta". It helps us to stop our natural hallucinating and mind-reading so that we can deal with the actual symbolic information available. We then stop inventing and filling in the details as we listen *just for the words*, and deal with them as symbols for our screenplay. This teaches us to make the distinction between sensory-based terms and non-sensory-based or evaluative terms, an essential for a professional communicator. The Meta-Model questions are all indexing questions, indexing specifics: where, when, how, in what way, which one? These questions help us to obtain precise and accurate sensory information from people.

In meta-modeling, we learn to take every word that we cannot *representationally track to the screen of our mind*, and ask questions until we can. This is what we mean when we say that some language is "ill-formed" and some is "well-formed". Language is *well-formed* when we can track it to the cinema screen and *ill-formed* when we cannot.

"You feel pressure about learning? What is this 'pressure' that you feel? How do you know it is pressure? Oh, you 'have to' do it? And how does that equate with 'pressure' for you? 'Pressure' in what way? Oh, mental pressure. And what do you mean by 'mental' pressure? You hear a voice telling you that you have to do it? That's interesting. Where is this voice? What is its tone, volume, speed? Whose voice is it?"

Artistry in using the Meta-Model begins when we can distinguish sensory-based terms from all others and from having a playful, curious, respectful, and explorative attitude that keeps asking "dumb" questions. All along, we stay meta to the content. We do not let the words hypnotize us.

As we hear vague and abstract language, we keep asking questions until we can operationalize the terms and use the information for our movie. It may be information for the content of the screenplay and what we see, hear, and feel, or it may be in the form of how we frame the cinema and the cinematic features that we edit into the movie.

EXERCISE

1. Take your daily newspaper and explore various news items, editorial statements, even classifies in terms of just *representationally* tracking the words to your internal mental movie.

2. What questions would you need to ask the writer or editor to fill in the missing pieces of the movie?

3. Evaluate how well you were able to step back from the content and notice the structure?

2. Meta-Programs

In learning and using the model of Meta-Programs, we similarly have to learn how to step aside from the *content* of the person's story or experience and consider structurally *how the person is looking* at things.

What is his or her *perspective*? What point of view is the person operating from? Is he matching or mismatching? Is she looking for options or procedures? Is he going at things or away from them? Is she operating at a global level or sorting for details?

Simply asking or sorting for meta-program distinctions forces us to rise above the content to the structure. Practice this regularly. As you do, refuse to overwhelm yourself by looking for twenty or fifty meta-programs at once. Instead, take one or two of the meta-program distinctions and practice looking for those. By practicing with one or two meta-programs at a time, you will learn to discern which sort or filter is occurring in the midst of the content of a conversation. It is very much like listening with a third ear. It's like asking, "If this person had colored glasses on and was seeing the world using this or that side of a continuum, which one seems to stand out?"

While the linguistic distinctions of the Meta-Model focus us on the *words* that a person uses to describe experience and direct us to representationally track the language to an internal mental movie, Meta-Programs invite us to a different focus.

"What channel is the person on? Is the person sorting for news, drama, comedy, cartoons, or what? How is this person processing? What thinking patterns is he or she using?"

Some meta-programs overlap or correspond precisely with Meta-Model distinctions. The words that we call *modals*, which indicate *how* a person is operating (necessity, desire, possibility, impossibility), occur in each model. The meta-programs of global/specific (general/detail) overlap very closely to the Meta-Model distinction of sensory-based words (specific) and abstract terms (global).

Artistry in using meta-programs involves recognizing a person's perceptual filter-how he or she has colored the world and then uses those filters.

EXERCISE

1. Return to the newspaper pieces of a news item, editorial, or classified ad and this time use a different-color pen or highlighter to identify meta-programs.

2. Take the checklist of meta-programs and go through the pieces looking for one at a time.

3. Evaluate the ease or difficulty in stepping aside from the content of the materials to identify meta-program distinctions.

4. How do your meta-program sorting styles influence and/or affect this search?

3. Meta-States

In learning and using the Meta-States model, we step aside from the *content* of the primary situation or state to notice the higher states or frames *about* it and/or we access resourceful states to apply to it. Without the ability to *access and apply* one state to another, we could not build up meta-states. The reflexivity of mind, which always and inevitably reflects back onto itself, begins spiraling around in vicious cycles if we are not able to *rise up* in our mind and notice it. When that happens, we get caught up in the loop, as if in a closed system.

With the meta-move we take control of the process. Paradoxically or counterintuitively, we typically have to learn to not "fear" our reflexivity (a meta-state itself) as we give ourselves permission to ride the loops and spirals, and to go on spins. Eventually we can meta-state our own mind-emotion-body expressions as just that—*expressions*. These are just expressions of state. As we "dis-identify" from them, we stop overidentifying ourselves as our thoughts or emotions or body.

With meta-states, we already have an internal movie playing (at the primary level) and it is already framed, structured, and formatted with certain sorting styles (meta-programs). Now we ask another meta-question: "When we bring this thought, feeling, or physiology to bear upon the primary-state movie, how does this affect that? How does it transform, texture, or qualify it?"

In Meta-States, we look for one of sixteen different *interfaces*. Perhaps the higher nullifies the lower, or intensifies it, or reduces it, solidifies, loosens, entrances.

Interesting enough, with Meta-States, we now recognize the source and origin of meta-programs. Meta-programs are solidified meta-states that have become so habituated, so integrated, that what was once a meta-state has become a perceptual filter or meta-program that colors our matrix. Mismatching as a state can become a sorting program. So can matching, options, or procedures. As states, these began as a thought or feeling and eventually were so well integrated that it became a default thinking program.

EXERCISE

1. As you return one more time to the newspaper items, look for meta-states explicitly described or implicitly assumed.

2. What state or states did the writer or editor have or operate from about the primary experience?

3. Evaluate the ease or difficulty in making this meta-move to notice the states, levels, and reflexivity that enable you to flush out the meta-states.

4. Meta-Modalities ("sub-modalities")

The fourth meta-domain of NLP comes under the deceptive label of "sub-modalities." This term actually makes it sound as if the distinctions within this category occurred at a *sub*level to the representational screen on which we record our sensed movie. But they do not. The distinctions are cinematic features that we edit into the movie from a higher level.

The "sub-modalities" of zooming in relate to the meta-program of details and zooming out to global thinking. So with the "sub-modality" distinction of "associated and dissociated" in every sensory system (visual, auditory, and kinesthetic), these are also meta-programs.

With "sub-modalities" we sort for the qualities, properties, features, and distinctions in our mental cinema. Accordingly, we ask: "When you view your mental movie, what does it look like? Is it a still snapshot on the screen or a moving picture? Is it clear or fuzzy? Is it close or far?"

We ask questions of its cinematic qualities. We do this of the video track (what it looks like), of its audio track (what it sounds like), of its movement and sensation track (what it feels like as somatic sensations), of its gustatory and olfactory track (what it tastes and smells like), and of its vestibular track (what it feels like in terms of balance or lack of balance). These are editorial questions that relate to the way we film and encode the movie.

The meta-modalities provide yet another unifying influence in our search for the structure of experience. Each domain provides yet another facet in the diamond of subjective experience.

The systemic thinking in a unified field theory

By definition, a "system" involves numerous interactive parts and it inputs one thing and outputs another. Because our neuro-linguistic system inputs information and outputs responses, a unified field theory of NLP will centrally highlight feedback and feed-forward loops.

In the last chapter we described systemic thinking using the meta-states structure about our neuro-semantic system. Systemic thinking is itself a meta-program. We noted this and identified it as such in *Figuring Out People* (1997). Now we want to use systemic thinking to create a unified field theory. For our purposes here, we will enumerate a few key distinctions about thinking systemically that are crucial for mastery and that contribute to our under-standing of a unified field theory of NLP.

1. System awareness and consideration

The first requirement in learning to think systemically is to bring into our focus an awareness of the entire system:

● What is the system?
● What are the parts of the system?
● What are the principles governing the operation of the system?
● What is the input into the system?
● What is the output from the system?

A unified field theory of NLP will first of all focus on the entire neuro-linguistic system of a person-as-a-whole-in-an-environment. The theory will include all of the sensory-based and empirical factors as well as all of the evaluation-based realities that we create or absorb from our social contexts. It will recognize all of the *input* channels from the outside (the sensory systems) and all of those on the inside, our internal *input* channels of internal thinking, processing, and imagining. It will recognize the *output* channels of behavior, gesture, and physiology and the mechanisms that we use to account for such (for example, calibration, eye accessing cues, linguistic markers).

2. Feedback and feed-forward thinking

Once we identify the system, we need to recognize the feedback and feed-forward loops that govern how the input travels inside the system. In systems terms, *feedback* refers to the information being input from the world and to the *output* of a system at one level as it *re-enters* the system at another level. For example, I receive feedback that what I said "hurts my daughter's feelings". That input comes from her, from outside. Yet, as soon as I receive it, I have thoughts and feelings about it and, as I do, both the external and internal feedback from myself re-enters my system at a higher level as I make a decision to not hurt her feelings and to find out what happened.

Feedback occurs as both as incoming information from the world and, in a strange way, as incoming information from one level of the mind to another level. It then becomes *input* (from myself) that will influence the next step. Feedback then is not merely "a comment about your performance". *Feedback* concerns the results and consequences of a process and how it *comes back into the system as additional information.*

Feedback in a system operates as the central mechanism for self-regulation and self-organizing processes. These work in a nonlinear way, as network patterns. We call the two most basic forms of feedback in a system positive and negative.

Self-balancing or "negative" feedback creates homeostasis so that the system maintains a balanced equilibrium. This is a self-correcting and self-adjusting process as seen in riding a bicycle or steering a boat. Here the outputs of the system cause a dampening and/or corrective effect. The more we eat, the less hungry we feel. The more hunger we feel, the more we eat. In systems terms, this sets up a "virtuous cycle".

Self-reinforcing or "positive" feedback is the basis for runaway systems or what we call "vicious cycles". An initial effect continues to be amplified as it travels repeatedly around the loop. Here the outputs of the system cause an amplifying effect so that we get more of what we put out. The more we save money, the more the savings grow. The more we spend, the more the indebtedness increases. The more we feel afraid, the more the fear grows and spreads to become anxiety, panic.

If we attempt to use linear thinking or to think in straight lines, that is, using direct cause-effect movements between things in a system, it becomes difficult to track and follow the flow of information in the system. This is where we have to shift to thinking in a more nonlinear way, and to visualize the system in terms of loops, circles, spirals. Visualizing or even diagramming such systems and feedback loops is not always easy. In fact, they can make the mind spin.

3. Both/and rather than either/or thinking

Systemic thinking involves a different kind of logic from the old Aristotelian logic that excludes the middles between two opposite poles. Given that systems have many interactive parts, very few facets of the system will operate in either/or terms. Instead, almost everything will involve a multitude of "causes" or more accurately, contributing factors. Either/or thinking comes from the Aristotelian model of the world that posits things using an either/or frame. As we apply this to mastering NLP, we realize that we cannot classify some things as either a meta-program or a "sub-modality". They are both simultaneously. We look at the thoughts-and-feelings of a state and they look to be that of a primary state *and* yet also a meta-state that has coalesced into it. A frame is not either a belief or a value, or an identity, but all of these at the same time.

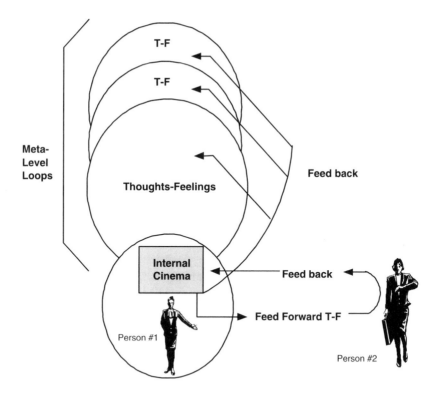

Figure 14.2: The multiple feedback loops

The problem with the Aristotelian model is that we exclude the middle and so blind ourselves to all of the factors in between the two extremes. For a unified field theory, we need the Meta-Model distinction of both/and (Chapter Thirteen).

4. Nonlinear thinking

In place of the linear thinking of Aristotelian thinking, thinking in terms of systems moves us to non-Aristotelian systems, which encourage a kind of thinking that's comfortable with going round in circles, simultaneous processes occurring, and categorizing the same thing in numerous ways. The nonlinear thinking in our meta-states arises from the mechanism of reflexivity. As we think about our thinking, our feeling, our neurological responses, or feel about our feelings, our thinking, our remembering, and our body, our mind goes in loops, in a circle so that down the line it can influence itself.

5. Self-organizing patterns

Living systems are self-organizing, and, as we noted in the last chapter, self-organization is an important facet of systemic thinking. The inputs to the system feed it, in that it is the "fuel" that makes the system grow, develop, live, and thrive. The output are the expressions of the life of a system.

In our neuro-semantic system, the only thing that ever enters the system is *information* or ideas. It is therefore *ideas* as meta-states and meta-frames that "feed" a system and cause it to self-organize through repetition and reiteration.

Immanuel Kant first used the terminology of "self-organizing". He said that we must think of each part of an organ "that produces the other parts (so that each reciprocally produces the other) ... because of this, [the organism] will be both an organized and self-organizing being." This defines the nature of living organism.

The quality of *self-organization* arises out of the chaotic nature of a system due to the ability of a system to create multiple iterations. In fractal geometry, the "fractal" shapes that occur in their characteristic patterns are found repeatedly at descending scales, so that at any scale their parts are similar in shape to the whole. This creates the quality of "self-similarity". You can see this everywhere: rocks look like small mountains; branches look like lightning, borders of clouds look like coastlines; a river delta looks like the ramifications of a tree or the repeated branching of blood vessels.

We see the same process creating a similar gestalt in neuro-semantic systems. In these, however, the self-similarity occurs as *patterns*. Patterned ways of thinking (meta-programs), of speaking (Meta-Model distinctions), editing our movies ("sub-modalities"), and feeling (meta-states). These arise from the iteration of some basic idea over and over again. A person may use the idea of "failure", "control", "resourcefulness", "love", or "fun" and reiterate it in his or her mental movie, feelings, or talk. Doing so creates a pattern. The pattern results from the iteration.

6. Thinking in terms of leverage points
The nature of systemic change in a nonlinear system is such that sometimes the *smallest of changes* can have the most dramatic effects. That's because they can be amplified repeatedly by the self-reinforcing feedback. *Iteration* is a nonlinear process that refers to *repetition or repeating* and describes what happens when a function operates repeatedly on itself.

7. Network and the structural patterning of nested loops
A network, like the neural network of the brain, is nonlinear; it goes in all directions. This endows a network pattern with nonlinear relationships and allows us to iterate messages repeatedly. When we make a meta-move to meta-state, we rise above some primary experience and now relate to that and about that. We transcend and include. And in this transcending and including process, we experience *holons*—parts in wholes; wholes with parts. That's why we can take a tiny part of a system and through unpacking it discover the higher frames that govern the whole

system or matrix. That's why we can begin with a larger level whole and install it so that it permeates every part.

When we have a network system that uses feedback for correction (learns from mistakes), we have a network of loops that can regulate and organize itself. Self-organization emerges and governs the life of the system. When we think in terms of networks, we ask such questions as:

- Is there a pattern of organization that we can identify?
- What is the nature of the nonlinear interconnections?

Every pattern is composed of both substance and form. We discover the substance when we ask, "What is it made of?" In this question, we focus on its elements and component parts.

Regarding form, we focus on it when we ask, "What is its pattern?" This leads us to focus on its patterning, structure, order, and how it does what it does. In our modeling of human experiences, thinking systemically allows us to synthesize these two approaches. Capra described it this way:

> In the study of structure we measure and weigh things. Patterns, however, cannot be measured or weighed; they must be mapped. To understand a pattern, we must map a configuration of relationships. In other words, structure involves quantities, while patterns involve qualities. [p. 81]

8. Holoarchies and emergent properties

At each level of complexity in a system, the observed phenomena will exhibit properties that do not exist at the lower levels. That's because things "emerge" in systems. "Temperature", which is central to thermodynamics, is meaningless at the level of individual atoms, where the laws of quantum theory operate. The taste of sugar is not present in the carbon, hydrogen, and oxygen atoms that constitute its components.

Similarly, such properties and qualities are typically destroyed when a system is dissected. That's why systems cannot be understood by analysis or a reductionist approach. The properties of the parts are not intrinsic properties, but can be understood only within the context of the larger whole. Capra again:

> Systems thinking concentrates not on basic building blocks, but on basic principles or organization. Systems thinking is "contextual," which is the opposite of analytical thinking. Analysis means taking something apart in order to understand it; systems thinking means putting it into the context of a larger whole. [p. 30]

To think systemically we think more holistically ("whole-istically") of integrated wholes, gestalts, the overall configuration that emerges. This we do in NLP and Neuro-Semantics as we use a meta-detailing perspective. We not only think globally, but, while thinking globally, we detail the expressions that give the meta-frame a reality. We not only think in terms of specifics, but, while thinking specifically, we do so from the larger perspective of what it means.

Summary

While Meta-States began as simply another meta-domain, it has grown to offer a theory and model for unifying all of the domains and components of NLP. It does so by providing an overarching framework for how all of our framing works and how framing works at all levels.

As a unifying model, Meta-States is uniquely nonlinear in its formatting. The mechanisms that drive Meta-States are systemic nonlinear ones, the reflexivity of consciousness. As such this offers an explanatory model of how we build up all of the meta-phenomena.

Chapter Fifteen
NLP Unified Field Theories
Dilts, Bandler, Hall/Bodenhamer

In the field of physics, Albert Einstein sought to create "a unified field theory" that would tie together all physical theories into a single model. His aim was to establish a larger level framework to unite everything.

Similarly, there have been several attempts to bring all of the facets, theories, and models of NLP together. Prior to the Meta-Domains Systemic Model, two major attempts had been made to bring together all of the rich facets in NLP (e.g., the Meta-Model, meta-programs, values, time-lines, perceptual positions, "sub-modalities," the Milton-Model, strategies, perceptual positions, and the techniques SCORE and SOAR). The idea is that if we could put together a *unified field theory* regarding how NLP works, this would simplify all of the detail complexity.

Robert Dilts created the first of these larger-level models and Richard Bandler the second. As we move to mastery of this field, it's important that we have some familiarity with these models and especially in terms of the unified field theory presented here. In this chapter we review these two attempts at creating a holistic and system model of NLP, and we offer a critique of each.

Why? Our purpose is to identify the strengths and weaknesses of the models and to use them as we build yet another model. By incorporating the most salient and powerful features of what Dilts and Bandler have already done we hope to move closer to truly designing a systemic model that embraces all of NLP. We offer the meta-domains systemic model as one version among many. It does provide one coherent way to think about human consciousness, experience, and NLP itself in a systemic (systems-oriented) way.

The first systemic NLP model: the Neuro-Logical Levels Network

As far as we can tell, Robert Dilts created the first systemic model of NLP in the mid-1980s. He constructed his model (the NLP jungle gym) out of several pieces. First he took the SOAR model: State, Operator, And Result. SOAR was developed in the 1950s as a general model for problem solving and was first applied to teaching a computer how to become a chess expert. Inside a *problem space*, the model first identifies a set of *States* describing the current situation. It then identifies the set of *Operators* or mechanisms that a problem solver can use to change the situation from one state to another.

When Dilts applied this to neuro-linguistics, he established three linear axes, Self, Others, and Goals, which he diagrammed as a cube. To that, he then took the linear continuum of the time zones (past, present, and future) and combined it with the depth continuum of the perceptual positions (first, second, third—self, other, and meta). Lastly, he added vertical levels comprising the higher levels of the network, the so-called "Neuro-Logical" levels (environment, behavior, capabilities, beliefs/values, identity and spirituality).

This gave him three axes: vertically, the Neuro -Logical levels; lengthwise, the three time positions; and the three perceptual positions for depth. This created the "Jungle Gym" as a conceptual workspace for "states" and NLP interventions.

With all of these pieces things added together, Dilts's multi-dimensional cube incorporates his SOAR model along with "the new code" (perceptual positions, Grinder and DeLozier, 1987). It also incorporates the SCORE model as Dilts used his 3-D-cube model to define and work with *problem spaces* and used neuro-linguistic *Operators* to manage systemic dynamics and to create change from present to desired state.

The operators for Dilts are the specific sensory representations and "sub-modalities" (neuro-), language patterns (linguistic), and physiological cues and expressions (programming). Using these processes, he said, would give us the ability to map problems through spatial and time-line sorting.

Various degrees of complexity arise whenever we put into one model this much information. Dilts's model brings together the basic format of *present state/desired state* as he took the pieces of SCORE:

Having put these pieces together in this rigid and hierarchical form, Dilts then worked on providing practical guidelines for sorting out different *kinds* of problems using Self-Organization Theory. He used two axes: stable versus unstable problems, simple versus complex problems. In doing this, he has pioneered the path for figuring out *what* technique or pattern to use *when* and *with whom*.

Critique
What are the strengths and weaknesses of this attempt at a unified field theory of NLP?

As a strength, this model utilizes a great many of the NLP distinctions, submodels, and patterns. It does provide a way to track the detail complexity of so many facets of NLP. Using the overall structure of the SCORE model, it provides a very basic and productive frame, what's called the NLP algorithm: present state to desired state through accessing and applying of resources. When one uses this model to think about working with problems and effectively applying NLP, one creates a solution-oriented frame and keeps one's focus on resources for bridging from current to desired state.

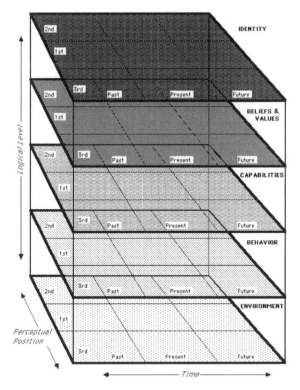

Figure 15.1: The Jungle Gym

On the positive side also is the development of higher levels in addition to linear steps. This was the problem with the NLP-enriched TOTE model. Although it had a *meta*-step inside the TOTE, the focus was almost entirely on a linear, step-by-step process. This first development of a systemic NLP model fully introduced the importance of meta-levels and the idea of the influence of embedded levels upon the primary experience. Dilts even played around with embedding the models of NLP inside each other (see figures 15.3 and 15.4).

Figure 15.2

Present State →	Bridging to →	Desired state
Causes	Resources	Outcomes
Symptoms		Effects
Past and present	Movement	Future and future of that future

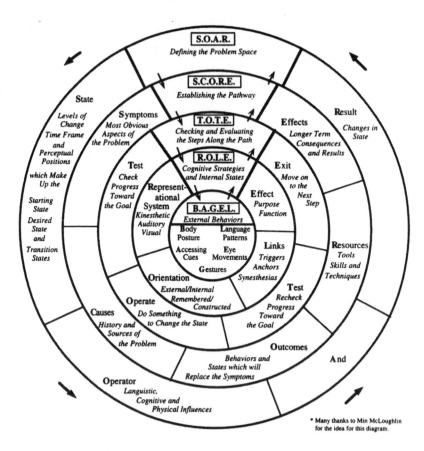

Figure 15.3: Overview of the 5 models forming the Dilts' unified field theory

Within this circling model, he used the following:

5. SOAR: **S**tate, **O**perators, **A**nd **R**esults
4. SCORE: **S**ymptoms, **C**auses, **O**utcomes, **R**esources, **E**ffects
3. TOTE: **T**est, **O**perate, **T**est, **E**xit
2. ROLE: **R**epresentational systems, **O**rientation (external/internal; remembered /constructed), **L**inks (anchors, synesthesias), **E**ffect (purpose, function)
1. BAGEL: **B**ody posture, **A**ccessing cues, **G**estures, **E**ye movements, **L**anguage patterns

From there Dilts put these five models into a framing structure as noted in Figure 15.4.

Regarding the weaknesses of the model, a central problem is its linear representation. Rather than being formatted as nonlinear it is framed as linear, static rather

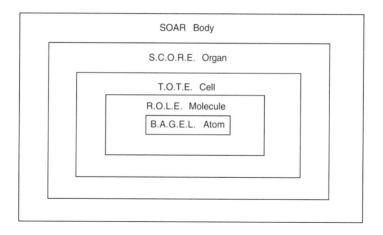

Figure 15.4: System of models

than fluid, and rigid rather than flexible. Of course, the picture of the 3-D cube that looks like the dreaded Borg spaceship from *Star Trek: the Next Generation* doesn't help. In other words, if we are going to speak and think about *systemic processes and dynamics* we also need a metaphor and diagram that looks nonlinear, dynamic, and fluid. Dilts's awareness of this has more recently shown up in his research on self-organizing systems. There he has shifted to using the metaphor of a ball rolling on an energy field—a much more dynamic metaphor. This portends a much more productive direction in terms of a more appropriate metaphor.

Yet even more important than this is the fact that the Neuro-Logical levels are *not truly a "logical level" system*. The six elements in this system (environment, behavior, capabilities, beliefs and values, identity, and spirituality) do *not* fit together so that each higher level is the class or category of the lower. Even when we apply Dilts's own definition of "logical levels"—with the higher levels governing and modulating the lower, and with the lower members being of the class of the higher—the neurological levels fail to measure up.

Several NLP trainers and theorists have noted the numerous inadequacies of the so-called Neuro-Logical Levels model. Woodsmall (1995), Munshaw and Zink (July, 1997), and myself (Hall, 1997, 2001) have detailed these in various articles and books.

And again, the primary problem is that the Neuro-Logical levels do *not* meet the criterion of being a "logical level" system. Many of the levels in that model do *not* engulf or embed the lower levels within it. "Environment", for example, is a much larger phenomenon than "Behavior". Every "Behavior" occurs within some "Environment". "Environment" is not a member of the class of "Behaviors". Running would be, gambling would be, so would reading, writing, consulting, and managing. These are *behaviors*. But not "Environment". We cannot have a *piece of behavior* separate from and not within some *Environment*.

"Capability" offers another difficulty. Does this term refer to "the potential to develop" or to an "ability"? If it means an actual ability, some- thing that a person does, then it occurs at the same logical level as "Behaviors." The word describes the source and foundation for the behavior itself. And every "Capability" in that sense occurs within some "Environment". In fact, different environments enable us to manifest different capabilities.

"Beliefs/Values" in this model refers to a meta-level awareness of consciousness. Here "mind" has gone beyond mere *representation* of the internal mental sensory movie. Mind here has reflected back onto its own thoughts and feelings and states to validate them with value, importance, and significance. This is what creates a "belief" as a validated thought. The meta-level functioning of consciousness in the role of *validating and valuing* denominalizes the terms "Belief" and "Value". How do we *believe or value* something? At a meta-level to our representation of that something (a person, a process, an event, a concept), we validate it by saying "Yes! That's important!"

Dilts presents "Identity" as supposedly above "Beliefs/Values". Yet when we denominalize this nominalization, we come back to another function of conscious- ness, namely, *identifying*. An "Identity" arises from what and how we *identify with*. This reveals that all identities are beliefs. We believe in identifying with something; we make it real to us on the inside as we value it. The nominalization of "Identity" is not a "thing", does not really exist apart from our mental-emotional identifying with it. Identities arise from the process of *identifying*, and whatever we identify with, we *believe* in and value. An "Identity" is not real, it is not an entity: it is a belief. We can either believe in it or question it.

"Spiritual" represents the highest level in the Dilts list of the Neuro-Logical levels. Yet, when we denominalize the term "spiritual", we see that it means relating to spirit. That gives us yet another nominalization, the term "spirit". And, when we denominalize that term, we are left with the original metaphor, "breath, wind, energizing essence". The same referencing metaphors occur in Greek and Hebrew—wind (*pneuma, ruah*).

This brings us back to yet another "Belief/Value". In the level of the "Spiritual" we have the validating and valuing of our inner "breath", which signifies metaphori- cally our *inner essence*, an essence that we use to refer to that which transcends the body.

In terms of meta-levels, the pieces of this model easily reorganize into three logical levels in the following way designated by Figure 15.3. This model fails to indicate the *fluidity* that we have with our reflexive consciousness. What happens to the model when we believe in our spirituality, identify with our capacities, believe in our beliefs?

Bandler's "Design Human Engineering" (DHE) as a second attempt at a unified field theory

A few years after Robert Dilts developed his Neuro-Logical Levels network and used it as a model of systemic NLP, Richard Bandler began designing his systemic model. He called it Design Human Engineering, using Korzybski's 1921 phrase. In doing this, Bandler went off in a very different direction. Rather than use meta-levels, he built the DHE model primarily out of "sub-modalities".

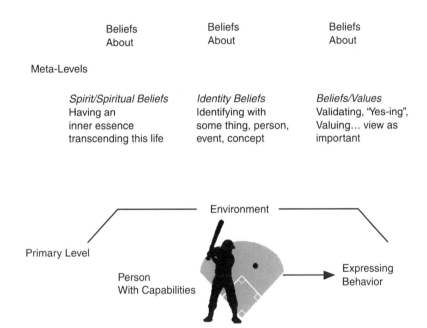

Figure 15.5

In this approach, Bandler sought to encode all of the pieces of NLP using imagined perceptual grids or globes. In that way he could encode all of the elements, models, and patterns as actual "sub-modality" images. To that end, he sought to find some metaphors that would carry and contain this idea. At first he came up with imagining grids around our pictures that could stand for more or less of each "sub-modality", more or less of meta-programs, and challenge our use of Meta-Model distinctions. Then, like a person working the "controls" of an audio system, you could push the "lever" up for more, down for less. Later he decided to put the continua on the longitude and latitude lines of a globe. Then, by imagining a globe over the life space of a person, we could adjust the lines to identify their critical "sub-modalities", meta-programs, linguistic distinctions, and so on.

Beginning with *An Insider's Guide to Sub-modalities* (1988), Bandler and Will McDonald played with various 3-D holographic images. In trainings around 1990 he created exercises for building holographic grids and projecting them into space.

In *Time for a Change* (1993), you can find the idea of *holographic grids* based upon "sub-modalities" that work with setting up control knobs for fast and slow time and "me" and "not-me" representations.

By the time Bandler began conducting DHE trainings (1991), he shifted to the idea of imagining crosshairs to build up the ability to construct various imagined tools involving *globes* and other configurations. These would be projected into space as participants were told to think of these as "tools" they could use to "see" into the internal worlds of people. Like the cyborg in the movie *The Terminator* who had a program for measuring distance, space, spanning a person's files for response patterns, participants were encouraged to stop modeling and just engineer the programs they wanted and to see what was possible.

The governing assumption in this new approach of DHE was actually a basic NLP understanding. Namely, as people organize their realities on the inside, that organization is projected and reflected on the outside by how they act and move and gesture. Watch these things closely and systemically, and you can figure out their internal structures. So, just as we can see "time" representations on the outside by watching where a person gestures when he or she talks about the "past", or the "present", or the "future", and just as we can learn to "see" a person's sensory systems at work via eye accessing cues or "hearing" it in linguistic markers, so we can see the holographic images inside their mind on the outside.

To that end, the DHE model and training started from the assumption that we can literally *see* a person's beliefs, values, or frames projected into actual space. This explains why they value "location" as the most important meta-modality ("sub-modality"). The model assumes that inside "sub-modality" distinctions we have the very building blocks of all subjective reality. They assume that as a tiny piece of a hologram contains all the information, the same occurs inside of "sub-modalities".

As a systemic model attempting to pull all of the pieces of NLP together, DHE operates from a certain understanding and theory about "sub-modalities". It assumes first that "sub-modalities" operate as the molecular structure of experience, and, second, that "sub-modalities" are all-important for explaining and controlling all responses. By assuming "sub-modalities" are the "building blocks of experience"—as the periodic table of elements describes the basic building blocks in chemistry—they applied the Bateson phrase, "the difference that makes a difference" to these distinctions.

In this way, Bandler cited such things as "sub-modality" shifting, altering, mapping over, and contrastive analysis as governing all experience. So, rather than moving *up* to the higher levels, his approach was to move *down* to the basement of the mind, to the so-called "sub-modalities".

Bandler's approach with "sub-modalities" led him to assume that we could transform "confusion" into a meta-level phenomenon like "understanding" by using the "sub-modality" *code*. Simply find something you "understand", identify the "sub-modality" form or code, and map all of the "sub-modalities" in the confusion to the "understanding" "sub- modalities". The mapping-over process will transform "confusion" into "understanding". So with "beliefs". All you have to do is map over from a doubt or weak belief to a strong belief and suddenly you will believe the new content. You have to if you so code it. The secret lies in finding and mapping over the critical "sub-modalities". For Bandler, this use and approach to "sub-modalities" equally applies to moving from bad decision to good ones, or from "unmotivated" to the intense motivation of a "fetish".

DHE processes tap into something else. They utilize the fact that there are some things about a person's model of the world that we can "read" on the outside. This takes the NLP understanding and skill of using neurological processes such as eye accessing cues, breathing, body shape, and predicates to recognize a person's representation systems. Others have explored how this applies to reading "sub-modalities" on the outside (Robbie, 1987; Hall, *The Spirit of NLP*, 1996). We even took the idea for reading meta- programs on the outside (Hall and Bodenhamer, *Figuring Out People*, 1997).

Yet DHE, as a systemic model, goes much further and assumes that we can learn to *see* just about everything, even all the meta-level phenomena of frames regarding a person's model of the world, as a 3-D holographic image in space. To achieve this level of perception, DHE exercises use trance states to train participants to hallucinate grids, control panels, or globes and then to stack "sub-modalities" inside these hallucinated structures. The aim is to include such things as meta-programs, "convincers", beliefs, time-lines, motivation strategy, trust.

In *Persuasion Engineering* (1996), Bandler and LaValle suggest that one should use all of these pieces in working with someone in a sales situation. By doing so, a "persuasion engineer" (e.g., a salesperson) could *see* a person's strategies for motivation, buying, and deciding. Then, seeing those structures, the salesperson could simply put a product into those places and the person then cannot but help to respond positively.

As a unified model, DHE not only sought to bring all of the individual pieces of NLP into one model, but also sought to extend NLP and to do something more. NLP was founded and based upon modeling, on *finding the structure* of excellence in experts. DHE shifted to a different focus. It asked, "What if we had a cyborg and could install any program we wanted into that cyborg and engineer human expertise from scratch? What would we want to invent and install?" Rather than look for an expert or genius with an actual skill, DHE sought to design it from scratch. The problem is that, after more than a decade of following this path, no new models were developed (see the article at www.neurosemantics.com: "Ten Years and Still No Beef".)

Critique
The strength of DHE is its frame of *pretending that anything is possible* and then using all of the pieces of NLP to playfully move these around while in a suggestive

and open state of trance. In this, DHE represents an advanced level of using and playing with the basic NLP model. In this also, many have found DHE very useful for expanding creativity, thinking outside the box, being more playful, developing a more ferocious attitude, and refusing to be limited by "can't". Many have also found DHE very useful in terms of learning to visualize more effectively and vividly and to use more of the cinematic features of our internal movies.

The chief problems and main weakness with DHE, however, is the overuse and overvaluing of "sub-modalities". The distinctions that we refer to when we talk about "sub-modalities" not only do not explain or control everything, but they are not "sub" at all, as we demonstrated in Chapters Seven and Eight. There we showed how the term itself is misleading and why there really are no "sub" levels to the modalities. It is the name that is a false-to-fact term.

The brain may be holographic, as Karl Pribram has suggested, and much of our thinking-feeling may operate in some holographic ways, but "sub-modalities" do not carry all of the meta-level knowledge, understanding, and frames, as DHE has claimed.

Another weakness is that the DHE model hardly even recognizes the existence of meta-levels, let alone take them into consideration. For that reason, it fails to integrate meta-levels and fails to show the relationship between "sub-modalities" and "logical" levels. DHE ignores the Bateson principle that higher logical levels or frames govern the lower frames. In doing this, it puts too much of a burden on the idea of "sub-modalities"—a burden that it cannot bear.

The DHE model also ignores the meta-levels in such human phenomena as "understanding" and beliefs, and the role that such levels play. By assuming that mere "sub-modality" shifting governs these experiences, DHE totally ignores the most important structures. In the earlier chapters on Meta-States, we described the meta-level structure of "beliefs" and the problem of attempting belief change by merely using the "sub-modality" mapping over.

In other words, if you have a piece of *subjectivity* that organizationally and structurally involves levels of abstraction, states about states (meta-states), embedded layering of consciousness, and so forth, then "sub-modalities" cannot run the whole show if they are "sub" to the sensory movie running in our heads. They operate at the editorial level.

Yet if "sub-modalities" are actually the framing structure that we bring to and edit into our movies, then they are *meta-modalities*. This explains why "sub-modality" mapping across seldom works to transform confusion into understanding, thought into belief. "Sub-modalities" actually work symbolically and semantically at a higher level to the movies playing in the theater of our mind.

The Meta-Domains Model: the third systemic NLP attempt

Given these first attempts, what have we learned that we can use as we pull together all of the component elements and models of NLP to create *systemic* NLP, a unified field theory? We have learned that a systemic model of NLP has to take into account and unify the following:

1. Representation systems that we re-present on the screen of our mind;
2. The cinematic features of the internal movie ("sub-modalities");
3. Detecting internal processing and states via external cues;
4. Feed-forward responses to the world;
5. Feedback information from the world;
6. Meta-level states and "logical" levels;
7. The embeddedness of many layers and levels;
8. Meta-Model linguistic distinctions;
9. Meta-Program perceptual distinctions;
10. Reflexivity, recursiveness, never-ending spiral looping;
11. Perceptual positions;
12. The time zones: past, present, future;
13. Algorithm from present state to desired state via resources-SCORE (Symptoms, Causes, Outcome, Resources, Effects);
14. Interface relationship between levels;
15. Trance states and uptime states;
16. Resourceful patterns: the technology of NLP.

Beginning with the reformulation of meta-levels borrowed from Robert Dilts's model, we began rethinking the many component pieces and domains of NLP in terms of Meta-States and wondered if that would provide a larger-level frame for fitting them together. A system, by definition, is any process of numerous parts that involves inputs and outputs and a feedback process.

We began the exploration originally when we worked out some of the details of the "logical" levels of "time" as we noted that there are many different kinds of "time", and "time" at different levels (*Time-Lining*, 1997). At the time we did not even think of such in terms of Meta-States, only of "logical levels". After that we more fully developed it as we reformulated the model of the Meta-Programs in terms of meta-levels (*Figuring Out People*, 1997) and began seeing that somehow meta-states and meta-programs were connected. We did not know how. That came later when we discovered that meta-programs were solidified meta-states that had become so habitualized that they moved from being meta to getting into muscle and neurology themselves. It was later that we finally described the process of how meta-states become meta-programs for perceptual sorting (*NLP: Going Meta*, 2001).

When those endeavors of remodeling NLP worked out so well, we applied the conceptual structure of meta-levels to the wild and chaotic list of the "sleight-of-mouth" patterns. Applying the meta-levels to those linguistic reframing patterns became the Mind-Lines model (1997). We chose the phrase "mind-lines" to get away from the negative connections of manipulation and deceit involved in the metaphor "sleight of hand". At first we did not even recognize that the Mind-Lines model and patterns were actually conversational meta-stating. But by the third and fourth editions of *Mind-Lines* (1999, 2001) that not only became clear, but we made it explicit in the model.

After that I (MH) worked on a book to revisit magic and to present a 25-year update on the Meta-Model itself, the model that launched NLP in the first place. In *The Secrets of Magic* (1998) and then later in a complete revision (*Communication Magic*, 2001), we not only explored the "logical levels" in the Meta-Model, but showed how the meta-levels of the Meta-Model are linguistic expressions of meta-states.

With so many interconnections between these four meta-domains we began to wonder aloud if we could actually use the four meta-domains to create a systemic model of NLP. We thought that by using these in much the same way that Dilts used SCORE, perceptual positions, time, and so on, and as Bandler used "sub-modalities" and trance, we could play with the various ways that the four meta-domains fit together. First we simply identified the four models.

(a) Meta-Model
A model of language, meaning, transformation from one level to another, questioning for precision, using for trance, an anchoring system of words and symbols that "stand for" some sensory or logical referent that we can track to the cinema of the mind.

(b) Meta-Modalities (or "Sub-Modalities")
A model of the distinctions, features, and properties that we can edit into the cinema that plays on the screen of our mind. These distinctions involve sensory-based symbols that stand for and represent yet higher-level semantic conceptual states. Some of them correspond to meta-program, Meta-Model, and meta-states distinctions.

(c) Meta-Programs
A model of processing, sorting information, perceptually seeing, filtering, and coloring the world that distinguishes between the content of thought and the thinking patterns or programs that format and structure that content.

(d) Meta-States
A model of states and "logical levels", reflexivity, the feedback and feed-forward loops of awareness that enables us to move to various levels of awareness, that creates higher and more complex states unique to humans.

Next came the question of how they fit together. Do they describe the same thing from different perspectives? Do they describe different domains of experience? Do they describe different domains that overlap one another?

What is the relationship between Meta-Model, Meta-Programs, Meta-Modalities, and Meta-States?

This last question is what opened up an entirely new way of thinking about NLP itself. As we realized that each of these meta-domains was *above* and yet *about* the same thing, experience, it was clear that we could look at the structure of subjective experience from four different venues:

- **Language:** linguistics, symbols
- **Perception**: seeing, filtering, sorting, thinking styles
- **Cinematic features:** distinctions for structuring and encoding our movies
- **State/levels:** experience, aboutness, reflexivity, recursiveness

At the same time we began realizing the overlap between these four *structural domains*. Each deals with structure and process rather than content, yet in structuring, formatting, and framing things, each influenced and governed the content. We discovered that some of the linguistic distinctions of the Meta-Model were, at the same time, perceptual distinctions of the Meta-Programs (i.e., modal operators). We discovered that some of the perceptual distinctions of the Meta-Programs were also the cinematic distinctions of the "sub-modalities" (global/specific, zoom in/zoom out; associated/dissociated).

As a system of interactive parts and components, pathways of information going in (inputs) and coming out (outputs), along with numerous feedback and feed-forward loops, *human experience* could look at the neuro-linguistic *states* from the point of view of *language*, *perception*, and *level*.

Tracking the structure developmentally

Which comes first? Language, perception, movies with cinematic distinctions, or state? Since we are not born with language, but learn language, an infant does not yet *map* his or her sense of the territory, but immediately *senses* it at the primary level. "Thought" for the infant is mere *representation*. And even that is very primitive. As infants we are not born with the ability to hold our images constant. What we see, hear, feel, smell, and taste on the outside comes and goes. When Mother leaves the room, she's gone and we can't see her in our mind. Constancy of representation will come later. In the meantime we holler and scream because we cannot comfort ourselves with an internal image of her. And we giggle and laugh when she plays peek-a-boo with us, constantly giving us a cognitive jar as she keeps reappearing out of nothing.

But with "constancy of representation" mental and emotional life takes on an entirely new dimension. We can now "record" our movies of what we see, hear, and feel and keep those movies in our mind to entertain us. Now we can "think" by playing the movies over and over for weal and woe. Yet it isn't long before we reach yet another developmental stage. Soon we can have "second thoughts" while experiencing the first thoughts. That is, *while* we are playing a movie of playing, eating, resting, or watching TV, we can have yet another thought *about* that.

At a training, an NLP participant said that whenever his eight-month-old little girl became constipated she experienced "going to the potty" as painful. He said that she had become afraid of going to the toilet but that he had found that if he would go with her and sing to her, it would distract her mind so she could go. But, he asked, as he began to learn about NLP anchoring, "Would this anchor of music in the bathroom set up any undesirable consequences in the future?"

An interesting question, and one that evoked a lot of laughter about those possibilities. Yet even more fascinating to me was the child's meta-state that she revealed. Even at that early age she could already *anticipate* with *fear* going to the toilet. She had already enough reflexivity in her little mind to not only anticipate and hold constant the idea and experience of going to the potty, and its being unpleasant, but had come to *fear* it.

The state of pain was one thing, her *fear of* anticipating that pain was yet another. It was a higher level of mind, a meta-state. She was already setting a frame of fear about her own experiences or states. And, once we begin to become reflexive, we develop *self-reflexive* consciousness and use *language* to track and anchor such, and, as we do so repeatedly, it becomes our way of perceiving the world.

So here are the four meta-domains of state, then sensory movie awareness, then language, then perception set forth in terms of developmental psychology all coming together. We felt we were onto something.

The six-stage developmental process

As a result we created the following six-stage developmental process, which summarizes how these four domains fit together in a systemicmanner regarding the structure of our experiences. Ultimately, these four models refer to the *same thing*: subjective human experience. They look at the experience but through four different lenses to thereby give us four different points of view.

The Neuro-Linguistic States model of Meta-States

First, we experience states, neuro-sensory states cued by our internal movie of the world, a movie that we eventually come to hold in mind and manipulate with symbols. As we re-present what we have experienced through our sense receptors (eyes, ears, skin) we reproduce inside on a mental screen of the mind.

The meta-modalities of our "sub-modalities"

Then we begin to add structural features to our movies as we make them richer, fuller, more lifelike, and vivid. With maturity we learn to see, hear, and sense more exquisitely. We learn to make more refined distinctions and to use them in our symbolic encoding of meaning in our internal cinemas.

The language model of the Meta-Model

This supplies us with lots of words, sentences, and symbols by which we can encode and name the movie and classify the movie as belonging to this or that category, and so takes us upward in the mind to higher conceptual states (meta-states). This gives us the meta-representational system of language and abstract symbols.

As we move up to thinking about our thinking, feeling about our thinking, feeling about our feelings, we experience ever more complex states, meta-states, that comprise our meanings, concepts, and abstract categories.

The perception model of the Meta-Programs

As we keep using the same state (matching or mismatching, option or procedures, global or specific) about other states, the way we see things from those states become our perceptual filters. They habituate so that they become a program or pattern that frames most or all of our thinking in a given area. The meta-states have coalesced into our very neurology so that we perceive from the thinking pattern.

The Neuro-Semantics States model of Meta-States

We then have thoughts and feelings about our meta-programs, liking them or disliking them, validating them or rejecting them, and these become even higher level frames. The never-ending regress of reflexivity keeps moving us up in our mind so that we create not only frames of reference but frames of mind—which eventually become the very frameworks of how we experience ourselves as persons, hence "personality".

The interfacing of the meta-domains

The linguistic distinctions that we have and use in the Meta-Model also occur in the Meta-Programs as perceptual distinctions and, further, they show up in the thought-feeling distinctions of our meta-states.

We see this in the *global* or *gestalt thinking style* as a meta-program. We create this by overusing the *generalization patterns* of the Meta-Model (e.g., nominalization, universal quantifiers, lost performatives) and in setting a *global frame of reference*. This not only becomes a filter, but it becomes a mind-body state that will generate in us the sense of a global state.

A *necessity thinking style* as a meta-program distinction shows up as the "modal operator of necessity" when we look at it as a linguistic distinction of the Meta-Model. It is also a thought-feeling frame of reference that induces us into a state of necessity, pressure, compulsion, or obsession.

In other words, when we have an experience, all of these facets and dimensions of experience occur. It is at the same time a linguistic, perceptual, and state experience. These are all components of the system and they work self-reflexively on each other. This explains the complexity that we know and recognize in our mind-emotions-body organism. And over time these dynamic facets of our consciousness influence and create each other. We language our states, we see and encode our movies, we feel our language, we perceive our states, we perceive our language, and so on. All of these interactive parts mix and mingle and do so in such a way that we can easily get into a situation where it becomes difficult to know which variable is occurring or what we are doing with it at any given level.

The meta-domains interface model

Four domains govern the NLP adventure into experience. These four meta-domains describe four different models within NLP and yet they all describe the same referent: subjective experience. This gives us four routes to travel as we adventure into states. We have four avenues for exploring, playing, and transforming human experiences and "personality".

In these meta-domains we see the structural genius of NLP at its best. We have the Meta-Model of language that identifies the linguistic encoding and form of the mapping that anchors the sensory video that plays in the mind. The Meta-Model describes the linguistic magic of the mapping and how we move from the senses to the meta-representation system.

From the cinema of the mind full of sensory-based information and language we move upward into the meta-linguistic domain of evaluative words. These supply the words for the movie and narrate whatever story plays out in the theater of the mind. And they induce states. States and then states about those states. With the repetition of these states comes habituation, and with that the *magic* of meta-programs, those habitual ways of sorting and processing information.

These perceptual filters then govern our everyday thinking-and-feeling and so create our style or of perceiving. Yet, because these show up in language, we also find them in the Meta-Model. The *modals* that are our favorite describe our basic *modus operandi* ("modal operators") for moving through the world: such as necessity, impossibility, possibility, desire. We also have styles of reasoning, inductive, deductive, abductive (gestalt and detail), which lead us to sort for specific details or deductive global understandings.

Similarly, via the habituation process, any meta-program can become a *driving* perceptual style reflecting the meta-state from which it arose. A person who always thinks in terms of gestalts, in terms of the big picture, will always bring global and general thoughts-and-feelings to all experiences. We can similarly count on a person who sorts for necessity to bring a state of necessity, compulsion, "have-to-ness" to bear on every other thought-and-feeling state. In these ways, *driver* meta-programs reflect meta-states and meta-states create meta-programs.

Together these meta-domains describe our experiential reality in everyday life, namely our mind-body states of consciousness. By uniting them we can describe our states as systems of interactive forces that generate our felt "force fields" within which we live, think, perceive, feel, and act.

From primary state to multi-layered meta-states

The following *stages* offer a theoretical model of the systemic development of human consciousness and "personality" in terms of these four meta-levels as they develop from a simple primary-level state of consciousness into a multi-layered and multi-leveled meta-state.

Stage 1
We track over from our sense receptions of the world via our eyes, ears, skin, and other sensory organs into a mental world of sights, sounds, sensations, smells (the VAK), the mental movie that plays out on the screen of our consciousness, our primary level or state. We sense or experience these sensory representations of the world of stimuli as an internal cinema.

Stage 2
We then add our soundtrack to the cinema as we say words about the movie that we encode and re-present. The ability to "hold constant" our representations allows us to manipulate them as symbols or maps of the territory. With the meta-representational system of language, we begin using symbols and abstractions to stand in for the movie as well as to classify the movie, to categorize what it means to us.

Stage 3
As we go meta, we reflect back onto our states or on parts of our mind-body-emotional states and thereby create meta-states or meta-frames. Self-reflexive consciousness uses meta-representations to set frames about our experiences, meaning frames encoded in linguistics (the structure given by the Meta-Model), belief frames, thinking frames (the structure given by Meta-Programs), value frames, understanding frames, intentional frames. The meta-stating process is reflexive and never-ending, an infinite regress that creates "logical" levels ("psycho-logical" levels) and the higher neuro-semantic or conceptual states. As a

systemic process it generates new gestalts, systemic configurations of layered consciousness, or multiordinal realities.

Stage 4

As this habituation of thinking-feeling styles and states continues and becomes incorporated into our meta-linguistics, these styles *coalesce* into our primary-state experiences and so become literally "in-corporated". This embodiment of the higher levels of "mind" into muscle translates habitual and valued meta-states into perceptual filters or meta-programs.

Stage 5

As the higher levels of states or frames habituate and coalesce into the lower levels, the meta-level frames of reference and frames of meaning from the higher levels coalesce so that they enter into neurology itself. We no longer can see, hear, feel, or experience the world simply or purely. The recursive loops of feedback and feed-forward have now integrated the meta-representations of hundreds and thousands of beliefs so that they are in the body now. The layeredness of mind at all the meta-levels not only created an embeddedness of our states, but a systemic holoarchy structure of mind, body, and emotion. These now merge so that they are often undistinguishable. Doing so is what allows the higher states to *qualify* the primary states from which we encounter the world. This gives us textured states such as *joyful* learning, *compassionate* anger, *calm* fear, *thoughtful* frustration. Now the meta-frame operates as a self-organizing attractor in the whole system.

Stage 6

As the entire mind-body-emotion system continues to grow and evolve, new properties emerge, especially the larger matrices of the mind. These are the belief *systems* around various dominating concepts that set the frame for all the games that we play at the primary level. As mind becomes increasingly more layered, ideas and concepts are embedded in each other as frames, and a dynamic system of consciousness emerges. Higher domains of knowledge as frames-of-reference give direction as we navigate life.

Key properties of the meta-domains

1. Fluid unpredictability

The fluidity of the meta-levels in this model stands out saliently in contrast to the specifically named "logical levels" in previous attempts at a systemic model. To conceptualize this we have to think about the entire neuro-linguistic or neuro-semantic system as *fluid*, in flux, forever changing. It is not static, rigid, or permanent.

This fluidity means that we can bring *any* thought-feeling-physiology to bear on any other; that the infinite regress of always being able to think-feel about any previous frame never ends; that we can create all kinds of wild and unpredictable configurations. We not only meta-state with identity beliefs, but we can apply all kinds of other concepts to these concepts. When Korzybski described these levels as "second-order abstractions" or "third-order abstractions" he also noted that this both makes for complexity and lies at the source of "morbidity" in human semantic states.

2. Dominance of meta-levels

All of the meta-domains operate according to the mechanism that higher levels inevitably drive lower levels. When we abstract or generalize about our experiences or learning, we conceptually move "up" "logical levels". This has the effect of setting a frame of reference for the systemic network of embedded thinking. So as and when we "go inside", we go *up* into domains of knowledge and understanding, into embedded belief frames and systems, and up into conceptual matrices. Metaphorically, we store our referent experiences as the learning, generalizations, and conclusions that we draw from the experiences. We store such as a domain of knowledge, our values, our beliefs, and so forth. We "go in" and *up* to our frames of meaning, which give significance to that internal universe.

3. Meta-levels as being outside of conscious awareness

In the habituation process we lose conscious awareness of our mental, emotional, verbal, and behavioral responses. At that point, the neuro-pathways run the learned-response program without the need for consciousness. From a practical point of view, all of our meta-frames, whether in the form of what we call beliefs, values, meta-programs, memory of historical events, intentions, pleasures, expectations, decisions, metaphors, or whatever, rise up to become our highest frames, the framework of our entire person or personality.

Then, as we live our lives *embedded* inside and *governed by* those frames, we live and operate without awareness of them. As this frees our conscious awareness from keeping track of those tasks, it frees us to move on to discover and create new learning experiences. When we habitualize healthy frames, this creates personal freedom. But, when we habituate unhealthy frames, it installs those toxic meanings so that they do us much harm.

4. Multi-levels govern the change processes

What we call "experience" differs at every "logical" level because the term "experience", as a nominalization, is also a multiordinal term. What we call experience at the primary state involves what our neurology and neurological sense receptors (eyes, ears, skin, taste buds) are processing. At the thinking level, the movie that we're playing on the screen of our awareness determines our "experience".

As we move up the meta-levels, "experience" is determined more and more by the structure of our languaging, embedded frames, and reflexivity. The mechanism that predominantly governs and drives "experience" in the matrices of our mind are the *meta-representational systems* and how we use language and various symbolic systems.

This means that *change* and transformation of "experience" at each level will also differ. While kinesthetic anchors work very well at the first levels, as we move up the levels, we have to anchor through more symbolic systems, through reframing, metaphors, and nonpropositional language.

Recognizing the role of meta-levels and the nature of human psycho-logics enables us to understand the power and the "magic" of primary-level technology, such as anchoring and meta-level technology, that shows up in such patterns as the phobia-resolution pattern, time-lining, reframing, mind-lines, and core transformation. As we move up, transformation occurs through reframing and outframing.

5. "Modeling" itself differs according to the level at which we use this term

As "change" plays a different part and role at various levels, so does modeling. We can easily and efficiently model simple stimulus—response types of experiences using the flow- chart of our neuro-linguistics (the NLP-enriched TOTE model). Yet this does not work so well when we have various meta- moves within an experience. Modeling that takes the meta- levels into consideration means that we shift to tracking the upward vertical moves as mind-body-emotion awareness jumps logical levels and embeds what we have learned into higher frames.

6. Redundancy

Since the four meta-domains view the same phenomenon (subjective experience) through four different filters (language, perception, cinematic features, and states), it provides a fourfold analysis that overlaps and reinforces itself, thereby providing redundancy. As a result, this gives us a fourfold analysis for "personality" and the factors that govern it.

7. Systemic recursiveness

Because the Meta-States model starts from the primary-level experience of *a neurological state* that operates holistically as a mind-body, thought-emotion, brain-body system, it highlights our holistic nature and the nature of our experiences. Here the cognizing-emoting nature of consciousness itself takes in and processes information to create the first level of meaning. Thereafter, our consciousness becomes self-reflexive. Then, whatever we experience in terms of thinking-and-feeling, we will then entertain second, third, fourth and more thoughts-and-feelings about that.

Recursiveness in some early NLP presentations was looked upon as an entirely negative and useless mechanism. Trainers constantly warned about getting caught up in a negative and vicious downward spiral. No one seemed aware that, as we can spiral downward, we can also spiral upward in a positive way. That's called a virtuous spiral. It uses recursiveness to keep looping back onto oneself with resources and with frames that increase pleasure, productivity, balance, ecology, and health.

8. Personality's "force field"

What happens when we access a *state* and enter that state fully and completely? What happens to us when we fully experience a state? The answer is that we experience state-dependency. It becomes our whole world. It affects our learning, memory, imagination, communication, behavior, perception, and other aspects of our life.

We then experience "state" as a dynamic and fully energized neurological reality. This is the wonder and magic of neuro-linguistic and neuro-semantic states. When we step into one fully, its a trancelike state, a focus or genius state, and then it becomes our internal universe, which we use as an energy field.

Neuro-semantic states literally generate somatic and neurological *energies*. And why not? All of our abstracting from the world of energy manifestations occurs through our embodied neurology. We abstract from the world and turn one form of energy into bioelectrical, chemical, and mechanical. So, when we are in a strong and focused state, it consists of an energy system. It consists of mental-emotional energy derived from beliefs and values, understanding and memories, imagination and dreams, hopes and passions.

When we speak about *state-dependency* of learning, memory, perception, speech, and behavior then, we speak about the "force-field" energy of our states and its actual physical embodiment. As an embodied state it is real and actually correlates in the body; it has manifestations that we can learn to see and utilize. In this way the four-meta-domains model integrates the spatial metaphors and understanding that come out of advanced NLP work in "sub-modalities" and DHE.

EXERCISE: Meta-domain awareness

1. **In groups of three, one person presents a problem or a challenge.**

2. **Then together brainstorm to identify the four meta-domains in the problem by questioning and exploring "the problem". Find and record the Meta-Model linguistic distinctions, the Meta-Program filters, "Sub-Modalities", and the Meta-State experiences.**

3. **The design is not to "solve" the problem, but to *model* it with these four perspectives.**

Summary

To create a unified field theory of NLP we need to bring together all the component pieces, models, submodels, technologies, and so forth. We reviewed two major attempts at this in this chapter in order to identify their strengths and weaknesses so that we can avoid the weaknesses and build on their strengths.

We have here offered a third attempt at a systemic NLP model using the four meta-domains. This is just a beginning. We offer it to suggest some possibilities as we build a model that truly unifies all of the pieces of NLP into a coherent system, backed up by a coherent explanatory theory.

Part Four

Modeling with Systemic NLP

Chapter Sixteen
The NLP-Enriched Strategy Model

With the four meta-domains as four models for mastery, we're ready for modeling. This is the heart of NLP. As a model, NLP began as a modeling project and it will continue to grow and develop from modeling. In this chapter, we review and expand the NLP Strategy model and describe how we use strategy elicitation as one of the foundational steps in modeling. In the next chapter, we add the meta-levels to modeling as part of our mastery of this field. The key to learning and mastering strategy elicitation and modeling is in the doing.

The strategy of experience

In NLP, "strategies" refers to how we accomplish or perform a task or gain an experience. We can identify a strategy for motivation and depression, for decision and indecision, for implementing tasks and procrastinating, for feeling happy and pleased and for feeling crabby and irritable. We have strategies for reading and comprehending, for getting along with people, dealing with hotheads, eating, exercising, staying healthy and vital, for loving and for feeling loved. We have strategies for every experience, for every state, for every skill.

A strategy is made of the same stuff as are all of the rest of our neuro-linguistic experiences—the sensory representations that make up our internal movie and the features of our somatic kinesthetics. So, when we unpack a strategy, we detail the specific representational steps that we engage in as we put ourselves in state and achieve some behavior performance.

Of course, it is not as simple as it sounds. The trick is being able to catch a strategy that operates sometimes in milliseconds.

In the beginning, there was the TOTE

It was not long after the discovery of the representation-systems model that the early NLP co-founders linked those pieces of subjective experiences and came up with the Strategies model. It would be interesting to know who of those early NLPers first read *The Plans and Structure of Behavior*. This was the book by the early developers of the Cognitive Movement in psychology (George Miller, Eugene

Gallanter, and Paul Pribram) that set forth the Test-Operate-Test-Exit (TOTE) model. It was the TOTE model that Bandler and Grinder used as their framework in their first formal modeling. They enriched it with the representational systems to create a TOTE-enriched model that we call the strategies model. The fullest description of all of this occurs in Robert Dilts's classic work, *Neuro-Linguistic Programming, Volume I: The Study of the Structure of Subjective Experience* (1980).

It is the NLP enriched-TOTE model or the Strategies model that provides the foundation of NLP modeling. This does not mean that strategy work *is* the same thing as modeling. It is not. Many have drawn that conclusion and confused strategy work with modeling, yet the two are different. This becomes obvious, in fact, when we think about the first NLP modeling. When we think about Bandler and Grinder modeling Perls, Satir, and Erickson, we don't find any descriptions of their strategies. That's not how they went about modeling them.

The Strategy model

The NLP Strategy model provides a way to track the steps of an experience. Using the TOTE format, a strategy identifies how we test things to see how they measure up to our expectations, standards and values, operates on things to change something, tests again to see if it now works according to the standards, and then finally exits the "program."

What do we mean by a "strategy" in NLP? The word refers to the series of *representational steps* that move from some original stimulus to some final response. As such, it gives more detail and richness to the old Stimulus-Response Model. Based upon the TOTE model, the Strategies model enriches TOTE with the representational steps.

We discover a person's strategy for a given piece of behavior by eliciting the strategy using elicitation questions. This means that we explore *how* a person does something.

- "What a skill you have in depressing yourself! How do you do that?"
- "If I could be you for a day, what would I need to do to take your place?"

After we elicit the strategy, we can then represent the strategy as a step-by-step procedure. Doing this enables us to replicate it, change or redesign it, or utilize it in a new situation. "First you make a picture, then you say these words to yourself, experience this sensation ..." "Strategies" refers to the specific sequences of representations (both internal and external) that lead to a specific outcome. We speak of strategies in terms of outcomes: motivation, decision, convincer, learning, selling, for example.

The development of the Strategies model

The TOTE model arose as an update on the old Stimulus-Response (S-R) model of the reflex arc that had dominated psychology in the twentieth century. It updated the S-R model by incorporating two very critical elements in its modeling of human experience: *feedback and outcome.*

Robert Dilts (1980) writes:

> There is feedback from the result of the action of the testing phase, and we are confronted by a recursive loop. The simplest kind of diagram to represent this conception of reflex action-an alternative to the classical reflex arc-would have to look something like figure 2.1. [p. 23]

The refined model of the TOTE offered a *formal format* of the internal processing sequence which gets triggered by a stimulus. The tests in the model referred to the conditions that the operation had to meet before the response would occur. In feedback phase, the system operates to change some aspect of the stimulus or of the person's internal state to satisfy the test.

Dilts, *et al.* illustrated the working of a TOTE with tuning in a radio station:

> When you adjust the volume dial on your radio or stereo, you continually test the sound volume by listening to it. If the volume is too low, you operate by turning the knob clockwise. If you overshoot and the volume becomes too loud, you operate by turning the knob counterclockwise to reduce the intensity of the sound. When you have adjusted the amplifier to the appropriate volume, you exit from the "volume-adjusting" TOTE and settle into your comfortable armchair to continue reading.

> What do the arrows represent? What could flow along them from one box to another? We shall discuss three alternatives: energy, information, and control. [p. 27]

The founders of the Cognitive Movement in psychology, Miller, Galanter, and Pribram, structured TOTE to identify the flow of information through a system. To do that, they used the method of measuring information that Norbert Wiener and Claude Shannon had only recently developed. Dilts *et al.* then discussed the concept of "control" in the system. Namely, they described information as "a set of instructions" controlling responses or behavior:

> It is the notion that what flows over the arrows in figure 2.2 is an intangible something called *control*. The arrows may indicate only succession. This concept appears most frequently in the discussion of computing machines, where the control of the machine's operations passes from one set of instructions to another, successively, as the machine proceeds to execute the list of instructions that comprise the program it has been given.

> Imagine you look up a particular topic in a book. You open the book to the index and find the topic. As you look up each page reference in turn, your behavior can be described as under the control of that list of numbers, and control is transferred from one number to the next as you proceed through the list. The transfer of control could

be symbolized by drawing arrows from one page number to the next, but the arrows would have a meaning quite different from the two meanings mentioned previously. [p. 30]

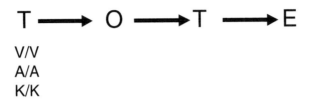

Figure 16.1

Operating in the test stage reveals congruity or incongruity. Does our map of the world (the ideas, expectations, desires, and so forth in our head) fit with our experience of the world? If we experience incongruity between the two, we loop back to the first test. If we find congruity between map and experience, we exit.

This model also maps out and demonstrates the importance of continually applying resources to a present state in order to achieve a new outcome state. We keep operating on the *difference* between map and territory. Success comes from repeatedly testing present states against desired outcomes, and then accessing and applying resources until we bring about a congruency between the two states.

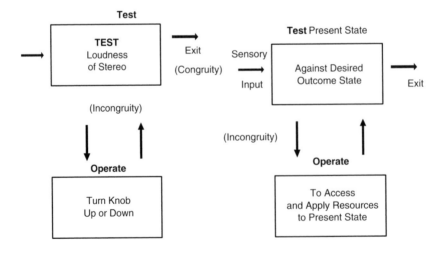

Figure 16.2: Diagram of TOTE model

In this way, the TOTE model presupposes that we can achieve *behavioral excellence* through having:

- Specified a future goal of what we want;
- The sensory and behavioral evidence or cues indicating the achievement of the goal;
- A range of operations, procedures, and choices by which we can reach the goal.

Bandler and Grinder did not invent the Strategy model out of thin air. They began with the TOTE model and enriched it with the distinctions that they discovered.

The enriched TOTE model

In this way, the co-founders of NLP discovered or invented or polished up the Strategy model from the TOTE of the cognitive psychologists who developed that model as a more complete elaboration on the old S-R model. This was their "time-binding". Korzybski explained that we bind time when we build upon the discoveries of earlier inventors so that we do not have to reinvent the computer.

The TOTE provided the basic format for describing a specific sequence of behavior. It described a sequence of activities that consolidates into a functional unit of behavior that typically executes below the threshold of consciousness. Then, designating this process as a mental strategy, Dilts, Bandler, Grinder, Bandler-Cameron, and DeLozier (1980) integrated the TOTE as a template into the NLP model. This enriched and extended the TOTE so that it included the representational pieces, such as sensory representational systems, the distinctions of these sensory modalities ("sub-modalities"), eye accessing cues, and linguistic predicates.

The result was a model that allows us to unpack an unconscious strategy, anchor the elements together, reframe the meanings involved, and design, redesign, and/or install a strategy. These new enrichments more fully articulated a model for modeling experience as it looked further and deeper into the "black box". At the same time it provided a much more extensive and precise language.

In these ways NLP refined the TOTE model. It specified how we do our testing and operating in terms of the sensory systems and the precise distinctions in those systems. As the NLP co-founders restated Test conditions and Operations as taking place through the representational systems, they greatly refined the S-R and TOTE models.

For instance, a person could compare external/internal visually remembered (V^e/V^i) to test something: "Does this spelling look like the way I remembered that it should look?"

Or one could do it in the kinesthetic system (K^e/K^i) or in the auditory (A^e/A^i). The experience of congruence (which leads to exiting a program), and incongruence (which can keep one looping inside a program) also shows up as represented through one of the representational systems.

In this model, a Test may take place between two internally stored or generated representations. Tests may be of, say, the intensity, size, or color of a representation. A person may require that a certain sensation, sound, or sight reach a certain threshold value before it produces a sufficient signal to exit a program.

Since most people seem to generally prefer one representational system (RS) over another, RS primacy describes how we use our most highly valued RS in performing Tests and Operations. We often do this even when it does not work very well for us and sometimes even when it creates difficulties and limitations.

In the refined NLP Strategy model, modeling effectiveness often involves matching the appropriate RS to the task (e.g., visual RS to spelling, auditory to music). In fact, one goal of TOTE and RS analysis is precisely this, finding the most appropriate RS for the TOTE steps that enable us to obtain our desired outcome in the smallest number of steps. When we can do this, we say that our model has elegance. The Strategy model provides a new focus and motivation about our RS. It shows that all of our RSs are resources for improving learning and performance.

For example, consider spelling strategies. A phonetic strategy for spelling entails a sequence of $A^e \rightarrow A^i/A^e$. Yet, because the visual coding of the English language does not follow phonetic rules, people who use a visual strategy for spelling consistently outperform those who use auditory strategies. The sounding-out strategy works very well for oral reading presentations. It does not work so well for spelling. A typical visual strategy for spelling involves a step of steps as in the following figure.

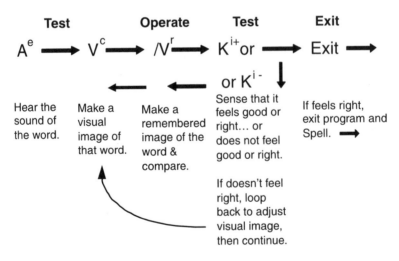

Figure 16.3: Spelling TOTE

Mastering NLP, Understanding the TOTE

Mastering NLP involves understanding the TOTE model for a number of reasons. First, TOTE provides a most fundamental tracking of "mind" through its representational steps. Further, the TOTE steps are implicitly inside most NLP patterns. Third, TOTE provides a basic organization of a system, any system, and so allows us to move from linear thinking to nonlinear or systemic thinking. It does this by working with the basic idea of feedback loops as part of representational steps.

Figure 16.4: The TOTE model

The first Test
The first Test is the cue or the trigger that initiates the strategy. We use the criteria as we feed forward what we want. Applying this to a decision strategy, we ask:

- What lets you know it is time to decide? How do you do that?
- When do you begin deciding?
- Are there any other external stimuli that cue you to decide?

The Operation
We can operate in a number of ways. We can access data that we need. We may remember such data, create it from scratch, gather information from others as required by the strategy. We can operate by changing things inside ourselves, our criteria and standards; we can operate by changing things in the outside world. In eliciting the information about the persons operating, we ask:

- What information do you want? How do you know to look for that information?
- What do you get the information from? How do you know to do that?
- You must recognize there are alternatives-how do you know this?
- How do you generate alternatives?

The second Test
The second Test occurs after we have operated on ourselves or the world. Now we take a new reading to see how things measure up, or fail to measure up, to our expectations and desires. In the second Test we make a comparison of some aspect of the accessed data with the criteria. We elicit this by asking:

- What are you measuring now?
- How do you do that measuring or comparing?
- How do you represent it?
- How do you evaluate the alternatives?
- What has to be satisfied in order for you to decide?

The Exit

The exit refers to the time when the strategy has fulfilled its purpose and is now exiting that program. In a decision strategy, we are at the decision point because that's what a strategy for deciding does. Typically, when a strategy completes its task and has succeeded, it exits; although sometimes we will run a strategy over and over without succeeding and then we will exit as a way of giving up on the strategy. Prior to giving up or succeeding, we will use the second Test as a cue to cycle back to the Operation stage if the evaluation fails to match its objective. In eliciting this facet of the strategy we ask:

- How do you know when to exit the program?
- How do you know when you are done—that you have succeeded in making a decision?
- How do you know to give up and exit the strategy?

A demonstration with unpacking a strategy

Randy had a terrible habit of confronting people whenever they would do anything "wrong". He had a style of moving through the world looking for errors and problems that affected him and immediately letting the person know. This was also his strength—he worked in quality control in a technology company. But Randy knew that it made enemies and put people off. He didn't have many friends, he didn't get along with people at work very well, he was not promoted or included in on decisions, and he couldn't keep an intimate relationship. When he asked for some assistance, I first wanted to find out how he created his limitations.

"So when do you know it's time to confront?"

"Well, just about any time something is wrong. When I see a mistake, I just have to tell a person about it."

"So if you're standing in line at the airport and you notice a couple fussing and one of them states something wrong, you have to confront them?"

"No, no. It's not like that. I wouldn't do that. It's not my business."
"So, when is it your business?"

"It's my business when it affects me. If someone makes a mistake that affects me, then I have to confront them about that."

"You have to straighten them out!"

"Well, yeah. It's more that I need to let them see their error."

"And straighten out their thinking so that they know better and see the error of their ways!"

"That sounds so harsh when you put it that way."

"So you don't have to straighten them out?"

"Well, yes I do."

"On any mistake?"

"Yes."

"If they misquote a date, or say that so-and-so is thirty-seven instead of thirty-eight?"

"Yes. It's the principle of the thing."

"What's occurring inside you to let you know that you have to do this?"

"It's an urgency. I feel that I just have to."

"Or ...? What will happen if you don't?"

"Well, error."

"And so what's the big deal if a person is thirty-eight but someone says thirty-seven? What's so bad about an error?"

"I just feel bad. There's a tension right here [*holding stomach*] and it then starts radiating out to my chest."

"So you get this feeling of a tension in your body, in your organs and muscles. And what is it that lets you know to experience that tension?"

"Their error."

"How do you represent their error? Is it something you see or hear or what?"

"Well, yes, I see their error and compare it to a more perfect picture, then I just know that it's wrong and I say so."

"So you have two pictures. Are these snapshots or movies?"

"Usually movies."

"And if I were to peek into the theater of your mind, what are they like? Color, close, three-dimensional, et cetera?"

"The perfect movie has more color and is bigger and closer and the other is much less so ... This is interesting. No wonder the other ones never measure up! My perfect movie is so much more real and compelling."

"Then the voice, is that your voice? What are the qualities of the soundtrack in here and the words themselves."

"The words are usually, 'This is wrong; this is not right!' And the tone is kind of angry, fairly loud, and there's a demandingness to the tone. It's like a surround-sound theater."

"As you experience that, then what happens?"

"I feel an urgency to do something, say something."

"And what is that urgency about? It's intent or purpose?"

"To stop the voice. That's interesting: I didn't know that. It's to make the voice stop. I hate that voice."

"So, when you say those words aloud to the person, do you use that same tonality?"

"Yes, I guess I do."

"Then what happens?"

"Then the voice goes away."
While there was a lot more in this elicitation, even with this bit we can see how the experience works, and the structure of its logic. Interesting enough, Randy found that, through the very process of the elicitation, things began to change. His own insights and awareness of how he created the experience put him at choice point. Later we found that by playing around with lowering the internal voice and making the "perfect" movie in the theater of his mind less compelling, he was much less driven to criticize. He also learned to turn this quality-control program off with personal relationships.

The pattern for strategy elicitation

Suppose you wanted the recipe for a delicious dish. What do you need in order to create that delicious dish? You would need specific information about such things as the ingredients to use, the amounts, the order for mixing them together, and the oven temperature. The same kind of thing holds with regard to detecting and using the structure of subjective experiences to create an experience of excellence. The following offers the basic pattern for eliciting a strategy.

EXERCISE
1. Prepare yourself for eliciting a strategy.
Step fully into an uptime state so that you are fully present with the other person. Access the beliefs, values, and states of mind and emotion that will enable you to establish rapport with the person.

2. Begin by establishing a positive frame for rapport.
Set the frame of your outcome with the person you are eliciting the strategy from.

"You do that very well! Would you mind teaching me how to do that?"

"Suppose I lived your life for a day, how would I do this?"

3. Access the state.
The person needs to fully and congruently associate with the skill or state. To fully elicit their strategy, you may want to take the person back to the place where the behavior naturally occurs. Doing that lets the context, with its natural anchors (e.g., sitting at typewriter), elicit the response. Or we can elicit the state by reproducing a portion of the context (e.g., tonality, gestures, playacting).

- What is the referent event?
- What strategy are you going to elicit?
- When, where, with whom does this occur?

Invite the person to step back into the experience: "I would like you to describe the event fully and to do so until you re-experience it congruently and intensely."

4. Intensify the state.
In elicitation, you will want to amplify and intensify the state. Doing this helps because the more of the state you evoke, the more of the experience you will have to work with. This will also enable you to more fully access the state.

5. Explore the "how".
"How do you do this?" If the person has conscious awareness of their strategy, they will tell you. If not, look for them to demonstrate it—and to do so unthinkingly. Eliciting primarily involves good questioning techniques by which you induce a person to carry out a task (actually or just in thought) that requires the strategy.

- "Have you ever experienced a time when you really felt really motivated to do something?"

- "When did you last feel naturally and powerfully motivated?"
- "How do you experience the state of feeling exceptionally creative?"
- "Have you ever gotten into a situation where you felt very creative?"

Typically, accessing questions involve a person recalling an experience.

- "What did it feel like?"
- "How did you do it?"
- "When do you feel best able to do it?"
- "What do you need in order to do it?"
- "What happens as you do it?"
- "When did that last occur?"

Questions such as these encourage a person to "go inside" where they then access their memory banks. Classic NLP used the phrase "transderivational search" (TDS) from transformational grammar to describe this process. This big mouthful of a phrase means that we search inside our mind for references and referent structures. We all engage in TDS processes to "make sense" of things, deal with stimuli, and recreate states and experiences. In elicitation, we use the TDS process to assist someone to go back through their constructs of past times to recover the structure of the experience.

In Neuro-Semantics, we use a different metaphor and framework in how we think about this. Instead of "going down" to a "deep" structure, we think about the structuring of the levels of mind as providing "higher" frames. Accordingly, we think about the referencing process as "going in" and then "up" to access our frames-of-reference. This offers a slightly different picture of the same process. We think of our history of experiences as a meta-level frame of reference, as our *history frame*. With this change of metaphor (up rather than down), we think about searching our reference frames as the embedded matrices of meaning.

6. Calibrate from an uptime state.
Unpacking strategies necessitates that we become fully alert and open to the person's external cues. Only when we are "up" and in the present moment can we effectively calibrate to the person's state as we watch our expert demonstrate the very strategy that creates the state. People will typically *demonstrate* their processing and structuring as they talk about problems, outcomes, or experiences. This mind-body connection gives us lots of redundant information. So we become attentive to such "instant replays", in order to note how the person cycles through the sequence of representations that leads to the experience or behavior.

7. Ask the person to exaggerate.
If you do not get the strategy upon first questioning, invite the person to exaggerate some small portion of the strategy. Exaggerating one step in a strategy may also access other representations linked to it synesthetically.

8. Stay meta to the content.

Since strategies operate as a purely formal structure, this necessitates that you "go meta" to the structuring process itself. This enables you to avoid getting caught up in the content and to notice the formatting itself.

Using strategy analysis for mind-tracking

Dilts *et al.* (1980) summarized strategies and strategy analysis in this way:

> All of our overt behavior is controlled by internal processing strategies. Each of you has a particular set of strategies for motivating yourself out of bed in the morning, for delegating job responsibilities to employees, for learning and teaching, for conducting business negotiations, and so on." [p. 26]

As we analyze the sequence and composition of a strategy by decomposing its structure into its components of representations, we discover its order or sequence. In doing this we *track* the activities and responses of the mind and follow where a brain goes in its representing as it creates neurological experiences. This involves performing Tests on input, Operating on the representations, perhaps looping around in the second Test until we eventually Exit the program in moving toward an outcome.

Taking this as a metaphor, we can think about the *representations* as functioning as digits on a telephone. To get to our desired party, we have to push the buttons on the phone in a certain sequence. Similarly, sequencing our internal representations also leads to various outcomes. It all depends on both the signals that we punch in and the order in which we punch them. If we punch in a sequence of representational activity (seeing this, hearing that, feeling this) that leads to accessing mental-emotional resources, then we have *modeled the structure* of that experience.

By the same token, we *mis-strategize* when we apply highly valued strategies in inappropriate contexts. We may use a strategy sequence that could work wonders in accomplishing some outcomes and creating some behaviors, but, when misapplied, can create problems and limitations. This happens when we use an auditory strategy to spell or a visual strategy to read aloud. Other problems can also arise in our strategies. For example, we may develop inflexibility or we may overgeneralize our strategies. We may get stuck in them, looping around without an exit, like certain phobic responses. We may build up less than useful strategies such as losing our temper and flying into a rage over small things, jumping to conclusions, acting without thinking, personalizing other people's misbehaviors. We may mis-strategize by tuning into inappropriate information in another representation system.

Mastering the Strategies model

Tracking a neuro-linguistic mind-body system through its sequences enables us to *replicate an experience*. To do this presupposes numerous skills. Given that a strategy identifies where the brain goes and how it responds along the way, then in order to produce similar results we have to minimally do the following:

- Identify and detect strategies
- Elicit and unpack strategies (using eye accessing cues, physiology cues, and linguistic markers)
- Interrupt and alter strategies
- Design new strategies and/or redesign old ones
- Install strategies and design installation plans
- Utilize a strategy in a different context

These are the *strategy skills*. They presuppose that we have developed awareness and sensitivity to the signs and cues that indicate the operating of a strategy. This means we need to develop high-level skills to manage a strategy as we elicit it. The strategy-elicitation process also presupposes other skills: anchoring, reframing, pacing, for instance. It implies the ability to do comparative analysis between strategies as well. When we can do all of this, we can design better strategies.

In strategy unpacking, we unpack unconscious strategies to make them conscious. Of course, when a behavior has attained the status of a TOTE, its signal level lies outside consciousness. We no longer know explicitly the details of each step. This requires much skill and practice in making these unconscious strategies explicit.

Using the SCORE model for modeling

Robert Dilts extensively uses the SCORE model in modeling and refers to it as an "Applied Modeling" strategy. The SCORE model essentially involves gathering information using the format, "present state leads to desired state". Using it allows us to specify the distinctions that define the "problem space"—the symptoms of that space and the causes that lead to the symptoms. From there we specify the distinctions that make up the desired outcome—the resources necessary to move us there and the effects that then result.

In unpacking a strategy and finding an expert's model, we look first at the symptoms and causes (present state) that an expert responds to. Then we look at the outcome of expertise that the expert has achieved. We then inquire about the resources that make that possible, that create the bridge from one place to the other, and then the effects of that outcome and how they play a role in the expert's motivation or intention.

In using the SCORE model, we will first need to identify the symptoms and causes that define the problem space. This elicits a fuller description of the problem state. Then we elicit a description of the resources that moves one from that present state to the desired outcome state.

SCORE modeling questions

Symptoms
What are the specific, observable, or measurable symptoms to be addressed by the model?

Causes
What are the causes, contributing influences of the symptoms?

Outcomes
What is the outcome (desired state) to be attained?

Effects
What long-term positive effects will be achieved by modeling the expert?

Resources
What resources does the expert have that creates the excellence?

Strategies for modeling

Strategy work begins the modeling process. For that reason, understanding what we do in gathering a strategy of an experience provides the foundational framework for modeling. As a summary, here are some of the most essential frames that allow us to effectively gather a strategy and begin a modeling project.

Begin with rapport. As with everything we do in NLP, we begin by establishing rapport with a person. In strategy work, this means matching and pacing the expert's experience and setting frames that make the process feel safe and respectful. We gain rapport not only at the level of physical matching, but also at the conceptual level. We match the person's values and criteria for being professional and respectful. Without this, we will not be able to obtain high-quality information from the expert.

Begin with a well-formed outcome in mind. This is another NLP basic. Even if we are not sure precisely what we are seeking to model, we at least need to develop some idea before we begin strategy elicitation. This is where a review of the literature regarding a specific area of expertise or field can catch us up on what has already been discovered. Then, using the well-formed outcome pattern, we can clarify our own mind with regard to what is relevant and what is not. Many a modeling project has floundered and crashed due to skipping this step.

Clarify if you are wanting to model a product (Modeling I) or a person (Modeling II) or both. This is part of having a well-formed outcome. Do you want to model *what* someone does, or the end result of that person's actions so that you can then replicate it as you train others? Or do you want to model the attitude, spirit, and higher states of mind of the expert that allow the expert to do what he or she does in the first place?

Set yourself for pattern detection. At the heart of strategy elicitation and modeling is seeing, hearing, and detecting patterns. This means the ability to think in terms of structuring, formatting, sequencing, and so on. It is in this sense that modeling necessitates the ability to move above content to structure. This is why we use the TOTE model. We want to get a sense of the beginning and end of the sequence. That structural understanding allows us to then punctuate where to start and when to stop.

Set yourself to look for structure, no matter how dynamic the state or experience. By recognizing that tornadoes, the way baseball players play ball, how a mathematician thinks, how we depress, panic, and traumatize ourselves all have structure, we set ourselves to detect that structure. Sorting for structure becomes our meta-frame.

Be prepared to go meta. In both strategy elicitation and modeling, we will want to know not only the sequence of steps but also the higher frameworks. This means the ability to be aware of and skilled with logical or meta-levels and to recognize when a person has made a meta-jump to a higher level. The nature of systemic processes—with forces, leverage points, feedback and feed-forward loops, and the emergence of new properties—necessitates this kind of skill. It means awareness of the interface connections between levels and what to anticipate in terms of the relationships between the variables in a system.

Be prepared to backtrack to keep focused. Not only will we be moving forward and upward, but also backward. Going backward, in fact, gives us the ability constantly to backtrack and to check where we are in the process. This allows us to recap where we are and to check with the expert if we are getting it.

Give yourself to extensive search and research in your explorations. In eliciting strategies and in creating models we need several very resourceful states: persistence, a no-quit sense of curiosity, the ability to tolerate ambiguity. After all, we are exploring unconscious competence and so have to ask lots of questions in order to tease out the pattern behind the experience.

Keep checking your own states. Because this work involves being in the right kinds of states, we need to make sure that we have access to the appropriate states. We will need states of, for instance, intense curiosity, sensory acuity, adventure, exploration, respect, wonder, persistence.

Keep developing your modeling tools. We have many tools now in NLP and NS for eliciting strategies and creating models. We have the four meta-domains. These allow us to model the language of an experience, the perceptual filters, the cinematic features of our internal movies, the states, and the levels. We can also use the SCORE model, the SOAR, the well-formed-outcome pattern. To effectively create new models, we need to use all the tools we can, practice using them, and continually be aware that sometimes we create submodels or patterns as stepping stones to yet other models.

Keep refining your skills of discrimination. In pattern detection and the use of multiple tools, we will want to continually refine our ability to make distinctions. This begins as we use our knowledge of strategy analysis, the sequencing of sensory representational steps through the TOTE model format, and it continues as we learn to make even finer discriminations as we separate what's important in a strategy from what is accidental. This distinguishes the things necessary for a process to work from the extras. It also leads us to what we call *modeling elegance*—a phrase that refers to obtaining the fewest variables that are absolutely necessary to make a pattern work. When we have that, we have "modeling elegance."

Summary

By *strategy* in NLP we refer to the step-by-step process that enables us to move from initial input to a system (some stimuli) to final output (response). This gives us the most basic structure for modeling.

When we get a strategy, we are only "modeling" in a very limited sense of the term. Actually, we are simply identifying the sequential structure of one strategy. Modeling involves much more.

In Neuro-Semantic modeling, we take the meta-levels of an experience fully into account as the embedded frames of reference that govern the entire embodied semantic system—the subject of our next chapter.

Chapter Seventeen
Modeling Using Meta-Levels
Strategy Models in NLP

There's a wonderful thing about identifying a strategy. When we identify a person's strategy for a behavior or skill, we can then create a rough model that describes how that person achieves his or her outcome. When we do this repeatedly with numerous experts, we gather multiple strategies. This then allows us to build an even more effective model that can be used more widely. Because one person's strategy may involve lots of idiosyncratic features that may not transfer to others very well, modeling typically begins by gathering many strategies. From there, we reduce the strategies to common features and then test to find out which variables are essential and necessary. This allows us to create a bare-bones model. From there, we can begin testing the model with experimental groups and adding other features to it to make it more practical for replicating the particular expertise.

Modeling grows out of strategy work. Through unpacking the strategies of experts, refining and redesigning the strategies, using the literature of a particular performance for adding required variables, we can build models.

It was in this way that NLP modeling began. It started with the exploration of a strategy: how could Richard Bandler as a college student pick up on the linguistic and behavioral skills of Perls and Satir and replicate their expertise? John Grinder took the transformational-grammar model about linguistic patterns, the general-semantics model about the map-territory distinction, and the TOTE model and began tracking the strategy. Then they went to Perls and Satir to find some of the distinctions and variables in how they produced their magic.

In this way they modeled the structure of the patterns that governed the magic these wizards performed with their words. Actually they performed very little modeling of the wizards themselves. Primarily they sought to find out what the wizards did in their language patterns that created transformation in people. Only later did they begin to wonder about the wizards themselves, and how they were able to train their own intuitions to function as they did. From that arose the set of general distinctions that we call the NLP presuppositions. In this way, Grinder and Bandler sneaked some theory into the field of NLP. These presuppositions actually contain the meta-levels of attitudes and meta-states that defined the frames of mind from which Perls, Satir, and Erickson operated.

This gives us two facets of strategy work and modeling. We can model what an expert does (his or her products and skills) and we can model how an expert actually performs the expertise (the attitude, state, and frame of mind that creates the products). Recognizing these two parts of strategy work, Wyatt Woodsmall has labeled them Modeling I and Modeling II. One occurs at the primary level of experience (the products of the experts); the other occurs at the meta-level of experience (the mind or spirit of the expert).

Figure 17.1: Modeling I and II

Modeling I: The art and skills of the expert that produce a behavior or skill. The strategy of *how something works.* Modeling I is getting the strategy for spelling, effective marketing, parenting, weight control, writing, motivation, creativity, and so on.

Primary Level:

— The What
— Content
— Products

Modeling II: The art and skills of getting the expert's strategy for his or her state of mind emotion, body—the attitude or frame that creates the expertise in the first place. The strategy of the mental-emotional structuring of the experts.

Meta-level:
— The How
— Attitude, Spirit
 Frame of Mind

The Strategy model gives us the ability to track the flow of a person's brain-body (neuro-linguistic functioning). With it we can create a flowchart from an original stimulus in the world to the expert's final response. As such, this model puts into our hands a more extensive description of how any subjective experience creates the results it does.

Rising above the limitations of the strategy model

In spite of the value of the TOTE model, and of the NLP-enriched version, the Strategy model, both models have a limitation. They are mostly and predominantly linear rather than nonlinear. Despite the fact that both models included within them a meta-move, both mostly represent the structure of experience as a step-by-step process. Both represent experience as sequential and linear. So, even though they include the system features of feedback loops, the models are weak in presenting things systemically.

That's why we have intentionally added meta-levels to the Strategy model to create Neuro-Semantic modeling. Doing this allows us to recognize and work with the meta-levels (also called "logical levels") in our work with strategies. Originally this arose from a modeling project, when I (MH) was working on resilience. Out of that work came the discovery of meta-states and the development of the Meta-States model.

Adding meta-levels to our work with strategies means that we recognize that every representational step occurs inside multiple levels of embedded frames. It is these embedded frames that serve as our reference systems for such concepts as meaning, purpose, value, belief, criteria, and self.

Using Meta-Levels in Strategies

Imagine trying to write out the strategy formula sequentially for the following:

> Sometimes I get really upset when John doesn't come through with what he said he would do, and I feel like yelling at him. But then I feel really bad for the ugly angry thoughts I entertain. I feel like I'm a really bad mother. I wonder if I can parent at all. So then I start to feel guilty. But, with the counseling I've had, I then feel ashamed that I've fallen back into the old guilt habit, and know that I'm going to be stuck in this dysfunctional way for the rest of my life. Then, feeling depressed about that, I go to the kitchen and eat.

Although we can track down all the representational steps, and can even then identify all the mind-body states of consciousness thereby elicited, we find that kind of strategizing and state analysis difficult and convoluted when it contains within it numerous logical levels.

The woman began with an anger state. Then to that state she went into the state of self-judgment ("bad" for ugly angry thoughts, "bad mother," questions parenting ability). About her self-judgment state, she then felt guilty. And about the guilt state about her self-judgment state about her anger state she accessed a state of shame. And about the shame state she went into depressed state.

To track and analyze this multilayered state of consciousness wherein self-reflexive consciousness keeps looping back onto itself with the Meta-States model provides a way to sort that includes meta-levels. This enables us to understand the kind and quality of states she brought to bear on her other states.

Modeling the higher levels of mind and meaning

These illustrations with spelling and anger demonstrate the importance of recognizing these higher (meta) "logical levels". The representations at the primary level do not solely determine the meaning of the experience. To discern what the representations mean, we have to recognize and consider the higher frames within which the primary experience is embedded. In terms of strategy elicitation and unpacking, this invites us to move up to the contexts within contexts in which a given person's thinking-and-emoting and behaving occur.

Not all meaning occurs at the same level. There are levels of meaning as there are levels of abstraction, as we noted in Chapter Five. For instance, we can sort out the levels of meaning in the following way:

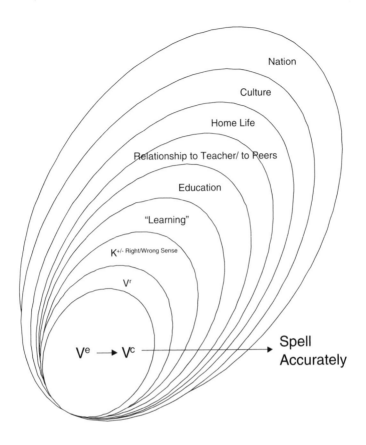

Figure 17.2: Meta-levels in the spelling strategy

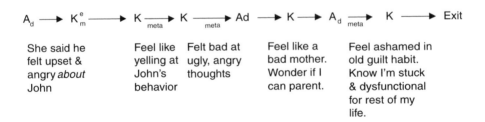

Figure 17.3

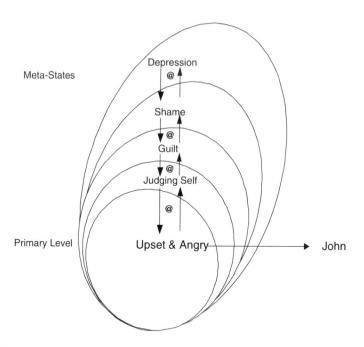

Figure 17.4

1. Associative meaning
At the primary level there is the meaning created by the way we link or associate things together. There is stimulus-response meaning. Which is linked to which? Which internal states or significance (IS) is linked to this external behavior or stimulus (EB)?

2. Representational meaning
At the primary level also, there is the meaning that is encoded in the brain in terms of representation. How have you encode this linkage? How do you represent this association? When you see it, hear it, or feel it, how do you encode it in the internal movie of your mind? What are the cinematic features of your movie? Are the pictures and sounds close or far, bright/dim, loud/quiet, fuzzy/clear?

3. Contextual or frame meaning
At meta-levels, we have contextual meaning, the meaning that is determined and governed by the contexts or frames. What concepts, abstractions, or understandings have we set as a frame about the representation of the association?

Thinking systemically in modeling

When we add meta-levels to our work with strategies, our eliciting, unpacking, designing, and installing of strategies becomes much more systemic. Then we can

313

track "mind" even when it goes round and round in circles and spirals. Mind, after all, does that. It reflects back onto itself. This is one of the factors that make strategy elicitation tricky. Our brains do not respond in a strictly linear, step-by-step process.

The system that comprises our mind, emotions, and body has numerous feedback and feed-forward loops, which occur at various levels simultaneously. Just as we are receiving information back from the specific environment in which we are engaged, we are sending other thoughts and feelings back to the higher frames of our mind. And, just as we are feeding forward our new adjustments down through the levels of our mind and then out into the world of events, we are feeding back some of our thoughts and emotions about that. Did we mention that the mind-emotions-body system is highly systemic?

It is. And, because it is, systemic features occur in our experiences. These include feedback and feed-forward loops, emergent properties, gestalts that are more than the sum of the properties, simultaneity, and looping.

As we add meta-levels to our work with strategies, we add a very rich dimension to our modeling. Failure to do this results in very limited models. Yet as we add the levels we also have to be careful in *distinguishing* the levels. Korzybski warned that when we confuse levels, whether meta and primary, or between diffe ent meta-levels, we inevitably feed a degree of "unsanity". With self-reflexive consciousness reflecting back onto itself, and ever moving to higher levels, the syntax and the relationship between abstraction about abstraction, state about state, level about level take on great importance. Earlier we noted sixteen effects that occur when one level interfaces with another. Failing to distinguish levels confuses levels and creates the "unsanity" of making less effective adjustments to reality.

Thinking systemically about "logical levels"

Throughout this work we have noted that the meta-levels (or meta-states) of layers of embedded frames are also described as "logical levels". This raises some important questions:

- What are "logical levels"?
- How do "logical levels" work?
- How are they related to meta-states?

Having worked extensively with logical levels, Robert Dilts *et al.* (1991) have provided an excellent operational definition of them:

> In our brain structure, language, and perceptual systems there are natural *hierarchies* or levels of experiences. The effect of each level is to *organize and control the information on the level below it.* Changing something on an upper level would necessarily change things on the lower levels; changing something on a lower level could but would not necessarily affect the upper levels. [p. 26, emphasis added.]

> Logical Levels: an internal hierarchy in which each level is progressively more *psychologically encompassing and impactful*. [Dilts, 1990, p. 217, emphasis added.]

Let's pull this definition apart and sequence out the specific features that make up what we call a "logical level". As we do, we need to remember that the term "logical level" is a nominalization of a process and therefore not a thing. Therefore "logical levels" are not externally real. There are no such things as "logical levels". But there is the process of mentally, emotionally, and even somatically layering these neuro-linguistic components upon one another. This is what we refer to when we speak about "logical levels."

Dilts's definition provides several crucial features about "logical levels". Five of these components enable us to begin to build an operational definition. They are:

1. A hierarchy of experience;
2. Higher levels organize and control information on lower levels;
3. The modulation effect of the system necessarily works downward;
4. The modulation effect of the system does not necessarily work upward;
5. Higher levels operate in a more encompassing and impactful manner than the lower levels.

In order to have "logical levels", we need a series of levels (two or more) where the items operate in a certain prescribed order with regard to each other. That is, they create a hierarchical system. We have "logical" levels when the level above "inevitably and predictably" ("logically") drives, affects, modulates, organizes, and controls the level below it. In true logical levels, the higher levels always and inevitably modulate the lower levels.

What does a "level" mean? A level is a line or surface that is horizontal or flat. As an adjective, it means having no part higher than another. Each exists on the same horizontal plain. The Strategies model provides an excellent example of a number of items (representational system distinctions) existing on the same level, yet designating different steps in a process leading to a final outcome.

Using the term "hierarchy" in this description of "logical levels" tends to set up a false expectation. It suggests that there is an order, a static order. But, in the mind-body-emotion system, the "logical levels" are not static or rigid. They are fluid. They move. They keep changing. And it is this fluidity of our layering of thoughts, feelings, and concepts upon each other that makes representing these levels difficult. Any and every static metaphor (e.g. ladders, steps, floors in a building) misrepresents the "logical leveling" of the mind.

Systems theory and language offer a better term than "hierarchy". They introduce the term "holography". Taken from the Greek word "*holos*", meaning whole, it refers to the part in the whole and the whole in the part. This is the nature of a holographic image.

Robert Dilts (1983) has written more that helps us to understand "logical levels":

> Logical typing occurs where there is a discontinuity (as opposed to a continuity, as with the hierarchies) between levels of classification. This kind of discontinuity is exemplified:
>
> a) in mathematics, by the restriction that a class cannot be a member of itself nor can one of the members be the class.
>
> b) in logic, by the solution to the classic logical paradox, "This statement is false." (If the statement is true, it is false, and if it is false, then it is true, and so on.) The actual truth value of the statement is of a different logical type than the statement itself.
>
> c) in behavior, by the fact that the reinforcement rules for exploration in animals is of a completely different nature than those for the process of testing that occurs in the act of exploration. [p. 24]
>
> The informational effects between levels and types is called feedback and is probably the major distinguishing feature of cybernetic systems. [p. 39]
>
> Differences of the same or different logical type interacting at different levels (hierarchical or logical respectively) will result in the modulation of the difference on the lower level. [p. 49]

Gregory Bateson (Bateson and Bateson, 1987) wrote:

> Logical Types: A series of examines is in order:
>
> 1. The name is not the thing named but is of different logical type, higher than the thing named.
> 2. The class is of different logical type, higher than that of its members.
> 3. The injunctions issues by, or control emanating from, the bias of the house thermostat is of higher logical type than the control issued by the thermometer.
> 4. The word "tumbleweed" is of the same logical type as "bush" or "tree". It is not the name of a species or genus of plants; rather, it is the name of a class of plants whose members share a particular style of growth and dissemination.
> 5. "Acceleration" is of a higher logical type than "velocity". [pp. 209-10]

All of this allows us to expand our operational definition of the nominalized phrase "logical levels". Now we add the following distinctions, which give more description to this leveling or layering of the mind with reflexive facets of our neuro-linguistics:

6. There exists a discontinuity between the levels—a break.
7. With the construction of logical levels, a relationship arises between levels that we must take into consideration. If we do not, "paradox" arises. Paradox does not exist "in the world". It arises and exists as a "mind" seeks to sort out and understand phenomena that merge from different logical levels.
8. Hierarchical logical levels function as a system so that not only do the higher levels arise out of the lower, but they also later feed back information into the system and therefore "influence" into the lower levels. This creates recursiveness within "logical level" systems.

9. Because it is a cybernetic system, as information moves up logical levels new features emerge that do not exist at the lower levels. This emergence at higher levels involves, in systems language, summitivity. In other words, the emergent property does not exist only as the sum of the parts, but new properties and qualities arise over "time" within the system.
10. Reflexivity describes one of the new features that emerge in logical levels. In living organisms this results in self-reflexiveness or self-consciousness.
11. In a system with feedback properties, logical levels operate by self-reflexiveness, the whole system becomes cybernetic. It becomes a "system that feeds back onto and changes itself" (Dilts, 1990, p. 33). This makes it self-organizing.

Remodeling the "Neuro-Logical Levels"

Much of the confusion today about "logical levels" has arisen not because of Dilts's explanation and definition of "logical levels". He accurately defined them there. It arose rather from his presentation of what he called the "Neuro-Logical Levels". Why? Because, surprisingly, that list of items is not a "logical level" model. The structure of these items fails to meet the criteria of "logical levels" just given. This means that the Neuro-Logical Levels lack the structure of "logical levels" in that each level "is progressively more psychologically encompassing and impactful" (1990, p. 217). While we noted this in Chapter Fifteen, we will here give further consideration to the matter.

Now as a list of beliefs and as a checklist of some meta-levels (beliefs, values, identity, mission, spirituality), the Neuro-Logical Levels model provides a list that we can use for many things. If we consider each level as a resource frame or state for the primary state of behaviors, then this list of beliefs insightfully shows how we can apply higher levels to lower levels.

Dilts (1990), wrote, "At this stage we find which resources are needed. And you might need resources at all levels." (p. 122)

So, while the idea of "Neuro-Logical Levels" was introduced by Robert Dilts very early in the history of NLP, and while it has had a very positive and useful influence, and while we continue to use it in numerous patterns, it is not a "logical level" system.

This is because it fails to fulfil the criteria and definition of a "logical level" system. The lower levels of that model are not always members of the class of the higher levels. For example, "environment" is a larger level than "behavior".

Woodsmall (1996) identified several problematic factors with this list:

1) "Environment" describes a larger phenomenon than "behaviors". Even though behaviors may affect environment, behaviors do not drive or modulate environment. This interferes with the structure of the levels and prevents it from operating

Figure 17.5: The neuro-logical levels or levels of beliefs

6. Why? (big)	Spiritual	God/Universe	Transmission
5. Who?	Mission	Identity	Mission
4. Why? (small)	Motivation/ Meaning	Beliefs/Values	Permission/ Motivation
3. How?	Process/Strategy	Capabilities	Direction
2. What?	Actions/Reaction	Behaviors	Actions
1. Where? When?	Opportunities/ Constaints	Environment	External context

as a system. If we eliminated environment, we would come closer to having a logical and orderly list wherein each higher level would govern, drive, and modulate the level immediately below it, and each higher level would operate in a "more psychological encompassing and impactful" way (Dilts, 1990, p. 217).

2) Environment is not a member of the class of behaviors. It does not have that relationship to behaviors. Behaviors are not a category that's more psychologically "encompassing and impactful" than environment.

3) There's no thread. In Bateson's logical levels, learning operates as the thread that goes through the system, uniting it as a system. Learning "drives" each level. But what thread goes through this list? Woodsmall noted that here is a very useful laundry list of items to keep in mind about beliefs and to check out regarding different kinds of beliefs. It obviously also acts as a memorable list by using the indexing questions (where, when, who, what, why). But it does not function as a holistic system of logical levels.

Dilts translates these levels into the "neuro-logical levels". He wrote (1990), "These different levels each bring a deeper commitment of neurological 'circuitry' into action." (p. 210)

Does the higher level of 'Behaviors' drive, organize, and modulate the lowest level of 'Environment'? Does our motor system of conscious activities drive and organize our peripheral nervous system of sensations and reflex reactions? Should we not reverse that order? Dilts later turned this into "examples of statements at the different logical levels" and this model led him to generate the following items.

On the bottom level, we have an evaluative statement loaded with a high-level generalization (a nominalization, "the cancer"). "The cancer is attacking me." Yet above that statement we have a simple declarative statement in sensory-based language. "I have a tumor." Now which statement represents a higher logical level?

Figure 17.6: Neuro-logical levels

6. Spiritual	Holographic	Nervous system as a whole
5. Identity	Immune system Endocrine system	Deep life-sustaining functions
4. Beliefs	Autonomic N.S. (heart rate, pupil dilation, etc.)	Unconscious responses
3. Capabilities	Cortical systems (eye movements, posture, etc.)	Semiconscious actions
2. Behaviors Motor System	(pyramidal and cerebellum)	Conscious actions
1. Environment	Peripheral NS	Sensations and reflex reactions

Figure 17.7

5. Identity	"I am a cancer victim."
4. Belief	"It is false hope not to accept the inevitable."
3. Capability	"I am not capable of keeping well."
2. Behavior	"I have a tumor."
1. Environment	"The cancer is attacking me."

Figure 17.8

5. Identity	"I am a healthy person."
4. Belief	"If I am healthy I can help others."
3. Capability	"I know how to influence my health."
2. Behavior	"I can act healthy sometimes."
1. Environment	"The medicine healed me."

Obviously the bottom statement, "The cancer is attacking me." Again, I would suggest that we reverse these if we want the higher level to classify the lower. Behaviors occur within environments.

In yet another example, Dilts (1990) has provided the following chart. "The following statements indicate the different levels in someone who is working toward a health goal." (p. 211)

This set of statements comes closer to a set of logical levels. An almost specific detail ("the medicine") acts upon the person to bring healing. Yet the phrase "the medicine" functions like a nominalization and the verb (taking a specific medicine into the body) has disappeared. Here "medicine" designates a class of items instead of specifying anything (e.g., taking aspirin).

Below "Behavior" should occur sub-behaviors or micro-behaviors that make up the class of "Behaviors". If we put "Environment" we put a much larger phenomenon below a specific behavior. Again, behaviors always occur within the context of some environmental situation.

In a chart in *Changing Belief Systems with NLP*, Dilts demonstrates his genius as he makes what seems to us to be a correction in the Neuro-Logical Levels. Here he integrates a time-line of a person's past, present, and future with the psychosocial developmental stages adapted from Timothy Leary (pp. 133-34) with his logical levels. In the following figure he drops the "environment" level from the diagram (p. 135).

This diagram brings us much closer to a true hierarchy of "logical levels." The only problematic facets that continue are the following:

There is vagueness implicit in the use of the word "capabilities". Does this term refer to the *potential* of doing something or *actually* doing something? If it refers to an ability, then it is a behavior—an actual doing (some speaking, thinking, emoting, behaving, relating). If it means potential, then it refers to an internal mental-emotional resource or strategy. In such cases, it refers to a member of the same class, some component of a mind-body state.

Then there is the vagueness of the term "beliefs". How does a belief differ from a representation? Can we represent something we do not believe? Of course. Mere representation, even when we juice that representation up by making it close, three-dimensional, associated, or in color, still does not, in itself, create a belief. To representations we have to add a meta-representation (i.e., language) of validation, which we articulate in saying yes to the representations. It is the higher-level frame that creates the new gestalt that we call a "belief".

Both internal representations and beliefs involve "knowledge". But in beliefs we have a meta-level validation about the knowledge. To disbelieve something we first have a primary-level representation and then a meta-level disconfirmation. We encode this by saying no to the primary representations.

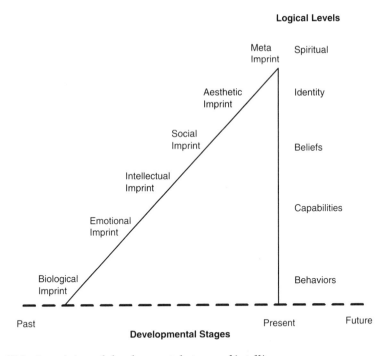

Figure 17.9: Imprints and developmental stages of intelligence

Dilts (1990) has insightfully described the nature of beliefs as meta-frames, that is, frames about frames. He has described beliefs as setting "a frame that determines how everything afterwards gets interpreted" (p. 133). Beliefs function as a higher logical level of thoughts about other thoughts. That's why, as Dilts noted, a belief "is not about reality", but about our ideas—ideas of meaning, cause, ability, self, mission, time.

If "capabilities" means potential, we have a belief on our hands. We have a belief about what we "have the ability" in the future to accomplish. "Identity" is also a belief about our concept of self. The same holds true for the term "spiritual". This describes, among other things, what we believe about the larger questions of origin, destiny, and higher intelligence in the universe.

Then there is the lack of a thread in the levels. The set of levels does not fit the definition of "logical levels" primarily because each higher level is not a category or classification of the lower level.

The meta-level of background knowledge

There are many, many more levels (logical levels) than the six distinctions in the Neuro-Logical Model. We have identified twenty or so that we regularly use in Meta-States. One of these is the meta-level of background knowledge.

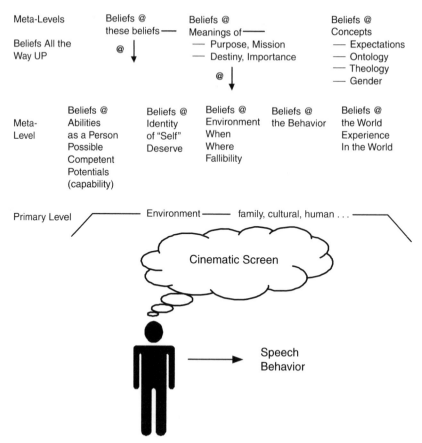

Figure 17.10: Re-modeling and neuro-logical levels

"Background knowledge" refers to the larger frame of reference of understanding that sets a context for a given expertise, skill, or performance. As we have noted, working with strategies and modeling does not occur in a vacuum. It always occurs within some domain of understanding. Even something as simple as the spelling strategy (as noted earlier) occurs within various frames of understanding—the language used, for instance, the intellectual context, the cultural context.

Background knowledge reveals that there is a certain level of knowledge, base of understanding, or comprehension involved in every action, behavior, skill, and expertise that we want to model. Consider the issue of "background knowledge" in terms of modeling when it comes to any of the following areas or domains:

Psychotherapy   Ericksonian hypnosis

Consulting in corporations   Expertise in the stock market

Olympic sports   Wealth building

Baseball

Managing a Fortune 500 company

Parenting

Weight management

Selling

Marketing

Women in leadership

Fitness

Healthy Eating

Skiing

Persuasion

Unpacking the strategy of an expert pilot

Suppose we wanted to model an expert pilot. Certainly we would start with the structural patterning about how to think, feel, and act in the cockpit. That would be the beginning. We could then access motivation, decision, understanding, navigating strategies and the like. Yet when we have completed all of that, we still would need to know and access the background knowledge of aerodynamics, aviation, and other subject areas in order to fly. We would want to ask:

- What do you know about aerodynamics that I should know before you turn over controls to me?
- What do you know about engines, mechanics, and so forth in an airplane that would be useful for me to know?

This highlights the importance of background knowledge of a field. Given that, how do we learn the sufficient and necessary background information so that we can enter into and engage an expert in modeling his or her expertise? We could begin by reviewing the literature of the field. In graduate work, we call this a literature review. We could also explore where, in a given field, is the current state of the art of that field.

Accessing the right states for modeling

What states and meta-states do we need to access and use in order to effectively model? This is critical since we can operate from the wrong states, states that would completely undermine our ability to model effectively. Given this, modeling excellence necessitates that we access the kinds of states that would support effective modeling. These include the following.

1. Openness
We model best when we operate from the openness of a naïve, innocent seeing, hearing, or feeling, a childlike willingness to play the fool and to be more present in our experiences. Such a state involves being in an intense uptime of pure sensory awareness.

2. Playfulness
There's a childlike innocence and playfulness that goes into the best modeling attitude. It's the attitude that asks, "What if ...?" questions and searches for possibilities in the most playful way.

3. Being explorative
From the open playfulness we can then be truly curious, searching, inquiring, investigating, and living on the edge of our curiosity. Such exploration inherently involves a respect for the person or persons being modeled and the ability to be empathetic and caring.

4. Flexibility
In gathering information from our expert we will need to be able to quickly and easily shift our perceptual positions and our perspectives. Later, as we build a tentative model, we will need to be flexible as we seek to prove ourselves wrong and to discover the limits and constraints of the model.

Whenever we build a model of something, flexibility and non-egoistic investment help us to avoid the danger of becoming too wedded to the model. We need the flexibility and openness to keep revising it, testing it. John Grinder says that at the testing stage of the model we actually seek to prove ourselves wrong. To pull that off we have to de-invest our identity and ego from the model. At that point we will need to take a more distant and objective view as we seek to disconfirm our confirmations and to put our models to the test thoroughly. We only get in the way of our own learning when we act as if our ideas were sacrosanct and unquestionable.

5. A sense of awe and appreciation
Another state that facilitates our best skills in modeling is that of being able to stand in awe of the wonder and mystery of the skill presented. Nothing kills freshness of perspective like the attitudes of boredom, taking things for granted, or snobbery. Conversely, it is the attitude of appreciation for the person, for the skill, or for the positive intentions that allows us to see with fresh and innocent eyes.

6. Recognizing patterns
In modeling we are looking for "the pattern that connects", to use another Bateson phrase. "What is the pattern or form or structure that connects or unites these disparate elements?" To ask this question and to go on this kind of a search means that we rise above content and dealing with the experience from a structural point of view. It means looking for larger-level forms by which we might punctuate the events. "How can we organize these elements? What patterns of organization may be occurring here?"

7. Persistence

If modeling were easy, quick, and simple, it would not be such a valued skill and experience. But it is not. It takes persistence and commitment to stay with a theme and to live with ambiguity and chaotic forces until one begins to see the internal self-organizing thread that weaves it all together. Persistence is needed for navigating the different stages of modeling, for thoroughly catching up with the literature of a field or area, for returning to the raw data, for trying out various formats, and for learning new skills in how to implement the model.

8. Tolerance of ambiguity

Ambiguity will dominate much of the modeling process. There will be the ambiguity and even confusion at the beginning as we formulate the research question that we want to address. There will be ambiguity about the amount of data that's available, and what's truly important. There will be ambiguity as we work with the systemic processes and try to understand and identify the organizing mechanisms and the self-organizing attractors. There will be many times when we will be called upon to hold several opposing ideas at the same time and wait until a new perspective emerges for how to unify the seeming contradictions.

Organizing data for building a model

There are numerous steps or phases in the process of modeling. These modeling stages reflect the movement from initial encounter with an expert and a piece of excellence to the final product. How do you structure and sequence the data to create a model of the expert?

1. Beginning orientation

Typically I (MH) begin the initial information gathering in one or two ways: by reviewing the literature in a field, domain, or discipline and/or questioning, interviewing someone with a high degree of expertise in a field. This usually results in my obtaining an overview of some, if not most, of the key items, ingredients, and variables involved in a particular area. In both instances, I ask:

- What are the key elements involved in this piece of excellence?
- What other things play a role in terms of the variables that we have to take into account?
- Of these elements, which are necessary and which are peripheral?

Then, still in the preparation stage, I will pick one or more experts whom I want to model and decide on such controlling influences as the following:

a. Context in which the modeling will occur. How will we set up, preframe things or the person, induce the best and most appropriate states, and so on? If we are going to work with a living expert, then when and where do we meet, under what conditions? How can we facilitate the structure of the meeting so that it allows the expert to feel relaxed, valued, and at his or her best? What is our relationship with the expert? Is it personal or professional? What are the understood arrangements in terms of the use of such things as the materials, confidentiality, crediting the person?

b. States. What are the most appropriate states for both the modeler and the one being modeled in terms of gathering the highest quality of information?

c. Materials. If the expert is not available, or even dead, then what are the materials used? Do we reply upon books, articles, film, personal associates, journals, or what?

d. Clarifying our purpose and the structure used in the modeling. What skill, expertise, or behavior do I want to model? What is the purpose in formalizing this model? Why do I want to do this? What will this offer to the expert? Will I be copying an unconscious competence, improving it, or designing a new one? Whom will I model? How will I find, contact, relate to the persons or structures to be modeled? What criteria will I use in selecting a model? Who will the model be for?

At the first stage of modeling, we will also want to distinguish between the kinds of experiences we are modeling. Are we modeling a behavior, a state of being, a dynamic function, or what? Along these lines we will want to do the following:

- First identify the overall structures of the experience to be modeled. This means establish our S-R (stimulus-response) parameters. Where does the behavior, state, or skill begin? Where does it end?
- Establish the time span of the experience. How long does the strategy or experience take from beginning to end? Are we speaking about a micro-behavior that occurs in seconds (e.g., the spelling strategy), one that involves days or weeks (e.g., delegating, managing, leading), or one that might involve years (e.g., innovating a new product, marketing, cultural change).
- Create a tentative model by sequencing the materials that you have from beginning to end. Then establish the steps or stages inside that framework. What are the key parts, stages, and facets of the processes?

The unconscious-uptake stage involves taking second position to the person to build up our initial intuitions about the skills of the person. Here also we can use mirroring and mimicking (if appropriate) to approximate our sense of the skills. Rather than seek to "understand", we here seek to "experience". Use a know-nothing frame, step out of your assumptions and use as unbiased an attitude as you can. Step into the expert's role and try out the skill "as if" you were that person.

2. Initial "model in mind"

We then create a *tentative* format, model, or understanding and then begin testing it against more of the literature, case studies, interviews, and other materials. The attitude of the modeler at this point should be one of testing and seeking to disprove the initial model to determine if it will hold up and work as a model:

- What am I missing?
- What else is there?
- What does this model not explain?
- How else could we formulate this understanding?
- What are my blind spots? The blind spots of this paradigm?

The multiple-descriptions stage is the stage where we seek to create several different descriptions of the skill, behavior, or state. Here we will use descriptions from first, second, and third positions. We will seek to obtain double and triple descriptions that allow us a richer understanding of the pattern. Doing this will make the final model richer and more flexible.

The art of decomposing a process is the stage in modeling where we take apart a piece of excellence and tease out its higher levels. We do this to develop an understanding of its motivations, agendas, dynamics, and the like.

- What micro-level behaviors are involved?
- What contextual and environmental anchors are involved?
- What feedback processes are involved or need to be involved?
- What calibration tools, models, and the like will be necessary?

3. Formatting and replicating

Once we have a structure, we can begin testing it with self and others by seeing if what we have is sufficient to replicate the same kind and level of expertise in another person.

What other variables or features may factor into this experience?

The subtraction process in modeling comes when we start sorting out everything that is absolutely essential to the working of the model from those extra and peripheral to replicating the skill or behavior. Here we seek to eliminate everything extraneous so that we can identify the heart of the structure. This allows us to clarify and define the specific steps that are absolutely required to attain the desired results in the given contexts. Systematically leave out various pieces and notice the results that you get. Keep subtracting to reduce the steps until you have the simplest and most elegant form that still produces the behavior.

The designing and redesigning stage of modeling occurs as we continue to develop the model and add other resources. We do this in order to go beyond the expertise of the expert or experts that we have modeled. Now we are synthesizing the qualities that will allow even more advanced properties to emerge, allowing us to go beyond the development of the expert.

Summary of the steps in a modeling process

1. Determine the expert(s) to be modeled, keeping in mind contexts, states, materials and clarity of purpose.
2. Gather initial information about that area of expertise. Review such things as literature, interviews, questionnaires, prototype modeling.
3. Develop the initial "model in mind": expand with double and triple descriptions, identify relevant patterns involved in the cognitive and behavioral stages of the skill's expression or development.
4. Organize and structure a fuller, logical expression of your model.
5. Filter out and reduce the model to only the necessary and sufficient variables.
6. Test the effectiveness, usefulness, power of the model: try it out in various contexts, situations, with various individuals and/or groups.
7. Redesign for greater quality, elegance, power.
8. Construct patterns, processes, and technologies for transferring, installing, and replicating the skills in others—a training program.
9. Test and retest the model: develop appropriate instruments for measuring results, specify the edges of the model's validity and usefulness, where is it not appropriate?

Figure 17.11: Modeling using meta-levels: frames all the way up

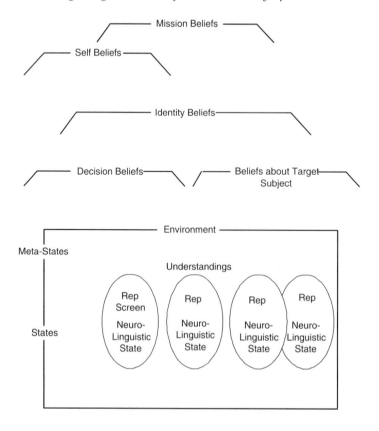

Summary

Modeling involves more than getting a strategy, yet it often starts there. We obtain a single person's strategy for some expert skill, then another's, and another's. Eventually we sit down to explore, refine, and redesign the idiosyncratic strategies and to generate a more universal model.

Modeling also involves looking at an experience or expertise via exploring the literature of the field. Doing this provides multiple lenses and perspectives about the experience. It establishes the background knowledge of that field or skill that contains some of the theoretical and hypothesis principles that may be crucial in building a model.

To engage in the modeling process takes some special states, attitudes, beliefs, and frames. These mostly involve a willingness to step aside from our paradigms and assumptions and to use a know-nothing frame of ignorance.

Part Five

Personal Mastery

Chapter Eighteen
Mastering Trance

It is really no secret that, in mastering NLP, we master our states and this especially means our *trance states*. As previously noted, the Meta-Model is as much a tool for de-hypnotizing as it is a tool for communicating with precision and gathering high-quality information. Very early in their work, Bandler and Grinder explored and created a model of Ericksonian hypnosis. So much Ericksonian thinking, attitude, presuppositions, and style were brought into NLP that the field is recognized as one of the many branches and models of Ericksonian thinking, therapy, and hypnosis.

As NLP practitioners we learned early the linguistic facets of the Meta-Model and the Milton Model. By these models we developed the basic skills for using hypnotic language and for inducing various states of trance. In this chapter, we will continue to develop this by adding the meta-linguistics of Meta-States to your hypnotic skills. That will comprise Part I. Then in Part II we will play around with some new patterns around the trancy meta-level of "time".

Part I
What is hypnosis, anyway?

First and foremost, hypnosis is the experience and process of altering one's state. In hypnosis, we specifically *go inside* and access meanings, memories, imagination, and understanding. This creates an inward focus of attention so that, from the outside, we may look as if we were asleep or had gone away. Actually, we have simply *transitioned* from one state to another. Nonreferencing words and noun phrases do not allow us to pick out anything actual in our immediate environment or immediately track to our representational screen. This evokes an inward focus. We have to go inside to create, invent, and/or recall the information that allows us to create our internal movie.

This means that hypnosis is a response to language, to ideas, and to meaning making. We hypnotize ourselves and others by communicating and swishing our awareness to another referent. Whether that state is an enhancing state or one that causes them to "freak cookies" is an entirely different matter. Bandler and Grinder (1979) described it in these words: "Hypnosis is fundamentally no different than any effective communication. There is no such thing as hypnosis as a separate and distinct process." (p. 2)

As we turn inward and become highly focused on some thought, idea, memory, or emotion, we develop a "deeper" or more powerful trance. Our concentration becomes more intense and focused. The "deeper" or "higher" we go into such trancelike states, the more it seems as if we were no longer here, but that we had gone elsewhere. And, in our mind, we are … somewhere else.

Understanding trance states in this way helps us appreciate that trance is a naturally occurring phenomenon that we all perform. We enter such states whenever we become engrossed in a task, captivated by a "spell"-binding speaker, lost in a movie, or daydreaming while driving on a highway. Anything that captures our attention and enthralls our heart can cast a spell upon us. A captivating story can do it. So can a piece of juicy gossip. Hypnotic states are not all that strange, they are not mysterious, supernatural, demonic, or the gift of a special few.

When we change our orientation to reality, we experience a different reality orientation. Typically in trance states we move from an external orientation and turn inward to the matrices of our frames. And, because these higher levels involve thoughts typically outside our conscious awareness, we say that our "unconscious" mind becomes dominant. Actually this terminology creates some of the misunderstanding about hypnosis. When we turn toward and attend that which is typically *not* conscious, on the inside we become very conscious of those thoughts *and* simultaneously we lose awareness (consciousness) of our immediate environment.

Are we "unconscious"?

Yes and no. We are simultaneously *not* conscious of one thing while being conscious of another. What was in awareness is now *out* of awareness. What we were *not* aware of, we now become aware of. In terms of the levels of the mind, we are never simultaneously aware of all of the things we know. George Miller's magic number of 7-plus-or-minus-2 bits of information come into play at this point. From a practical point of view, we only need to layer several layers of awarenesses and distract attention among them to create different kinds of unconscious states. Mostly "unconscious" means *outside* of awareness. Sometimes when we refer to the "knowledge" of our immune system, autonomic nervous system, or other "subconscious" information we also use the term "unconscious".

As we use these terms to describe the different kinds, levels, and styles of knowing in our mind-body system, it's useful to remember that we have only *one* mind. We do not have "an unconscious mind" *and* then a conscious mind. As our *mind* focuses on some things, we experience *conscious awareness* of those things *while* simultaneously letting 99 percent of our knowledge slip *outside* that focus so that we are *not* conscious (*un*conscious) of all that.

The appearance of being asleep to the world, unconscious of that world, contrasts to how we experience our internal focus. An outside observer might think that we are not aware, yet on the inside our experience is that of being more aware and more focused than usual. On the inside, the experience feels like a *heightened state*. Many times people will say, "I wasn't hypnotized—I heard every word you said."

One characteristic of the hypnotic state is how we experience a heightened degree of suggestibility in trance. Erickson said that trance is a "state of autonomous responsiveness to suggestion without any conscious understanding" (*Healing in Hypnosis*, 1983, Vol. I, p. 10). We experience this intense receptiveness to ideas when we are entranced by a story.

So what is hypnosis? It is getting lost in our mind to the internal movie we are revisiting or creating in response to a story, emotion, memory, our imagination, whatever. The movie playing in our mind becomes so compelling, and we enter into it so fully that it seems as if the world goes away.

Figure 18.1: The hypnotic state

What is the nature of the hypnotic state?

This everyday experience is a natural process that we all experience. It's only a matter of degree.

How lost can you get? How easy can you get lost? What do you get lost in? Does the experience enhance or impoverish your life?

We call trance by lots of names: deep thinking, concentrating, praying, meditating, just thinking, just listening. That we don't think of them as "hypnotic" doesn't make them any less so. The question is more one of how much skill we have in using them systematically to induce preferred altered states—ones that will enhance our lives.

Because we become more receptive in such states, we can use them to amplify our experiences as a tool for taking charge of our brain. We can also use trance to get more intense responses from others. In hypnotizing we never "control" another's mind: we only work with the mind in leading and suggesting. We can amplify powers and skills, intensify states of energy, induce numbness (pain control), alter time (giving the impression of time speeding, time going really slowly), and increase the potentialities of our most subconscious nervous systems. Yet for all that, it is not a panacea and we cannot do everything with it.

In fact, recipients can always resist inductions, refuse suggestions, and "break state" (come out of the trance). Only in the Hollywood movies can hypnosis *make* people do things against their wills. But that's movie fiction. Trance work involves providing stimuli to give something for another to respond to. Resistance and cooperation in trance demonstrates a person's ability to respond.

When we play the role of inducer (hypnotist), we are mostly operating as a biofeedback mechanism to that person. That's why *pacing* verbally and nonverbally is *the central way to create trance*. Realizing that we are not going to hypnotize without pacing, who do you think is in charge of the experience: we or the person going in? When we say words that do not fit, the person will come out of trance. Why? Because it does not fit. It jars consciousness.

Unlike traditional hypnosis, which talks about the hypnotizability of people or the *depth* of trance, it is, according to Bandler and Grinder, more a matter of *how* any given person prefers to go in, when, with whom. "Depth" in NLP has now become a question of pacing, rapport, and trust.

We hypnotize by talking, using words, and creating stimuli for ourselves and others to create internal movies. Erickson said in *Healing in Hypnosis*, Volume II (1984), "Hypnosis is a process of distraction, fixation, and generalization. It's fixating a person on ideas that evoke wonder and questioning and then utilizing the need for answers."

What does trance or hypnosis feel like?

The feeling of a trance can take on the feeling tone of a great many states–it depends to a great extent on the content toward which you are turning inward. Are you inwardly focusing on relaxation, energy, love, healing, learning, or what?

What is the language of hypnosis?

Entering into a hypnotic state occurs when we hear words that invite us to create an internal movie in our mind. The more artfully vague the words, the more we turn inward to create sense and meaning of those words. Artfully vague words are the most trancy of all words. What we say and how we say it are our two powers for hypnotizing.

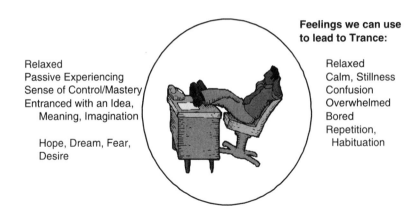

Feelings we can use
to lead to Trance:

Relaxed
Passive Experiencing
Sense of Control/Mastery
Entranced with an Idea,
    Meaning, Imagination

Hope, Dream, Fear,
Desire

Relaxed
Calm, Stillness
Confusion
Overwhelmed
Bored
Repetition,
    Habituation

Figure 18.2: The feeling of trance

The Meta-Model identifies linguistic distinctions that are naturally vague and therefore hypnotic. The more ill-formed the term or phrase, the more trancy. When we *use* and apply such, rather than question, we use the Meta-Model hypnotically. This means that unspecified nouns, verbs, references, and nominalizations form the language that hypnotizes. Use the Meta-Model distinctions with all of their glorious ill-formedness and those who hear you have to go inside to fill in the meanings. If they ask you to be more specific, they come *up* into sensory awareness of the present moment. Questioning the vagueness in language brings us out of trance.

We can use the Meta-Model then in two very different ways:

1. To de-hypnotize and bring people out of trance. Asking questions of specificity reduces vagueness in expressions and increases awareness about the old trance states. This de-hypnotizes as it invites us into a new and higher level of awareness about the movies we're playing in our minds.
2. To hypnotize by using the linguistic distinctions to move a person *up* the scale of abstraction and into higher abstractions. This invites us to build new generalizations and models of the world as we produce and edit our new internal movies.

What are the nonverbal hypnotic processes?

While words predominate in hypnotizing, in addition to hypnotic language patterns, there are hypnotic ways of talking that contribute to creating a hypnotic effect-that is, in inviting people to go inside in using their references to create and get lost in a new movie.

1. *A tone and tempo that paces and suggests*

We can use our tempo to match the other's breathing to pace them, which develops a more hypnotic voice. We can speak in a steady voice using the other's breathing as the rate and speed of our talk. We can slow our tempo down to convey "more significance" and speed it up to convey "excitement".

Using our inflection we can modulate our voice to raise it at the end of a statement to engage the conscious mind, keep it level to make a statement, and drop it to indicate a "command".

2. *Nonverbal pacing and then leading*

In hypnosis, pacing and leading is the central meta-pattern. First we pace to get rapport, then we lead. We let the other lead and reflect responses. We mirror the other's output channels and calibrate to responses. This is the interpersonal feedback nature of hypnotic communicating.

We can select messages outside a person's awareness and feed it back. We can gauge the tempo of our voice to their breathing, blink at their rate of blinking, nod as they nod, rock at the same rate, say things that must in fact be the case, or things that you notice are the case. As a person listens, this immediately verifies our words: they realize their truth and this builds credibility.

In pacing we can utilize anything that happens and incorporate it into the ongoing process. "And the noises in the room can help you relax even further … because as you notice them, you can feel comfortable …"

3. *Using content to distract*

In a strange way, as we engage a mind in some various content—a story, emotion, hope, dream, or fear—this can so entrance and engage the person that we can simultaneously set other frames that will remain *outside* the person's awareness, which then slide in without resistance. We can do this through marking out words, ideas, questions, and commands. These *embedded commands* or questions can then be communicated with, say, a different voice, tone, space.

4. *Facilitating response potential with suggestive ideas*

Another hypnotic process that's not linguistic involves the *implied* frames and suggestions that come along with other thoughts and ideas. Using a child's tone of voice, pedo-grammar, or talking about experiencing the first day of school are all indirect suggestions for age regressing. Describing in detail the sensations of putting a hand in a bucket of ice water indirectly suggests numbness and anesthesia. Talking about comfortably staring at one spot and wanting to blink, but being unable to, suggests eye closure.

What is the metaphorical direction of trance?

In terms of direction, is trance "down" or "up"? The traditional metaphor of choice has been the depth metaphor. "Allow yourself to float down, deeper and deeper...." And that's certainly one choice.

Yet the structure of the Meta-Model implies that in trance we move "up." It is up despite the fact that Bandler and Grinder used the "depth" metaphor. While they continued to talk about "the deep structure" (transformational grammar) going "down" into trance, their *meta*-model of language put the higher and more abstract language *up*.

In working with trance states in Meta-States, we have chosen to consistently stay with the height metaphor and to consciously "go in" and access our *higher* frames of mind. This makes every meta-stating pattern a hypnotic pattern because it inevitably invites a person to go in and then go up, up and away into the higher realms of the more abstract and conceptual states.

Meta-Trance turns the metaphor upside down so that we think of our *reference system* not as down in the basement of our personality, but as the canopy of our consciousness, as our *frames* and as the matrices of our *references*. We make our transderivational searches upward to the canopy rather than downward to the basement.

Conceptually, in *meta-stating* ourselves (and our states) we access layer upon layer of states—of thoughts, emotions, memories, imaginations, feelings. This takes us up, up and away into the ozone layer. When we do this, we "space out". We can track only so far and then we zone out. It's the experience of hypnosis. How can we go *up* into trance? Isn't the direction of trance *down*? Don't we have to float down deeper and deeper into ourselves? This identifies the structuring or patterning nature of *metaphors*.

The meta-stating shift from primary state of awareness (focusing on what's "out there") to a meta-level awareness (focusing on what's "inside" our mind and emotions) describes a transition from primary to meta-levels. This describes a trance phenomenon. As such, it opens up all kinds of insights into the nature of trance as well as how to use trance more conversationally in everyday life. As a trance phenomenon, meta-stating layer upon layer of thoughts-and-feelings, it is trance all the way up.

"Have you ever had an experience that you found so exciting and so thrilling, that learning it didn't seem like learning at all, it was just pure fun and absorption? You know, something like skiing or rollerblading. Some people learn woodworking, painting, even reading like that. It's just so much fun ... and I don't know if you can just allow yourself to recall an instant like that ... but if you give your brain a chance to *scan through* your history now and identify something like that ... and when you find it, just be there again, fully and completely ... seeing, hearing, and

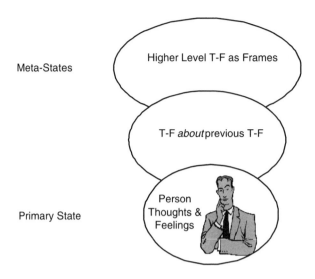

Figure 18.3

feeling it afresh ... because when you do, you can begin to *recover the feeling of focused learning*. And as you do, notice just how much you *enjoy and appreciate that experience* ... Because as you do, you can *appreciate yourself as a learner*, can you not, for the skill of joyful learning? And, as you *appreciate yourself*, you can also feel a growing sense of passion or ferociousness increasing about that self-appreciation and about that joyful learning, can you not? And about that ferociousness, you can rise up in your mind to feel a sense of respect for people ... and if you felt a little bit outlandish in your outrageousness about appreciating so fully and completely your total joy of learning ... of course, you could then become *courageous* about the outrageousness of your appreciation of your joyfulness of learning ..."

Meta-stating trance states

We use meta-states for installation by inviting a person to texture a primary state with higher-level frames. The higher frame operates as an *outside*-of-conscious-awareness structure. We take thoughts-and-feelings and *go meta* to apply them to other thoughts-and-feelings. We transcend one level of thinking-feeling and include that level inside of another level. All of this layering or texturing occurs *in the mind*, which is working at multiple levels of awareness.

New hypnotic language distinctions

Moving into meta-levels moves us from sensory-based language into more and more abstract terms. The language here involves the language of the Meta and the

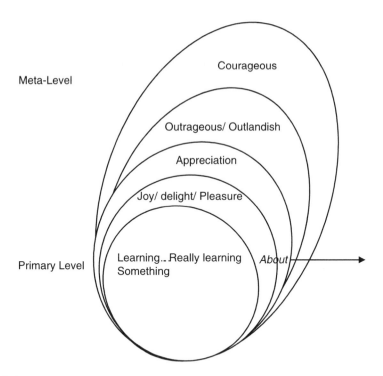

Figure 18.4

Milton models *and* it offers yet other new linguistic distinctions. The following offers some of these linguistic cues.

1. State-about-state syntax

Look for phrases that create or structure a state-about-a-state. "I fear my fear." "I feel calm about my anger." Whenever we juxtapose two states so that one state references another, we have a framing format.

Any time we presuppose one state upon another state, we set up this kind of syntax. "It seems that you'd like to say or do X, but to do so you'd be selfish, mean, [or whatever]" "What would you feel if you could pretend to do X thinking it meant you knew how to protect your personal boundaries, and then forgot you were pretending?"

2. Meta-words

Many words imply a meta-position: of, about, regarding that, beyond, concerning, transcending. "I feel *upset* about my stress ..." "Well, *regarding* my grief about my dad's death, I feel ..."

Buried underneath the concept of ... limitation

Bear in mind	Hidden in an upper corner of the mind
Keep in mind	Uppermost in mind
Above and beyond	In terms of
In view of	As you realize
With this realization	As you remember those feelings
From a more X—(realistic, objective, compassionate) point of view	
What are you holding in mind about ...?	
Let's now apply that to ...	Even more importantly,
Rise up in your mind	Overall
Overview	As an overriding principle
Get on top of your X (depression, anger, anger)	

3. "Self"-words
Generally speaking, the word "self" with a hyphen indicates a meta-state: self-confidence, self-esteem, self-celebration, self-contempt, self-analysis, self-consciousness, and so it goes.

4. Classifications
Whenever we hear classification kinds of words (groups, levels, degrees) or statements that describe or presuppose levels of classifications, we probably have a rare and unprecedented opportunity to pull back the structural curtain on the reality before us and discover meta-states.

5. Quotations and narratives
A sneaky way that Bandler and Grinder often worked with meta-states (without using this terminology) involved layering consciousness through the use of "quotes". They would tell a story, open up a narrative, and within that description put another quote of a quote. Such layering of various thoughts-representations-emotions (states) would create larger and larger levels of frames and contexts (each inducing or accessing various states). To do this we can open up a quotation, narrative, or story and then another, and another, and so on.

6. Logical-level shifts
Some words, terms, and phrases shift one from one level of consciousness to a higher level. Consider this: "I know that she means well, but I feel really hurt by what she did."

Here, the word "but" tends to negate the previous words. It negates, "She means well". The speaker now shifts the focus to "she hurt me". It does not say, "She does not mean well", although we often hear it as meaning such. It simply shifts to a higher logical level.

We experience the "but" as shifting us from the lower level of awareness and emotion to a higher state that then drives and permeates the lower state. By contrast, notice the effect of "and": "I know that she means well, and I feel really hurt by what she did."

This keeps the thoughts-emotions on the same logical level, which then has an additive effect (adding this state to that state), which in NLP usually has the effect of collapsing the two states together.

7. Adjectives that qualify states
Adjective and adverbs are words that modify people, places, and things (nouns) and actions (verbs). As such, they describe the frames for viewing the subsequent things or actions. In this way, adjectives and adverbs encode and hide meta-states.

Gladly embrace	Bitterly criticize
Tolerable anxiety	Sharing hesitantly
Unacceptable grief	Stubbornly insistent
Unconscious thinking	Helpless defeatism
Deliberate inhibition	Ferocious resolve
Forgetting to deliberately inhibit	Ferocious attachment
Proudly stubborn *about* my resourcefulness	

8. Pseudo-feeling terms
We call many things "emotions" or "feelings" which are not emotions at all. We do so by using the syntactic environment, "I feel ..." and then add a judgment to it. If you ask, "And how do you feel about that?" you can usually get a real feeling that has kinesthetic qualities.

- I feel like a king (royal)
- I feel like I need closure
- I feel spectacular
- I feel helpless
- She felt horrified that she might learn something new!
- I feel alienated (unreal, weird)
- He felt like he was being born again
- I feel dumb/stupid

- I feel marvelous (fantastic, incredible, clever)
- I feel like an object (at loose ends)

9. Multiordinal terms

We noted this linguistic distinction in Chapter Twelve. Korzybski designated a nominalization that can mean different things at different levels as a *multiordinal* term. These *ambiguous* terms convey ambiguous meanings until the level is specified. Multiordinal terms have definite meanings on a given level only when we specify the level and context. We fix the meaning when we identify the level. Examples of such nominalizations include: reality, state, science, meaning, love, yes, no, true, false, function, relation, difference, problem, cause, effect, evaluation.

Each multiordinal term invites us up the levels of the mind. That's because as we love to explore new domains of the mind we can even explore love or love that exploration, or explore that exploration even further.

10. Meta-State questions

When we ask questions that presuppose a higher state over the experience, this serves as meta-trancing language. "Would you enjoy feeling confident that you can and will really learn these new skills? And how surprised would you be if you found that the learning was accelerated by the joy and play-fulness?"

11. Nominalization of nominalizations

- The ugly side of his personality comes out under pressure
- His lack of moral fiber
- The pace of modern life goes too fast for me
- His ego is very fragile
- His emotional health
- The pressures of his responsibilities

If nominalizations are the "tranciest" terms as we have, then the idea of nominalizations of nominalizations increases the need of a listener to go instead and invent his or her own understandings and meanings.

12. Incorporating meta-state techniques inside trance inductions

Take any meta-state process and put it inside of any induction for a person to "go inside" and think-feel-experience an idea.

"And as you relax comfortably in the growing knowledge that in just a moment you will turn to your right or your left and see something of importance, something that causes you to feel the ultimate value and important of that thing, whether it be a newborn baby and the mystery of life or whether it be the scary sky at night and the vastness of the universe ... because, while I don't know what your unconscious mind will bring forward to you, I know that you can *feel the sense of awe and wonder* at the immense value and importance of that ... and as you *feel that awe fully* ... you can just let it grow and increase ... that's right ... and fill your own body, because this is such a valuable experience in itself, is it not? Because it really lets you *feel value* and to know that you can *attribute value* to things ... and I wonder just how good you will feel as you *feel this value* about your-self-the mystery and wonder of your own mind and neuro-linguistic system knowing that you are a human being ... inherently valuable just because of that ... and notice how that affects your breathing and posture ... because you can *feel that value* all over, can you not? Growing ... expanding and giving you a center of value to operate from ... Now."

EXERCISE: *Language*

1. In a small group of four persons, brainstorm to invent three to five questions that will elicit some useful and powerfully positive meta-states in others.

2. After you come up with the statements, try them out on each other to see if they work.

EXERCISE: *Conversational meta-stating*

1. Write five sentences that you can use in your work that conversationally meta-state.

2. Meta-stating blessings—write five meta-stating statements that pronounce a blessing or benediction.
"May you thoroughly enjoy *your discoveries* as your curiosity *explores* afresh and activates *your memory* in new and delightful ways, making you more creative and insightful than ever before, now!"

"I trust that you will find yourself enraptured *in an ecstatic kind of joy* about your new knowledge as you read and discover either afresh or anew more powerful and impactful ways to apply all of what you have learned in NLP, knowing that you will begin to surprise yourself in applying your more refined skills in ways that make life more enjoyable."

Meta-State invocation
"Now as you begin to learn with an excited anticipation of the curious and wonder-filled things you might find in this model, may you ferociously *enjoy* your learning and find yourself *appreciating* your skill for implementing just those things that would truly enhance and ennoble your life! And you can do this with a growing sense of appreciation for your *creativity* as you enjoy *watching yourself* with confidence and *wondering* excitedly how much this will improve your *flexibility* and *resourcefulness*."

Part II

The trance states of "time"

Because "time" is an abstraction and nominalization, it occurs only in the mind and not "out there" in the world. We create the concept of "time" as a meta-level frame and then use it as an organizing principle and a category. "Out there" in the world all we have are events occurring.

If "time" does not exist at the primary level, then how do we get to this experience or feeling of "time"? We get to "time" by recognizing that it does not occur in the process world of events, actions, happenings, and movement. Only then can we *rise above* that level, in our mind, and map or construct the conceptual category of "time". It takes a meta-level of awareness to make comparisons and evaluations about those events and to create the idea and concept of "time".

As we experience events, rhythms, and activities repeatedly we come to know them as *times*, or instances, of events. From that awareness we develop a "sense" of duration as a higher-order feeling that results from the summation (or abstraction) of many individual occurrences. This represents one meta-state of "time", namely, "a sense of duration" (an abstraction that compares and relates that configuration of events).

As we talk about these "times" we begin to manipulate this symbol. We begin to number these "times", compare them, sequence them. Then we can say, "Time has elapsed", or, "It took three years to complete the project", or "In another couple of days". Yet what have we actually seen come and go? Not "time" but events. Our abstraction of these numerous events and our representation of their duration, order, and sequence occur at a higher level of abstraction.

Then we begin to use the verbal shorthand involved in the short nominalization, "time". That leads us to begin to objectify it as we talk about *it* as if *it* had physical properties, as do sensed objects. So we end up languaging the nominalized concept as if it were a real thing. We say, "time" flows, moves, races, slows down. We talk about wasting "time", saving it, misusing it. Actually, we have reference to times of something occurring somewhere, and not our concept of "time".

"Time" arises, then, as a *gestalt abstract awareness* that holds past, present, and future together into a structure-as-a-whole configuration, as in a time-line. "Time" emerges from our awareness of events, our sense of duration, our summation of development and growth that occurs "over time", and from our abstraction of "time" as a dimension as in the space-time continuum. When we analyze "time" (as we do other higher-level abstractions such as beauty, love, and happiness) and find the component pieces out of which the structure-as-a-whole emerges, we do not find "time" in any of the pieces. It seems to vanish with analysis.

All of this is trance. None of it is real. This means that our concept of "time" is a meta-state and operates as a mental state *about* the primary level of "times"—times of events occurring. When we number these elements and compare them with set standards we get what Weinberg called a "times of times" or "time". We compare our "feeling of an event's duration" with previous memories of the same, then as we think *about* such we create another meta-level awareness of "time". In creating the gestalt sense of "time", we begin with our kinesthetic sensations of rhythm and rhythmic activities. To that we code and remember these repetitions of cyclical phenomena, and the repetition of occurrences generates a sense of duration—a higher-order feeling.

Figure 18.5: The logical levels of "time"

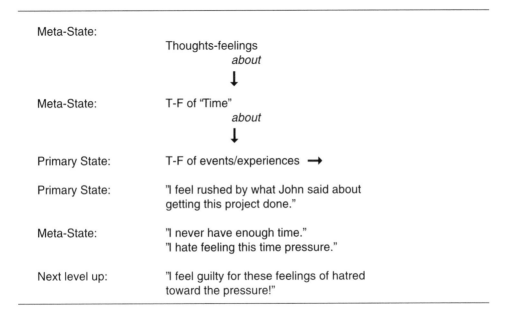

Meta-State:	Thoughts-feelings *about* ↓
Meta-State:	T-F of 'Time" *about* ↓
Primary State:	T-F of events/experiences →
Primary State:	"I feel rushed by what John said about getting this project done."
Meta-State:	"I never have enough time." "I hate feeling this time pressure."
Next level up:	"I feel guilty for these feelings of hatred toward the pressure!"

EXERCISE: Changing your time-line

Would you like to change your time-line or time-lines? Since our time-lines are not real but a mind-body encoding of the concept of time, the process of changing these internal representations of "time" can occur relatively simply. But a warning: when you change your time-line, you may initially experience disorientation, even feel dizzy, strange, or weird.

First, do notice how you sort time. You may have a different time-line configuration for the way you relate to "time" at work, at home, when on holiday, when engaged in a hobby. So simply think about some simple activity in a given realm and notice your representations of that today, yesterday, last year, two years ago, five years ago, twenty years ago. Then notice it today, tomorrow, next year, two years from now, five years into your future, and then twenty years.

347

As you now step back, in your mind, from these representations, notice *how you know* and distinguish past, present, and future. What images or configurations do you use? Most of us sort in different places and so a line, a path, a road, or some linear symbol typically can encode this. Others will use such thing as circles, spirals, boomerangs, or calendars.

Because *location* tends to be an easy and common way in most cultures, notice that first. Then any other differences in the audio-video film in your mind: color, closeness, whether you're in or out of the movie, its tone, its volume, and any other ingredients.

EXERCISE: *Changing a through-time orientation*
1. Float up above your time-line.
From there straighten your line so it runs left to right. Then, rotate your time-line ninety degrees (or rotate yourself ninety degrees).

2. Then drop down into your time-line.
Do so with the realization and feeling that you now have your "past" behind you. And as you let your represent your "past" as behind your head, you can open your eyes to see the "present" directly in front of your face while the future seems at arm's length or further in front of your face. Take a moment with this ... How does it feel?

EXERCISE: *Changing an in-time orientation*
1. Float up above "time".
Straighten your time-line and then rotate your line ninety degrees (or rotate your body ninety degrees).

2. Drop behind your time-line.
Do it so that everything lies directly in front of you. Make the images about six inches to one foot square and place "past" images an arm's length to your left (if right-handed). Notice that your "future" has moved to the other side. The present goes directly in front of your face about a foot out. Imagine the tops of all three images to stand at eye level. You have now taken on the codings of an ideal *through-time* person. Take a moment with this ... How does this feel?

Some people will experience profound changes as they do this exercise. Others will not. Almost everybody finds it easier to experience these patterns after they first work with someone well trained in time-line processes. You may wish to leave your time-line in its opposite position for a while just to experiment with it.

The trance states of fast and slow time

Richard Bandler has said that two hypnotic phenomena that are his "all-time favorites are fast and slow time distortion".

Our *brains* can create two very special kinds of psychological "time"—the sense of "time" moving very fast and the sense of "time" moving very slowly. The fact that chronological and cosmic "time" does not do this, nor do the events of life, at the macro-level, move any more quickly or slowly, but we *feel* as if this were the case, informs us that all of this occurs inside. It operates as a psychological function of representation.

How does our brain pull this piece of subjectivity off? What comprises the internal structure of "fast" and "slow" time?

The following instructions can be used for yourself or as you coach a partner through the process.

The pattern
1. Identify your time-line.
Ask yourself how you organize "time". What are the structure, shape, and configuration of your time-line? How do you differentiate between the past and the future?

2. Access states of fast and slow times.
Identify several examples of times when "time" seemed to move quickly and slowly. Use your voice and tone congruently as you do this. As you coach the person into the state to access the critical information, use your tone, tempo and voice.

When was the last time you experienced *slow* time? Recall it fully and be there again. (Anchor this state.)

Has there ever been a time when time just flew? Where were you? What was happening? Return to that experience fully.

In eliciting these states use quotes, metaphors, and stories to layer the person's internal sense of contexts and context-of-contexts. Remember that as "time" operates from a meta-level, so fast and slow "time" operate by means of the comparisons we use.

Menu list: You are blowing down the freeway going really fast and suddenly pull off into a twenty-mile-an-hour zone on the off-ram. It feels as if you're crawling. If you went from the slow zone into a modern zone, you would feel as if you were going fast.

3. Identify the cinematic features or qualities of fast and slow time.
How do you represent fast time? Slow time?

What are the "sub-modalities" features that define the difference? As you contrast fast time and slow time, what features in your movie encode the difference?

Be sure to find pleasant instances of slow "time". List some experiences where "time" slowed down *and* was pleasurable: for instance, a wonderful day that took forever or the first day of a long-awaited vacation when "time" just stood still.

What is the coding in your memory or imagination that creates the sense that you have lots of "time"? How do you create slow time?

What is the coding when "time" zooms by? The moment came for something and before you turned around, the event was over. It passed as if in no time. You sense, "Where did the time go?" "Two hours have passed? No, it can't be!"

4. Juxtapose the "times" to identify specific differences.
Take the two kinds of "time" and compare them. What are the differences between fast and slow time? Is the difference in where you see, hear or feel the two? Is the slow-time movie associated and the fast-time one dissociated?

Look for very unusual things to occur in these representations. In time distortion we sometimes have a difference of speed of movement between parts of the images—is that occurring? Is the center of the images moving quickly, while other parts are moving slowly, or are the side of the images moving fast?

5. (optional step) Utilize the time-line if you have any difficulties.
Turn your time-line so it is out in front of you. Turn physically if you have to, stand up and *back up* to the last time you remember experiencing exquisitely slow time.

Back up associatedly to an instance of fast time. As the person backs up into the memory, the future disappears in front of them.

"Good, now literally pull up the events around you as you back up and see what you saw, hear and feel what you felt. Pull the events around you until you are fully in the even again. And take a moment as you relive this fully and just enjoy the process as you notice the distinctions."

6. Anchor and Apply both fast and slow "time".
Every time the person accesses slow time, inquire about a difference in one feature to accentuate it. As you do so, anchor it. Establish an anchor on one knee for fast time and one on the other knee for slow time.

Apply fast and slow time to two experiences. What experience would you like to experience with a greater sense of more time? Does anything go by too quickly that you would like to have last a lot longer? What things would you like to get over a lot more quickly?

8. Meta-state while in a trance state.
"Allow yourself to close your eyes and go away to another time and place so that you can begin to make preparations to feel yourself *let go* deeper into a trance than you have before … now, so that you can begin to float back on the wings of time and change. And go way, way back. Because what I want to do, speaking to you as a child, involves beginning to get a little bit younger with each breath, a year at a time … becoming younger and younger. Seeing perhaps a birthday or a pleasant event from each year as you *step back* in your mind, getting a little bit younger, and a little bit younger with each breath.

"And as you get younger you can recapture that childlike ability to learn, really learn, and to experience things. Because when you were very young, a month seemed like forever. And as you get older, months seem to just zip by. And, when you were a child, a month seemed like a long time, and an hour took forever. In fact, five minutes seemed to last an eternity …

"Now let your unconscious remember how to feel time as slow and fast and to feel it fully [*fire anchors*]. Because your unconscious remembers how you experimented to find out those distinctions, and it can remember fully … now.

"And in a moment when I reach over and touch your knee like this [*fire anchor for fast time*] you will zip back to an event that went really fast … but, because you want it to last a lot longer, when I touch this knee [*fire anchor for slow time*], you can experience time as moving v-e-r-y slo-o-o-ow-ly. It will almost stand still. And as it does you can relive that event in real time of two minutes, but it will seem like an hour."

Meta-state a new decision in "time"

The following is a time-lining or meta-stating process using the decision-destroyer pattern. To use the concept "time" so that it serves our empowerment and effectiveness we sometimes first have to undo false, useless, and toxic mappings from past events that we no longer need to drag with us and use to torture ourselves. A decision map created at some previous time does *not* have to be treated as unchangeable. We can recode an old decision and update it.

The pattern
1. Identify your time-line.
Think of some simple activity that you did this morning, then think about it last week, last year, two years ago, five years ago … next week, next month, next year, two years from now, five years from now.

Where do you locate these memories and imagination? What kind of a configuration do you have these in: a line, circle, drawer, Rolodex—what?

What are the differences in pictures, sounds, feelings?

2. Float above your sense of "time" and draw a time-line.
Now float back to a specific memory, then float forward through now to a time in the future.

3. Identify a limiting decision to change.
What decision (or belief or experience) that you once made is now a limiting and even toxic decision? Are there any old decisions, beliefs, or memories that you would like to change?

4. Access, anchor, and amplify some resources.
What resourceful states, ideas, understandings, beliefs, or decisions would have totally transformed that old experience?

5. Float up and then back on your time-line to fifteen minutes before the event.
In just a minute, when you float back down into your time-line so that you are fifteen minutes prior to the old experience, you will look into your future. This means that you will *not* see the old decision because it has not happened yet. It does not exit. So, as you now fully reaccess the resources that you want to apply to the old experience … just those resources totally transform things.

Ready? Good. Now float down … with the resource … and bring it through the experience and up to the present.

6. Future-pace and check ecology.

Spiraling resource experiences

The pattern
1. Access the here and now.
Imagine yourself in a wide-open space in this moment in time fully associated and fully present to your thoughts-and-feelings. Think back to a number of delightfully resourceful experiences of your past—beginning by thinking of such an experience that occurred last year … And, once you see and hear and feel that experience, step back into *this moment in time* and imagine that experience circling around you as the planets move around the sun. Watch it circle around you as if you stood in the middle of a spiral.

2. Let it settle.
Eventually let it settle back to where you first found it—a year ago—and do the same thing with a resourceful memory from two years ago, and again with one from three to five years ago. As you find and re-experience each resource, let it become another orbiting event as if it were a planet of resourcefulness moving around you as in a spiral.

3. Imagine fully and completely a delightful resource.
Imagine a resource that you want to experience in the coming year, in the year after that, and then in the time between three and five years from now. Again, let each experience move around you in a circle as a another rotating planet of resourcefulness.

4. Step into the spiraling resources.
Stepping into the middle of these spiraling, circling resources, just allow yourself to notice them moving around you at different distances, perhaps moving at different speeds, moving into your past, moving into your future. And as you allow them to rotate as a spiral you know that you can breathe deeply and fully in the center of all of these colorful, bright, and exciting resources that surround you and you can wonder, really wonder, what will happen, in just a moment when they collapse into you … fully and completely so that you can again experience them fully from within …

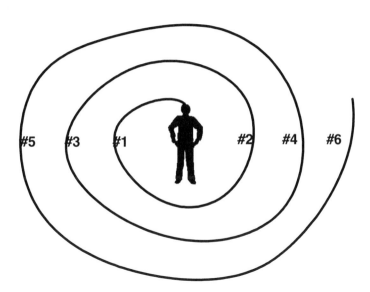

Figure 18.6

Developing instant patience now

Patience and impatience are "time" emotions. They arise from the thoughts-and-feelings we have *about* "time"–whether schedule time–psychological time, sacred time, or some other meta-level awareness of "time".

In the state of patience we think, represent, believe and therefore feel that we have plenty of time, or enough time; whereas in impatience we do the opposite: we think-feel that we don't have enough time, that we have a scarcity of "time", that

353

we need to hurry, rush, go faster.

These emotions, like all emotions, operate primarily as internal representations *drive* them. When we track back an emotion to the "thought" (the internal coding) out of which it comes we find representations that encourage impatience, frustration, anger, upsetness, demandingness, and so forth. To undo this unpleasant and, generally, useless emotional state, we need to recode our sense of "time".

The pattern

1. Use your time-line to specify the structure of impatience.

How do you know you think-feel "impatient" about this? What lets you know that you feel "impatience"? (Elicit the strategy.)

2. Elicit the higher frames for this structure.

Ask, what does it mean to me if I don't get all of these things accomplished? What does it mean if I have this and that project demanding a deadline? What does it mean that this activity seems boring?

Where is the necessity or the demandingness (from yourself or others) that creates the sense of impatience?

3. Challenge the frame of demandingness.

Ask, why must I accomplish this by Tuesday? I agree that I would prefer to do so, but why *must* I? What would happen if I don't get everything done today that I want to get done?

What happens as you expose the *demandingness*? Have you simply been operating from an old impatient program of disliking delayed gratification? Have you simply conditioned yourself for low-frustration tolerance? Do you actually have no logical reason for the impatience?

4. Accept the thoughts-and-feelings of impatience.

Access *acceptance* and then from a meta-level apply to impatience. What happens when you fully *accept* your thoughts-and-feelings of impatience? Do you now feel you can relax comfortably in this higher knowledge and perspective?

Meta-state the impatience also with appreciation, with calmness. What resources best transform the old impatience?

5. Give yourself more "time".

As you go meta again, this time alter your future "time" representations so that you see more space, more room, more distance, notice what happens.

As you do this, relanguaging yourself: "I have plenty of time and refuse to threaten myself in an erroneous way by thinking of 'time' in terms of scarcity. I will take effective action to do what I can and leave it at that."

What happens?

6. Quality-control the experience and future pace.

Summary

Whenever we *go in* and develop a strong *inward focus* we thereby make the transition from the uptime state into a meta-level state. This is meta-trance. It's just a different metaphor for thinking about trance and for working with trance processes.

As NLP is through and through a communication model, it is at the same time a model of hypnosis, hypnotic language, and hypnotic processes. In meta-trance we have enriched this by thinking about the meta-language that allows us to enter "Meta-Land" and rise up in our mind to some of the highest conceptual states known to us.

Chapter Nineteen
Mind-Lines
Conversationally Reframing

Historically, the patterns for conversational reframing have been called "sleight-of-mouth" patterns. Robert Dilts along with Todd Epstein developed these as they collected some of the language patterns in Richard Bandler's speech patterns. Dilts tells the story of the origin in his book *Sleight of Mouth* (1999). We have developed a piece of that on the website under the title, "When Richard Bandler Played the Paranoid Game" (www.neurosemantics.com/Articles/paranoid.htm).

Over the years, the "sleight-of-mouth" patterns appeared as a section or perhaps a whole chapter in numerous books. I (MH) recorded them as a presentation from Chris Hall in *The Spirit of NLP* (1996). Yet the first full-length book on these patterns for conversational reframing was *Mind-Lines: Lines for Changing Minds* (2002).

In renaming the patterns mind-lines, we decided to not use the sleight-of-hand metaphor. Our reason for this is simple. There are a lot of negative connotations to the "sleight-of-hand/mouth" metaphor such as trickery, deception, and manipulation. While any reframing pattern can be used in a hurtful and manipulative way, that is not their primary use and certainly was not their design. Rather, they are designed to enable us to *frame* meaning in new and more productive ways. So while this domain of NLP training began as "the Sleight-of-Mouth Patterns", and while many people have used them to pull the wool over the eyes of their victims, that is *not* their design here or their place in mastering NLP.

Our use of these *patterns, as patterns for transforming meaning* is to use them to make our experience in life richer and fuller for ourselves and for others. Here we will use them to empower ourselves in having more fun and in accessing more resourceful states. We will use the "magic" of these re-framing patterns to blow out objections and excuses, to create win-win relationships, and to increase our powers of persuasion.

Have you ever heard a line that changed your mind?

Lines can do that. Lines can change our minds. After all, a line is just a statement that frames our understanding. A line invites us to produce and edit a movie in our mind—a film that we can then play and use to feel and act in new ways. With that in mind, consider each of the NLP presuppositions as a line, a mind-line, giving screenplay information that can change your mind. This was especially true when they were first presented. As they have become more and more accepted, we take them more for granted. But, when psychology was primarily focused on "fixing broken people", the idea that "people are not broken: they have all the resources they need" was a mind-changing line and initiated a radically different video to play in the mind.

The NLP presuppositions succinctly and powerfully summarize a whole new way of thinking about a number of things. As such, they provide us a new perceptual grid as they set a new frame of reference or frame of mind about things. Where did the NLP presuppositions come from? From the attitudes that Perls, Satir, and Erickson demonstrated and expressed. Later, as Bandler and Grinder identified and adopted them for themselves, they became part of the very spirit of NLP. We see this in the early NLP writings. For example, notice the following lines from the 1985 book, *Using Your Brain—For a Change*. Here Richard Bandler presents many mind-lines and he does so in a playfully seductive way that challenges additional ways of thinking. Enjoy his artistry because soon you will be replicating this form of linguistic elegance.

On learning

The problem with brains is that they learn things too quickly and too well. Human beings have an amazing ability to learn ... the bad side ... you can learn garbage just as easily as you can learn useful things. [p. 10]

It's an amazing thing to be able to remember to get terrified every time you see a spider. You never find a phobic looking at a spider and saying, "Oh damn, I forgot to be afraid." Are there a few things you'd like to learn that thoroughly? When you think about it that way, having a phobia is a tremendous learning achievement. [p. 11]

Phobics are people who can learn something utterly ridiculous very quickly. Most people tend to look at a phobia as a problem rather than an achievement. They never stop to think, "If she can learn to do that, then she should be able to learn to do anything." [p. 46]

On human nature and behavioral "problems"

People work perfectly. I may not like what they do, or they may not like it, but they are able to do it again and again, systematically. It's not that they're broken; they're just doing something different from what we, or they, want to have happen. [p. 15]

Another difficulty with most psychology is that it studies broken people to find out how to fix them. That's like studying all the cars in a junkyard to figure out how to make cars run better. If you study lots of schizophrenics, you may learn how to do schizophrenia really well, but you won't learn about the things they *can't* do. [p. 15]

I always keep in mind that anything anybody has done is an achievement, no matter how futile or painful it may be. *People aren't broken; they work erfectly!* The important question is, "*How do they work now?*" so that you can help them work perfectly in a way that is more pleasant and useful. [p. 143]

On getting depressed

There are times when you don't get what you want from someone else. But when you don't get what you want, feeling bad is extra! Did you ever think of that? First you don't get what you want, and then you have to feel bad for a long time because you didn't get it.

To a man who claimed to have been depressed for sixteen years, Richard said, "That's amazing! You haven't slept in that long?" (*Counterexample*)

The structure of this statement as much says, "I have encoded my experience such that I am living in the delusion that I have been in the same state of consciousness for sixteen years." I *know* he hasn't been depressed for sixteen years. He's got to take time out for lunch, and getting annoyed, and a few other things. People spend a lot of money and time learning to meditate in order to stay in the same state for an hour or two. [*Counter-example*] If he were depressed for an hour straight, he wouldn't even be able to notice it, because the feeling would habituate and thereby become imperceptible ...

You can cure people of what they've got, and discover that they never had it. "Sixteen years of depression" could be only 25 hours of actually being depressed. [Bandler, 1985, pp. 28-29]

On change

Psychologists are always looking for the "deep hidden inner meaning." They have taken too many poetry and literature classes. Change is a lot easier than that, if you know what to do. [Bandler, 1985, p. 16]

On confusion

Confusion is always an indication that you're on your way to understanding. Confusion presupposes that you have learned a lot to date, but it's not yet organized in a way that allows you to understand it. [p. 83]

Years ago I realized I had been wrong so many times, I decided I'd just go ahead and be wrong in the ways that were more interesting. [p. 85]

The healthiest thing you can do ... is to become confused, and [while] many people complain about how confusing I am, they don't yet realize that *confusion is the door-way to a new understanding*. Confusion is an opportunity to rearrange experience and organize it in a different way than you normally would. That allows you to learn to do something new and to see and hear the world in a new way. [p. 95]

So whenever you get confused, you can get excited about the new understanding that awaits you. And you can be grateful for this opportunity to go somewhere new, even though you don't yet know where it will take you. [p. 96]

On influence, control, manipulation

Many therapists even have a rule against being effective. They think that influencing anyone directly is manipulative, and that manipulation is bad. It's as if they said, "You're paying me to influence you. But I'm not going to do it because it's not the right thing to do." When I saw clients, I always charged by the change, rather than by the hour; I only got paid when I got results. [p. 53]

A lot of people think that NLP sounds like "mind control" as if that were something bad. I said, "Yes, of course." If you don't begin to control and use your own brain, then you have to just leave it to chance. [p. 118]

On relationships

The greatest error of all is in thinking that the only way for you to feel good in certain situations is for someone else to behave in a certain way. "You must behave the way I want you to, so I can feel good, or I'm going to feel bad and stand around and make you feel bad too." [p. 62]

One thing that has always amazed me is that people are seldom nasty to strangers. You really have to know and love someone before you can treat her like dirt and really make her feel bad about small things. Few people will yell at a stranger about important things like crumbs on the breakfast table, but if you love her, it's OK. [p. 64]

On interrupting a dad who was overcontrolling and very angry

The father dragged his daughter into a counseling office with her arm twisted up behind her back and shoved her into a chair ...

"Is there anything wrong?" I asked.

"The girl's a little *whore*."

"I don't need a whore; what did you bring her here for?"

"No, no! That's not what I'm talking about ..."

"Who is this girl?"

"My daughter?"

"You made your daughter into a *whore*!!!"

"No, no. You don't understand ..."

"And you brought her here to *me*! How disgusting!"

At this point the man who had come in snarling and yelling is now pleading with the speaker to understand him. This means that he had totally switched from attacking his daughter to defending himself. Meanwhile, his daughter was quietly cracking up about all of this. She thought that was wonderful.

"You brought her in here with her arm twisted up behind her back and threw her around. That's how prostitutes are treated; that's what you're training her to do."

"Well I want to force her to …"

"Oh, 'force'—teach her that men control women by throwing them around, ordering them around, twisting their arms behind their back, forcing them to do things against their will. That's what pimps do. Then the only thing left to do is to charge money for it." [pp. 64-65]

We call these mind-lines, "Apply to Self" and "Content Reframing", as you will soon discover:

"Let me ask you … look at your daughter. Don't you want her to be able to feel love, and to enjoy sexual behavior? But how would you like it if the only way she learned to interact with men was the way you brought her in that door a few minutes ago? And she waited until she was 25 and married somebody who beat her up, threw her around, abused her, and forced her to do things against her will?"

Here we have a mind-line that outframes the old frame as it applies a person's values to a belief or understanding. We also have a mind-line that "post-frames" the situation by entertaining thoughts of the outcome, and then the outcome of that outcome.

"But she may make a mistake, and it will hurt her."

"That's possible. Two years from now that guy may drop her like a hot rock and go away. And when she feels bad and lonely … she'll have no one to go to, because she'll hate your guts."

This is more "outcome-of-outcome" reframing.

"Isn't it more important that she learn to have losing relationships? Or should she learn to have the morals of any man that can force her around? That's what pimps do." [p. 66]

This mind-line engages in the prioritizing of values.

On certainty and uncertainty

Certainty is where people stop thinking and stop noticing. Any time you feel absolutely certain of something, that's a sure sign that you have missed something. [p. 97]

Whenever you think that you understand totally, that is the time to go inside and say, "The joke is on me." Because it is in those moments of certainty that you can be sure that the futile learnings have set in, and the fertile ground has not been explored. Obviously, there is always a lot more left to learn, and that is the fun part of NLP, and its future. [p. 156]

There is so much more inside our minds than we suspect. There is *so* much more outside than we are able of being curious about. It's only that growing sense of curiosity that allows you to capture the enthusiasm that makes even the most mundane, or the most fascinating task worthwhile, fun, and intriguing. Without that, life is nothing more than waiting in line. [p. 159]

Lines frame minds

What is it about statements or lines such as these that catch our fancy and that can change our minds about how we have been thinking? How do lines or assertions about things work in the first place?

Lines work by framing. *Framing* refers to the perspective that we take as we view things, the perspective we use in our internal movies. For example, we normally *frame* confusion and depression as "bad" things, as "problems", as "experiences to avoid". Yet, in the former statements, Bandler framed them as "good" things, as opportunities, and as desirable experiences.

Confusion is really the gateway to new learning. Depression is a creative skill that has structure. Normally we frame "being certain" as a good and desirable thing. Bandler framed it as a problem. Certainty means we have stopped thinking.

The structure of any line, statement, or assertion that we make is a trait, quality, or category. And as we frame it, so it is to us. It establishes its meaning. When we *frame* it in a different way, we *reframe* the very meaning of that trait, quality, or category.

The daughter wanting to explore her sexuality meant "rebellion" and "being a whore". Then it was framed as wanting to be her own person, knowing her own mind, refusing to be used. The dad's actions were framed as caring and trying to prevent her from being a whore. Then he was framed as treating her as a pimp, as mistreating a woman.

This shows that *meaning* is a function of *framing*. Apart from frames and framing, activities and behaviors do not mean anything. It takes a mind to *frame* sensory-based responses to give it this or that *meaning*. We do this in two ways. First, we can use our minds to *link* one thing to another. This gives us associative meaning, stimulus-response meaning. "This X is linked to or associated with this Y." Dog salivates in the presence of meat so we ring a bell and link the presenting of the meat with the ringing of the bell until the ringing of the bell becomes associated with the meat. Classical conditioning.

We can diagram this as a formula:

This X (the stimulus) leads to ➜ this Y (the response).

The harsh tone of Dad's voice when he's upset or angry leads to one's being punished and to feeling bad. Harsh tonality leads to feeling hurt.

Second, when we associate things repeatedly, the reference experience itself eventually becomes our frame of reference for how to think of other things that we can put into the same category. This creates a second kind of meaning, *framed meaning* or *conceptual meaning*. As we abstract from the experience and categorize it, we create classifications. "Dad" as an "authority figure" now stands for other "authority figures". This gives us a new and higher-level structure of meaning.

Authority figures are scary (i.e., they are dangerous, hurtful, able to punish and inflict harm).

In this way the influence of an experience spreads. We now come to use it as a model or frame for how to think-feel about other things. As this happens, the stimulus-response format develops from a mere *causation* structure into an *equation* structure. Now the X *is* or *equals* the Y: harsh tonality = being hurt; authority figures = danger.

Lines that encode the structure of "meaning"

What does "meaning" mean? Literally, it refers to anything that we "hold in mind." Whatever we "hold in mind" constitutes what something *means* to us. And what do we hold in mind but associations and frames? And that's it. Where do we get such associations and frames? From referent experiences. We experience something and then bring it into our minds through representation. We see it again, hear it again, feel it again. We *re*-present it to ourselves.

At this point the *reference* has become a *represented reference*. It plays out on the screen of our mind and, as we play out the movie again, we *experience* the reference again. The internal cinema in our mind sends signals to our nervous system and body as if we were again the player or actor in the movie-and in that way the linguistics become neurology. We then re-experience it. Then, through habituation, the movie becomes a familiar one. We begin structuring or framing the world in terms of the X leading to the Y. Stimulus-response.

But it doesn't stop there. As our mind grows, we begin to abstract from the experience to create categories and classifications. We generalize from the specific and we let it *stand* for a broad class of things. These broad classes are more abstract terms: learning, confusion, depression, self, failure. Every time we generalize from our specific cinema of a represented referent experience, we create a frame of reference. Now we see the world in terms of that frame of reference.

All of this shows up in the formula that we use in the NLP Meta-Model as summarized by three linguistic distinctions.

Cause-effect statements:	X leads to Y
Complex-equivalence statements:	X equals Y
Identification statements:	X is Y

Together these statements create what we can only call neuro-linguistic and neuro-semantic "magic". It's "magic" because *saying* (or *representing*) *makes it so inside*. Saying that X leads to, equals, or is Y does not make it so in the physical world of forces and impacts, but it does *make it so* in the internal world of information, communication, and structure.

Confusion does mean or lead to or cause ignorance or badness or lack of success. Confusion is, leads to, and means you are at the gateway to new creativity.

This is the heart of meaning, of magic, of human reality, of the making of our mental maps, and of transformation of our models of reality. The map we construct is not the territory. It is a map of the territory—a symbolic representation of the territory. The territory is one thing, and the map is yet another. Bateson said, "It [the territory] never gets in." What gets in is our representations of the territory. And it gets in at different levels.

First we let in a straightforward sensory-based representation as our mental movie. I hear the harsh tones and I represent the kinesthetic pain of being spanked. I play a movie from Dad's upset to my sore backside. I play the movie over and over and keep re-experiencing it and can do so long after the original referent experience is done and over. I encode the movie with certain cinematic effects—size, brightness, color, soundtrack, smells, words.

Then I have other thoughts and feelings about that harsh tonality/painful backside movie. I can conclude all kinds of things *about* it. And, with a child's mind, we usually compute things in such a way that the maps we make are not the maps that really help us to succeed in life.

- "This is the way life is."
- "Dad hates me."
- "I'm no good."
- "Authority figures are scary."
- "Life is worthless."
- "I deserve to be punished."

Whatever we conclude, whatever generalized classifications we create, we believe them, assume that they are real, and let them become our unquestioned *frame of reference*. As we make this meta-move to a higher level of mind, we become the director and producer of our movies. It's not just that we have the old movie playing in our minds, but we play it and use it to interpret and make sense of other things. It becomes part of our referent structure for thinking, for making sense of things. This is the way it is.

The magical cube

The Mind-Lines model operates from a visual digital diagram, the magical box or cube. This is where the magic of meaning occurs. Inside that box or cube, we all have a neurological and linguistic formula that governs how we construct "meaning." In brief, it is "X leads to or equals Y." The X stands for something "out there," some external behavior (EB). The Y stands for some processing or experiencing inside, some internal state (IS). This gives us the magical formula: EB → IS.

It is this formula of neuro-linguistic magic that induces us into mind-body states, neuro-semantic states. Structuring it as a formula inside of a box gives us a way to think about and learn more than two dozen explicit ways to reframe beliefs, ideas, and understandings. As you tune into your own internal dialogue of meaning-making or as you listen to someone else's, and you hear ideas that could poison a mind, disrupt emotions, or sabotage effective living, you will have at least twenty-six ways to transform that conceptual reality.

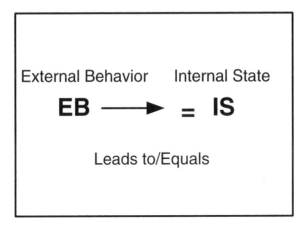

Figure 19.1: The magic box or cube

Mind-lines: lines that frame meanings

Now you know the secret of the magic. The structure of neuro-linguistic magic operates according to how we use language to encode our internal cinema, which in turn signals our body and neurology about how to feel and how to respond. It's magical.

If you *think* that not reaching your goal on first attempt is, equals, and leads to the category of "failure", then any error-detection signal becomes the semantically loaded experience of *failure* to you.

If you *think* that not reaching your goal on first attempt is, equals, and leads to the category of "feedback", then any error-detection signal becomes the semantically loaded experience of *feedback* to you.

How do you experience an error detection signal? A mistake? An unsuccessful activity? Do you feel and experience it as failure or feedback? How have you framed the meaning of a mistake? Are mistakes okay in your neuro-linguistic system? Do you feel excited and thrilled to get an error message so that you can make course corrections? Or do you feel bad, ashamed, guilty, or inadequate when an error message comes up?

An error message doesn't mean anything apart from how you have framed it. Most of us have learned to map "error" messages as bad. Why? Because we were punished for making mistakes. Parents spanked us, teachers humiliated us in front of others, authority figures made life more difficult for us. So we used our referent experiences to chart out, X (error message) leads to (→) Y (emotional distress). We kept some same movies of that in our mind to remember. Then we drew higher-level conclusions about all of this and encoded such in linguistic structures. "I can't stand being made wrong. It's so humiliating." Then, it is that line that we keep feeding our mind that frames our reality.

Mind-lines: lines to reframe the meanings we hold in mind

The Mind-Lines model begins with this understanding of mind, referencing, representation, language, and neuro-linguistic states. It begins with the "magic" formula. This is the heart and core of understanding reframing.

$$X \rightarrow = Y$$

But it doesn't end there. That's just straightforward reframing. The content of X (an error message) can be reframed to mean numerous things. X is the external behavior, the thing or activity that occurs out there in the world. Y is the internal experience—the internal mental or emotional state, the internal significance. As such X and Y do not even exist in the same dimension. One is external (the territory), the other is internal (the map). Linking them, equating them, and identifying them is the "magic" that makes it so.

From here we have six additional ways to reframe. If we dissect X or Y we can *deframe* this meaning equation. That breaks down and analyzes the component pieces to give us the internal strategy of how the person mapped a particular X leading to a particular Y. When a map doesn't work very well or is especially toxic, *deframing* works as a dissolvent on the map.

Next we step aside to look at the immediate box into which we have put this X ➜ = Y formula. That allows us to then *reframe the context*. "Where this formula would really work in a beneficial way is Z."

We can also reframe by *applying* the very pieces of the statement (the X and the Y) to the person to see if it equally applies to self and to other. This *reflexive* framing enables us to put the formula to the test to see if it will hold up under scrutiny. Many limiting belief statements map things in a way that creates a double standard. Typically, this shows its weakness.

We can even do this *reflexive reframing* on the entire formula of meaning. Doing that allows us to do *counterframing* as we look for exemptions and counterexamples to the belief statement. This too challenges and puts the statement to the test.

From there we can step outside of the entire formula and look at the formula in terms of *time*. When did the person construct this map and why? What was the *positive intention* for building this belief? What was the *positive cause* for building it? This allows us to *preframe* the statement so that we take an empathic understanding of it.

With regard to *time*, we can also look at it in terms of where this map will take a person over time If you let this formula govern your neuro-linguistic experiences in the days and years to come, what will it do for you? What outcomes will result? And from those outcomes what other consequences will occur? And if you live your whole life this way, then what? This gives us *post-framing*, as we can look at the statement from the perspective of short-, medium-, and long-term consequences.

Stepping outside the box of the meaning formula is actually an *outframing* process. Yet it is only one of scores of ways that we can outframe the meaning locked into the formula. We can also outframe in terms of universality, values, mapping, identity, or ecology. Outframing moves to a higher level to bring a higher frame of reference to it. In this way we can test it and/or transform it. What happens to the belief statement when we apply one of a few dozen other frames to it?

Finally, there is the move of applying a *metaphorical frame*. We can outframe the original framed equation analogously by bringing a metaphor, story, narrative, or some other referent. This allows us to move beyond deductive and inductive thinking to abductive thinking.

In all of these ways, we can frame the original movie and its frames afresh. We can tear the frame apart, turn it on its head, twist it around, pseudo-frame it in the past or in the future, outframe, and frame it with analogies. Each move alters the very structure and form of the meaning and thereby affects either the cinematic features of the movie or the entire movie itself.

That, in a very brief overview, describes the *seven directions for sending a brain* as we reframe in seven different ways.

How do mind-lines work?

Mind-lines work through how they encode *representation* and *reference*. At the primary level of thinking, we represent the content and details of the cinematic movie. This makes up what's on our mind, the content of our thoughts. Then, at multiple meta-levels, we set frames of reference that create the higher contexts and framing structures that form the mega-meanings of the representations.

Let's play with the NLP mind-line that says, "Behind every behavior is a positive intention."

1. Representationally-how do you represent that?
In the movie of your mind, think of some behavior. See that behavior, hear it, feel it. If it is obnoxious, hurtful, and nasty behavior, then step out to watch it as an observer. Adjust the cinematic features of the movie so that you can watch it comfortably. Now edit into the movie the understanding that, "behind" or "above" that piece of behavior, the person is attempting to accomplish some positive value of some sort for him- or herself. How do you *represent* that? How do you represent layer upon layer of intentions until you find a level that's sufficiently positive?

In the movie in my mind, I see a person in a bubble—the bubble represents his or her state. I color that bubble so that the color symbolically represent the state (e.g., red for anger, pink for gentle, black for sad and depressed). As the movie plays, behaviors pop out of the bubble, and above and beyond the bubble I see a white aura that indicates the higher positive intentions that the person is attempting to express.

2. Referentially-how do you frame this movie?
What does it mean to you? What conceptual contexts do you apply to it? When you look at your movie of behavior having positive intentions behind it, what does this mean to you? The basic goodness of people? The possibility of creating higher intentions through using this frame? The recognition that people are more than their behavior?

How did you do that? To become masterful in NLP, take each and every one of the NLP presuppositions and put it through this process. Do it very specifically and with lots of vivid details. Create an internal movie that represents the idea in the presupposition. If you have to shift to caricature images, cartoons, or diagrams, feel free to do so. This is where you will find using the visual digital system very useful. That's because concepts typically need the visual digital system for epresentation.

Let's do one more. Consider the mind-line that drives the very epistemology of NLP and NS: "The map is not the territory." This statement from Korzybski summarizes the distinction between map and territory and uses the metaphor of

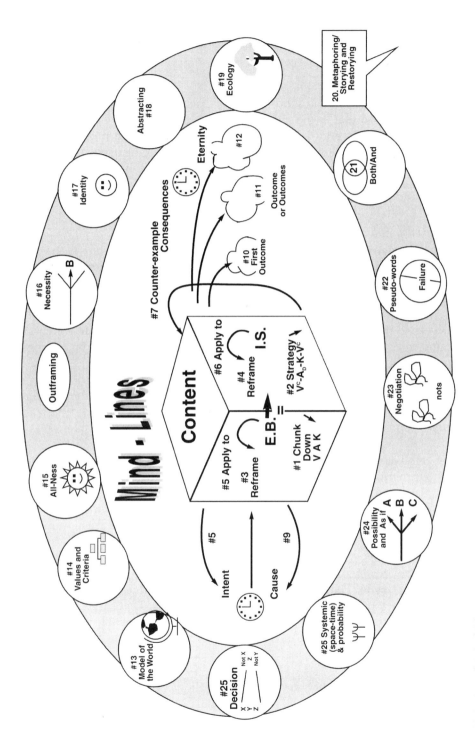

Figure 19.2: Pascal Mind Lines

"map" for all of the internal processes of abstracting and mapping. The fuller statement asserts not only the negation, but also that the usefulness of our mapping depends upon the symbolism in the map having a similar structure to the territory.

1. Representationally-how do you represent that?
This invites us to make a movie about the events, people, and things that we experience in the world so that in the movie we distinguish between what's going on "out there" in the world and the mappings that we make about it on the inside. *How do you represent that?* How do you *encode* that your mapping of events is *not* the same thing as the events themselves? Again, you will probably need to use some nonliteral visual graphics to encode this higher-level understanding.

2. Referentially-how do you frame this movie?
What meaning, significance, and value do you give to it? What do you say to yourself about this? What do you feel about it? What higher-level frames of meaning support and empower the movie? What frames make the movie increasingly more compelling for you?

The answers to these questions will tell you how you can then create conversational mind-lines that you can use with friends, loved ones, associates, in trainings, in writing, wherever. When you have effectively *represented* and *framed* the idea, then you can more effectively communicate that idea to others and do so in an influential and persuasive way. Notice how Bandler (1985) did it with the idea that people aren't broken, but work perfectly (see "On human nature and behavioral 'problems' " above).

Consider this view from the standpoint of representing and referencing. On the screen of our mind, we see "people," we see people doing what people do—living, working, playing, parenting, insulting each other, being abusive and nasty, yelling, blaming. This gives us *representation*. We have a movie. Then the word "perfectly" comes but as a qualifier for how people function, it jars things. The movie comes to a halt, it stops. "Perfectly"?

Then comes the line, "I may not like what they do ..." Yes, that's right! Pacing. The movie starts up again. People doing things ... and I not necessarily liking what they do. "[O]r they may not like it ..." Another pacing line. That's right. They also may dislike what they are doing. I know that one. "[B]ut they are able to do it again and again, systematically." As the movie continues, as I observe the disliked behavior going on and on and on ... I not liking it, they not like it. Hey, this movie sucks!

"[S]ystematically. It's not that they're broken: they are just doing something different from what we, or they, want to have happen." Here's the *frame*. This is what it *means*. It works! People work perfectly. "Perfectly" refers to the structured and predictable nature of the actions, that the behaviors are actually achievements, accomplishments.

Representationally tracking *how we encode words* and then how we *frame* those representations gives us the ability to understand what we are *doing*, neuro-linguistically and neuro-semantically, with our words. It gives us the ability to analyze how our lines actually *work* in our minds and in the minds of those to whom we speak. It is the analysis of a film critic.

Let's try this on another statement. Let's look again at that quotation we saw above from Bandler (1985) conversationally reframing a phobia:

> It's an amazing thing to be able to remember to get terrified every time you see a spider. You never find a phobic looking at a spider and saying, "Oh damn, I forgot to be afraid." Are there a few things you'd like to learn that thoroughly? When you think about it that way, having a phobia is a tremendous learning achievement.

Did you notice what went on cinematically in your mind as you read that statement? If not, then read it again and notice how you can make sense of it. It starts with a statement that's shocking to our normal way of thinking and so it has a tint of humor in it. "It's an amazing thing to be able to remember to get terrified every time you see a spider."

Representationally, the line invites us to "see a spider". That's the movie. Referentially, it frames seeing a spider as a member of the class of something to "get terrified" about. But, prior to introducing that category, we have a yet higher frame: "remember to get terrified". In those four words there are frames by implication. This suggests that getting terrified is a task, something that you have to do, something to remember, something that not everyone can do. And yet prior to that is the line, "It's an amazing thing to be able ..." So before the movie starts we are *pre-framed* with three levels: (1) amazing feat, (2) able to remember, (3) to get terrified every time. Then comes the movie: "seeing a spider".

To that give vividness and humor and compulsion to the movie, Bandler says, "You never find a phobic looking at a spider and saying, 'Oh damn, I forgot to be afraid.'" This gives some specific details to the movie playing in the mind. And the ridiculousness of that mini-scene makes the imagery all that much more memorable.

Finally, to *post-frame* the idea, he adds a couple more lines that set an even higher frame *about* the whole movie. "Are there a few things you'd like to learn that thoroughly? When you think about it that way, having a phobia is a tremendous learning achievement." Above the previous frames we now have 4) Such thoroughly learning and a tremendous learning achievement.

The 26 mind-lines

Now that we've wetted your appetite for the Mind-Line patterns, here is a brief overview of them. We have given each one a name and then supplied a description about it. At this point just read them and enjoy getting an overview of the patterns.

1. Specifying the Magic
Inquiring about the specific component pieces that make up the EB (external behavior) or the IS (internal state). Asking, "How do you know to call it this?

2. Detailing the Magical Strategy
Detailing out the specific order and sequence that the representations take to create the experience. Asking what comes first, second, third, and so on.

3. Reframing the EB Content
Offering a different meaning or label for the EB: "If you want to really see this EB, take a look at …"

4. Reframing the IS Content
Asserting that the EB is not really that IS but another: "This isn't IS Number 1: it is IS Number 2."

5. Reflexively Apply the EB (X)
Applying that EB to itself.

6. Reflexively Apply the IS (Y)
Applying the IS to the person or the speaker.

7. Counterexample
Looking for or asking about exemptions and counterexamples. Does this always happen?

8. Positive Prior Intention
Declaring that the person actually had *positive intentions* in generating the behavior and declaring them. A pacing move. "Weren't you attempting to accomplish the positive purpose of …?"

9. Positive Prior Cause
Declaring that positive causes outside the person actually created the behavior.

10. First Outcome
Challenging the behavior or belief based on its consequences. A confrontational move.

11. Outcomes of Outcome
Amplifying the consequence over time showing the disasters it will create.

12. Ultimate Outcome
Taking the consequences to the end of life and exaggerating it to a lifetime of it. A Provocative Therapy move.

13. Model of the World
Framing the belief or behavior as a map and therefore not inevitable.

14. Value Outframing
Frame with things more highly valued than the belief or behavior.

15. Allness Outframing
Inquiring about the universality of the belief.

16. Necessity Outframing
Inquiring about the rules or laws that "necessitates" the belief. Getting to its compulsory nature.

17. Identity Outframing
Inquiring or framing it as an identification, an identity?

18. All-Other-Abstractions Framing
Catch-all category for any other concept or frame of reference to apply to the belief. Mind-lines 21-26 also fit into this category of "other abstractions".

19. Ecology Outframing
Inquiring about the overall usefulness and balance of the belief.

20. Metaphor or Story Outframing
Telling a story that might contain one or more of the previous mind-lines but in the form of a narrative.

21. Both/And Framing
Questioning whether the belief is an either/or situation or whether there may be shades of gray in between or as a matter of degree.

22. Pseudo-Words Framing
Questioning whether the words that make up the belief are even real symbols that actually stand for something.

23. Negation Framing
Framing or questioning that invites the construct of a negation that nullifies the belief.

24. Possibility and "As If" Framing
Using a pretend or possibility frame to imagine the unimaginable to try on a new belief or concept.

25. Systemic and Probability Framing
Framing in terms of probabilities or other systemic factors that might contribute, influences that are nonlinear and circular in nature.

26. Decision Framing
Framing in terms of choice and volition rather than thought, wish, emotion.

Making lines work in the mind for transformation

How do we make the *lines* that we utter really work in human minds to alter the very structure and framing of reality? What have we learned from these examples?

First, aim to layer line upon line. When you do, you set frame upon frame. And you have to layer only three to seven such frames before most people can no longer track the layers. When this happens, the first levels just slide in. So don't depend upon just one line. In fact, that's one reason many people find that they have not well integrated the NLP presuppositions. They rely upon just one line to do all of the work. "The map is not the territory." Yet, if you don't have the rest of the lines that frame and outframe that statement, the one-liner will suffer from too much reductionism. In this, we frequently do ourselves and others a disservice when we reduce the NLP presuppositions to one-liners.

Second, utilize the power of frames by implication. We also do a disservice by overstating things. When we try to state everything we typically come across as pedantic and even condescending. So learn to practice *not* saying everything. Imply. Suggest. Hint. Seduce. Don't tell all. Leave enough unsaid so that the mind of the listener has to become active in filling in the ambiguities. Activate the imagination and then leave it to the imagination. If you're not convinced about the power of succinctness, return to the mind-lines of Richard Bandler that we quoted at the beginning of this chapter and notice the succinctness and suggestiveness in his statements.

Third, use many different mind-lines for the same idea. Say what something is, then what it isn't, then offer a metaphor, then outframe with its importance, ecology, or some other higher frame. Think about all of the mind-lines as steps that give you many ways to dance with an idea.

Fourth, continually calibrate from sensory awareness. Stay in sensory aware-ness so that you can continually calibrate which mind-lines work and which ones do not. Then reinforce the ones that work and drop the ones that do not work. Be playful and flexible in the process of creating and delivering the lines. In fact, this may be one of the most important keys to effective conversational reframing, staying playful. The danger is getting serious. Why? Because when we get serious we then set out to "get it right" and we aim to avoid being wrong. Yet that very attitude prevents us from experimenting, playing, discovering, and learning by trial and error.

The fact is that, when we get serious, we typically get stupid. It all happens very quickly, almost at the same time. The stupidity that arises is the stupidity of thinking that our representations and frames are real. They are not. If we treat them as real, they become real to us. The need to be right actually undermines learning, discovery, and creativity. The only worse thing is "the pride of being right" that leads many to feel self-important because then they are "right". When that happens, kiss learning, discovery and creativity goodbye.

So, now that you realize that seriousness increases stupidity, how do you feel about being more playful with these lines? But, if you get serious, then just stop, in your mind, and know that, the more you get serious, the more you will begin to loop around that seriousness until it becomes painful, really painful, until you lighten up and enjoy your stupidity, realizing that it is the gateway to new creativity.

Using mind-lines to enhance powerful beliefs

The NLP trainer Frank Daniels suggested during a mind-lines training in Nottingham, England, that we use mind-lines to *change* limiting beliefs. While he watched some demonstrations, it dawned on him that the Mind-Lines model could equally well be used to build up and reinforce an empowering belief. During the training, he suggested this and asked what I thought about it. It put a new light on yet another way to use mind-lines. So it was there that we first took the mind-lines questions and intentionally used them with participants to build up, extend, and expand an already powerful and wonderful belief. Since then I have used the series of mind-lines questions to do that in many other places. The following exercise will give you the chance to do the same with the mind-lines questions.

Pattern

1. Form a group of three persons and designate them experiencer, coach, and meta-person.
The experiencer will be the person who gets to go first. The coach is the person who will coach or facilitate the first person through the exercise. And the meta-person will be the person who will watch and record the process and track where the coach is in the process.

2. Identify and express a positively enhancing belief.
Do you have any empowering beliefs that really make life good for you? What do you believe that you'd like to amplify? What belief serves you well that you would like to make even more magical?

First express the belief in a clear and succinct statement. Then express it congruently, expressively, and in a way that you find is compelling. Write the belief statement down.

3. Coach the person through the Mind-Line questions.
Use the Mind-Line questions and conversationally inquire about what it means, how the person knows to call it that, their positive intention about that, and so forth. As the experiencer, just respond naturally and easily to the questions, letting

yourself fully experience the representations, frames, and feelings of the belief. The coach should use lots of confirmations and affirmations in the process.

4. Ask the questions in whatever order seems most appropriate for the experience.
There is no "right" procedure for asking these questions. Begin with the following arrangement and adjust them to the experience as it unfolds.

- What do you believe? Is this an empowering belief for you?
- How does it empower or enrich your life? What does it enable you to experience?
- What do you mean by X or Y?
- And what do you mean by that?
- How do you know that you believe this? And how do you know that?
- So this means X to you? (Reaffirmation and confirmation.)
- And does it mean anything else?
- How does this benefit you? How does it enrich your life?
- And how does this serve in a positive way for you?
- Do you do this in reference to yourself? To others? Does it apply to itself?
- Did you create this map yourself or did you learn it from someone else?
- When did you first learn to think this way?
- What was your positive intention in doing this? What do you get from that? (You can expand on this line of questioning.)
- What does this lead to?
- And when you get those benefits, what does that tend to lead to?
- When you think this way and use this belief to move through the world, how does it affect your identity or the way you define yourself?
- Do you have to do it this way?
- What other values does this have for you?
- Is it fully ecological? For your business, profession, personal life and relationships, health?

Summary

The Mind-Lines model pulls together into a linguistic model a great many of the features and facets of NLP so that mastering mind-lines facilitates our skill and competency in NLP mastery.

The conversational reframing patterns in mind-lines enable us to shift consciousness in seven basic directions. Recognizing that enables us to think of it as a directionalizing model.

Meaning shifts and changes according to how we frame it and the framing is a power entirely at our disposal.

Chapter Twenty
Using Mind-Lines in Everyday Life

Can we really "run our own brain" if we don't know how to frame things to empower us and to put positive spins on things? Of course not. That's why *reframing* is so critical. Reframing gives us the power to control our frames and hence our meanings.

Knowing as you do that *lines* can change minds, it's time to play with how we can create new lines. Here we begin with the toxic idea of "failure". We do this to encourage you in deepening your understanding and appreciation of *language as magic*. This will give you some practical experience with the reframing directions. Here, then, is an example of how *lines* can change our mind and reframe our life. We offer this practical example because many people operate from the toxic *idea* that anything that blocks immediate success is "failure" and that means "Failure" with a big F. Here are 26 ways to put new frames around this idea that will expand your thinking and give you more ways to frame things.

Twenty-six ways to reframe "failure"

Consider the toxic ideas in this statement: "Whenever I don't succeed, it really bothers me. It makes me feel like a failure. Not reaching my goals is such a bummer. I get depressed. No wonder I put things off and hesitate about other things. I just hate being a failure."

1. Specificity or "chunking" down
So you think you "are" a "failure", do you? As you think about something for which you feel like a failure, and define yourself as such, *how* do you know to do this? If you lost a job once, are you a failure? Twice? Three times? What standard are you using to make this judgment? How do you know to use *that* standard? When, where, and with whom did this occur? How do you represent this generalization of being a "failure"? What pictures, sounds, feelings, and words do you use to create this meaning?

If I were to get a sneak peek into the mental theater of your mind, what would I see? How would I know to give it the same name that you have, that is, to call it "failure"? How do you represent the action of failing at one thing as "making" you a failure?

2. *Sequencing a strategy*
So, up until now, you have accepted the idea of viewing and defining yourself as "a failure". Well, let's try to understand this. *How specifically* do you know that failing at one thing on a particular day makes you "a failure"? What do you see first, then what do you say about that, and so on as you think about this? If I were someone from the Temporary Job Agency and I would take your place so that you could have a vacation from this, teach me *how to do this the way you do*. What would I have to think, see, hear, sense?

3. *Reframing the external behavior*
This doesn't mean "failure": it means feedback. *Not* reaching some important goals really means that you now have some crucial information about how *not* to get there. So, with that in mind, you can feel free to explore new possible avenues, can you not?

4. *Reframing the internal state*
How interesting that you say that. What I really find as a failure, and I mean Failure with a big "F", is someone who doesn't reach a goal, and then sits down to wallow in whining and refuse to try again. When a person rolls over in the mud and won't learn or try again, I'd call that a "failure".

5. *Reflexively applying to self*
Does that mean if you don't reach your goal in presenting this limiting and painful belief to me, that just talking to me will turn you into an even bigger failure? You have to succeed at this communication or it will mean that and *that* only?

So, as you think about not reaching a goal and labeling it as making you a "failure", I take it that you do this a lot. You take a specific instance and overgeneralize it into a whole category? And you do this so successfully, don't you? Would you like to fail at this success?

6. *Reflexively applying to a listener*
So, with that way of thinking about things, if I don't succeed in coming up with a good way of responding and helping you with this limiting belief, I will also become a failure? In other words, my success or failure as a human being depends on succeeding in this conversation in just the right way? There's no room for experimenting, feedback, or dialogue?

7. *Counterexample framing*
When you think about some of your successes—and how good and resourceful you feel about them—you mean that, if you mispronounce a word, or fail in any

aspect of any goal surrounding *that* goal, that would turn you into a failure? "Success" is that fragile and "failure" is that solid?

8. Positive-prior-intentional framing

Reaching the goals that you set for yourself must mean a lot to you. I can imagine that you develop this perspective to protect yourself from messing things up and to push yourself to higher levels. Since you want that, perhaps some other attitudes about failure might help you to really succeed in your goals.

9. Positive-prior-causation framing

It strikes me that it's important for you to set and reach goals. So you probably have taken on this limiting belief because you have had some painful experiences in the past and you now want to protect yourself against such. Perhaps it was those experiences that actually seduced you into that limiting belief. What other beliefs could you build that you would find even more effective than this one?

10. First-outcome framing

What results when you move through life defining experiences and yourself as "failures" just because you don't reach a goal in precisely the way you want to? Does this serve you well in setting and reaching goals or in feeling successful? Do you like those negative unresourceful feelings?

11. Outcome-of-outcome framing

Imagine going out, say, five or even ten years from now, after you have defined every unsuccessful attempt at reaching a goal as turning you into a "failure", and then living from that "failure" identity and from feeling unresourceful. What will come out of that? Will you take on many risks? What other outcomes emerge when you feel like a "failure" and take that into your future?

12. Eternity framing

When I think about this, I wonder what you will think when you look back on this belief about failure when you step over into eternity, and I wonder how you will think and feel about this limiting belief that you used as you moved through life?

13. Model-of-the-world framing

It really is an interesting way to think about events because it really does overload them with so much meaning! Do you know where you got this way of mapping about "one lack of success equals failing"? Do you know that most people don't use that map to torture themselves?

14. Criteria and value framing
When you think about your values of enjoying life, appreciating people, doing your best, experimenting, learning, do you not think of those values as more important than making judgments about the "success" or "failure" of your actions?

15. Allness framing
So, since everybody has failed at something at some time in life, that must make everybody on this planet a "failure", a complete and absolute "failure".

16. Have-to framing
So you *have* to frame your attempts at reaching a goal in this way? What would it feel like for you if you did not evaluate events in terms of success or failure? What would happen if you didn't do that? Suppose you got to frame attempts as experiments, feedback, or playing around.

17. Identity framing
What an interesting belief about your self-identity—so totally dependent on your behaviors. Do you always *identify* people with their behaviors? Do you really consider that people "are" their behaviors and nothing more than their behaviors?

18. Ecology framing
How enhancing do you find this belief when learning a new skill, trying a new sport, taking a risk and practicing new social behaviors? Would you recommend this belief as a way for others to succeed with greater ease and positive feelings? Does it empower or limit your endeavors?

19. Other-abstractions framing
The idea of "failure" really seems like a distressful and painful idea and yet you say that it really doesn't serve to enhance your actions or motivate you, so I'm just wondering if maybe this isn't a faulty map that just needs to *evaporate or vanish from the screen of your mind* because it isn't sufficiently real to be useful, but of course, if you allowed it to just *fade away* so that you focused more on using feedback for success, how would that empower you to get on with things?

20. Metaphoring and storying framing
1. So if you brush your hair but do not get every single strand of hair in just the right place, that also makes you a failure?

2. When my daughter Jessica turned nine months, she began the process of learning to walk, but she couldn't walk upon the first attempt—nor upon the first hundred attempts. She constantly fell down. And she would sometimes cry. But most of the time she would just get up and try again. As she did, she learned more and

she developed more strength in her legs, and more balance and movement, so that eventually she got the hang of it, and had a lot of fun in the process. And I wonder if this says anything that you can *take* and apply to yourself now.

21.Both/and framing

It sounds like so much of life is either success or failure and that there's hardly anything that you notice in between. It seems like the boundary between what you call "success" and "failure" has hardly any distance so that you can step from one to the other in a moment. How useful would you find it to be able to measure *the degree* of these states? Or, perhaps, even better, to recognize that they can both occur at the same time?

22. Pseudo-word framing

So you're using this term "failure" with a lot of abandon and yet we haven't been able to actually point to any specific reference, either in the world or even in concept. This suggests that it's actually a pseudo-word and that you've been tricked by the linguistic fraud of the label itself. And since it refers to nothing real or tangible, but only to a mapped construct in your mind, do you really need to use this non-referencing term?

23. Negation framing

I know this isn't possible, but I'm just wondering what would it be like for you if you couldn't compute the meaning of "failure". As you think about "failure" as a nonexistent concept, as an experience you cannot experience, because you always get information and feedback, and discover how not to do something, I'm curious about how much more resourceful that would be.

24. Possibility and "as if" framing

Since the state and experience of "failure" has been so unproductive and painful, take a moment to imagine the possibility of living in a world where being a "failure" could not occur, because you were so focused on always gathering more data about how to refine your actions. Now just pretend that you are there fully and completely and, as you do, show me the face of that state, and the posture, and the breathing, good …

25. Systemic and probability framing

What's the probability that when you start this new project that you will totally and absolutely fail at it to 100 percent like someone who knew nothing at all about it? To what extent do you think you'll fail at it within the first fifteen minutes? The first day? What about the first month? What are some of the other factors and contributing influences that could improve your odds at making this successful?

26. Decision framing

So now that you have entertained several new ideas about this whole realm of suc-ceeding and failing, what have you actually decided serves you best? What frame would empower you to get on with life, bounce with the ups and downs, and for-ever put yourself in a learning orientation? Have you decided to feed and nurture your mind on that idea? Which one thing will you do today to begin this new way of moving through the world?

Lines can change minds

Lines change minds because we use them to shift the meaning frames we give to experiences and ideas. Lines can persuade us to think about things in ways that support our ongoing empowerment. In Mind-Lines, we have several other exam-ples that you might want to check out. We have provided examples of reframing the idea that "Complex things are hard to learn", "Confrontation is bad and dan-gerous and always leads to trouble", and "Saying mean things makes you a bad person."

Getting into the right state to create and use mind-lines

What kind of a state do you need to access in order to operate optimally when using mind-lines? Like everything else in life, being in the right kind of state is cru-cial to success. Our state of mind, emotion, body, and neurology makes all the dif-ference in the world. So, recognizing that our mind-body state comprises our thoughts and physiology, let's make sure that we begin from the most supportive state.

EXERCISE: Accessing a magician state

1 Form groups of three persons.
Select someone to go first as the experiencer, someone to coach the person through the process, and a meta-person to observe and record.

2. Induce and anchor a playful and mischievous state.
Use the two NLP inductions:

"Think about a time when you experienced X ..."

"Imagine what it would be like if you fully and completely were X ..."

When the experiencer reaches a high-level experience of the playful state, perhaps a 7 on a scale of 0 to 10, nod head or indicate to the coach so that he or she can anchor the playful state.

3. Switch roles.
Make sure that everybody gets into the *right kind of state* to learn, absorb, and play with these mind-lines.

Empowering states for mind-lining

What are your top ten states for exploring meaning, playing around with it, and empathizing with the struggles of others so that you can be effectively helpful?

What are the states that support your ability to handle the magic of language and meaning so that others recognize that you do it with respect for them?

As we search for the best *states* for conversing, dialoguing, listening, sharing, and presenting, we begin to orient ourselves to this domain. Use the following as a beginning list for your repertoire:

1. Energetically flexible
"I can vary my responses!"
The most basic and primary state that empowers the use of this word magic involves our own personal *flexibility*—i.e., an open, changeable, flexible state of mind-and-emotion. This contrasts with states of rigidity, closeness, and Aristotelian thinking in terms of map/territory confusion: "This is that!"

How about the flexibility to jump logical levels at a single bound? Can you do *that?* Okay, stretch those mental muscles and loosen up your rigid thoughts and get ready to move up and down the levels, to "go meta" to any and every concept (e.g., time, causation, values, identity, ecology, consequences, abstraction, modeling).

Only when we can jump concepts at a single bound will we be ready to truly mind-line. This means we need a mind that has sufficient energy and mental alertness and that suggests taking care of ourselves in terms of such considerations as eating, exercising, and sleep. It's hard to be mentally alert when we are fatigued and worn out.

2. Playfully creative
"Let's play around and see what else this could mean."
The playful state, in contrast with seriousness, reflects a light and easy attitude toward the existence and construction of meanings. You have probably noticed the degree of playful creativity that's needed in order to think outside of the box and to come up with other perspectives.

What makes thinking outside of the box hard? When we confuse map with territory. When we think words are real. Conversely, when we know, "Everything everybody says is just words"; "What people say and write is just symbols. None of it is externally real. We are just engaging in a symbolic process, the mapping of our understandings."

So what do you need to do to get yourself into a playful mood about language? To the degree that you think either language or truth is externally real, or that they have an existence apart from a human mind, the map-territory confusion will cause you to *identify* and to get serious. That's when the game is over. Once we get serious, then we get stupid, and playful creativity goes out the window.

Along with playfulness, access a state of bantering that allows you to engage in teasing. Have you ever just bantered back and forth with some good friend? Do you know what it means to playfully banter ideas and words? Remember a time or just pretend that you have had such an experience and step into it fully. How much fun do you think you'll have in just bantering back words and frames? Double it.

3. Uninsultable

"Come on, throw a term at me."

For a moment just imagine that you have stepped into a state where you feel so centered that nothing, but nothing, could insult you. Once you have fully accessed the state of uninsulta- bility, then imagine receiving the gift of an insult, a good, gut-retching insult. Now, as you receive that insult, do so from a feeling of being centered and focused, that it has nothing to do with you as a person, and that, with this awareness, you can say, "No thanks, I already gave at the office." Now go forth and be playful.

Uninsultability is a high-level meta-state that allows us to become unselfconscious because we can now forget about ourselves. It enables us to get our ego out of the way so that we are not trying to "prove" anything. We can then be graciously proactive, calm and relaxed, centered, gentle, respectful, and loving without fear, apprehension, or worry.

4. Mischievous

What would you say is one of the most mischievous things you've ever done in your life? As you step into the state of feeling mischievous, add a dash of seduc- tiveness to it, dip it in charm and stir thoroughly. When you're ready, let all of these feelings pop out in your neurology with a very special smirk—you know, the smirk that your parents used to hate and yell at you about. Remember that one?

I think that Richard Bandler's ability to see the world from a tilted point of view is part of his genius. He would not only twist things around and see things from the most ridiculous points of view, but in the early days of NLP he often pushed it so far that he came across in a totally iconoclastic way and so scared a lot of people. Most of Bandler's mind-lines occurred as an expression of his mischievousness. He always seemed to thoroughly enjoy taking someone's limited view of reality and twisting it inside out. He seemed to really enjoy getting people going. The problem was that it was often difficult to tell if it was good-hearted mischievousness or if he was really going to hurt you.

5. Empathy and antagonism
When you form a preframing mind-line, you look for positive intentions and try to put the best spin on things. What state will you need when you do that? You will need a sense of caring and compassion. You will need states of empathy and thoughtfulness for the person.

By way of contrast, when you use the post-framing mind-lines you will be rubbing the dangerous consequences in someone's face. Then you will need a different state of mind. You will need a more antagonistic state wherein you have the power to provoke and confront.

6. Communicational knowledge and elegance
To flexibly play with these mind-lines, you will need a really good knowledge base of the patterns or at least of the pattern you want to play with. Use your ferocious learning state to read and comprehend the pattern, then make lots of mistakes so that you can learn from all of the marvelous feedback that will come your way.

Supporting beliefs for an empowering "magical" state

Above and beyond our states are higher states. These meta-states take the form of beliefs, understandings, knowledge, expectations, decisions, and values. These meta-level frames either support or hinder our resourceful states. They either enable us to get into the kind of states optimal for learning and using mind-lines or they sabotage our best efforts at such.

Several years ago, we began to explore this question and to model each other regarding our ability to create reframes that we could use conversationally. We also began modeling those who seemed skilled in quickly, easily, and automatically producing effective *word magic* in the context of objections, "problems", or difficulties. From that exploration, we collected the following list of supporting and empowering beliefs.

1. Every statement or objection has within it an answer
Suppose you believed that no matter what objection a person may raise with regard to a project, product, or service that you offer, that deep within the person's objection you could find an answer. Imagine that. Every objection carries within it its own solution.

Using this as an operational directive puts us into states of curiosity, interest, and respect. It empowers us to keep exploring, gathering information, and finding out numerous things about another's model of the world: his or her drives, motives, values, objectives, interests, understandings.

Could this be true? Of course it could. After all, if a statement that encodes someone's point of view is just a map, a map of some territory, then exploring that map will do two things. It will elicit a fuller representation, one that suffers from less impoverishment, and it will invite the mapper to update the map while he or she is talking about it. The errors in perception, as mapping errors, self-correct with the right kind of questioning. And the right kind of questioning can empower a person to map in higher and more exquisite ways to redirect the brain. In this lies the magic.

2. It's all feedback and never failure

This frame brings us back to the key presuppositions about communicating and the systemic nature of thoughts and responses. It says that whatever happens in our lives is actually just the next step in some process. It could simply be just communication about how another person perceives or it could be a description of how a process works or doesn't work. It does not have to mean anything more than that. It is just feedback.

This means that we do not have to take statements and semantically load them to mean "success" or "failure" in any absolute sense at all. We do not have to personalize it at all. We can let it just mean "feedback" to a stimulus. Then it becomes only information to us, only a "response".

Why would we want to do this? To stay emotionally neutral when an undesired response comes our way. Then, staying resourcefully curious, we are empowered to keep exploring, seeking to understand, and thinking creatively of other alternatives.

3. Personalizing communication interchanges reduces effectiveness

Whatever someone says is just words and information. Instead of personalizing, I shall recognize that I "am" *so much more* than all of my thoughts, feelings, speech, and behavior. I shall not reduce either myself or others by labeling, name-calling, insulting, or contempting due to some piece of communication that seems disrespectful.

The giving and receiving of information in a communication exchange has really nothing to say about my identity or destiny. Therefore I can refuse to allow myself to put my "self" on the line due to someone else's grumpy state. Sometimes I may have to write down a statement, and play with it for a while, but eventually I will identify the magic formula within it.

4. Assuming responsibility is an empowering rush

At first glance almost everybody thinks that assuming responsibility for the responses we get is connected to blame, accusation, and feeling bad. Could that be an old mind-line equation that someone fed us? Yet, as a map, blaming others for "not getting it", "being stupid", "not paying sufficient attention", "being obnoxious", "resisting", and so forth takes us nowhere useful. It doesn't build a positive relationship. It doesn't create rapport. It doesn't induce states of openness or receptivity in others.

This is the surprise and magic that occurs in this new map. By assuming that "the response I get is the meaning of my communication" we actually step up into our power zone. This gives us more control over things, not less.

Applied to conversation and even arguments, it means that, because we know that *meaning* is an internal thing, meaning doesn't exist out there. We use such devices as words, signals, and gestures as symbols to convey our meanings, but these symbols do not *mean* in and of themselves. Meaning arises inside of the mind of a meaning maker.

That's why we can say, "I really never know what I have communicated. I can know what words I used, what metaphors, what gestures, what tone and volume, but I really never know what I have communicated. I don't know what the other has heard. That's why I have to constantly ask, calibrate to the other person's responses, seek for feedback, and use such to keep adjusting myself to the person's current reality."

Doing this keeps me *proactive*, involved, engaged, tuned in, and using all of my powers for the communicating feed-forward and feedback loops. What a rush! It keeps me from thinking or feeling like a victim. It gives me a sense of control over my own life and destiny.

5. Detecting and recognizing meaning and frames as people talk and interact is simple once you start paying attention

This belief enables us not to feel overwhelmed by language, by words, by objections, or by statements. These are *only* human constructs at best—constructs that we can detect and recognize. As we do, we can formulate an understanding of the meanings involved and *play* with such—framing and reframing to our heart's content.

6. Meaning works by associations and frames; this induces people to live in conceptual worlds of their own making

This understanding empowers us to understand "meaning" as an internal job, as inside the mind of a meaning maker, and as an association between things. Recognizing such as a mental map and not externally really saves us from the insanity of confusing map and territory. Just because someone says something, that does not make it real or actual. I do not have to react and take offense at any word. I do not have to feel bad because of the words they use. At best whatever someone says exists only as a symbol.

7. Thinking about my thinking enables me to jump a logical levels in a single bound

Knowing that meaning exists at many levels of mind allows us to jump logical levels in a single bond. We can now recognize the *aboutness* structure and negotiate the meta-levels. In communication exchanges, the person with the most flexibility in jumping logical levels will have the most influence.

8. People deserve the chance to have their maps expanded and will appreciate the jar after they recover from the dizziness you induce

Mind shifting does a person good. In the long run, it makes mind more flexible and adaptable; it develops good ego strength for facing difficulties, bouncing back from setbacks, and constructing the most appropriate, healthy, and ecological maps. Most people will love you for it.

EXERCISE: Mind-lines

1. Select some ideas to mind-line.

In a group of three or four persons, brainstorm about various objections, complaints, statements, and beliefs of others that you would like to have more choices and options in how to respond.

2. Select some personal lines for more resourcefulness.

Include in your brainstorming a list of internal self-talk lines that put you into not so resourceful states with which you would like to have more resourcefulness.

3. Invent some great lines.

Come up with three or four of the very best lines that you will share with the whole group to use as we play with mind-lines.

Summary of the mind-lines

The following provides the seven directions for sending a brain as we create various kinds of lines for changing a mind.

1. Deframing: tearing a magic formula apart

We first go down. We move to pulling part the *meaning equation*. We take apart the component pieces of the see-hear-feel movie (the VAK) along with the words that make up the soundtrack of the movie. Analyzing the structure in this way involves a moving down or deductive kind of thinking. In deframing a frame of meaning we discover the component pieces that went into structuring and sequencing the belief. Frequently, with a limiting belief, such analysis will cause the magic spell to evaporate.

#1 Chunk down on EB or IS

#2 Reality-strategy chunk-down

2. Content reframing: the lateral pass

We reframe in the center of things, inside the box itself, when we look at the X and the Y and how they have been linked or associated. This is the heart of meaning within the box. Linguistically, what ties the X and Y together are complex-equivalence, cause-effect, and identification statements. These meaning equations and attributions define the heart of neuro-semantic reality. Here we shift the meaning associations: "It doesn't mean this: it means this." This entails various facets of content reframing. In *content reframing*, we say, "Don't think that about this thing, event, or act, in that old way: think about it in this new way."

#3 Reframe EB

#4 Reframe IS

3. Counter-reframing: when an exception stares you in the face

In counterframing we move to offer a reframe that *counters the content*. We let our consciousness reflect back onto its own content (the ideas within the meaning box) and apply the meaning equation to the other side of the equation to see if it coheres or if that breaks it up and deframes it.

This reframing involves what we call "reflexivity" or self-reflexive consciousness—"mind" that can think about its own thoughts. In *counter-reframing*, we ask, "What do you think of the belief when you apply it to yourself?" "What do you think of the belief when you apply it to those cases, times, and events, where it does not fit?"

#5 Reflexively apply EB to self/listener

#6 Reflexively apply IS to self/listener

#7 Counterexample

4. & 5. Preframing and post-framing: the magic of the "time" frame

In these conceptual moves we frame things with "time". We reframe by mentally moving to a prior or a post state to the meaning construction (the formula in the box). Then, we "run with the logic" to see if the meaning equation will make sense when we expand the time frame. In doing this we essentially ask, "Does the magic still work?"

This reframing move introduces the "time" frame into the equation as we frame the meaning box with the concept of time. We bring various "time" conceptualizations to bear upon our belief-thoughts in the meaning box. In preframing, we say, "Put this thought in the back of your mind." In post-framing, we say, "Keep this thought in the front of your mind about that belief as you move into your future." Again, this challenges the magic in the box.

Before Time:
#8 Positive prior framing (intention)
#9 positive prior cause

After Time:
#10 First outcome
#11 Outcomes of outcome
#12 Eternity framing

6. Outframing to meta-levels: meta-stating magic

In outframing, we move up the level of abstractions about the meaning construction. We move upward to higher and higher levels of mind and then apply many new and different facets to our neuro-semantic construct of meaning. All of these chunking-up moves involve inductive thinking and reasoning processes.

In Outframing, we say, "Wrap your mind around the belief in this way." Frequently, these moves not only challenge the old magic, but bring new and higher magic to bear on the belief.

#13 Model-of-the-world framing
#14 Value framing
#15 Allness framing
#16 Necessity framing
#17 Identity framing
#18 All other abstractions
#19 Ecology framing
#21 Both/and framing
#22. Pseudo-words Framing
#23. Negation framing
#24. Possibility and "as if" framing
#25. Systemic and probability framing
#26. Decision framing

7. Analogous framing

Finally, we shift from inductive and deductive thinking as well as horizontal and counterthinking, and we move to analogous thinking (or "abduction"—Bateson, 1972). We do this by shifting to storytelling, metaphor, and narrative. In this abducting type of framing, we essentially say, "Forget all of that, and let me tell you a story …"

#20 Metaphoring/storying and narrative framing

Cues for remembering the mind-lines

Here's a succinct way that summarizes how to think about and remember the mind-line statements and questions. Use the following as cues to prompt your thinking. As you use these, they will eventually become automatic. Use them as semantic environments and prompters for your creativity. After you use them for a while and begin to customize them to the way you talk, they will become natural.

The deframing mind-lines
1 Specifying the magic
- What component pieces make up this idea?
- How do you know to call or label this X?
- What lets you know to think, picture, or hear it in this way?
- What do you mean by X?

2 Detailing the magical strategy
- In what order and sequence do these parts occur?
- What comes first, then second, and son on?
- What lets you know to first see this and then hear that?
- When and where do you do this?

The content-reframing mind-lines
3 Reframing the EB content
- What really is EB is …
- What else would be a case of this EB?
- If you want to really see a case of this EB, consider … .

4 Reframing the IS content
- This isn't IS Number 1: it is IS Number 2
- What other IS could we just as well attribute to this EB?
- If you really want to see a case of this IS, consider …!

The counterframing mind-lines
5 Reflexively apply the EB (X)
- What an X statement!

6 Reflexively apply the IS (Y)
- So you are doing Y to me?

7 Counterexample
- Has there ever been a time when you did not do or experience this?
- When does this magical formula about yourself or life not apply?
- So you have never experienced the opposite?

The preframing mind-lines
8 Positive prior intention
- You probably did that because of *stated positive intention.*
- Weren't you attempting to accomplish the positive purpose of ...?
- What would you guess the person sought to accomplish of value to him or her?

9 Positive prior cause
- You did that because X or Y occurred, did you not?
- What else could have caused the idea or behavior outside your control?

The post-framing mind-lines
10 First outcome
- This belief will lead to you experiencing the consequences of ...
- What will happen if you run with this idea or behavior?

11 Outcomes of outcome
- If you experience that outcome, what will it then lead to?
- As you get the first outcome, that will then lead to X, is that what you want?

12 Ultimate outcome
- Ultimately, this belief will lead to X & Y. How do you like that?
- When you look back on your life, having experienced all these consequences, how will you think or feel about it?

The outframing mind-lines
13 Model of the world
- Who taught you to think or feel this way?
- When you think of this as just a mental map, how does that change things?

14 Value outframing
- What do you find more important than this?
- How does X (some other value) affect this?
- When you compare this with X (value), what do you think?

15 Allness outframing
- Always? To everyone?
- Would you recommend this for everybody?
- Has there never been a time when you didn't?

16 Necessity outframing
- What forces you to think this way?
- What would happen if you did not?
- Do you have to?
- What would it be like if you couldn't?
- What stops you from doing this other thing?

17 Identity outframing
- What does this say about you as a person?
- When you think or do this, how does that affect your identity?
- Who would you be if you didn't believe this?

18 All-other-abstractions framing
- When you think about A, B, or C *about* that, how does that influence things?

19 Ecology outframing
- Does this serve you well?
- Does it enhance your life?
- Do any parts of you object to this?

The analogous framing mind-lines
20. Metaphor or story outframing
- I have a friend who just last month
- Carrying over and applying a referent story was telling me about … to the belief.

Additional mind-lines
21. Both/and framing
- Is this really an either/or situation? Black or white?
- There's no grays? No middles? Do degrees or extent of?
- Could it be both and at the same time from different perspectives?

22. Pseudo-words framing
- Is this a true word that stands for a real thing or a valid concept?
- Could this be a pseudo-word? Just a noise or spell mark?

23. Negation framing
- What if this were not real and did not really exist?
- What would it be like if this just faded away from your internal cinema? How would that affect things?

24. Possibility and "as if" framing
- What if there were a possibility of your doing this?
- Suppose for the sake of discussion for a moment that you had the resources to … Would you like that?

25. Systemic and probability framing
- What's the probability of this happening? Or not happening?
- What other systemic factors or influences affect this?
- Is this truly linear or is there anything circular or systemic in this?

26. Decision framing
- Have you decided that this is so? Is that what you what?
- Will you do this? Will you keep choosing this path that doesn't work?

Summary

As you learn the Mind-Lines model remember that it is like learning to play the piano. First you have to learn the keys—where they are, what they are called, what sounds they produce. Then you have to go through the *drills*. But, eventually, the day comes when all of the practice, the memorizing, and the repetition pay off. Eventually the day comes when you can play, can really, really play. You can sit at the piano and just let it rip. You can invent new tunes. You can play by request. You have become an artist.

Chapter Twenty-One
Presuppositional Languaging
Part I

Using presuppositional terms to set frames that direct awareness and create hypnotic effects

In the last two chapters, we have talked about directing our brains to send our minds into new areas. We do that in order to "run our own brain" more effectively. We do that to influence the minds of others, to become more persuasive, and to add the most influential frames. In fact, doing this with mindful intention and with respect for others propels us in mastering NLP.

When we speak about directing our brains or the brains of others, we do not mean this in an absolute way or in an unethical way. Just as there are limitations and constraints when we practice the art of running our own brains, so there are with influencing others. That's why we use a coaching or facilitating model rather than one of forcing.

In the art of influencing others, we essentially offer instructions. This respects the right of others to reject the influence and this avoids the conflict and war over "control". We cannot "force" anyone to think or feel anything. Such is not within our control. Only we can control our own thinking and feeling, speaking and behaving. In the art of directing, we provide for ourselves or another the most compelling and influential messages possible. Yet as professionals we do so in a way that respects the integrity, values, beliefs, and principles of others.

When we engage in directing another's perception toward an outcome we take a coaching role to facilitate the process. This does not guarantee that the other will accept the outcome: it only makes the outcome more of a possibility. In this process we invite the other to consider new options and alternatives. As we do this conversationally, we simply talk with another person and then offer our persuasion more subtly and gently. Our aim is to enable the other person to focus in a new way, to consider other alternatives, and to try on more enhancing perspectives. We do this all the time anyway whenever we communicate. What we did in the mind-lines chapters and now here is to make the process explicit and do it with expertise.

The NLP model on representing reality

Before we delve into the intricacies of how we direct our perception, a brief review. Our starting premise is that *all perception is a construction*. The only thing we experience is our map *of* the territory, and not the territory itself. As we experience the world through our senses and as we re-present that world by mapping those perceptions via our representation systems and constructing our mental movies, this and this alone is all we "know". All we know of "reality" is what we map. We then navigate the world with that map or instructional video-film.

To do this we create a series of images (snapshots and movies) within our minds. We create pictures, sounds, feelings, smells and tastes as a facsimile of the world. That movie operates like an instructional video for how to operate. In this way we create strategies. It doesn't stop there, though. We also give significance to these videos via the words we use to describe, evaluate, and classify things. And we do this at multiple levels of abstraction.

What explains the "magic" of NLP? Namely, we change and are transformed as we change our internal mappings. When we pull out the old videos and put in new ones, we get to play a different role and get to feel and experience a different "reality".

This means that all of our limiting beliefs, values, decisions, or memories are neuro-linguistic constructs or movies. Transformation therefore ultimately involves deconstructing the limiting frames and reconstructing more resourceful frames. Or, to run with the movie metaphor, transformation is cleaning out the old video library of outdated films and B-rated movies that we didn't like in the first place, and replacing them with quality films.

There's more. In addition to recognizing that the map is not the territory, we also recognize that each person operates from his or her own map. That's why we listen, ask questions, explore, and seek first to understand. Until we explore, we don't know what movies others have been playing in the theaters of their minds. And frequently neither do they. First comes awareness, then choice. If a map no longer serves us or another well, we create a more useful one.

In all of this we cannot *not* utilize our representational systems in creating our internal cinemas. That's how we "think" and that's how we move to meta-levels to establish the frames that allow us to believe, understand, reason, anticipate, and imagine. Every time we open our mouths and talk both we and those who hear us track images, sounds, and sensations onto our internal screen.

Of course, this becomes more complex when we use concepts. For example, consider the concept of negation. We say, "Don't think of a blue tree." To map out in our mind we represent a tree, a blue tree, and then we attempt to "no" longer hold that image, to negate it.

Ultimately, we direct our conscious mind and our mental-emotional-somatic processes by giving our minds "information" to process. Bateson noted that that is all that ever enters into mind—information. And because we cannot *not* process information (what we say and how we say it), our words and gestures greatly influence how we map things. This is the foundation of "persuasion". When we are persuasive, when someone is persuasive with us, we entertain new ideas and new frames.

With mind-lines and presuppositions, mastery comes in part as we learn how to speak with an outcome in mind. Our purpose is to lead ourselves or others to construct certain images on the screen of the mind and to set frames of meanings. Doing this will direct perception toward the desired outcome.

How do we direct a person's perception eloquently?

We skillfully use our linguistics and nonverbal signals to direct thought and awareness. What follows here then flows naturally from the Meta-Model (Chapters Eleven and Twelve), the Mind-Lines model (Chapters Nineteen and Twenty), the Meta-Programs, Meta-States, and the Milton Model of hypnotic patterns. Here, in focusing on presuppositional language, we simply add another focus onto how to use hypnotic language patterns skillfully.

Each of these models views the same linguistic process from a slightly different point of view. From the point of view of the Meta-Model, using the vague language of the "ill-formedness" or "violations to well-formedness", we induce a person to go *inside* to fill in the vagueness and to create idiosyncratic meaning. This entrances a person into his or her own world of meaning. From the point of view of the Milton Model, we create response potential by artistically using nonreferencing words so the person goes into a trance to create or find his or her own references. In both cases, it's the same process, just different explanatory models.

Here we specifically consider the following presuppositions, a few central ones for directing brains:

1. Existence
2. Awareness
3. Possibility and necessity
4. Temporal and spatial
5. Ordinal
6. Exclusive/inclusive or
7. Cause-effect
8. Complex equivalence

What is a presupposition?

A presupposition answers the following questions:

- What has to be true in order for the sentence to make sense?
- What does a person have to hold in mind to make sense out of a given sentence or phrase?

● What assumed frames and ideas are necessary for a word, term, phrase, or sentence to be processed as information?

We are not here talking about the presuppositions of NLP. We are rather talking about the Meta-Model linguistic distinction of presuppositions. As noted above, there are extensive lists of linguistic presuppositions in several NLP books. We recommend the list in Appendix B of *Structure of Magic, Vol. 1* (pp. 211-14).

"What does a person have to hold true in order to make sense of a statement?" Using this description, what does the following sentence presuppose?

"I am typing this chapter in my computer."

1. I am typing.
2. I know how to type.
3. I have a referent concept for the someone that I refer to as "I".
4. This self owns or has access to a computer.
5. The computer can be used for the behavior of typing.
6. The computer has a keyboard, monitor, CPU, and perhaps a printer.

Stop and notice Number 6 again. The statement presupposes several components of a computer and it may include a printer. Yet it does not *necessarily* presuppose a printer. Is there anything else that this sentence presupposes without actually mentioning?

7. What about a chair?
8. What about a room?
9. What about a "front" to the room?
10. What about a "back" to the room?
11. What about "sides" to the room?
12. What about what is not room?
13. What about my believing that I have some knowledge of some subject that I can type?
14. What about my belief that someone would want to read this information?

Some things are *presupposed* (a place) while others are not (a room, a chair). The computer could be outside. The computer may be on a high stand requiring someone to stand. And we can continue to extend this line of thinking. Yet to what use? What is the value of this?

Recognizing *the unspoken frames* within and above our words and statements allows us to recognize the *frames by implication* that we are setting and the unspoken assumptions by which we are operating. Setting frames has profound effects and use as directional language for where we send our brains and how we create response potential. Often it is not what is explicitly mentioned in our communication that creates the most potential: it is what we have not explicitly mentioned.

How do we question, or challenge, a cause—effect statement? Someone says, "You make me mad." Then you respond: "Really? So if I understand you accurately, you believe that I am 'making' you mad? Would you be so kind as to tell me what I am doing that *causes or forces you* to have to choose to feel angry?"

Note the words *"causes or forces* you to have to *choose* to feel angry." This statement does not explicitly say that anger is your choice, but it certainly *presupposes* it. The statement paces the person's complaint about being "made", "caused", or "forced" to feel something. It focuses the person's attention on "what am I doing" that creates this causation? What causes or forces you to have to choose to feel angry? Implied also is the opposite of choice. You could *choose not* to feel angry. This sends a message to the higher frames of mind that are typically outside of conscious awareness and so bypasses the more conscious part of the mind. It says by implication, "You have choice as regarding whether to respond with being mad or not."

In this way, using words with presuppositional implications can very *subtly* provide more resourcefulness and leverage as we direct awareness. Yet in using such linguistic presuppositions, we do not expect one term or even one sentence to carry the entire transformation. We layer. Once we *plant* a suggestion, even subtly, we follow up by planting even more. We build up the desired representation (e.g., being responsible) with multiple layers and so move a person to a desired outcome. With this person, we have planted a thought of *choice*. From there we can lead with other statements to invite the person to own his or her anger responses, or even *choose not* to respond with anger but some other mental or emotional response (e.g., questioning, curiosity, action).

We begin with the realization that every time we make a statement, we reveal our model of the world. Every time I open my mouth, I give you many of the implied frames that make up my conscious and unconscious model of the world. Therefore listening to the "surface structure" we can make fairly accurate evaluations regarding what lies in the "deep structure" (or the high structure of embedded frames upon frames). Because language (as a representation system) can and does operate from presupposed structures, the ability to *hear* and *recognize* that structure gives us the power to pace and lead.

Consider this example. Suppose I say, "I love sharing NLP with others." What does this statement presuppose about my beliefs? About what I hold important? Does it not presuppose that I have a passion for NLP? I have studied NLP and know it well enough to share it or believe I can share it? I love assisting and helping other people in utilizing the NLP tools to run their own brains?

It presupposes these things and much more. Every statement of language ontains hidden presuppositions that inform us about the frames of the speaker. Mastering this facet of language enables us to move to a higher level of NLP mastery.

1. Existence

Consider the presuppositions of existence in the statement, "Jason goes to college." What do we presuppose as *existing* to understand the statement?

The sentence presupposes there is a person named Jason, that there is a college. Could we not also say that Jason has ability to learn, that he has completed high school, that he has been accepted by a college? We could say there are such things as colleges. These are some of the assumptions we make. They are not stated, but they must exist in order for the statement to make sense. As such we can use them for leverage when we want to speak hypnotically.

Language makes sense only if we draw such conclusions. Some describe this as a function of the "unconscious" mind. That's shorthand (and vague shorthand at that) for recognizing that what we frame at one level has to have higher assumptive frameworks to make sense. The "unconscious"—or what is outside the conscious—part of our mind presupposes the necessary frames. This higher part of our mind works from these assumptions. That's how such terms work so subtly. It subtly lies in what we assume.

Listen then for the *implied frames and understandings* within words, terms, and statements. Even when you flush out one level of assumed ideas, listen further for the things next implied. When we have identified the presuppositions above and beyond the first statement, and we have statements like, "He is of age", "He has the ability to ..." and "He has the motivation to ..." there are yet more things implied.

Here's another example. Use it to explore the presuppositions within it. "He rose from his seat, went to the front of the room, and began writing the answer on the flip chart."

What presuppositions of existence do we have in this statement? There is a flip chart. There is a room, a front of the room, a back of the room, people, a male, a seat, a question.

The language, as a sentence in English, contains multiple assumptions. Focusing on the phrase "flip chart" invites us to make a picture of such in our mind. As we do that, we give it existence, at least in our mind. There may be no flip chart in reality. The speaker may have misspoken and meant blackboard or whiteboard. The speaker may be making up a story. But, in our mind, we create a flip chart and a man and a room and all that goes into making that scenario real to us.

For us to use the phrase, "a flip chart", we have to create a conceptual space in our mind and then fill that space with a flip chart. Prior to filling the mental space with the flip chart, we have an empty *conceptual space*. We have all of the things that are implied in the existence of a flip chart. At that nanosecond, we have "the *not* of the flip chart".

That is, we construct a background onto which we then map the foreground. The background is implied, assumed, and presupposed. It has to exist in order for us to see or imagine a flip chart. Flip charts don't exist in a vacuumless space: they exist in space. So the *spatial context* must exist also. And, as it is *not* the flip chart, it is the *not* of the flip chart. So with Jason. When we speak about "Jason" then everything around Jason is "not" Jason.

This means that for every *presupposition of existence* there is the *not* for what we posit as existing. There is background for everything we put in the foreground. There are all of the things and processes that have to be in order for the other to exist.

How is any of this useful? It becomes useful when we talk about "problems" and construct "problem" frames. Frequently, the *not* will provide the solution to the problem. That's because the not will take us to the negative or the reverse of the problem—that is, the lack of the problem. In mental space, this frequently opens doors for solutions. It is in this sense that we sometimes say, "Problems typically carry their own solutions."

As an example, consider the statement, "I am suffering from depression."

First we have to posit that "depression" exists. Then we have to assume all of the background of "depression". So then, what would be *not* depression? If depression is standing out in the foreground, what are all the things in the background? As you go *outside* your frames to answer that question, what did you find? Was it joy, happiness, glee, excitement, calmness, serenity? The *not-depression* is the background for *depression*. "Depression" can only make sense if we have a contrast frame of happiness, motivation, vitality. This explains the power of the question, "If you were not suffering depression, what would you be feeling?"

How can we use this hypnotically to direct perception and awareness?

Suppose I am a car salesman wanting to sell you a new car. I will want to focus your mind on "a new car" and on all those things about the car that appeal to your values. I will also want to pace what you believe about purchasing a car that's important to you. So I ask some questions. I ask questions to discover what you want. If I find that you want a medium-priced car that has a reputation for quality and value, then I will use my language to direct your attention toward those values so that you produce a fill of that in your mind.

"I hear that *you* want a medium price car that has a reputation for *quality* and *value*? Let me show you this *model* that *we* have over here on the *lot*. As you can see from the *sticker* on the *window*, it is a medium-price car. It is a *Toyota*, which *Consumers Report* rates as one of best-quality *automobiles* on the *market*. It *also* has a *reputation* for having a high resale *value* with a very moderate per-mile *cost*."

Note all the presuppositions of existence (terms in italics) that direct the person's attention to those things that match his or her beliefs and values about purchasing an automobile.

This lets us send a brain (our own or another's) toward anything in existence. We simply direct the person's attention to that item simply by naming the item. *Naming* calls it into existence. *Naming* makes it so. We make language directional by using presuppositions and by focusing attention on whatever it is that we want to direct attention toward. Therefore, to speak skillfully, we will talk of those things that we want to present on the screen of consciousness.

2. Awareness

I don't *know* whether or not you have *realized* just how important presuppositions are in your communications and persuasion, but as you *think* about their impor-tance, do *consider* that as beliefs they define our model of the world and the very frames of our minds.

Presuppositions of awareness are terms that cue us for a psychological *state* of awareness. Do you see and hear them (again, italicized) in the previous paragraph—the words *consider, think, realize*? We could add *notice, sense, aware, feel, touch, taste, smell, hear, see*. Any *sensory terms* are presuppositions of aware-ness.

Of course, awareness presuppositions *direct attention* and emotion and experience.

As you can *see*, I can influence your mental map and invite you to map things along certain lines as long as you *listen* to me because you will then obtain a *sense* of what it means to truly operate as a master practitioner. And, as you *sense* that *awareness*, you *know* that it will affect you and those who are important in your life in your communications with them because you can *see* and *hear* your-self communicating more effectively, can you not? Also as you *realize* that you have control over your own communications to the extent that you *think* about it, your growing *knowledge* about communication will give you a certain advantage.

And, as you are *listening* to the *sound* of my voice about the "place of pure poten-tiality" the "place" *before* words and the "problem" and the "not-problem," you can let it increase your *realization* that you are more than what you *think* you are; you *know* that you are much more than those *thoughts*.

And, as we *look* at and explore the presuppositions of existence, it increases our *awareness* that, no matter what we *think* we are, we are always more than that. So, when there is a problem and we are *focused* on that problem, we can choose not to *focus* on that problem and to open our eyes to *see* the bigger picture. In fact, we can choose to go all the way back in our *awareness* to the "not," or even before, and become *aware* of our spirituality.

And being there now will only make us *think* new thoughts and *see* things, things that we have never *seen* before now, and hear voices and relanguage ourselves in a way that will produce more motivating behavior. And it will cause us to ... *think* ... that problem it is really not problem that is an old memory.

Presuppositions of awareness provide us some very useful tools in hypnosis, assisting us as we direct a person toward a desired outcome. They also provide a great way to pace and lead people. Presuppositions of existence provide the "object" for a person to focus on, whereas presuppositions of awareness highlight the "thought" for internal attention.

EXERCISE: Presuppositions

1. In pairs, take any of the hypnotic language patterns in the Milton Model.
Use any of those patterns along with the presuppositions of existence and awareness to create an induction.

2. First the person or persons you would like to address. Identify where you want to send their brain.
What do you want to accomplish? What state do you want to induce? What emotion to elicit? What awareness to know and realize?

3. Then write out a two or three paragraph induction that direct that person's brain along that course.

4 Take turns inducing a light trance state and then reading the induction.
Afterwards test by seeing how it worked and what it elicited in the other person.

3. Possibility and necessity

As terms, we classify "possibility" and "necessity" in the Meta-Model linguistic distinctions as "modal operators." When we *use* these terms to induce trance states, it puts into our hands hypnotic patterns. As noted earlier in the chapter on trance, this uses the Meta-Model, not for precision, but for artful vagueness, and so induces altered states. This *inverse use* of the Meta-Model allows us to use the same model for one of two purposes: either for precision and well-formedness or for trance and inducing inward searches for meaning.

If we use the linguistic distinctions of modal operators of possibility and impossibility, necessity and desire, and probability and improbability, we can create corresponding presuppositional frames. Doing this allows us to induce a mental-emotional world with these qualities.

- Trances of impossibility and/or possibility. These will be constructed through the use of such words as: impossible, can't, possible, able, can.
- Trances of improbability and/or probability. The key terms for these trances will be could, would, may.

- Trances of necessity and compulsion. These will be driven by the terms must, should, ought, have to, need to.

Could, would, may are words of probability. They invite us to imagine a *probable* situation. "You could learn these patterns and have a lot of fun doing so, couldn't you?" We can represent that as a possibility and as a probability.

Modals in linguistics refer to one's *mode* or *style* of operating. Such terms describe *the way* we move through the world, our *approach, orientation*, and even *attitude*. The modals of *probability* describe life in between those of impossibility and possibility. Sometimes, in thinking to ourselves or talking to others, it is too big of a jump from a problem state to a desired state if we attempt to shift from "I can't" (impossibility) to "I can". (possibility). We need something in between. We need something that encodes a probability without its jumping all the way to a possibility.

"I know now that you have believed that you couldn't do this, but I'm wondering if you have *considered* that *perhaps* there is a probability that you *could* possibly do it because as you *consider* the probability of that possibility now, the possibility that you *could* do it, it *gives* you a chance to find out the *degree of probability* that you can do it even now, if you know what I mean."

This process involves linking *modal operators* together in such a way that it functions as a linguistic form of the Chaining Anchors pattern. It connects one modal state to another, and then to another, and in this way paces where a person is as it gently leads to a more useful and desirable outcome. Using this kind of languaging typically assists a person in moving from a problem state to a desired state by setting up some in-between states for a smoother transition.

Did you noticed the kinesthetic sensations and emotional states that the *different modal* operators elicit? How does the term "must," "should," "have to" or "need" work for you? What does it elicit in you in terms of an emotional state?

I *must* do _____."

I *need* to do _____."

What kinesthetic sensations do you experience from those lines? Are they positive or negative? Now try this one:

I *can* do _____."

I *get to do* _____."

I *want to* do _____."

Do you experience a more positive kinesthetic when you use these modals? For most people, *necessity* words typically create a more negative motivation than a positive one. Conversely, *possibility* words generate more positive motivation and emotional states. Similarly, modal operators of *probability* provide a nice way to move from a negative state to a more positive state. We can use it as a jumping off point from the negative (the modals of impossibility and necessity) to the positive states (using the modals of possibility).

This allows us more choices in responding and directing a brain when a client says, "I just can't learn these new ways to run my own brain. It's just too hard!"

"Yes, I can see that there is a part of you that believes you *can't* do it, at least not now, and so I would like to ask that part of you if it *would*, just for a moment, consider the *possibility* that, if you applied the right resources to this learning, you *may* very well find that it is *possible* that you *can*, or at least much more probable. What do you think?"

In this response we start by pacing the impossibility (the "I *can't*") to the probability (*would*) to the possibility (*possible*) to another probability (*may*) to possibility (*can*). This nicely paces. As it does so, it simultaneously chains a series of states from unmotivated to motivated. You might have noticed that the statement also used other presuppositions, those of existence and awareness.

When we listen to and use another's modal operators, we use the ones that the person gives us from their mapping style and then feed it back to that person. We can use this to set up a series of states and link them together so that it creates a direction for their neuro-linguistic system. Of course, if we use our own modals, then we use our own presuppositions, frames, and beliefs. When, however, we hear and pace the *modals* that a person gives us, feeding them back to that person you, especially in the order given to us, immediately fires off their neurology in a way that makes sense. It's a powerful way to build rapport.

EXERCISE: *Modal operators*
1. State a limiting belief as an impossibility.
With a partner, make a statement that contains a modal operator of impossibility that defines an actual limiting belief that you have or have had.

2. Explore new possibilities.
The partner will then explore what you would like to believe instead. In gathering this information, the partner should listen for modal operators in your language.

3. Design a pacing-leading statement.
Your partner should now devise a pacing-leading statement to chain you from impossibility to possibility through probability. The statement will begin with the limitation, then elicit and chain states so that you will move from limitation state to desired state. Your partner can utilize any hypnotic language patterns including presuppositions to assist you in this process. Afterwards test to refine the statement.

4. Practice the new lines.

Express to your partner the limiting belief and listen as your partner delivers the lines of the hypnotic language. Notice and fully calibrate to the person's nonverbals to recognize the effectiveness of the pattern.

What does it do for you? How does it feel? Does it set up the new direction for you?

5. Continually refine, test, future-pace.

Continue until you both find the lines that work, then check the ecology and future-pace.

Modal operators and meta-states

How do these modal operators work so powerfully to create emotional states and change patterns in our lives? The answer lies in the meta-stating effect of the modals.

Consider the example of chaining modal operators in terms of being an elegant linguistic pattern. In terms of creating "commands to the nervous system", that chain induces a series of states and behaviors that moves us in a certain direction, and of course, as it does, it directs us toward that change. How does this work?

It works because the modals, as modifiers of verbs, set the frame for so modifying. The verb in this case refers to whatever action or process under consideration. It's the action of the movie in your mental theater. The *modals*, not being the verbs themselves, are not the actions but the *style of operation* of the verb. To illustrate, read the following statements and notice the emotional states that each statement elicits in you.

Figure 21.1

Modal operator	Meta-frame set	State elicited
"I *must change*."	A frame of necessity	Pressure, demand
"I *have* to change."	A frame of necessity	Pressure, force
"I *desire* to change."	A frame of desire	Hope, passion
"It is *possible* to change."	A frame of possibility	Hope, excitement
"I *can* change."	A frame of possibility	Confidence, courage
"I *choose* to change."	A frame of choice	Power, control

In each of the above examples, the modal operator modulates the action of the verb, and in doing so affects the state and the perception. It does this by putting the specific modal operator in a meta-position to our primary state of the specific action—in this case, changing.

What does this mean? It means that the modal operator *meta-states* the verb and so determines the frame of the verb. Because "all meaning is context-dependent" (Bateson), as modal operators set the context or the frame for *how we operate*, they determine the meaning of the corresponding states.

In meta-stating another state, the higher *state textures* the lower state. We now see this in these modal-operator patterns. When I *must* go to work, the *must* textures the quality of the set of actions that I refer to in "going to work". What a different texture of mind-and-emotion when we get up in the morning with the intention of going to work! Or say, "I *can* go to work." The higher state (as a meta-state) does the job of an adverb in that it defines the *quality* of the primary-level activity.

This leads to the conversational trance work that we do with Meta-States. Since every adverb and adjective, as a modifier, sets the frame for the qualities that we want to "bring to bear upon" (or apply to) an experience, it allows us to meta-state experiences very easily.

And as you *comfortably* relax in the *growing* confidence that you can and *will* understand these things about your *modus operandi* in the world, you can *really* wonder and do so *excitedly* about the possibilities for change and transformation, knowing that in NLP and NS we focus on positive changes that enable people to be at the best, and you can feel that in a *delightful* way, can you not? Because you can manage your mind at its highest levels to achieve the kind of quality that makes excellence fun and delightful. Because you know that, if you don't do that, then you will get into a negative state that will burden everything you do."

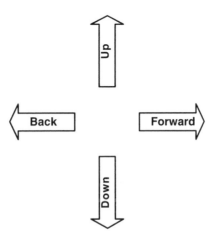

Figure 21.2: The "directions" of the mind

407

(We have an article on the website entitled, "The Power that Drives Modal Operators"—see it at www.neurosemantics.com.)

4. Temporal and spatial

The Mind-Lines model identifies how we can send our perception in seven different directions. As a process, Mind-Lines lets us take a person's perception outside of his or her perceived problem or challenge. Doing so empowers us to present various meta-level resources and frames that can enable a person to reframe the problem in numerous ways. In a similar way, presuppositional languaging provides another way to think about this process.

Here we will combine temporal and spatial presuppositions into one category. Doing so provides an excellent tool to use as we send another's awareness in these directions. Below are listed several words and terms that encode these space-and-time presuppositions.

EXERCISE: Temporal presuppositions

1. Identify a problem or a challenge.
2. Specify the cinematic features in the movie.
With the problem in mind, notice the "sub-modality" features that make up this problem or challenge. That is, as you create a visual image of the problem, notice where you see it and its distance, how far away or close it is.

3. Observe cinematic changes.
Notice what happens to the problem when you use the following presuppositional line:

"And *aside from* that _____."

What happens to the "sub-modalities" of the problem's location?

Debriefing

For most people, processing the spatial-presupposition phrase, "aside from", the content of the visual image will move further away in space. Sometimes the images will immediately move over. In the moment of that movement, cognitive space is created and it is at that moment that we can insert one or many resources. For example:

"And, *aside from* your depression, how are you feeling?" ("Apart from" works in a similar manner to how "aside from" works.)

Using this pattern in sales

Imagine this type of languaging in the context of sales. Suppose someone makes an objection to an offer or proposal that you've made. Now suppose that you then comment, "You know, *aside* from that objection, how will this product meet your needs?"

And, if we have good rapport, the people may very well push the objection aside as they attempt to answer the question. As they do so, they will be creating space and filling that space with their own answer about how the product will meet their needs. Isn't that pretty magical? As we remember that it is the internal representation that a person focuses on (i.e., the internal movie running in the mind), that controls a person's state, the more we facilitate a person to direct attention to *how a product could be useful*, the more those considerations will become the foreground of that person's internal cinema.

"And *aside* from that *objection* how does this *product* actually meet your *needs*? And as you *see* [or hear, feel] how it meets your *needs* [*match the person's representation system*] you *can* really *consider* how these *benefits* will enhance your future and what it will feel like to enjoy the *benefits* of *this product, now.*"

In this last sentence, notice how we have used all of the presuppositions of existence: awareness, modal operators, and spatial and temporal terms. In utilizing all of these presuppositions, now you can examine more intentionally the person who objects to your product, how you can respond, and the effects this will probably have on the person's internal processing.

Aside (temporal) from your *objections* (existence) how do you *see* (awareness) this *product* (existence) meeting your *needs* (mark out "needs" with a special tonality and make the modals an existence presupposition) and *now* (temporal) you *can* (modal operator) *get* (modal operator) a *sense* (awareness) of how *this* (awareness) *product* (existence) *will* (modal operator) totally change and enrich your *future* (temporal) *lif* (existence).

Prepositions

Space

Across	By	On
After	Down	Onto
Along (-side)	Except	Out of
Apart from	From above	Outside
Around	From below	Over
Aside	In	Relative to
At	Including	Short of
Before	In front of	Through
Behind	In place of	Toward
Beside	Inside	Under
Between	Into	Up
Beyond	Off	With (in/out)

Other spatial predicates

Here	There
This	That
Away	Above

Time

Past	Present	Future	Atemporal
Before	Here	After	Looking
Then	Now	When	Until
Look back	Already	Look ahead	Like
Just	During	Soon	Being
Did	Happen	Want to	Making
Happened	Happening	Would be	Deciding
Was	Is	If	
Made	Make	Will happen	
Did	Differently	Will be	
Decision		Will make	
		May	

Using temporal presuppositions

In a training context, a young man by the name of Tommy said he would like to work in front of the group during a master practitioner course. His complaint was that he felt that there were too many things to learn. Bob here uses the Mind-Backtracking pattern to meta-state the frames above his immediate perception.

"I have a problem with the fact that there are *so many things to learn*. They are all right there in front of me."

"Good. Now, Tommy, what thought do you have behind the thought that you have so many things to learn and that they are all right there in front of you?" (Pacing.)

"I guess that an effort to learn is like horses galloping in one path. I want to get it all together galvanizing them in one direction."

"And, what thought do you have behind the thought of your wanting to galvanize them into one path?"

"I want to be on God's path. Just to be on God's path."

"And is there any thought behind the thought of being on God's path?"

"God himself."

"Good. I want you to right now, so just go there … that's right … and be there, and be with that awareness right now. And being there now, what happens when you apply your awareness of 'God' to your thoughts about having so many things to learn that is right before you?"

"I think, 'Well, in his own time, he will get them all galloping in one direction.' And that's OK!"

Meta-stating with a higher spatial presupposition

This use of the spatial presupposition "behind" can actually be quite powerful to invite a person to step aside and dissociate from a problem state, and to then let the person move up several meta-levels and find or create higher resources. From there we can meta-state the person with the resources as we simply invite the person to *apply* the discovered resource states to the problem state.

You can use this same type languaging with other spatial and temporal presuppositions to get similar results:

- What is *above* that?
- What is *beyond* that?
- W
hat is *below* that?
- As you *transcend* that level of awareness, what comes into mind?

Each one of these spatial presuppositions will take a person's awareness to a place *outside* the problem space. It will invite the person to make a meta-move to a higher level where higher resource states can be identified and used to bring healing to the problem. Which direction would you like to send your brain? Try it. Think of a problem or challenge. What is *above* that problem? And when you step into that space, what is *above* that? Keep reprocessing this question until you run out of responses and then notice where you are.

EXERCISE: Spatial and temporal presuppositions
1. Find a partner to play with.
Pair off with a partner and think of a problem or challenge to play with.

2. Meta-model a problem.
The coach will meta-model the problem until the problem has been stated in the form of a cause-effect or complex-equivalence statement: "This X causes Y"; "This X equals Y."

3. Choose a spatial or temporal presupposition.
The coach will choose a spatial or temporal presupposition and then, just with

language, invite the other to make a meta-move, access a higher resource, and apply it to the problem state. Use such terms as "above", "beyond", "beside", "apart from".

4. Continue until resourcefulness emerges.

Keep meta-stating the problem with various resources until the problem shifts and/or until the person seems to be experiencing the problem in a more resourceful way.

5. Check ecology and future pace; then shift roles.

Summary

The presuppositions in language operate as powerful outside-of-consciousness frames. This makes them valuable for setting frames and especially for setting frames covertly.

Using linguistic presuppositions enables us to meta-state our statements with conceptual frames and assumptive frameworks. This allows us to build the embedded matrices of frames that can work for persuasion elegance and for spreading resourcefulness around.

Chapter Twenty-Two
Presuppositional Languaging
Part II

We began exploring the power, nature, and usefulness of the presuppositions in our everyday conversation in the previous chapter. That continues in this chapter as we explore and apply them for the purpose of sending our brains off into new and more resourceful directions. These seemingly tiny and insignificant words are actually the terms and ideas that we can use for frame setting and inducing powerful hypnotic states and we can do so in everyday conversation. So let us continue where we left off.

5. *Ordinals*
We have now covered several presuppositions, yet in this next group, the second thing that's critically important about what an ordinal is and how to use it is as follows.

Did that jar you? Did you catch yourself stopping and rereading that sentence to see if it was right? Did you wonder, "What was the first thing about ordinals? Did I miss something? Did the computer or typesetter delete a line? What happened? Where is 'the first thing'?"

Typically, most people (but not all) would have responded by creating a cognitive space in their minds as it were as they would wondered about "the first thing". Not everybody not do this. Some global thinkers will miss it completely. Some options will also miss it. But specific detailed thinkers and especially procedure thinkers will catch it. So the working of this presupposition depends, to some extent, upon one's meta-programs and thinking style. Those who judge rather than perceive might notice it.

Ordinals, as the term implies, assign order or rank, to a "one, two, three" list. Use words such as "first", "second", or "third", or "next", or "later", and it cues the idea of an ordered sequence. When we say "first", we set up a direction for the brain to go. It presupposes an order, a sequence, and a series of items. When we say "second" to a sequential thinker without having previously mentioned "first", it does something different. It jars that person's awareness. That's because such individuals are highly primed to sort for series, sequences, lists, and order and care about such. So to start in the middle without a transition violates and interrupts the person's way of thinking. It invites that person's brain to go into a search mode. "What was first?" If this happens often, it can invite anger, frustration, and stress. Typically it creates an internal space wherein they go inside and begin searching.

Of course, at that point, we have a place for saying other things, for planting suggestions, without the person's hearing it consciously. This describes one of the hypnotic ways we can use ordinals.

Ordinals are about syntax. It is about everything occurring in an order, and usually in a correct or right order. So what happens when we turn the order of things around? What happens when we put things "out of order" or into a reverse syntax? Actually, with structures that require a specific sequence, we can have a lot of fun with language as we *reverse the syntax* of problem statements.

As an example, Carol said she felt worried when her teenage daughter did not come home on time.

To that I (BB) replied, "Your teenage daughter not coming home on time and that caused you to feel worried?" (Pacing.)

Carol said, "Yes."

"What would happen if you did not come on time with that worried feeling?"

Carol broke out in laughter in response to that. Reversing syntax and reversing cause-effect statements often completely interrupts a problem, blows it out, or disorders it. The linguistic structure of what Carol said can be put into the following formula:

Daughter's not coming home on time (A) causes mother to worry (B).

This gives us a classic cause-effect statement. "A" happens first, this is followed by the occurrence of "B". As such, this describes how to construct an "apply-to-self" *mind-line* reframe. By reversing the syntax, we can put "B" on top of "A". That is, we can bring "B" to bear on "A", or apply "B" to "A". We can also meta-state "A" with "B". When we reverse syntax with an ordinal, complex-equivalence or cause-effect statement, we bring the problem to bear on itself. We meta-state the problem with the problem.

Presuppositional play with fear of heights
In another training, a participant Bill said that he would be willing to work in front of the training group to work on his fear of heights.

"You have a fear of heights? Tell me, what do you have to do first, in your mind, in order to be afraid of heights? *How* do you know you are afraid of heights?"

"How do I know?"

"Yes. *How* do you know?"

"Well, because I feel it? I feel afraid."

"You feel it? How do you know *when* to feel it?"

"When I look down, I guess."

"When you look down?"

"Yes. If I'm on a ledge or high up and look down, I feel afraid."

"Do you have to actually be looking down before you feel it?"

"When I open my eyes and look down I feel it. I sure do."

"You can't do it just in your mind ... here ... now?"

"Oh, sure. Yes I can do that."

"Good. What a skill! So right now I want you to just imagine yourself up on a high place and looking down, and go ahead ... *feel* it."

"I don't want to."

"I know. I can see that. But would you just do that for a moment? Let's make sure you have not lost this skill. That could happen, you know. That's why we have to test these things."

"OK ... Whew!"

"And, how is that a problem for you?"

"How is it a problem?"

"Yes, is it a problem? Maybe it is not. How does having this fear of heights when you look down on things, even in your mind, and you feel this fear of heights—how is this a problem for you?"

"It paralyzes me."

"You get paralyzed?"

"Yes."

"You know, Bill, if I were you, I think I would just paralyze that fear of heights—now—because if you *paralyzed* that fear I wonder what would happen."

Bill didn't say anything for a few moments. But it was obvious that he was processing things inside. I'm sure the gears were turning inside because it seemed that smoke was coming from his ears. Shortly, the entire group broke out in laughter. I gave him some time to process the reversal of the syntax and let things settle.

"OK, Bill, let's go back up to that image of height again. How high do you have to be in order to feel that fear?"

"I have to be on the rooftop of my house."

"Good. Then, Bill, let's go on a field trip. In fact, everybody here, let's all go with Bill on this field trip—to the top of Bill's house."

Actually I had Bill walk out to a deck in the building where we were and to stand up and to look out. The deck stood approximately 15 feet (4.5 meters) above the ground. To test the process, I asked him to walk over to the edge of the deck. His fear was gone. Prior to this he said he would have been clutching, white-knuckled, to the banister. Actually we tested this resolution of his fear of heights several days later as well to see if it had maintained as his new frame. He did. He reported that he had undergone other therapies in an attempt to fix this fear of heights, yet none of them work. Yet this worked by the use of a linguistic presupposition, the paralyzing a paralyzing feeling. And that, of course, is part of the magic of our neuro-linguistics.

6. Inclusive/exclusive or

One of the oldest linguistic structures in hypnotic language is the double-bind pattern. Milton Erickson's genius really shone in his ability in setting a benevolent double-bind. He would casually talk with a person and ask whether it would be most appropriate to get well within thirty minutes or thirty days. He would ask if the person wanted to go into trance in his favorite trance chair or just in the chair where they were sitting. In each case, the specific answers were not as important as the fact that the person was hearing and processing and making some response.

By positing *either this or that*, the higher frame of getting well or going into a trance was thereby accepted. And you might be interested to know that we couldn't make up our minds about whether we should focus this chapter on practical applications of transformation or on mastery, so we did.

When we set up a benevolent double-bind, we do so by using the linguistic patterning that we call Inclusive/Exclusive Or. We can see this in the following statements:

"Would you prefer to resolve this issue and feel satisfied with the solution by the end of our coaching session or would it feel more real if it took thirty days?"

"As you develop mastery of NLP do you prefer to mark and measure each and every step of your progress so that you can consciously recognize it, or would it be okay if you just continually move in that direction so that it becomes your basic life orientation?"

How does this presuppositional language work? Notice that it seems as if the speaker were offering a choice. The speaker describes resolving an issue and then

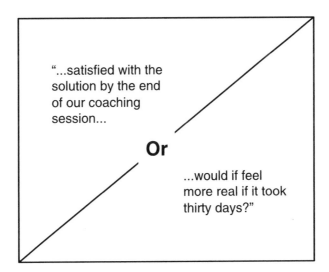

Figure 22.1: Inclusive/exclusive or

offers the choice in terms of time: when do you want it resolved to your satisfaction? Shall it be in this session or in thirty days? In order for this simple double-bind to work, a person focuses on the *content question* about time, the details of how long. In focusing on that question, by presupposition the person has already *accepted* the higher frame of the benevolent double-bind, namely, that he or she *will* resolve the issue. That is no longer in question.

At the primary state, the person's mind (conscious awareness) is on the details of time. Yet the very process of focusing on that in itself necessitates the *acceptance* of all of the higher implied frames. It accepts the original intent above and beyond the Inclusive/Exclusive Or. This terminology means that the statement both *includes* the choice of resolving the issue (whether in thirty minutes or thirty days) and *excludes* the possibility of not experiencing the higher frame (resolving the issue).

By presupposition, the Inclusive/Exclusive Or includes all the lower levels of choices. This is what gives the *illusion* of choice. By presupposition, it excludes the person from escaping the "frame box" that has been set, whether it's getting well, resolving an issue, going into trance, or whatever. This higher-level choice occurs by the acceptance of the either/or choice at the lower level. Typically we do not hear the higher-level choice: we merely accept it "unconsciously" to the extent that it lies outside of our conscious awareness.

For more elegance in persuasion, we will want to ask such questions. We will want to ask questions that contain within them such resourceful presuppositions, that, in the very answering of the question, it presupposes the acceptance of the higher-framed presuppositions. In this way we communicate the higher frames while distracting conscious attention with primary-level questions. So, while the lower questions direct a person's mind toward various details, the very answering of the question enables the person to accept the presupposed frames that support some desired outcome.

Given the structure of this Inclusive/Exclusive Or, we can sometimes use it to pull off a linguistic "visual squash". Suppose, for example, a person says, "I don't know whether I should stay in this relationship or if I should leave." As we gather more information we discover the person's positive intention in saying this and in struggling with this decision is to feel more secure (and less insecure) and to have more of a sense of freedom.

With that information, we could now reply, "How will you ever *experience the real freedom* to relate to anyone if you don't learn to *feel secure* with yourself?"

In this case, we have moved up the levels by finding the highest positive intentions and then we have applied those intentions to the speaker's situation. We have applied freedom and security back onto the speaker in such a way as to give him or her a new meaning, a new frame of mind. In the classic NLP visual squash we take two conflicting parts, states, ideas, or beliefs and we bring them together, forcing them to exist in the same time and space. Here we have done that linguistically.

Demonstrating the Inclusive/Exclusive Or

Terry presented a classic description of an inner conflict when he said, "If I do therapy in my office at home it causes problems with the wife because I have people coming in and out of our private home. But, if move out and rent office space, that will increase expenses and overhead, and I will have to charge my clients more."

This describes a classic problem of internal conflict. Two parts of him were at war about what to do, what to decide.

If Terry works at his therapy practice at home, he can keep his rate low and work at home, but his wife doesn't like that. And that leads to arguments. If he moves his practice out of the home, he has to rent space. That increases overhead, and will force him to raise his rates, which will be hard on some of his clients.

I (BB) immediately asked Terry about his motivations. Why practice at home? Why keep the rates as low as possible? What did he get from that? He said that he felt that was yet another way of helping his clients.

"Terry, I get the sense that you want to stay home mostly because of your compassion for your clients?"

"Yes, that's right."

"So what would it be like for you if you gave yourself as much compassion as you give your clients?"

I played with the word "compassion" in this exchange. Terry had not specifically used that word, so where did I get it? I sensed it from our discussion. It was a generalization that put into words what I felt Terry was feeling. I sensed that this was his driving meta-state that put him into the conflict. People regularly use the words that they most value and, if we have our ears attuned to such value words, we will hear them. I knew that compassion rated as a very high value and positive intention for Terry, and from his double-bind I also knew that it was the compassion for both his clients and for his wife that created his difficulty. I knew that he valued his wife more than his clients.

So, guessing at his highest positive intention, I brought that to bear on the double-bind of the problem. At the moment of this linguistic intervention, neither his wife nor his clients were present. So I invited him to apply his value of *compassion* to himself and to his map. I did it this way:

"So, Terry, here you're facing a double-bind situation, caught between wanting to be compassionate to your clients and keep the costs down and to your wife, to create a safe and private home environment. You are in an Inclusive/Exclusive Or format. So, I'm interested. What would happen if you gave your wife the same amount of compassion you give your clients and yourself?"

A long pause occurred as Terry went inside, into a deep trance. As he did, I said, "Yes, that's right. And just let those thoughts and feelings sink in—sink in very deeply. And you can decide that you can trust that the answer will come to you with regard to what you need to do about your clients and what is most important in your life."

In this case, I meta-stated Terry by asking him to access the state of compassion and to apply it to the problematic state wherein he felt a conflicting double-bind. This gives us, as it were, a linguistic visual squash. At the primary level Terry was aware of two contexts: his relationship to his wife and their home and his relationship with his clients and his work. At the first meta-level, the frame that drove both was *compassion*. Yet what one frame wanted conflicted with what the other wanted.

As I helped Terry to become more conscious of compassion as his positive intention for both of these two parts, I also asked him to meta-state *himself and his mapping* of these things with compassion. What happened? What was the effect of the higher-level *compassion* on the structure of the Inclusive/Exclusive Or?

By having him apply *compassion* to both of his relationships and to his own mapping, I helped his awareness to expand. He realized that his marriage was first and foremost in his life and that making his marriage work was crucial. So, as *compassion* rose up to function as an even higher and larger frame, it outframed even the entire the Inclusive/Exclusive Or structure so that it no longer was an *either/or* structure.

7. Cause-effect

A presuppositional frame that we all assume as we move through the world is the neuro-linguistic structure of cause-effect. This refers to how we frame and construct our mental maps to posit that some things (ideas, events, or activities) are "causes" and others are "effects" of those causes.

What are the cues or linguistic markers of cause-effect structures? The Meta-Model lists such words and phrases as "like", "because", "if then", "made", "makes", "causes", and "force". Actually, any active verb presupposes a level of causation. "Since" and "so" also assume cause-effect.

In terms of the Meta-Model, we question and challenge such the cause-effect statements that are ill formed. "He makes me angry" is ill formed *because* it does not describe *the process* for how one person is causing another person to experience an emotion. "Rain makes me wet", by way of contrast, is a well- formed cause-effect statement. So is "He makes me lose credibility with the boss by making me late more than fifty percent of the time that I ride with him."

When we use presuppositional languaging, we do not question even ill-formed uses of causation terms: we use them to evoke a response in others. In fact, our words and how we say them *hypnotize* people and *make* them go into trance where we coach them to access the resources that facilitate healing, response potentials, or new resources.

If you reread that last sentence, you will see (a verb assuming a cause-effect action) that using causation can be quite useful in directing awareness and perception hypnotically. And *since*, as master practitioners, we *are becoming* skilled communicators, we *will* use linguistic structures that will *cause* us and our listeners to go where we *invite* a mind to go—*because* brains (ours and theirs) cannot *not* process such words and create such mapping because as people track such words it *causes* them to construct such maps.

When we use cause-effect statements (whether hypnotically or in everyday conversation), it effectively allows us to link thoughts. Causation terms enable us to link one thought to another, one state to another, one resource to another. This *works* wonders not only for the hypnotist, but also for the therapist, the sales person, the parent, the employer, or the marketer. Even trainers will find them powerful in training and installing new skills and competencies.

Since you are becoming ever more masterful as a practitioner, it must mean that you *are learning* advanced language structures that will only *make* you a more superb communicator.

Examine that sentence. Notice how it has two cause-effect statements using the presupposition terms "since" and "make". We used the cause-effect word "make" to link the thoughts of becoming masterful as a practitioner to the idea of become more superb as a communicator. Complex equivalences also serve as great linkage language and so, "it must mean" provides the linguistic marker of an equation.

Reversing syntax

We can do more with cause-effect structures. In the following statement, consider how Suzanne maps your problem.

"My sister *makes* me feel guilty."

In its simplistic format, the problem is: A (sister) *makes* B (Suzanne's feeling of an emotion).

"Suzanne, is this an ongoing problem for you? Or does it just come and go."

"It is an off-and-on type of problem."

"It goes *off* and then it comes *on*? So when do you know to turn it on rather than off?"

"You mean, when do I know when it's time to feel guilty?"

"Yes. I need to get a little more information to get it into a little clearer form. When we do that, then we can reverse the mapping. I can't do that yet: I need some more information about the problem. So, when do you know when it is time to feel guilty?

"Well, when she's not happy—that's usually when I feel guilty."

"Good. So, when she's not feeling happy, you know that it's time to feel guilty about that?"

"Yes."

"So, when she's not happy, that event causes you to feel guilty. Okay, now let's chunk down from that level. What I want to know now is this: how is that a problem for you?

"Well, I can't be happy when that happens."

"You say you *can't* be happy? 'I can't be happy if she is not happy'? 'So, when she is not happy, I *can't* be happy; it prevents me from being happy.' That might work.

"It does work. That's my problem!"

"So, Suzanne, what would happen if you could not be happy with your not being happy over her not being happy?

(Laughs) "I think it just went! … Yes, it just went." (*Snaps her fingers.*)

At this point, Yvonne spoke up: "My brother-in-law makes me angry."

"He does? Hmm. So, what would happen if you got angry at your anger at your brother-in-law? Right now just feel angry at your anger at your brother-in-law so that your anger just disappears."

It did.

As with the *ordinal* presupposition terms, we can format a problem as a *cause-effect* or a *complex-equivalence* structure. Once we do that, we can then reverse the syntax. We can take how we have mapped it and reverse the things we say are "causes" and exchange them with the things we call "effects." Frequently this will eliminate or blow out a problem linguistically.

The Meta-States model explains how this works. With Suzanne, we applied "not being happy" with "not being happy". We brought *not-happiness* as a state, put it at a meta-level to *not-happiness*. Doing this, in her case, functioned as one negative canceling out the other negative. With Yvonne we applied "anger" to "anger and her getting mad at being mad" and that caused the anger to be canceled out. In terms of the Mind-Lines model, we describe this as the linguistic pattern of "apply to self".

EXERCISE: Cause-effect
1. Identify the problem.
In pairs, the first person identifies a problem or challenge to play with.

2. Formulate the problem in cause-effect structure.
The person being the coach will ask questions until the problem can be put into the form of a *cause-effect* or a *complex-equivalence* statement-to the satisfaction of the first person.

3. Reverse and test.
Then reverse the syntax and present it to the first person. Calibrate to how the person responds. Continue until you reframe, blow out, or change the problem.

4. Check ecology and future-pace.
We do this to install as a new way of thinking. Reverse roles.

Intervening with detailed questions
We have taken a pattern that originally came from Richard Bandler and have adapted it to create a process exercise. This demonstrates the use of cause-effect presuppositional language in directing a person's awareness from a problem state to a resource state.

EXERCISE: Problem to solution
1. In pairs, identify a problem to play with.

2. Entertain focus questions.
The second person will then ask the following questions (see below) of the first person. Be sure to give each other time to process each question.

3. Process internally.
The person being questioned is not to respond verbally to the questions, but only process them internally. When the person has processed a question, nod to signify the questioner to move on to the next question.

List of questions for the questioner:
A. What's wrong?
B. What caused this problem?
C. How have you failed to resolve this problem so far?
D. How can you overcome this problem?
E. What would you like to change?
F. When will you *stop* it from being a limitation?
G. How many ways do you know you have solved this?
H. I know you are changing and seeing things differently, aren't you?
I. How good will you feel when you have fully resolved this and moved on with your life? And what will be some of the key resourceful states you'll experience?

Debriefing the working of this languaging
A. What's wrong?
Because this question is in the present tense, it invites us to associate into the problem. We make our internal movie and *step into it* so that we are there as the key actor in the film. In terms of the SCORE model, this is where we identify the current problematic *symptoms*.

B. What caused this problem?
This temporal presupposition presupposes that something in the past ("caused"—past-tense verb) brought the problem about. Now we *step out* of the movie to create another movie, an old movie of something that previously happened. In SCORE, this is *cause*.

C. How have you failed to resolve this problem so far?
With this question we *step back* into the movie and experience the problem and our failing to solve it. It refocuses our awareness so that we are not sorting for the cause but for the *failure* to solve it. With the presupposition of existence, the question does introduce the idea of resolution ("resolve"). But this is framed as a "not" ("failed to"). It moves us from the *cause* of the problem to the failure to resolve, and yet one step closer to the direction of resolution. It presupposes the possibility, but not reality, of resolution. It therefore paces with this focus. The final "so far" presupposes that it is just the current state of nonresolution and that resolution will come.

D. How can you overcome this problem?
This question contains a *process* term ("how") that looks for structure, a spatial presupposition ("overcome"), and a *modal of possibility* ("can"). It presupposes that we can move from the cause of the problem to the *solution* of the problem; that it's possible and just a matter of strategy ("how"). When we find or discover that how-to knowledge, we will then be able to *overcome* the problem. This presupposes that the solution is possible, and is possible for *you*.

E. What would you like to change?
"What" gives us a presupposition of existence, "like" a modal of desire, and "would" a modal of choice and will. "You" makes it personal. Having moved to the place of mapping "overcoming the problem" as a possibility, we have *stepped into* the movie of change. We are moving toward solution. "What would you like to change?" This puts us "at choice". Solution has a form or structure (D). Next we have an embedded command to the past problem.

F. When will you *stop it* from being a limitation? (Use a different tone or volume for the phrase in italics.)
With the questions having invited a person to start moving toward a solution and mapping the possibilities of choices for changes, "when" invites us to make yet another choice, to stop letting the "problem" "be" (existence) a "limitation" (complex equivalence). This presupposes a "no!" to the old frame thereby creating space for saying "yes" to a new frame. The embedded command is the invitation to say "no". "Stop it!" Stop framing the experience as meaning "limitation". "When" (a temporal presupposition) becomes the focus, "When will you ...?" Answering that question means accepting the higher frame of "Stopping it". Being *in the movie* invites us to look at this moment or in the future for "when" to do this. We are no longer focusing on the problem, but on the solution.

G. How many ways do you know you have solved this?
"How many ways ...?" presupposes there are many ways, many choices; "you have solved ..." presupposes "solution", and solutions in the past. This invites us to map that we have already solved it. Our movie shifts to a solution movie and we look backward to resources in the past, previous solutions that we have not yet mapped as solutions. This reinforces that we have many choices in solving this problem. It invites us to view the past as solution-filled rather than problem-filled. The implied frames in this: "What new behaviors and choices do you now have that confirm that you have solved the problem?"

H. I know you are already changing and seeing things differently, aren't you?
This invites the person to lock in the changes by noticing them. Using the awareness presupposition ("know") invites the person to share in the knowing. Present-tense active verb ("*are* already changing and seeing") invites stepping into that movie. The tag question ("aren't you?") invites a confirmation to the awareness. It invites a rhetorical "yes".

I. How good will you feel when you have fully resolved this and moved on with your life? And what will be some of the key resourceful states you'll experience? "How" as a process word again focuses on strategy. Accepting the question as legitimate presupposes that we will feel good upon completion, it's just a question of *how good* we will feel. Presupposed also is getting the problem "fully resolved" so that one is moving on with life. The second question presupposes that resolution leads to more resourceful states.

We have three ways to utilize cause-effect statements hypnotically. We can use them in hypnotic languaging by linking ideas. We can set a problem up as a cause-effect (or complex-equivalence) statements and then reverse the syntax. And, we can use the detailed questioning pattern to move a person from problem state to solution state and focus.

8. Complex equivalence
We construct a *complex equivalence* whenever we use a part of an experience (some aspect of external behavior) and set it up as equivalent to some internal significance (meaning) or state (internal state). This gives us the basic formula for the magic box and cube that we use in the Mind-Lines model: EB = IS.

When we have mapped things in this way, "magic" occurs. Then, to an external cue, we are able to assume that it carries a whole load of semantic meaning.

"You spoke harshly to me again; you just don't love me any more."

With a map like that, a person can experience *semantic reactions* any time of day or night, in the presence of the person or when just thinking about the voice quality. Yet in this case, the ill-formed structure of this Meta-Model distinction creates an impoverished map of the world that creates unnecessary pain. That's why we question or challenge such. Yet, presuppositionally *complex-equivalence statements* provide us with an outstanding linguistic structure that we can use to direct perception. It also makes for effective transitional languaging patterns for hypnosis.

Because we can link one thought with another thought with both cause-effect and complex equivalences, reading this now and using this understanding *means* that you are mastering this field and in the days and weeks to come will be utilizing these language patterns for directing your own awareness and that of others.

Identity
There are many other things we can do with the complex-equivalence structure. By definition, a complex equivalence refers to the *meaning* that we give to the sensory-based things of our world. What do those things mean? We equate them to our internal representations. This means that *meaning* is not only an abstraction, but a very personal abstraction.

What does anything mean? It depends on what any given person *represents* and *references* on the movie screen of the mind. Whatever internal state or significance we link to the external subject, that is the meaning, the complex equivalence. This also shows that we can change meaning at will. We call this reframing the meaning. We had *framed* it one way: "harsh tonality" *means* or is associated with, classified as, and categorized as "unloving behavior". Now we can *reframe* it: "harsh tonality" means "stress", "unresourceful state", "lack of skill in communicating when experiencing a negative emotion", and so on.

Since meaning is always subject to change, we can suggest new meanings linguistically easily and subtly. We can set other frames for the behavior or event "out there". This is what hypnosis is all about: changing frames.

This becomes especially useful when we think about the complex equivalences that we have used (consciously or unconsciously) to set up the frames of our identities. In the Extended Meta-Model (Chapters Eleven and Twelve, Hall, 1997, 2001), we have an additional form of complex equivalence as *identification*.

Actually, we create this complex equivalence very easily because we have the language to do it so easily. Via identification, we create the mental-emotional entity of "identity". All we have to do is use any form of the verb *"to be"*. The "to be" verb gives us the linguistic markers for identification and identity, "I *am* depressed". "I *am* a loser". "He *is* so dumb". "They *are* inferior".

When we say "I *am* …" we *identify* ourselves with what lies we put on the other side of the equation. A (I as a self, as a person) = B (some behavior, experience, or concept). We identify ourselves with the "B." We are Americans, Africans, teachers, selfish, Catholics, Muslims, alcoholics, sex offenders, whatever.

If I say, "I *am* a therapist", then is that *all* that I am? Even in the context of career and work, *am I just* a therapist? Perhaps I *am* also a writer. Could I also do some other things or are all other things eliminated?

Identification statements are prevalent all over the world. It seems to be a human predisposition and need to *identify* with something and to *identify* oneself. This is one way to map things. Yet it is not the only. We could also map that these are just experiences, behaviors, skills, functions. Instead of mapping things in terms of our identity (as an abstract concept), we could map them as actions and performances.

"I do therapy and I write, but I am always more than those two behaviors. I also mow the grass, straighten up the house, and work on websites."

"I engage in reading, researching, writing, training, talking to people, coaching, running, sleeping, eating, and watching television."

Korzybski said that all use of the "to be" verb was "unsane". He believed that every process of identifying and identification was the source of all ill-formed mapping. While we may not want to go that far, we do think its best to eliminate the "am" (or other inflections such as is, be, being, been, are) altogether from your self-identification. Sometimes I do therapy, sometimes I write, sometimes I read books, sometimes I mow grass …

For us, we seek to avoid identifying ourselves with what we do. *Doing* is but one facet of experience. And *doing* always occurs at a given time, in a given context, for specific purposes, and, at best, is but an *expression* of us, not "us". When we identify with what we do (or any other identification), we then invest all of our physical, mental, emotional, personal, and spiritual energies into it. Then we experience ourselves as that identification. We *are* our jobs, our titles, our relationships. Yet, when we *identify* ourselves with things that can be taken away from us, we set ourselves up to be threatened at *our sense of self*. This is the structure of what we call an "identity crisis". "Identity" can be put into a crisis only if we create a complex equivalence and identify ourselves with something external that can be threatened.

For a long time, I (BB) identified myself as a minister. Then the day came when I lost a large pastorate. The identification caused me to ask, "Who am I now?" I had identified my *self* with what I was "doing." What I *did* equated with *me*. So when I lost the "position" I identified with, status, right to do what I had done, I lost my *identity*. At the time I went through quite an identity crisis and transformation. I began identifying myself with my "being" rather than my "doing". Realizing this now, I know better than to equate self with actions and that is very liberating.

How do we dis-identify ourselves from what we do? Begin by using the infinitives of the nominalizations that you use in your identity statements. We express these in the form of, "I am" statements. This creates a tremendous *nominalization*. All of our actions, processes, and activities are frozen into the first person. To denominalize such limited identity maps, restore the infinitive. Restore the activities. Question the "I am" statements by meta-modeling them.

- To *be* that, what do you do?
- What actions, activities, and processes do you engage in?
- When you do those things, is that *all* you are?
- What else do you do? What other things do you express?
- When you identify with the "EB" side of the complex equivalence, do you really want to identify yourself with that?

This also works powerfully when people *identify* (or overidentify) with an emotion, an emotional state, or a label. When someone says, "I am depressed" or "I am angry" or "I am sad" they have *identified* with one emotional state and yet we know that they "are" and experience much more than just that.

Dis-identification through presuppositions

When Suzanne said, "I *am* sorry." I (BB) asked, "Is that who you are? Are you sorry?" And she said, "Yes."

"Is that all you think you are?"

"Well, no, but I am always saying that 'I'm sorry' about things."

"What are you that is more than sorry?"

There was a long pause. "Thoughtful," she said. "I am thoughtful."

"You are thoughtful? And, what are you that is *not* thoughtful?"

"I am much more."

"And beyond much more, what are you?" (Long pause.)

"I am covering new ground."

"And much more than covering new ground, what are you?" (Pause.)

"I am trying to bring the big picture on."

"You are trying to bring the big picture on. And do you know you are trying to bring the big picture on?"

"I care."

"How do you know you care? What kind of behaviors do you do that show you care. What are you doing that lets you know you care about people?"

"I see a lot of good in people."

"You see a lot of good in people. And what does that mean about you as a person?"

"There is a lot of good in me."

"What happens when you bring a lot of good in you to bear upon that limiting belief that you are sorry?" (Long pause.)

"It goes away."

"That's right, just disappear that limiting belief that you are sorry, now." (Long pause.)

EXERCISE: Presuppositions for dis-identifying pattern
This pattern provides a useful model for challenging and transcending boundary conditions associated with complex equivalences. It can be used both reflexively and when coaching others. For other patterns for dis- identifying see *The Sourcebook of Magic*.

1. Elicit an identity complex equivalence using the verb "to be".
Who are you? As you think about identifying yourself, how do you think about yourself? Listen for the form of "I am X".

2. Pace and feed back the complex equivalence to the person for validation.
So you *are* X; is that right?

3. Question and challenge the identification.
Is that all you think you are?

(Calibrate to physiological shift.)

Are you not more than that?

(Calibrate to agreement.)

4. Invite new higher-level mapping that goes beyond identification.
What are you that is not X?

(You want a verbal answer here.)

You *are* what? What Y?

(As a more expansive identification map is formed, find a word or term or way of expressing this understanding to solidify it.)

5. And beyond that Y (word elicited in 4), is that all you are?
How much more are you than that? You do know you are more than that, don't you? How do you know?

6. Confirm new self-defining, check ecology and future-pace.

EXERCISE: Redefining using pure potentiality
The following pattern uses temporal and spatial presuppositions to tear up limiting complex equivalences at the identity level. This pattern can be used in everyday language. Even with mild things the language will take you up, up and away to the higher levels of the mind for a more expansive perspective.

It's important in this pattern that after the person has moved up the levels that you begin feeding back what the person says. This pacing will not only validate and confirm, but it will have the effect of lighting up their neural networks as they associate more and more into the higher levels of awareness.

1. Pace current situation and move up the levels.
Starting where the person is at, invite the person to move up the levels of the mind. Repeatedly ask, "What do you think or feel *about* that?"

2. Travel to the heights; go up, up, and away.
Invite the person to move up the levels beyond words, beyond what can be expressed in propositional language. Take them to the formlessness void beyond that level. Use all of the meta-level words and levels.

"What do you believe about that? What does that mean to you? What ideas come to you about that?"

3. Confirm they have moved beyond words, then repeat.
"How do you know that you are there?" (Validate that they know: "I just know.")

What's beyond that? How do they know that?

4. Push it as far as you can.
"Great, and yet, are you not more than that?"

(Eventually, they will constantly be saying, "Yes.")

"Is that all you think you are?"

(Utter this statement, with an astonished tone. Do so holding the belief that the person is always more than what he or she thinks about him- or herself. Ask with a questioning and incredulous tonality, "Is that all?" Doing this sets the frame that they are more than whatever they think they are. People are so much more than anything they can map about themselves.)

5. Reverse the question and ask the negation.
"What are you that is *not* X, Y, or Z?

(All of the things they told you previously. Find out what the previous rung on the ladder is to get the person to move up to the next rung.)

6. Come back down the levels.
Once the person has moved well beyond any physiology that gives any hint of the problem, start going back down the levels and verifying at each step:

"You do know you are more than that don't you?"

[Anchor this as you come down as you continually ask—]

"How do you know that?"

7. Check ecology of the new self-definition and future-pace.

Debriefing the pattern
As we begin using this pattern, we want to get content about self and self-identification. Doing this will be easy and natural because you are engaged in a regular

everyday conversation. Conversely, you will not need to get any content about the problem. Rather than know such details, or the length of the problem, you need to know only the belief.

Starting up the levels may be slow at first, but then will begin to move very quickly. As soon as you sense that you are getting agreement, say, "Well what are you that is not X, Y, Z?" They tell you. Then say, "And, beyond that, is that all you are? How much more are you than that?" The person will go up in one place and come down in another. With the expansive awareness the person achieves at the higher levels, we will ground that awareness back into reality by bringing it back down with them as we ask for evidence.

Demo with Nancy

Nancy wanted to work in a training on her weight problem. She began by making an identity statement: "*I am* overweight."

"Is that all you think you are?"

"I am a woman."

"Aren't you more than that?"

"Yes."

"What are you that is not overweight?"

"I am a mother, business lady, I am going to write a book."

You are a mother, business lady and you are going to write a book. And beyond that is that all you are?" (Pause.) "How much more are you than that?

"I am child of God."

"And, how do you know you are a child of God?"

"He has promised it."

"He has promised it. And, how do you know it is yours?"

"I believe in him."

And being a child of God, now, and believing in him, how do you feel about that? "I feel very good about that."

"Which state is better: the one you came out of or the one you have now?"

"This one."

At this point Nancy broke out in laughter.

With this pattern you can burst limiting and impoverished complex equivalences in an ever so simple way. Using temporal presuppositions we invite a person to expose the complex equivalences that they have used for identification. We then "chunk up" the levels until we move to a place that's outside the person's box and to the representations of "not". When the person gets to the "not", and to the place of pure potentiality, they will find numerous resources there. At that point we can set the frame above the current reality strategy that "they are more than that".

Summary

We have now explored several linguistic presuppositions around such key conceptual categories as existence, awareness, possibility and necessity, temporal and spatial, ordinal, the Exclusive/Inclusive Or, cause-effect, and complex equivalence.

So, as we now have and recognize this sense of just how *effective presuppositions* are, *would* you *consider* the *possibility* of skillfully utilizing them in your *speech*, which will enable you to *move* your or another's *perception* in any *direction* that you *choose* to *move* that *awareness*? Because you *can take perception and move it backward* or *forward*, *up* or *down*, or in several other directions. And you *may choose to move it step by step* either leading to *resources* in the thoughts in the *back* of the *mind* or *maybe* in the *higher mind*. And, *as you* lead a mind *out* of the *problem state* and *up* into *resourceful states*, *then* that *will only cause* the realization that we are more, much more than any problem we could experience. And, as we *realize* this, we *will* even now begin to see ourselves as *being* not a person with a problem but a person with *innate resources* that occur at many, many levels. *We are resourceful*, and far more resourceful than we have dared to imagine before ... now.

We can direct perception through the skillful use of language by using numerous linguistic presuppositions that give us a structure for how to think about doing this. Presuppositions simply define what has to be true in order to make sense out of something.

Chapter Twenty-Three
Practical NLP
NLP Applied to Therapy, Business, Relationships, Health, Personal Development

"NLP is an attitude backed up by a methodology that leaves a trail of techniques."
- Richard Bandler

Why are you wanting to *master* NLP? When you finally reach a place of mastery, then what? What will that do for you? What will you be able to do then?

Neuro-Linguistic Programming, as a model, presents a cutting-edge way to think about human nature, human functioning, and human potential. Using the hyphens and dashes that link body-mind-emotion, neuro-linguistic, neuro-semantic to remind us that these are systemic processes, NLP describes how we as living beings operate. It describes how our very neurology maps the territory "out there" via our sense receptors and how we map that map to create our internal mental movie, and how we map that movie map with words, and map that map with more abstract and conceptual words, and so on. In the end, it is all mapping. In the end, we do *not* deal with the territory (the energy manifestations out there), but through our maps upon maps *of* that territory.

The foundational NLP presupposition from Korzybski and general semantics that says that the map is not the territory establishes the epistemology of NLP. Our operating theory of *how* we know what we know is the epistemology of constructionism. We construct our image of the world and use that facsimile as our representational reality.

Practically this cognitive-behavioral discipline means that we can change our lives by changing our maps. Finding the strategy for how a behavior or skill or even neuro-linguistic state works puts us in control of running that strategy or choosing to not run it. It puts us in the driver's seat so that we can "run our own brain". This also turns us loose on the world of experiences. As "the study of the structure of subjective experience," it provides us with the tools we need to model any experience. Using the tools, patterns, and models of NLP, we can model pathology as well as genius.

In modeling, we can design and redesign our experiences. Again, Korzybski (that original neuro-linguistic trainer) called this human engineering. From his engineering perspective, he believed that, as the human race could *time-bind* the best learning experiences of those who have gone before and start where they left off in the hard sciences, we can learn to do the same in the soft or human sciences as soon as we develop a sane language and semantics of such. This was his primary purpose in *Science and Sanity* (1933/1994).

Today we have begun to do precisely this. Bandler and Grinder began by modeling the therapeutic wizards Perls, Satir, and Erickson and thereby created numerous models for effective therapeutic functioning, communication skills, information-gathering skills, hypnotic language skills, somatic healing skills, and more. The first models that they gave us not only created the content and patterns of NLP, but offered some of the first effective strategies or patterns for change.

Neuro-linguistic technologies

We call NLP patterns *human technologies*. Such patterns or processes offer a step-by-step way to "run your own brain" to obtain a certain experience. How many patterns are there? *The Sourcebook of Magic* (1997) lists 77 of the most central and foundational of the NLP patterns. That suggests that there may be upwards of 200 NLP patterns. These provide specific strategies for high-quality functioning in a variety of areas, including:

- business
- education
- psychotherapy
- personal development
- sports and athletic coaching
- interpersonal relations
- communication: negotiation, mediation
- conflict resolution
- medicine, health

The 77 from *Sourcebook* include the following:

The basic meta-patterns
1. Well-formed desired outcomes
2. Pacing and matching
3. Calibration
4. Checking the ecology of a pattern
5. Flexibility of responses
6. State elicitation
7. State induction
8. State interrupt
9. Anchoring
10. Accessing positive intention

Patterns for incongruity of "parts"
11. The collapsing-anchors pattern
12. The parts-negotiation pattern

13. The Six-step reframing pattern
14. Aligning perceptual positions
15. The agreement-frame pattern
16. The aligned-self pattern
17. The resolving-internal-conflict pattern
18. The visual-squash pattern

Patterns for identity and "self"
19. The belief-change pattern
20. The dis-identification pattern
21. The reimprinting pattern
22. The time-line pattern
23. The change-personal-history pattern
24. The swish pattern
25. The circle-of-excellence pattern
26. The decision-destroyer pattern
27. The core-transformation pattern
28. Meta-transformations
29. The making-peace-with-parents pattern
30. The loving-yourself pattern
31. The self-sufficiency pattern
32. Receiving wisdom from internal sage

Patterns for neuro-linguistic states
33. The V/K dissociation, phobia cure
34. Accessing resourceful states
35. State-of-consciousness awareness
36. The "as if" frame pattern
37. The chaining-states pattern
38. The "sub-modality" overlapping pattern
39. The threshold-compulsion blowout
40. Transforming mistakes into learning
41. Becoming intentionally compulsed (Godiva Chocolate pattern)
42. The decision-making pattern
43. The pleasure pattern
44. The reducing-pleasure pattern
45. Breaking up limited synesthesias
46. Filing away memories

Patterns for languaging and relanguaging
47. The Meta-Modeling pattern
48. The Meta-Model III pattern
49. The denominalizing pattern
50. The problem-defining/formulating pattern

Patterns-for-thinking patterns, meta-programs, and cognitive distortions
51. Identifying/pacing meta-programs

52. Recognizing and challenging limiting meta-programs
53. The meta-programs change pattern
54. Disputing cognitive distortions

Patterns for meanings/semantics
55. The content-reframing pattern
56. The context-reframing pattern
57. "Sub-modalities"-reframing pattern
58. Six-step reframing as meta-stating
59. Pulling apart belief synesthesias
60. Establishing your value hierarchy
61. Kinesthetic hierarchy of criteria
62. The thought-virus inoculation

Patterns for strategies
63. The new-behavior generator
64. The forgiveness pattern
65. The allergy-cure pattern
66. The grief-resolution pattern
67. The pre-grieving pattern
68. The healthy-eating pattern
69. Resolving co-dependence
70. The speaking-assertively pattern
71. The responding-to-criticism pattern
72. The establishing-boundaries pattern
73. The magical-parents pattern
74. Transforming mistakes into learning
75. Thinking/evaluating wisely and thoroughly (SCORE model)
76. A Disney strategy for creativity
77. The spinning-icon pattern

The trail of techniques

This sampling of the techniques left by NLP suggest the possibilities of hundreds, even thousands, of more processes that are being and will be created in the years and decades to come. With the methodology of modeling the structure of experience and continually redesigning the multilevel maps and frames of mind, we can move into any practical area of life to build models of how best to function at this point in history and extend the range of human possibility through ongoing time-binding.

NLP and therapy

Psychotherapy differs from psychology in that it is a direct application of psychological principles and practices to the hurts, limitations, instances of impoverishment, and inadequate mapping as people grow and develop. Psychotherapy facilitates human development and potential.

Because traditional therapy in the twentieth century focused on problems and on all the ways humans were broken, it developed an orientation to "fixing" people (called patients) and remedying problems. It also was focused on the symptoms of such problems as emotions and defensive mechanisms, and assumed that "insight" or understanding would automatically "fix" things.

It was in this context that NLP took a very different approach. Assuming a meta-position to numerous therapeutic approaches, NLP entered the scene with a focus on modeling *what worked* without investing in any theory as to *why* it worked. Bandler and Grinder, in an iconoclastic attack on the field of psychotherapy, medicine, and psychiatry, galloped into the arena of therapy saying that they had no theory and wanted to indulge in no psycho-archeology or theo-archeology: they were modelers and cared only about what worked and how it worked.

Actually, this wasn't true, but for that time it worked wonders as a great reframe. They did have a theory, as we have noted throughout this work. Their theory was that the world isn't impoverished in such a way that there aren't enough choices for people for success or to be happy. If people are limited it is because they have an impoverished map of the world. And their choices in terms of emotions, thoughts, behaviors, and responses all made sense—given their map of the world. They make their maps through the modeling processes of deleting information, generalizing their ideas, and distorting their understandings. By sending them back to the "deeper" (or higher) levels of their map making and inviting them to revisit their map making through asking open-ended questions, they can construct more enhancing maps that will expand their choices, perceptions, understandings, meanings, and responses.

Thus was invented *the Meta-Model of language for therapy*. This model was simply a set of recursive questions to ask someone that had the "magical" effect of expanding their maps. With the expanding of the maps, one's relationship to the world would change.

Interesting enough, Bandler and Grinder did not model a cognitive therapist, but a family-systems therapist, and a gestalt therapist, and a medical hypnotist—and yet they ended up with a cognitive-behavioral model of psychotherapy. Beginning with those foundations, NLP as a meta-discipline extended to many other therapies including psychoanalysis, behaviorism, reality therapy, and many more.

Because of the NLP focus on *solutions*, it has always had an affinity for the solution-focused therapies, especially brief psychotherapy, Ericksonian therapies, and the cognitive-based therapies. Also, because of NLP's holistic model of mind-body (neuro-linguistic), it has also had a strong affinity to many of the body therapies. Yet, in all of its modeling, it has remained a meta-discipline, modeling whatever works in any and every branch of psychotherapy. This is not only its interdisciplinary strength, but also its appeal. NLP is eclectic in that it picks and chooses among various processes within many disciplines. Yet there's a reason and order to the eclecticism. From the meta-frame of looking for structure, NLP chooses what works and models that to identify the overarching frameworks.

Therefore, we cannot really describe "NLP therapy" as such, at least not as a separate discipline. Rather, we talk about this or that pattern, process, or intervention using an NLP modeling of various psychotherapies. Those patterns that we might describe as uniquely "NLP" would be those that fit all of the NLP presuppositions and would be considered generally as part of the training in an NLP practitioner course.

Reimprinting pattern

Traumatic episodes and reactions arise from traumatic experiences and from negative stories, movies, and imaginations. Once we map a "trauma" those representations govern our functioning, believing, valuing, and perceiving. They set an "imprint" frame upon us that feels solid and stable. Such imprints can involve both positive and negative experiences. Because *imprints* typically set a "That's the way it is" type of frame, this makes them feel ingrained and not easily altered.

Like beliefs, imprints operate as self-fulfilling prophecies. This explains the futility of trying to argue with a belief or an imprint. The person feels that he or she has far too much data gathered over time to support the belief or imprint for it to change. So, rather than directly fight with it, we operate more indirectly. We go back to a time prior to the original imprint, to a time before the person has reinforced the map with many later confirmations, and set some new frames that will undermine it from within.

In the mapping of imprints, expect to frequently find one peculiar abnormality. The abnormality is that, in the person's mental movie, he or she may actually switch positions with the person inflicting the harm or trauma. In making this switch, the person will also experience the perpetrator's reality. When this happens, it will create many of the confusing symptoms of thoughts and feelings in the person.

This is especially true for children who do not have a clear sense of their self-identity. It is part of the mentality of children to pretend that they are someone else, to take on the thinking, feeling, and acting of others. Sometimes they take on the role model—lock, stock, and barrel—with very little discrimination as to what that acceptance will entail. These dynamics can lead us to have multiple selves that actually incorporate many of the models we grew up with. Look for this kind of *introjection* of a significant other in traumatic imprints. It will not always occur, but will frequently be there.

Reimprinting works by the updating of internal maps, highlighting resources, and changing the old codes. In reimprinting, we will even give the people who perpetrated hurt against us the resources they needed that would have prevented them from creating the hurt in the first place. Doing this does not excuse or condone the hurtful behavior: it rather maps more appropriate resources and behaviors. Often, victims of crimes build limiting beliefs, then they maintain them through their angers and fears.

The pattern

1. Identify the problem.
What belief, behavior, or emotion do you want to change? What associated feelings go along with it? [Anchor this state.] What have you already attempted to change about that belief or behavior? What stands in the way or stops you?

2. Use the anchor to locate the experience in history.
I want you to *feel this* [fire the anchor] and just go back … in time … floating back until you find this feeling again … [Use the anchor to locate the imprint experience.]

3. Travel back in time with the emotion.
Whether explicitly or implicitly, use your time-line and invite them to go back to the imprint experience.

Just stay with *this feeling* (hold the anchor) and you can just begin to remember the earliest experience of this feeling.

As you are now experiencing that again, you can begin to verbalize the beliefs and generalizations that you originally formed from that experience.

Feel that negative emotion again … and just take that feeling back in time … Floating back … And what do you experience? Does it involve anyone else? … Do you see the person looking at you? … Go ahead and put yourself inside that younger you back then for just a moment. What beliefs do you make about this experience? … What beliefs about others, about the world, about God?

(Sometimes in the verbalizing of the belief a person will become aware of it for the first time and just expressing it will cause the old limiting belief to evaporate.)

4. Break state and review the experience.
I want you to step off your time-line and to review that imprint experience, to identify the situation and those involved. Just come back here to this room and to this now, and leave that past memory.

Good. Now let's review that experience as if we were watching a movie. As you now look back at that experience, put it way out there so that you have a sense of distance from it, so that you are no longer in it. but that you are just watching that younger you in it … How has that experience affected you since that time? What are some of the other beliefs that you constructed after that event?

5. Find the positive intentions in the feeling or belief.
What were the positive intentions of the others involved in that situation? If you don't know, go ahead and ask the characters in that remembered movie. Ask each character, "What were your positive intention for doing that?" Were they trying to make you a worthless person, trying to screw you up? Also, what are your positive intentions for keeping this movie alive in your mind?

6. Identify and anchor the needed resources.
What resources did you need back then but did not have? What understandings, beliefs, feelings do you have access to now that you did not have access to back then? (Access and anchor each of these resources. Do so for yourself and for each unresourceful character.)

What would the other persons in that movie have needed so that they would have been able to respond more effectively? More acceptance? Compassion? Calmness? Self-control? Respect? Self-esteem?

7. Apply the resource.
I want you now to review the imprint experience from the perspective of each of the characters involved in that event and, as you do, we will access each of the resourceful states that each character needed and give that to them so that the movie will begin to change … to transform … That's right. Just take these resources and give them to that person. After all, this other person … right now … is in your brain as an image or memory that you have created and that you keep alive. So take this resource and give it to him or her. And notice, what does he or she do differently with it? … What new beliefs can you now build from this experience? … Just go inside, and allow your unconscious mind to review each experience with this experience knowing that they now have the resources they needed. We know that this person didn't have that resource at that time, with your memory, you can update that model now …

There is a younger self back in that experience that needs resources that he or she didn't have then. What resources do you have now that would have allowed you to build a different set of beliefs back then? What insights, skills, abilities …? What is the closest you have come to having that resource? Now take that light and shine it back through your history. Shine it on that younger you … so that as that younger you begins to feel this resource, you can allow yourself to imagine how that would have changed things. And you can now allow yourself to be relaxed and secure, calm and comfortable with yourself in that memory … see that younger self in front of you building resourceful beliefs and abilities.

8. Associate and relive the imprint experience.
With each resource that you access you can now *step back* into that old memory and give it to each character; you can step back into time *feeling this* (hold the anchor) with all of these resources and even into the minds-and-bodies of the other persons … letting them have these resources. And as you do you can now update your own beliefs about these things, creating beliefs that will enhance your own life as you move into the future.

9. Receive resources.
Now you can step back into that time and into your younger self and fully receive all of these resourceful qualities and states, the very ones you needed to give the other persons in your movie.

10. Review and future-pace.
Now come back here to the present for a moment and turn around so that you can review all the changes in that experience. How satisfied are you with the transformations so far? Now step back into that younger you with all your resources and very quickly move up into the new and into your future.

Change-personal-history pattern

Since the "past" exists only in our mind as information and is not externally real, we can keep it inside the theater of our mind and body only as our "memory". Yet these memories are continually changing. With every new understanding, development, and experience we have, our memories keep changing. For this reason, "It is never too late to have a happy childhood."

What we remember, *why* we remember, and how we use our memories are our personal choices. We can "accurately" represent hurtful and traumatic memories and thereby so keep our body and emotions all filled up and stirred up with negative tensions. Or, if you don't like that as a way to run your own brain, you can use the following pattern to *change your personal history*.

The pattern
1. Identify a problem event.
Think about a time and place in your history that still troubles you … How does it trouble you?

What problems does it create for you?

When you step into that memory, what emotion arises? What meanings? Just notice them and now step out of that problem state.

2. Take an observer's viewpoint of that experience.
If that problem state is a primary state, then, as you *step aside* from it and just observe it, this will give you a more resourceful meta-state frame from which you can think about that primary state.

Just float above your time-line … And, as you do, go back to the problem event and observe it as a witness to it. From this meta-position, see that younger you going through that event.

3. Make resourceful learnings from the event.
As you just observe, you can now choose to learn, really learn from that event. What resources did that younger you need? What resources did the others in the situation need? Make a menu list of the resources that you would have needed to have changed things.

4. Return to the present and fully access the resources.
Good. Now return to this moment and place, and from the position of being in the here-and-now, access and anchor each and every needed resources. Amplify these and let's make sure that we have some good anchors for these resources.

5. From the observer meta-position, transfer the resources.
Close your eyes again and return to that past event with all of your resources, and, as you do, find yourself giving them to the younger you. Give each resource as a gift from your present self. Good … And now let the event play out with the resources. Imagine the younger you now acting, thinking, and feeling in a transformed way. From this position, you can also give the others in the movie the resources that they needed.

6. Come forward through your history with the added re-sources.
As you fully step back into the movie and become that younger you for the moment, imagine moving up through your time-line experiencing the resources so that, as you move through each subsequent year of life, the resources transform your history and enrich your life. Let the resources transform yourself and the others.

7. Return to the present and run an ecology check.
Does this new edition of your memory provide you a sense of closure? Does it encode better learnings and responses? Does it enhance your life? Would you like to live with this new edition? Does it provide you a more useable map for navigating life?

8. Future-pace.
Look out into your future from the perspective of having made these changes in your sense of your personal history and imagine them continuing into your future.

The decision-destroyer pattern

Sometimes in moving through life, we just make some poor decisions. Afterwards, those decisions become part of our mental map and then operate as a psychological force in our mind-body system that undermines and sabotages today's actions and feelings. This pattern *destroys* such limiting, destructive, and unenhancing decisions.

Decisions, as part of our mental maps, provide specific instructions about what to do. While a decision in one context and at one time may function very well for our benefit, as contexts and times change, these decisions can become outdated and useless. This pattern allows us to alter the decisions that we have constructed.

The pattern

1. Identify a limiting decision that you still live with.
Have you ever made a limiting and self-sabotaging decision? What did you decide and how was it limiting for you?

When did you adopt this decision? How long have you lived with it? How has it become ineffective for you now?

2. Identify an enhancing decision you'd like to live life by.
What would be a much more powerful, enhancing, and desirable decision? What would you want to accomplish by this new decision?

How would it help you to feel and think and act more resourcefully? As you now fully access that enhancing decision that served you so much better ... feel it and anchor it.

3. Float above your time-line back to when you made the limiting decision.
Now float back on the wings of time and relaxation to a time when you made a poor or limiting decision and see that younger you from above your time-line... . That's right ... and now float down into the experience so that you can feel it again for the last time ... and let's anchor this feeling. And now with this feeling (fire anchor) ... just float back even further to perhaps other instances of this limiting decision and do so until you get back to the earliest instance of this limiting decision.

4. Access resourceful decision.
Now let's step out of that and float back up above your time-line so that you can fully reaccess your enhancing decision (fire anchor). Good. And as you do let's go back fifteen minutes prior to that old limiting decision. That's right and now just float back down and into that younger you, bringing with you that enhancing decision fully and completely.

5. Experience the old situation with new resources.
As you do, bring these enhancing resources with you, letting them completely change your awareness and feelings as you experience the effects of this new decision.

6. Then quickly zoom up through your time-line to the present.
Now with all of these new resources vibrating and filling up your awareness I want you to very quickly zoom up through time with them ... letting them affect and transform many, many other things in your life ... and come all the way back up to the now... to this moment.

7. Stop and integrate in the present.
And now stop … here … in this moment … and fully integrate this experience and wonder, really wonder, how this empowering decision will play out into your future in the days and weeks and months to come.

Meta-stating negative-emotions pattern

Generally, bringing *negative emotional energy* (the psychic energy of negative emotions and thinking) *against* ourselves, or any conceptual facet of ourselves, puts us at odds with ourselves. It turns our psychological energies *against* ourselves in less than useful ways. While exceptions do occur to this, they operate as the exception rather than the rule. Use this pattern as a general process for handling "negative emotions and thoughts."

The pattern
1. Identify an emotional state with which you have difficulties handling, controlling, or managing.
For example: anger, fear, disgust, a sexual emotion, a religious emotion. What negative emotional state of thought-or-emotion do you not like, can't stand, hate, wish you didn't experience? What negative states do you feel as "taboo"? Describe this state. How is this a problem? What do you think and/or feel about this?

2. Check your permission level.
Go inside, quiet yourself and say, "I give myself permission to feel X." Upon doing this, notice your internal responses in terms of sights, images, sounds, feelings, or words chatting away inside your mind-body system. Identify any objections that arise. What would happen if you did accept or experience this negative emotion?

3. Design-engineer a new meta-stating structure.
Go inside and give yourself permission congruently with a strong and resourceful voice that reframes the objections. "I give myself permission to feel anger because it allows me to recognize things that violate my values and to take appropriate action early." "I give myself permission to feel the tender emotions because it makes me more fully human."

4. Meta-state the negative emotion with a powerful outframing resource.
For example: acceptance, appreciation, calmness, thoughtfulness. Use the basic meta-stating format: access, amplify, anchor, and apply.

5. Check ecology and add needed reframes.
Imagine fully and completely moving into your tomorrows with this outframe on the negative emotion … Does any part of you object to letting this operate as your orientational style? If so, recycle to Step 3.

6. Future-pace and install.

Now, as you imagine taking this new way of being out into your future, into tomorrow and all the tomorrows that follow, just notice how that fits and are all facets of your mind-body fully aligned with this?

NLP and business

Is there an NLP model of business? Of entrepreneurship, of corporate life, of coaching, of negotiating, sales, wealth building, career development, professional effectiveness? No, not really. Once again, as with therapy, NLP operates primarily as a meta-discipline and really has no theory of business, econ-omics, politics, social change, or cultural progress. At best, utilizing the NLP presuppositions about maps, flexibility, communication, systems, or feedback builds models from strategy elicitation of the best practices in each of these facets of business.

Over the years, many business models and patterns have been developed. Earlier Bandler began modeling great salesman and developed his Persuasion Engineering model. As the field of sales itself changed in the mid-1980s, other sales models have been developed. These newer models actually fit more congruently into the NLP model and presuppositions. Steven Heiman revolutionized the field of sales with his Strategic Selling model. This initiated a whole host of new approaches that focused on relationship, finding needs, coaching, facilitating, and respecting people.

This perhaps illustrates the value of NLP as a meta-discipline that not only finds the strategy of the best examples in a field, but also examines the meta-level structures and framework that governs the field. In that way, as a field changes, grows, and evolves, so will our models of that field. This happened in sales. The old hard-selling approach as exemplified in Persuasion Engineering has been replaced by models of persuading through relationship in ethical ways.

Today there are undoubtedly more published books, tapes, trainings, CDs, and videos on NLP applications to business than to any other field. This is especially true since NLP is most essentially a communication model and therefore has tremendous applications for any process that involves information processing and transfer. This makes NLP especially relevant and powerful for management, leadership, or persuasion. Anything that involves the transformation of meaning in the minds of people is subject to the modeling influence of NLP. Here NLP offers a way to identify the patterns of those who are at the cutting edge of their field.

The "as if" frame

The "as if" frame refers to the idea of *pretending to experience* a state, emotion, behavior, or way of operating in the world. Developed from Vaihinger this process provides a way to use our constructive imaginative skills in order to instruct our brains-bodies about what a particular "reality" would look like, sound like, or feel like. This process allows us to expand our maps and thereby our repertoire of choices.

If a person seems unable to even "imagine" a particular experience, have them model another person. Use this process to practice via pretending until you construct and install the resource.

While we can equally well use the "as if" frame for therapeutic and self-development issues, it provides a tool in business for developing new skills as we first play the role. This allows us to try out new behaviors and ways of operating without needing to "feel" that we are "really" there yet.

The pattern

1. Identify the desired experience.
What way of thinking, feeling, speaking, behaving, or relating would you like to have and experience? As you fully describe this desired experience in descriptive (see, hear, feel) terms, notice what you are beginning to feel.

2. Give yourself full permission to step into the desired frame.
Go inside and say, "I give myself permission to use the 'as if' frame to turn this new behavior, feeling, or belief into my reality."

What happens when you say this inside? Any sense of an objection? If so, then add, "I give myself permission to use the pretend frame as a step to truly believing ..."

3. Construct the "as if" frame and step into it fully.
What is it like when you fully pretend that you have stepped into that experience so that you are beginning to see, hear, and feel things through that perspective?

How are you experiencing that state in your body? What would someone else see as they look at you?

4. Run an evaluation check.
At this point don't worry about what it feels like. If it is new and different, then it will (and should) feel weird, strange, uncomfortable, not-me.

How useful would this be for you? What can you learn from this in terms of how it might empower some aspect of your life or relationships?

5. Future pace.
Suppose now that you took this way of thinking, feeling, or acting into your future and went out a year, five years ... Just imagine ...

6. Permit yourself to use the "as if" frame until it becomes installed.
Do you like the benefits and consequences of this experience enough to give yourself permission to keep using it and experimenting with it until it habituates as your style of responding?

Transforming "mistakes" into "learning"

Making a mistake is one thing. Making the same mistake again and again is another thing. If you ever find yourself repeatedly falling into the same old pattern again and again and wondering, "Did I not learn anything before? Why am I doing this again? When will I learn?" then you may have somehow built a self-organizing frame that has put you into a closed loop that keeps repeating.

Sometimes we organize our thinking, emoting, and behaving to accomplish an outcome, and then simply get into a pattern of repeating it mindlessly. If the pattern even partially works, we may subsequently simply fail to update it. We may no longer run a reality test or a quality-control test on it any longer.

The pattern

1. Identify the overused pattern.
What pattern or cluster of negative responses occur over and over that you have had enough of? What self-defeating behavior do you keep indulging in?

2. Identify supporting limiting beliefs that keep the pattern operating.
What are the limiting beliefs that contribute to or support this pattern?

What ideas, frames, understandings, decisions, and feelings keep using you to persevere in this pattern?

What context, feedback, or other factors do you somehow keep ignoring?

3. Identify an experience of similar structure.
What is another negative experience that exemplifies this response?

4. Worst-case-scenario comparison.
When you compare the negative experiences to something worse that could have happened, but did not, what do you feel?

Do you feel thankful that something worse did not happen? Relieved?

5. Explore positive side effects.
How did the negative experience actually cause, or contribute to, something positive at some later point in time?

Which useful things in your life would never have happened without these seemingly negative events?

6. Find the positive intentions behind the negative events.
What were the positive intention behind that negative event? What were the positive intentions of the others involved?

7. Find positive meanings to negative events.
What positive significance could that event have meant on some other level?

8. Re-edit.
Take these positive learnings and resources and return to a time before all the negative events occurred and use them as you relive them

Decision-making pattern

Sometimes we struggle with indecisiveness as we attempt to make a decision. Yet, because our experience of "making a decision" involves using our internal mental movies, producing better decisions involves using the appropriate representational systems in the most efficient sequence. We generally find it difficult to "feel" a good choice and to make good decisions without comparing alternatives visually. With this pattern we can produce decisions of higher quality.

As a nominalization, the word "decision" refers to the process of *deciding* between alternatives. As we move back and forth between alternatives, first considering or choosing one then the other, we need to doso from a meta-position that allows us a larger perspective of things. The most effective decision making involves using resourceful meta-statesfor clear-minded observing and for applying the highest values and principles.

The pattern
1. Identify a decision area.
What decision would you like to make? Do you have a well formed outcome regarding what you want the decision to do for you?

2. Access one visual possibility.
First allow yourself to see one possible decision and the solution that follows from it. (When working with someone, gesture up to the right and track to make sure the person follows visually.)

3. Meta-comment about the option.
As you think about the possible options and see what you do, what thoughts and feelings come to mind?

(Gesture down and to the right as you express this to facilitate the talking about the picture, or gesture up to a meta-position.)

4. Access a kinesthetic response.
As you do this, just notice what it feels like for you to have this option.

Do you like this option as you look at it?

5. Repeat for other alternatives.
What other possibilities do you have? See them, feel them. Does this take into consideration all of the significant options you can think of?

6. Go meta to select the best.
Now that you have seen and felt all of these possibilities, I want you to step back from them and take up a meta-position above them. As you do, what criteria will you use to make your decision?

Which of these standards is the most important? Second? Which option do you think meets most of your criteria?

7. Future-pace.
Having selected the most desirable solution, when you put this option into your mental movie and play it out in full sensory awareness, how does it work and fit into your life and future?

8. Check for objections.
Are you fully aligned with this? Does any part object to this option? What do you need in order to integrate that objection into the option?

What price will you pay for this choice? What price would you pay for another choice?

NLP and education

Given NLP's inherent focus on communication, information, and the structure of meaning, it is equally applicable to education, training, development, coaching, presenting, and the like. NLP starts from the premise that people are incredible learners. It begins from the understanding that, unless a person has brain damage by birth or accident or disease from cancer or a tumor, they do not have "learning dysfunctions" or disabilities but are fabulous learners. The problem is not that. The problem is that because they learn too well they learn a lot of non- sense, things that are not so, and things that undermine their success.

The NLP model starts from the revolutionary premise that all behaviors and responses are accomplishments. The NLP practitioner starts by examining any response pattern not as a problem, but as an achievement. This then allows us to begin modeling the structure of that experience. "What a skill! How in the world do you do that?"

From a Meta-States point of view, this tames the dragon of judgment, self-contempt, shame, and self-hatred. Many people have framed any learning that differs from the prominent cultural learning as somehow wrong, bad, and therefore proof of their inadequacy or inferiority. Of course, setting that frame about their learning is accessing a state of contempt, shame, or judgment and applying it to their previous state of learning. This meta-state structure then creates a "dragon state". Structurally the person has just turned his or her psychological energies against him- or herself.

When that happens, several very unpleasant and unfortunate things occur. First, turning one's negative thoughts-and-emotions (as a state) *against oneself* puts one in odds and in conflict with oneself. Then the mind, emotions, and/or body will pay the price for this attack. This is the source of many psychosomatic illnesses and diseases. This creates an impoverishment rather than an enrichment of human experience.

Second, one has just split one's mind, focus, emotion, and concentration so that there is much less "mind" left to deal with the process of learning. That further impoverishes one's situation. A person will now double-track rather than be of one mind about the subject at hand. No wonder learning ability, skill, comprehension, and retention are all reduced.

Conversely, by starting with appreciation, wonder, curiosity, and affirmation of the learning as a learning, as an achievement, it engenders a very different focus. These qualities and values of thought-and-emotion set a very different set of meta-states or frames of mind *about* one's experience. They allow one to stay focused on the achievement. "How do I do that?" "When, where, what contexts, in what way?" These modeling questions have the fascinating effect of empowering a power to recognize *the process* regarding how they systematically, regularly, and methodically create the "disability." We say fascinating, because once a person realizes that he or she *creates* the experience, that person has a choice point to and can choose *not* to run that program.

This reframes the learning situation entirely. The real problem isn't being able to learn something, but *learning stupid stuff* that does not enhance life. In other words, the person does not have a meta-level problem of being unable and incapable of learning or is too damaged too learn: the person has a primary-level problem of bad taste. They are just constantly refreshing some old limiting beliefs, understandings, and mappings.

Summary

As a model of human functioning, NLP offers a wide range of applications from therapy, to education, to business, to personal growth and development.

Chapter Twenty-Four
NLP Mastery

The User's Manual of the Brain, Volume II has been all about the art and process of mastering NLP. To achieve such mastery, we have focused on two primary things:

1. Using the four meta-domains of NLP as the larger framework and seeing the four domains as providing a systemic understanding that redundantly models the same thing-human experience.
2. Getting the spirit of NLP as the frame of mind or attitude that allows us to use the various models, patterns, and insights in a masterful way.

In addition to systemic thinking and setting the kind of belief, value, and understanding frames that will give us the passionate attitude of exploring, playing, and discovering, we have also woven a thread about meta-detailing throughout the text. By meta-detailing we are able to develop the flexibility of consciousness that allows us to work at multiple levels simultaneously and to move up and down the scale of abstraction and specificity as a situation demands.

Consider what such meta-detailing then leads to. When we are able to see the larger perspective (the *meta*-frame) and then *detail* it out to operationalize it, we synthesize both global and specific thinking in such a way as to experience a flexibility creativity. And, since the person with the most flexibility in a system will have the most long-term influence in that system, this empowers us within our personal mind-body system, our relationship systems, and in the embedded systems that we live in at work and in our culture.

Setting mastery frames

Throughout this work we have been talking about mastery in various terms. We have explored what it is in terms of NLP. We have explored what it means when we have developed a level of mastery (not perfection, flawlessness, and arrogance, but such an ease with mistakes that we know how to use them for feedback and continual improvement). We have described the processes for attaining mastery and the price we pay for it. In all of this we have also been setting numerous frames for mastery.

What are the mastery frames you have set for yourself? What are the attitudes (beliefs, values, understandings) that you have set for yourself that support moving to becoming more masterful with this model?

In setting such frames and exploring the process, we have discovered that *mastery* involves focus, concentration, passion, intention, commitment, and discipline. Given this, it's important that we recognize that we cannot achieve mastery in everything. None of us have the time, energy, or ability for that. Mastery involves honing in on one or a few areas and focusing intensely on them. It involves making some hard decisions and deciding not between "good choice" and "bad choice" but between two good choices. Between good and better.

George Leonard in *Mastery* describes four types of people that he experienced over the years: Dabblers, Hackers, Compulsives, and Masters. We may dabble in one area, hack in others, be compulsive in some, and master only a few. Those few areas of mastery usually include personal relationships and our careers.

- *Dabblers* get into one thing, develop a certain level of skill, then feel bored with it and so drop it and move on to something else where they then repeat the same pattern. They dabble without long-term commitment or focus.
- *Hackers* develop a certain level of basic skills and then begin to feel content with that and so they sit on the plateau, never to rise above that in their skills or abilities. Hackers can evolve to new levels of skill, but usually do so only in response to some immediate need or crisis. An aikido student who finds his or her skills insufficient in a fight may choose to learn more, but will soon settle into a new plateau and stay there. An employee threatened by a new employee's abilities with the computer may choose to learn just enough so as not to look totally ignorant.
- *Compulsives* are those who reach the first plateau and then become uncomfortable with their level of performance. At that they then push harder and harder to get better faster, so that, while they may reach another plateau or two, they ultimately burn out. They fail to pace themselves.
- *Masters* understand that the plateau is part and parcel of the mastery process. They recognize that there is a never-ending series of plateaus on the path toward mastery. They frame things so that they look at being on the plateau and make practicing every bit as exciting as when the spurts of growth come. So they are undaunted by plateaus, and view them as an expected part of the ebb and flow of life.

In all of this, the path of the master involves getting instruction, practicing, surrendering to the practice, keeping a clear intention to be the best, periodically pushing the "edge of the envelope". All in all, it is a process and never an end product. Most of the fun is the process itself, in getting there.

The pathway to mastery

As a summary for how we move on to mastery in terms of what's involved, here are a few of the things to consider as you now take the content material of this work and use it to master NLP:

1. *Getting or receiving instructions*

There's a paradoxical thing about mastery: those who become masters are *not* adverse to learning more, to receiving instructions, to admitting what they don't know. In fact, they know how to use their ignorance as one of their best learning tools. About mastery, George Leonard described an attitude that gets in the way and blocks further development when he wrote: "Most people have spent their lives reinventing the wheel, then refusing to concede that it's out of round."

What does this mean? It means that mastery takes an ongoing openness of attitude and humility if we really want to a master a field. We start out ignorant, then we become aware of our ignorance and aware that there is so much more to learn. Then, with practice and more learning, we become skilled and competent. But not masterful. Mastery comes when our learnings drop out of conscious awareness and an automatic, intuitive part of our skills and while we are still open to learning from others-even those whom we mentor. Nothing blocks mastery more than arrogance and self-importance.

2. *Getting lots of practice*

Practice is not only something we do: it is something we give ourselves to so much that it becomes an intimate part of our self-definition. How much is the idea of forever practicing and trying out new things and experimenting and then practicing some of the fundamental skills again a part of "who you are"? Every spring in the USA, world-class baseball players who get salaries in the millions of dollars get out for spring practice. And what do they do? They *practice* throwing and hitting the ball. As we also keep practicing the basics, we put ourselves on a road of continual improvement. We continue to practice even when we are on the plateau—in fact, *especially* when we are there.

3. *Surrendering to the practice*

Surrendering to practice describes the attitude that's a part of mastery, and that's the recognition that we have to *stay in shape* and that practice is just part of the game. To do this we suspend our disbelief, doubts, and ego as we surrender to practice. We just keep at it because we know that, for the master, there are no experts, there are only learners. Again, George Leonard wrote: "The beginner who stands on his or her dignity becomes rigid, armored; the learning can't get through. To be a learner, you've got to be willing to be a fool."

And it was Benjamin Disraeli who described surrendering to practice in these memorable words: "The secrets of success is constancy ofpurpose."

4. *Intending to be the best we can be*

A master develops a clear intention of his or her vision, the next step to actually take the steps to make it happen. "Intentionality fuels the master's journey." Regarding mastery, Arnold Schwarzenegger said, "All I know is that the first step is to create the vision, because when you see the vision there—the beautiful vision—that creates the *want power*."

Leonard wrote: "Masters are zealots of practice, connoisseurs of the small, incremental step. At the same time, these masters are precisely the ones who are likely to challenge previous limits, to take risks for the sake of higher performance."

5. Willingness to push to the edge

This refers to taking risks, pushing the envelope, exploring our ignorance, trying things even though we don't know whether they'll work, and asking lots of dumb questions to find out the edge of our maps. Here the attitude of passionate curiosity becomes crucial as well as the playful attitude that there is no failure, just feedback.

Summary

Howard Gardner says that it takes most experts in a field ten years to master that field, to get to the edge of that field and to be in the place of contributing something new. May you now take your knowledge of the NLP and Neuro-Semantic models and give yourself to them so that in the years to come you will experience your own mastery in running your own brain and being able to touch the lives of others with magic.

Bibliography

Andreas, Connirea & Andreas, Tamara, 1991, *Core Transformation*, Real People Press, Moab, UT.

Bandler, Richard, & Grinder, John, 1975, 1976, *Patterns of the Hypnotic Language of Milton H. Erickson*, Meta-Publications, CA.

Bandler, Richard, & Grinder, John, 1975, 1976, *The Structure of Magic, Volumes I & II: A Book About Language and Therapy*, Science & Behavior Books, Palo Alto, CA.

Bandler, Richard, & Grinder, John, 1979, *Frogs Into Princes: Neuro-Linguistic Programming*, Real People Press, Moab, UT.

Bandler, Richard & Grinder, John, 1982, *Reframing: Neuro-linguistic programming and the transformation of meaning*, Real People Press, UT.

Bandler, Richard, 1985, *Using Your Brain for a Change: Neuro-linguistic Programming*, Connirae and Steve Andreas (Ed.), Real People Press, Moab, UT.

Bandler, Richard, & McDonald, Will, 1988, *An Insider's Guide to Sub-Modalities*, Meta Publications, Cupertino, CA.

Bandler, Richard, 1993, *Time For a Change*, Daniels (Ed.), Meta Publications, Capitola, CA.

Bandler, Richard, & LaValle, John, 1996, *Persuasion Engineering*, Meta Publications, Capitola, CA.

Bateson, Gregory, 1972, 2000, *Steps To An Ecology of Mind*, University of Chicago, Chicago, IL.

Bateson, Gregory, 1979, *Mind and Nature: A Necessary Unity*, Bantam, New York.

Bateson, Gregory & Bateson, Mary Catherine, 1987, *Angel fears: Toward an epistemology of the sacred*, Macmillan Publishing Co., New York.

Bodenhamer, Bob G., & Hall, L. Michael, 1997, *Time-Lining: Advanced Patterns in "Time" Processes*, Crown House Publishing, Wales, UK.

Bodenhamer, Bob G., & Hall, L. Michael, 1999, *The User's Manual for the Brain: A Comprehensive Manual for Neuro-Linguistic Programming Practitioner Certification*, Crown House Publishing, Wales, UK.

Bourland, David D Jr & Johnston, Paul Dennithorne, 1991, *To be or not: An e-prime anthology*, International Society for General Semantics, San Francisco, CA.

Candice B. Pert, 1997, *Molecules of Emotion: Why You Feel the Way You Feel*, Scribner, New York.

Chomsky, Noam, 1957, *Syntactic Structures*, Mouton Publishers, The Hague.

Chomsky, Noam, 1965, *Aspects of the Theory of Syntax*, MIT Press, Cambridge, MA.

Dilts, Robert B, 1983a, *Applications of Neuro-Linguistic Programming*, Meta Publications, Cupertino, CA.

Dilts, Robert B, 1983b, *Roots of Neuro-Linguistic Programming*, Meta Publications, Cupertino, CA.

Dilts, Robert B, 1990, *Changing Belief Systems with NLP*, Meta Publications, Cupertino, CA.

Dilts, Robert B, 1999, *Sleight of Mouth: The Magic of Conversational Belief Change*, Meta Publications.

Dilts, Robert B, 1994, *Strategies of Genius, Volume I: Aristotle, Sherlock Homes, Walt Disney, Wolfgang Amadeus Mozart*, Meta Publications, Capitola, CA.

Dilts, Robert B, 1994, *Strategies of Genius, Volume II: Einstein*, Meta Publications, Capitola, CA.

Dilts, Robert B, 1995, *Strategies of Genius, Volume III: Freud, Mozart*, Meta Publications, Capitola, CA.

Dilts, Robert B, Dilts, R W, & Epstein, Todd, 1991, *Tools for Dreamers: Strategies for Creativity and the Structure of Innovation*, Meta Publications, Cupertino, CA.

Dilts, Robert B, Grinder, John, Bandler, Richard, & DeLozier, Judith, 1980, *Neuro-Linguistic Programming, Volume I: The Study of the Structure of Subjective Experience*, Meta Publications, Cupertino, CA.

1997 millennial Project

Erickson, Milton, 1983, *Healing in Hypnosis*, Vol I, The seminars, workshops, and lectures of Milton H. Erickson, Irvington Publishers Inc, New York.

Erickson, Milton, 1984, *Healing in Hypnosis*, Vol II, Irvington Publishers Inc, New York.

Gardner, Howard, 1983, *Frames of Mind: The Theory of Multiple Intelligences*, BasicBooks, Cupertino, CA.

Gardner, Howard, 1991, *The Unschooled Mind: How Children Think and How Schools Should Teach*, HarperCollins, New York.

Gardner, Howard, 1993, *Multiple Intelligences: The Theory in Practice*, BasicBooks, New York.

Gordon, David, 1978, *Therapeutic Metaphors: Helping Others Through the Looking Glass*, Meta Publications, Cupertino, CA.

Grinder, John, & Bandler, Richard, 1985, *Reframing: The transformation of Meaning*, Steve Andreas (Ed.), Real People Press, Moab, UT.

Grinder, John, & DeLozier, Judith, 1987, *Turtles All the Way Down: Prerequisites to Personal Genius,* Grinder & Associates, Scotts Valley, CA.

Hall, L Michael, 1995, 2000, *Meta-States: Mastering the Higher Levels of the Mind*, Neuro-Semantic Publications, Grand Junction, CO.

Hall, L Michael, 1996, *Becoming a Ferocious Presenter*, ET Publications, Grand Junction, CO.

Hall, L Michael, 1996, *Languaging: The Linguistics of Psychotherapy*, ET Publications, Grand Junction, CO.

Hall, L Michael, 1996, *The Spirit of NLP: Mastering the Art*, Crown House Publishing, Wales, UK.

Hall, L Michael, 1997, 2001, *NLP: Going Meta—Advance Modeling Using meta-levels*, Neuro-Semantic Publications, Grand Junction, CO.

Hall, L Michael, 2000, *Dragon Slaying: Dragons to Princes*, 2nd edition, ET Publications, Grand Junction, CO.

Hall, L Michael, 2000, *Frame Games: Persuasion Elegance*, Neuro-Semantics Publications, Grand Junction, CO.

Hall. L Michael, 2000, *Secrets of Personal Mastery*, Crown House Publishing, Wales, UK.

Hall, L Michael, 2001, *Communication Magic* (formerly *The Secrets of Magic*), Crown House Publishing, Wales, UK.

Hall, L Michael, & Belnap, Barbara, 1997, *The Sourcebook of Magic*, Crown House Publishing, Wales, UK.

Hall, L Michael, & Bodenhamer, Bob, 1997, *Figuring Out People: Design Engineering Using Meta-Programs*, Crown House Publishing, Wales, UK.

Hall, L Michael, & Bodenhamer, Bob, 2002, *Mind-Lines: Lines for Changing Minds*, 4th edition, Neuro-Semantics Publications, Grand Junction, CO.

Hall, L Michael, 1998, *The Secrets of Magic: Excellence in Communication for the 21st Century*, Crown House Publishing, Wales, UK.

Hall, L Michael, & Bodenhamer, Bob, 1999, *The Structure of Excellence: Unmasking the Meta-Levels of "Sub-Modalities"*, ET Publications, Grand Junction, CO.

Hall, L Michael, Bodenhamer, Bob, Bolstad, Richard, & Hamblett, Margott, 2001, *The Structure of Personality: Modeling "Personality" Using NLP and Neuro-Semantics*, Crown House Publishing, Wales, UK.

Harris, Randy Allen, 1993, *The Linguistic Wars*, Oxford University Press, New York.

Holland, Norman N, 1995, *The Brain of Robert Frost: A Cognitive Approach to Literature*, Routledge, London.

Korzybski, Alfred, 1921, reprinted 1994, *Manhood of Humanity*, Atlantic Books.

Korzybski, Alfred, 1933, 1994, *Science and Sanity: An Introduction to Non-Aristotelian Systems and General Semantics*, 5th ed., International Non-Aristotelian Library Publishing Co., Lakeville, CN.

Lakoff, George, & Johnson, Mark, 1980, *Metaphors We Live By*, University of Chicago Press, Chicago, IL.

Lakoff, George, 1987, *Women, Fire, and Dangerous Things: What Categories Reveal About the Mind*, University of Chicago Press, Chicago, IL.

Lakoff, George & Johnson, Mark, 1999, *Philosophy in the Flesh: The Embodied Mind and its Challenge to Western Thought*, Basic Books, New York.

Leonard, George, 1992, *Mastery: The Keys to Success and Long-Term Fulfillment*, Dutton/ Plume, New York.

McClendon, Terrence L, 1989, *The Wild Days: NLP 1972 to 1981*, Meta Publications, Cupertino, CA.

May, Rollo, 1969, *Love and Will*, W.W. Norton & Co., New York.

Metacalfe, Janet, & Shimamura, Arthur P (eds.), 1995, *Metacognition: Knowing About Knowing*, MIT Press, Cambridge, MA.

Miller, George, 1956, The magical number seven, plus or minus two: Some limits on our capacity to process information, *Psychological Review*, 63, 81-97.

Miller, George A, Galanter, Eugene, & Pribram, Karl H, 1960, *Plans and the Structure of Behavior*, Holt, Rinehart and Winston Co., New York.

Munshaw Joseph, & Zink, Nelson, 1997, SDA—A Self-Organizing Toolbox, *Anchor Point*, Vol. 12, July, pp. 23-29.

O'Connor, Joseph, & Mc Dermott, Ian, 1997, *The art of systems thinking: Essential skills for creativity and problem solving*, Thorsons, London.

O'Connor, Joseph, & Seymour, John, 1990, *Introducing Neuro-Linguistic Programming: The new Psychology of Personal Excellence*, Hartnolls Limited, Bodmin, Cornwall, UK.

Petersen, C, Maier, S F, & Seligman, M E P, 1975, reprinted 1995, *Learned Helplessness: A Theory for the Age of Personal Control*, OUP, Oxford.

Pribram, Karl, H, 1971, *Languages of the Brain*, Prentice Hall Press, Englewood Cliffs, USA.

Robbins, Anthony, 1989, *Unlimited Power: The New Science of Personal Achievement*, Simon and Schuster, New York.

Robbie, Eric, 1987, Sub-Modality Eye Accessing Cues, *Journal of NLP International*, Vol. I, No. 1, NLP International, Indian Rocks Beach, FL, pp. 15-24.

Robbins, Tony, 1987, *Unlimited Power*, Simon & Schuster Publishers, New York.

Searle, John R, 1995, *The Construction of Social Reality*, Free Press, Simon & Schuster, New York.

Seligman, M E P, 1991, reissue 1998, *Learned Optimism: How to Change your Life and Your Mind*, Alfred A Knopf, New York.

Watzlawick, Paul, Weakland, John, & Fisch, Richard, 1974, *Change: Principles of Problem Formation and Problem Resolution*, W.W. Norton & Co., New York.

Watzlawick, Paul, 1978, *The Language of Change: Elements of Therapeutic Communication*, Basic Books, New York.

Watzlawick, Paul (ed.), 1984, *The Invented Reality: How Do We Know What We Believe We Know?*, W.W. Norton & Co., New York.

Woodsmall, Wyatt, 1990, How To Select a Modeling Training, in *NLP Practitioner Trainer Manual*.

Woodsmall, Wyatt, 1996, What is Wrong With Logical Levels?, IANLP Conference, April 26, 1996, Austin, Texas.

Woodsmall, Wyatt & James, Tad, 1988, *Time-Line Therapy and the Basis of Personality*, Meta Publications, Cupertino, CA.

Zink, Nelson, & Munshaw, Joseph, 1997, *SDA—A Self-Organizing Toolbox*, Anchor Point Associates, Vol. 11, July, 1997, pp. 23-29.

The authors

L. Michael Hall, Ph.D.

PO Box 8, Clifton, CO 81520, USA; (970) 523-7877

(Michael@neurosemantics.com, NLPMetaStates@On LineCol.com)

Dr. Michael Hall, psychologist and entrepreneur, lives in the Colorado Rocky Mountains. For twenty years he had a private psychotherapeutic practice and then began teaching and training—first in communication training (assertiveness, negotiations) then in NLP.

He studied NLP with its co-founder, Richard Bandler, in the late 1980s, when he became a master practitioner and trainer. From that came *The Spirit of NLP and Becoming More Ferocious as a Presenter*. He also edited *Time For a Change*. As a prolific author, he has written and published more than two dozen books including *The Spirit of NLP, Dragon Slaying, Meta-States, Mind-Lines, Figuring Out People, The Structure of Excellence*, and *Frame Games*.

Hall's earned doctorate is in cognitive-behavioral psychology with an emphasis on psycholinguistics. His doctoral dissertation dealt with the languaging of four psychotherapies (NLP, RET, reality therapy, and logotherapy) using the formulations of general semantics. He addressed the Interdisciplinary International Conference on General Semantics (1995) presenting an integration of NLP and general semantics.

In 1994, Hall developed the Meta-States Model while modeling resilience and presenting the findings at the International NLP Conference in Denver. He has hundreds of articles published in *NLP World, Anchor Point, Rapport, Connection, and Meta-States Journal*.

Hall is the co-developer, along with Dr. Bob Bodenhamer, of Neuro-Semantics having co-authored a unified field model using the three Meta-Domains of NLP. They initiated the Society of Neuro-Semantics, and have begun to establish Institutes of Neuro-Semantics in the USA and around the world. Elvis Keith Lester joined the team in 1998, and then established the LEARN Institute of Neuro-Semantics in Tampa, Florida.

Today Hall spends his time researching and modeling, training internationally, and writing. Recent modeling projects have included modeling excellence in sales, persuasion, accelerated learning, state management, wealth building, women in leadership, and fitness and health. These are now Meta-State Gateway Trainings.

Books:
Defusing Strategies (1987).

Languaging: The Linguistics of Psychotherapy (1996).

The Spirit of NLP: The Process, Meaning & Criteria for Mastering NLP (1996).

Figuring Out People: Design Engineering with Meta-Programs (with Bodenhamer) (1997).

Mind Lines: Lines For Changing Minds (with Bodenhamer) (2002).

NLP: Going Meta—Advanced Modeling Using Meta-Levels (1997).

Patterns for "Renewing the Mind" (with Bodenhamer) (1997).

Time-Lining: Advance Time-Line Processes (with Bodenhamer) (1997).

The Secrets of Magic: Communicational Magic for the 21st Century (1998).

Instant Relaxation (1999, with Debra Lederer).

A Sourcebook of Magic, formerly, *How to Do What When* (with Belnap) (1999).

The Structure of Excellence: Unmasking the Meta-Levels of Sub-Modalities (with Bodenhamer, 1999).

The User's Manual for the Brain (1999, with Bodenhamer).

Dragon Slaying: Dragons to Princes (2000, 2nd edition).

Frame Games: Persuasion Elegance (2000).

Meta-States: Managing the Higher States of Your Mind (Self-Reflexiveness) (2000, 2nd edition).

Secrets of Personal Mastery (2000).

The Structure of Personality: Modeling "Personality" Using NLP and Neuro-Semantics (with Bodenhamer, Bolstad, and Harmblett, 2001).

Games Slim People Play (2001).

Games Business Experts Play (2002) .

Bob G. Bodenhamer, D.Min.

1516 Cecelia Dr. Gastonia, NC 28054, USA; (704) 864-3585; fax: (704) 8641545

Bob@neurosemantics.com, www.neurosemantics.com

Dr. Bob G. Bodenhamer first trained for the ministry, earned a doctorate in ministry, and served several churches as pastor. He began NLP training in 1990, studying with Dr. Tad James and receiving master practitioner and trainer certifications. Since then, he has taught and certified NLP trainings at Gastona College.

Beginning in 1996, Bodenhamer began studying the Meta-States model and then teamed up with Michael Hall to begin co-authoring several books. Since that he has turned out many works as he and Hall have applied the NLP and Meta-States Models to various facets of human experience.

In 1996 also, Bodenhamer co-founded with Hall the Society of Neuro-Semantics. This has taken his work to a new level, taken him into international trainings, and set in motion many Institutes of Neuro-Semantics around the world.

Books:

Figuring Out People: Design Engineering With Meta-Programs (with Hall, 1997).

Mind Lines: Lines for Changing Minds (2002).

Patterns for "Renewing the Mind" (with Hall, 1997).

Time-Lining: Advance Time-Line Processes (with Hall, 1997).

The Structure of Excellence: Unmasking the Meta-Levels of Sub-modalities (with Hall, 1999).

The User's Manual of the Brain (1999, with Hall).

Hypnotic Language (2000, with Burton).

Games for Mastering Fears (2001, with Hall).

The Structure of Personality: Modeling "Personality" Using NLP and Neuro-Semantics (with Hall, Bolstad, and Harmblett, 2001).

Trainings

The Institutes of Neuro-Semantics

Meta-NLP Practitioner: An intensive seven-day training in the essential NLP skills. This training introduces NLP as a model for discovering the structure of human functioning with a focus on how to run your own brain and to manage your own states. Learn the basic rapport-building, listening, and influence skills of NLP, as well as how to access and manage states through anchoring, reframing, and using dozens of NLP patterns. Discover how to use language both for precision and hypnotic influence. Required reading: *The User's Manual for the Brain* and *The Sourcebook of Magic.*

Meta-Masters NLP Practitioner: An intensive thirteen-day training in mastering all three of the meta-domains of NLP: language (Meta-Model), perception (Meta-Programs) and states and levels (Meta-States). This training focuses on the pathway to mastery and how to develop the very spirit of NLP, including curiosity, accelerated learning, flexibility, confidence, passion, playfulness.

Accessing Personal Genius: Introduction to Meta-States as an advanced NLP model (three days). This training introduces and teaches the Meta-States Model and is ideal for NLP practitioners. It presupposes knowledge of the NLP model and builds the training around accessing the kinds of states that will access and support "personal genius".

Advanced Modeling Using Meta-Levels: Advanced use of meta-states by focusing on the domain of modeling excellence. This training typically occurs as the last four days of the seven-day Meta-States Certification. Based upon the modeling experiences of Michael Hall and his book, *NLP: Going Meta—Advanced Modeling Using Meta-Levels*, this training looks at the formatting and structuring of the meta-levels in resilience, uninsultability, and seeing opportunities. The training touches on, among other things, modeling of wealth building, fitness, women in leadership, and persuasion.

Secrets of Personal Mastery: Awakening Your Inner Executive: This training presents the power of Meta-States *without* directly teaching the model as such. the focus instead shifts to personal mastery and the executive powers of the participants. Formatted so that it can take the form of one, two or three days, this training presents a simpler form of Meta-States, especially good for those without NLP background or those who are more focused on meta-states applications than the model.

Frame Games: Persuasion Elegance: The first truly user-friendly version of Meta-States. Frame Games provides practice and use of meta-states in terms of frame detecting, setting, and changing. As a model of frames, Frame Games focuses on the power of persuasion via frames and so presents how to influence or persuade yourself and others using the levels of thought or mind that lie at the heart of Meta-States. It is designed as a three-day program, and the first two days presents the model of Frame Games and lots of exercises. Day Three is for becoming a true Frame Game Master and working with frames conversationally and covertly.

Wealth-Building Excellence (Meta-Wealth): The focus of this training is on learning how to think like a millionaire, to develop the mind and meta-mind of someone who is structured and programmed to create wealth economically, personally, mentally, emotionally, and relationally. As a Meta- States application training, Wealth-Building Excellence began as a modeling project and seeks to facilitate the replication of that excellence in participants.

Selling & Persuasion Excellence (Meta-Selling): Another Meta-States application training, modeled after experts in the fields of selling and persuasion and designed to replicate these skills in participants. An excellent follow-up training to Wealth-Building Excellence, since most people who build wealth have to sell their ideas and dreams to others. This training goes way beyond mere persuasion engineering, as it uses the Strategic Selling model of Steven Heiman, also known, among other things, as relational selling and facilitation selling.

Mind-Lines: Lines for Changing Minds: Based upon the book by Michael Hall and Bob Bodenhamer (1997), now in its third edition, Mind-Line Training is a training about conversational reframing and persuasion. The Mind-Lines model began as a rigorous update of the old NLP "sleight-of-mouth" patterns and has grown to become the persuasion language of the Meta-State moves. This advanced training is a highly, and mainly, linguistic model, excellent as a follow-up training for Wealth-Building Excellence and Selling Excellence. Generally a two-day format, although sometimes three and four days.

Accelerated Learning Using NLP & Meta-States (Meta-Learning): A Meta-States application training based upon the NLP model for "running your own brain" and the Neuro-Semantic (Meta-States) model of managing your higher executive states of consciousness. Modeled after leading experts in the fields of education and cognitive psychologies, this training provides extensive insight into the learning states and how to access your personal learning genius. It provides specific strategies for various learning tasks as well as processes for research and writing.

Defusing Hotheads: A Meta-States and NLP application training for handling hot, stressed-out, and irrational people in fight/flight states. Designed to "talk someone down from a hot angry state," this training provides instruction in state management, first for the skilled negotiator or manager, and then for eliciting another into a more resourceful state. Based upon the book by Michael Hall, *Defusing Strategies* (1987), this training has been presented to managers and supervisors for greater skill in conflict management, and to police departments for coping with domestic violence.

Advanced NLP Flexibility Training Using General Semantics: An advanced Neuro-Semantics training that explores the riches and treasures in Alfred Korzybski's work, *Science and Sanity*. Originally presented in London (1998, 1999) as "The Merging of the Models: NLP and General Semantics", this training now focuses almost exclusively on *developing advanced flexibility* using tools, patterns, and models in general semantics. Recommend for the advanced student of NLP and Meta-States.

Neuro-Semantics Trainers Training: An advanced training for those who have been certified in Meta-States and Neuro-Semantics (the seven-day program). This application training focuses the power and magic of Meta-States on the training experience itself-both public and individual training. It focuses first on the trainer, to access one's own "top training states", and then on how to meta-state or set the frames when working with others in coaching or facilitating greater resourcefulness.

Instant Relaxation: Another practical NLP and Meta-States application training designed to facilitate the advanced ability to quickly "fly into a calm". Based in part upon the book by Lederer and Hall (Instant Relaxation, 1999), this training does not teach NLP or Meta-States, but coaches the relaxation skills for greater "presence of mind", control over mind and neurology, and empowerment in handling stressful situations. An excellent training in conjunction with Defusing Hotheads.

USA & Canada *orders to:*

Crown House Publishing
P.O. Box 2223, Williston, VT 05495-2223, USA
Tel: 877-925-1213, Fax: 802-864-7626
www.crownhouse.co.uk

UK & Rest of World *orders to:*

The Anglo American Book Company Ltd.
Crown Buildings, Bancyfelin, Carmarthen, Wales SA33 5ND
Tel: +44 (0)1267 211880/211886, Fax: +44 (0)1267 211882
E-mail: books@anglo-american.co.uk
www.anglo-american.co.uk

Australasia *orders to:*

Footprint Books Pty Ltd.
Unit 4/92A Mona Vale Road,
Mona Vale NSW 2103, Australia
Tel: +61 (0) 2 9997 3973, Fax: +61 (0) 2 9997 3185
E-mail: info@footprint.com.au
www.footprint.com.au

Singapore & Malaysia *orders to:*

Publishers Marketing Services Pte Ltd.
10-C Jalan Ampas #07-01
Ho Seng Lee Flatted Warehouse, Singapore 329513
Tel: +65 256 5166, Fax: +65 253 0008
E-mail: info@pms.com.sg
www.pms.com.sg

South Africa *orders to:*

Everybodys Books
Box 201321 Durban North 401, South Africa
Tel: +27 (0) 31 569 2229, Fax: +27 (0) 569 2234
E-mail: ebbooks@iafrica.com